Silvia Luraghi, Elisa Roma (Eds.)
Valency over Time

Trends in Linguistics
Studies and Monographs

Editors
Chiara Gianollo
Daniël Van Olmen

Editorial Board
Walter Bisang
Tine Breban
Volker Gast
Hans Henrich Hock
Karen Lahousse
Natalia Levshina
Caterina Mauri
Heiko Narrog
Salvador Pons
Niina Ning Zhang
Amir Zeldes

Editor responsible for this volume
Chiara Gianollo

Volume 368

Valency over Time

Diachronic Perspectives on Valency Patterns and Valency Orientation

Edited by
Silvia Luraghi and Elisa Roma

DE GRUYTER
MOUTON

This project has received funding from the Italian Ministry of Education and Research, grant n. 20159M7X5P_002 PRIN 2015 "Transitivity and argument structure in flux", PI Silvia Luraghi (Pavia).

 UNIVERSITÀ DI PAVIA

ISBN 978-3-11-127779-0
e-ISBN (PDF) 978-3-11-075565-7
e-ISBN (EPUB) 978-3-11-075571-8
ISSN 1861-4302
DOI https://doi.org/10.1515/9783110755657

This work is licensed under the Creative Commons Attribution-NonCommercial-NoDerivatives 4.0 International License. For details go to http://creativecommons.org/licenses/by-nc-nd/4.0/.

Library of Congress Control Number: 2021940737

Bibliographic information published by the Deutsche Nationalbibliothek
The Deutsche Nationalbibliothek lists this publication in the Deutsche Nationalbibliografie; detailed bibliographic data are available on the Internet at http://dnb.dnb.de.

© 2023 with the authors, editing © 2021 Silvia Luraghi and Elisa Roma,
published by Walter de Gruyter GmbH, Berlin/Boston
This volume is text- and page-identical with the hardback published in 2021.
The book is published open access at www.degruyter.com.

Typesetting: Integra Software Services Pvt. Ltd.
Printing and binding: CPI books GmbH, Leck

www.degruyter.com

Contents

Silvia Luraghi and Elisa Roma
Valency and transitivity over time: An introduction —— 1

Eitan Grossman
Transitivity, diachrony, and language contact —— 13

Chiara Zanchi and Matteo Tarsi
Valency patterns and alternations in Gothic —— 31

Elisa Roma
Valency Patterns of Old Irish verbs: finite and non-finite syntax —— 89

Guglielmo Inglese
Anticausativization and basic valency orientation in Latin —— 133

Silvia Luraghi and Dionysios Mertyris
Basic valency in diachrony: from Ancient to Modern Greek —— 169

Riho Grünthal, Heini Arjava, Jyri Lehtinen and Johanna Nichols
Basic causative verb patterns in Uralic: Retention and renewal in grammar and lexicon —— 209

Sonja Riesberg, Kurt Malcher and Nikolaus P. Himmelmann
The many ways of transitivization in Totoli —— 235

Michela Cennamo
Anticausatives and lability in Italian and French: a diachronic-synchronic comparative study —— 265

Denis Creissels
Phonologically conditioned lability in Soninke (West-Mande) and its historical explanation —— 305

Index of Authors —— 329

Index of Subjects —— 335

Index of Languages —— 339

Silvia Luraghi and Elisa Roma
Valency and transitivity over time: An introduction

1 Introduction

In this book, we present a collection of papers devoted to verbal valency that share a common orientation by addressing this issue in a diachronic perspective, either discussing changes in the behavior of verbs or discussing verbal valency at different historical stages of specific languages.[1]

Verbs and their semantic and syntactic behavior have long been at the center of linguistic research. This is not surprising: indeed, as remarked by Croft (2012: 2) "A central part of the grammar of every human language is the encoding of events and their participants in a clause." For this reason, Tesnière (1959) argued that the verb is the center of the "petit drame" staged in any given sentence.

Language specific and cross-linguistic studies approaching verbs and their constructions synchronically or diachronically abound, and it is impossible in this introductory chapter to account for decades of research developed within different theoretical frameworks. In what follows, we focus on two issues, since they are also the focus of the papers in this book, that is, valency patterns, especially as they have been investigated within the ValPaL project (see Malchukov and Comrie 2015 and below, Section 2), and valency alternation of the causative/anticausative type. The structure of the article is as follows. In Section 2 we briefly introduce the notion of verbal valency and different approaches to verbs and their constructional patterns, focusing especially on the methods and results achieved with the ValPaL project. Section 3 contains a discussion of transitivity and transitivity scales, as ensuing from cross-linguistic research partly based on the ValPaL

---

[1] This book collects some of the papers presented at the conference "The shaping of transitivity and argument structure: theoretical and empirical perspectives", which took place in Pavia in the fall of 2018 in the framework of the research project "Transitivity and Argument Structure in Flux" (https://sites.google.com/universitadipavia.it/tasf/stas2018-conference-the-shaping-of-transitivity-and-argument-structure/program?authuser=0), funded by the Italian Ministry for Education and Research (MIUR) in the framework of the 2015 PRIN call, grant no. 20159M7X5P (https://sites.google.com/universitadipavia.it/tasf/home?authuser=0).

Silvia Luraghi, University of Pavia, e-mail: luraghi@unipv.it
Elisa Roma, University of Pavia, e-mail: elisa.roma@unipv.it

∂ Open Access. © 2021 Silvia Luraghi and Elisa Roma, published by De Gruyter. This work is licensed under the Creative Commons Attribution-NonCommercial-NoDerivatives 4.0 International License.
https://doi.org/10.1515/9783110755657-001

data. In Section 4, we address the issue of valency alternations, and introduce the notion of basic valency, as developed in Nichols, Peterson, and Barnes (2004). Section 5 surveys the content of the papers collected in this book.

2 Valency in cross-linguistic research

The tendency for specific meanings to be instantiated by verbs that can be grouped into a limited number of classes based on the type and number of nominal constituents they tend to occur with, along with the possibility for certain verbs to undergo changes in this respect (e.g. to have active and passive counterparts), has raised the interest of linguists working in various theoretical frameworks. Among possible ways to capture such peculiarities of verbs, the notion of valency introduced by Tesnière (1959) is perhaps the most widely employed.

The notion of verbal valency captures the inherently relational nature of verbs: as verbs denote events, they necessarily imply the event's participants, i.e. the verbal arguments. For this reason, valency can be viewed as referring to argument realization. This provides a direct link to research on the syntax-semantics interface (Levin and Rappaport Hovav 2005), which regards argument realization as crucially determined by the meaning associated with specific verb classes. Such an approach immediately raises the issue how to distinguish between arguments and adjuncts. In fact, in Tesnière's terms, valency is projected by the verb, and marks a sharp distinction between arguments (obligatory) and adjuncts (nonobligatory), which is often problematic (Aldai and Wichmann 2018: 255–256). Still, the notion of valency remains a useful tool for linguists, and has enjoyed steady popularity.

In cross-linguistic research, comparing valency patterns, valency alternations and valency changing operations has proven an extremely revealing practice, as comparison has provided evidence for the common intuition that certain verbal meanings tend to select similar patterns across languages. A major effort to make possible comparing verbs with the same meaning in different languages on a comparatively large scale is constituted by the Leipzig Valency Classes Project, or ValPaL (see Malchukov and Comrie 2015 and the online database available at http://valpal.info). Within the ValPaL project a cross-linguistic investigation has been carried out, dedicated to argument structure properties of verbs of different valency classes, i.e. groups of verbs that have similar syntactic patterns (coding patterns and alternations). The ValPaL verb selection was semantically based: a number of verb meanings were chosen and paired with the semantically most fitting *basic* (i.e. underived and sufficiently frequent) verb in the languages under scrutiny. Subsequently, all attested coding frames were recorded for each basic verb. The database contains data for 80 verb meanings from 36 languages; additional verb meanings were added for specific languages, up to a total of 162 verb meanings currently included.

Problematic aspects of the original notion of valency are acknowledged by the ValPaL contributors. Concerning the distinction between arguments and adjuncts, for example, Haspelmath and Hartmann (2015: 50) write: "for quite a few cases we did not have a unique way of distinguishing between arguments and adjuncts, and the ValPaL database is therefore not consistent in this regard." In certain cases, the ValPaL contributors pragmatically adopted a less strict view of the role of the verb as projecting its valency. This is the case when Haspelmath and Hartmann (2015: 45) claim that:

The terms in [a-e] all have basically the same meaning ...
a. complementation e.g. Quirk et al. (1985: 1069–71)
b. subcategorization Chomsky (1965)
c. argument structure e.g. Goldberg (1995)
d. government model Mel'čuk (1974) (Russian *model' upravlenija*)
e. clause blueprint Grebe (1959) (German *Satzbauplan*)

In fact, the terms mentioned above all have the same referent, i.e. the constituents that verbs tend to occur with, but to say that they have the same meaning is somewhat farfetched. Let us for example consider the notion of argument structure as understood in the framework of Construction Grammar. According to Goldberg (1995), argument structure constructions are stored as independent form-meaning pairs: in other words, they are not projected by verbs. Rather, they are in principle independent of verb semantics. However, as highlighted by Stefanowitsch and Herbst (2011), the two approaches, i.e. the verbal valency approach and the constructions approach, may be seen as complementing each other.

Notably, this has implicitly been acknowledged by Goldberg as well, when she discusses constructional homonymy. Indeed, Goldberg (2006: 38) acknowledges the possibility of homonymy and stresses the relevance of the verb's meaning, along with the meaning of co-occurring arguments. She writes:

> In fact, there do exist instances of constructional homonymy: a single surface form having unrelated meanings. In order to identify which argument structure construction is involved in cases of constructional ambiguity, attention must be paid to individual verb classes. In fact, in order to arrive at a full interpretation of any clause, the meaning of the main verb and the individual arguments must be taken into account.

In practice, this amounts to saying that homonymous constructions are disambiguated in conjunction to the verb's meaning and the meaning of the NPs that function as fillers. Hence, following Goldberg (1995: 16): "the meaning of an expression is the result of integrating the meanings of the lexical items into the meanings of constructions."

In spite of these caveats, the ValPaL database provides a solid foundation for research on verb classes, as it allows cross-linguistic comparison and highlights common tendencies and discrepancies in the coding of verbal arguments based on the verb's meaning. The publication of the ValPaL data has had an impact on further research on verb classes, valency patterns and argument structure constructions, and also provided a foundation for studies on transitivity scales (e.g. Aldai and Wichmann 2018) discussed below.

3 Valency and transitivity

Since Hopper and Thompson (1980) the definition of transitivity embraces several parameters, and views it as a property of whole sentences/utterances and as a scalar notion, whose degree is determined by various factors related both to event structure (Tsunoda 1985, 2015) and to role- specific features that characterize participants (see especially Næss 2007). Malchukov (2005) argues that the transitivity hierarchy should better be split into two sub-hierarchies departing from the transitive prototype, i.e. decreasing patienthood (decreasing degrees of affectedness in Tsunoda's terms), instantiated by change-of-state verbs, contact verbs, pursuit verbs and motion verbs, and decreasing agenthood, instantiated by experiential verbs, as shown in Figure 1.

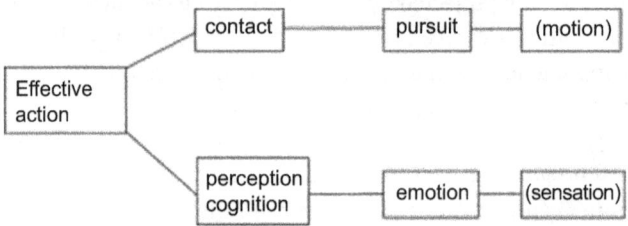

Figure 1: Two-dimensional verb type hierarchy.

The study conducted by Aldai and Wichmann (2018) on the ValPaL patterns and the morphosyntactic correlates of the transitivity scales in Figure 1 provides evidence for the relevance of valency patterns for the understanding of universal tendencies concerning argument realization and the coding of semantic roles (Haspelmath and Hartmann 2015).

Aldai and Wichmann (2018) found that coding is cross-linguistically relatively uniform in the sub-hierarchy of decreasing patienthood and that differences along the scale consistently concerns the coding of the second argument. On the other hand, valency patterns of verbs instantiating the sub-hierarchy of decreasing agenthood show a much wider range of coding variation, concerning not only the coding of the first argument, as expected (e.g. Malchukov 2006), but also the coding of the second argument. Interestingly, the sub-hierarchy of decreased agency mostly includes experiential verbs. The great cross-linguistic diversity in the coding of experience has been pointed out by researchers (e.g. Bhaskararao and Subbarao 2004; Verhoeven 2007; Luraghi 2020) and indicates a much more versatile nature of experiential situations that leads to a complex construal, crucially connected with embodiment and with common beliefs about situations. Hence, cross-linguistic research on valency patterns sheds light on the construal of situations: meanings that are lexicalized by verbs consistently showing the same valency patterns cross-linguistically point toward a uniform conceptualization of certain situations by humans, while meanings that are lexicalized by verbs showing a wider range of variation as to their valency patterns indicate situations that humans construe less consistently.

4 Valency changing operations and basic valency

The ValPaL database provides a survey of both valency alternations and valency changing operations. The distinction between the two groups is based on coding: while the former contains alternations that are not coded by the verb ("uncoded case alternations"; Malchukov 2015: 33) the latter includes alternations that are overtly indicated by verbal morphology ("verb-coded diathetic alternations"; Malchukov 2015: 35). Semantically, the two groups overlap: the anticausative alternation, for example, is uncoded in English, as in the case of *open* in (1) and (2), but it is coded in numerous other languages.

(1) *The door opened silently.*

(2) *The wind opened the door.*

The preferred coding and the morphological realization of valency changing operations have been investigated since at least Nedjalkov and Sil'nitsky (1973; see further Haspelmath 1993) and have given rise to a strand of research on 'basic valency'. According to Nichols, Peterson, and Barnes (2004), with change-of-state verbs indicating events that can come about spontaneously or be caused by some external entity, such as *open* in (1) and (2), differences in coding point to the existence of four basic groups of patterns. Two involve the addition/deletion of morphological material and are called oriented, either augmented as in (a) or reduced as in (b), while two do not involve the addition or deletion of any morphological material, and are called unoriented, either undetermined as in (c) or neutral as in (d). Augmented correspondences show a transitivizing orientation, while reduced ones conversely point to a detransitivizing orientation.

(a) Augmented correspondences: the basic form is intransitive; the transitive form is morphologically more complex; example: German *enden* 'finish, come to an end' / *be-enden* 'finish, bring to an end' (special case: the basic form is an adjective, e.g. Old Irish *is marb* 'be dead, die', *marbaid* 'kill')
(b) Reduced correspondences: the basic form is transitive; the intransitive form is morphologically more complex; example: Italian *sciogliere* 'melt, liquefy'/ *sciogliersi* 'melt, become liquefied'
(c) Undetermined correspondence:
   – Suppletion; example: English *eat/feed*
   – Ambivalent (labile); example: English *change* ('alter')/ *change* ('undergo alteration')
   – Conjugation class change; example: Italian *imbianchire* 'become white'/ *imbiancare* 'make white'
(d) Neutral correspondence:
   – Ablaut; example: English *lie/lay*
   – Double derivation (equipollent); example: Latin *fervesco* 'boil'/ *fervefacio* 'make boil'
   – Auxiliary change; example: Italian *è aumentato* 'it has grown, it has become bigger', *ha aumentato* 'it has increased, it has made bigger'

The notion of basic valency and of valency orientation as defined in Nichols, Peterson, and Barnes (2004) has introduced a useful tool to compare verb classes and their valency patterns synchronically and diachronically. Being based on morphological and lexical comparison, this tool is fruitfully applied to investigate genetic relationship, and has recently also been approached in an areal perspective (see for example Grossman and Witzlack-Makarevich 2019).

5 Adding a diachronic dimension

As highlighted in Section 1, this volume approaches valency and transitivity patterns from a diachronic vantage point. In this section, we briefly provide a frame for diachronic research in the field (Section 5.1) and then proceed to illustrate in greater detail the issues addressed in the chapters that compose the book.

5.1 Valency in diachrony

The data collected in the ValPaL database, in spite of having been used in cross-linguistic studies (see Aldai and Wichmann 2018), do not easily lend themselves to diachronic research, as the database only includes synchronic data from modern languages, and no historical stages of these languages have been investigated thus far based on the same verb pairs and the same methodology.

On the other hand, studies devoted to changes in verbal valency abound. To limit ourselves to valency alternation as described in Section 4, Nichols, Peterson, and Barnes' (2004) paper on valency orientation paved the way to a sway of language specific studies, including a number of diachronically oriented ones, such as van Gelderen (2011) on English and Plank and Lahiri (2015) on German. Various papers have discussed basic valency in ancient Indo-European languages, such as Hittite (Luraghi 2012), Gothic (Ottósson 2013), Homeric Greek (Sausa 2016) and in the reconstruction of Proto-Indo-European (Luraghi 2019). Other language families have also been investigated in diachronically oriented research: in particular, Grünthal and Nichols (2016) have shown how basic valency may change or remain stable based on data from Indo-European, Uralic, and Nakh-Daghestanian languages, while the issue of language contact has been addressed by Nau and Pakerys (2016) in a study of the influence of Finnic and Slavic languages on Baltic and by Grossman and Witzlack-Makarevich (2019), who assessed the integration of Greek-origin loan verbs into the valency and transitivity patterns of Coptic (Afro-Asiatic).

It appears then that the rich amount of data collected within the ValPaL project could be profitably exploited for diachronic research by supplementing it with data from historical stages of languages: this is one of the aims of the papers in this collection. Moreover, new research on the diachrony of valency alternations can deepen our understanding of mechanisms of language change and of the propensity of languages or language families to exploit different constructional patterns related to transitivity, especially when less investigated languages and language families are brought into the picture, as shown in some other chapters.

5.2 Content of the chapters

This volume grafts a diachronic dimension in the study of valency and transitivity patterns, either by addressing the evolution of valency patterns and valency orientation in single languages (Totoli, Soninke) or groups (Uralic languages), including languages with a long documented tradition (Greek and Romance languages), or by providing a thorough description and discussion of basic valency orientation and transitivity-related phenomena in well-studied ancient and medieval Indo-European languages such as Latin, Gothic and Old Irish.

In addition, the first chapter, by Eitan Grossman, titled "Transitivity, diachrony and language contact", frames the diachronic dimension of transitivity with research on contact-induced change, by highlighting the role of language contact in the emergence of broad areal patterns in morphosyntactic encoding. It shows how low-level changes in transitivity due to contact may be crucial in the evolution of valency patterns, calling into question purely functional explanations and suggesting that frequently observed morphosyntactic patterns may not be the result of and therefore proof of general tendencies rooted in semantics.

Chiara Zanchi and Matteo Tarsi's chapter applies the methodology of the ValPaL project to Gothic, a corpus language. It groups valency patterns and alternations of 87 Gothic verbs, thereby focusing on the encoding of the causal : noncausal alternation and showing how the causal domain was quite clearly tied to suffixation with -*ja*, while the noncausal domain could be expressed by a variety of morphological means, including the passive. It thus confirms recent conclusions on a much debated issue (Ottósson 2008).

The third chapter, by Elisa Roma, addresses the relationship between argument marking with finite and non finite forms of verbs in Old Irish, again applying the ValPaL framework in gathering data on valency patterns and alternations from a medieval language. It argues that the likelihood for finite forms to occur with an accusative argument and the likelihood for the genitive argument of non-finite forms to correspond to the same argument can be measured through a transitivity index, which may supply a criterion that substitutes acceptability judgments. The scale ranking a sample of 26 Old Irish verbs according to the transitivity index is then compared with cross-linguistic hierarchies of transitivity which have been put forward in the literature (Tsunoda 1985, 2015; Malchukov 2005; Haspelmath 2015).

Both chapters show how the ValPaL framework and methodology can be fruitfully applied also to past varieties in order to investigate valency patterns, verb classes and their evolution. Together with Guglielmo Inglese's chapter on Latin, they also illustrate accurate procedures devised to choose meaning equivalents for verbs in corpus languages.

Valency changing operations and the morphological encoding of the basic opposition between causal and noncausal verb pairs (in the strand of Nichols, Peterson, and Barnes 2004) also form the core of the remaining chapters.

Guglielmo Inglese's chapter on Latin analyzes data from 24 Early and Classical Latin verbs, splitting plain (noncausal) members of each pair into continuous and bound (e.g. *ferveo* 'be boiling' vs. *fervesco* 'come to boil'), following the updated guidelines in Nichols (2017). Latin widely displays suppletion, and a certain tendency for intransitivization via either verbal voice or the use of the reflexive pronoun *se* with so-called inanimate verbs. Verbal compounds with *-facio* 'make' and lability (P-lability) appear to be marginal strategies. Latin is clearly shown to occupy an intermediate position between Proto-Indo-European, reconstructed as a transitivizing language, and the Romance languages, which widely use intransitivizing strategies or lability. Through the data from Latin, the drift from transitivization to intransitivization that characterizes the Indo-European languages of Europe (Comrie 2006) can be framed chronologically and single steps can be focused.

Silvia Luraghi and Dionysios Mertyris' chapter on Greek offers a picture of the changes that occurred in the encoding of basic valency and valency alternation since the earliest stage, Homeric Greek, up to present-day Greek. Diachronic evidence comparing various stages shows an extension of voice alternation in Classical Greek, while lability, which emerged at the end of the Classical age and developed in Middle Greek, plays a relevant role for inanimate verbs in Modern Greek. The replacement of a detransitivizing strategy (voice opposition), which developed and was well established in the earliest documented phases of the language, by an undetermined one (lability) is clear-cut with inanimate verbs, while animate verbs show marginal adherence to either pattern and rather a tendency toward suppletion.

The sixth chapter, authored jointly by Riho Grünthal, Heini Arjava, Jyri Lehtinen and Johanna Nichols, gives a diachronic picture of the evolution of causativization strategies in the Uralic languages, taking into account a sub-sample of six verb sets (three animate verbs and three inanimate verbs) in 22 Uralic languages. The sub-sample, drawn from a larger database of 21 non-causal and causal verb pairs, allows to highlight diachronic developments within the family. Uralic languages clearly prefer valency changing affixal morphology. Other less consistent strategies result from verb-specific and language-specific historical developments that turn up to originate from former valency changing affixal morphology patterns as well.

The transitivization strategies of Totoli, a western Austronesian language of Indonesia, are the focus of the seventh chapter, by Sonja Riesberg, Kurt Malcher and Nikolaus Himmelmann. Totoli displays many transivization strategies, including causativization proper, transitive-intransitive alternation within the stative paradigm, alternation between the stative and the dynamic paradigms, and the use of applicative morphology. Among Western Austronesian languages, it is exceptional in that it employs the same set of formatives for different alternations (voice and applicative, depending on the argument structure of the verbal lexical base). After a description of Totoli's intricate system of valency changing operations, the authors suggest an hypothesis for the evolution of the puzzling polysemy in the voice-changing and valency-increasing paradigms: they argue that Totoli occupies an intermediate position between Philippine-type languages, which have a rich symmetrical-voice system but lack applicatives, and typical non-Philippine-type languages, which have applicative markers that are cognate with voice formatives in Philippine-type languages. The development of applicatives as a system independent from voice alternations in Philippine-type languages may have arisen through an overlap stage exemplified by Totoli, with the emergence of transitivity and valency as distinctions relevant in the grammar of Western Austronesian languages of the non-Philippine-type.

Michela Cennamo's chapter compares anticausativization strategies in Latin and in the history of its offspring Italian and French, taking into account aspectual, argument-based and lexical factors that determined different encodings, along with their developments over time. More specifically, it investigates the distribution of the different strategies available to mark anticausativization in French and Italian, both on a synchronic and on a diachronic plane, in the light of the interplay of the aspectual template of verbs with the verb's inherent meaning and features of the subject such as animacy and control. Cennamo shows that in both languages the SE-reflexive strategy comes to be gradually associated with telic, change-of-state verbs. Its interaction with the voice domain started from the alternation between the reflexive and the active intransitive in Old Italian, while Old French featured lability to a high extent. Cennamo further argues that the aspectual specification of verbs also affects the synchronic distribution of the anticausative strategies, whereby the reflexive morpheme *se* consistently indicates the presence of a final state/result/target state in the lexical meaning of a verb. It occurs with verbs lexically encoding a scalar change, either in all their uses, or in part of them.

The last chapter, by Denis Creissels, casts light on a curious feature of Soninke, a West-Mande language spoken in Mali, Mauritania, Senegal, and Gambia: all monosyllabic transitive verbs ending in a front vowel are labile (classical P-lability, as exemplified in Section 3), while transitive verbs that end with a non-front vowel are not labile. Creissels shows that this property is due to the evolution of a detransitivizing suffix-*i* that fused with the ending of non-monosyllabic verb stems, which eventually became homonymous with the transitive stems from which they derived. The Soninke case illustrates nicely how the emergence of a whole class of labile verbs may be due to phonetic development, being therefore not directly related to any semantic classification. It also strengthens the caveat in the first chapter of this volume against generalizations that are only based on synchronic verb classifications.

As these brief remarks show, the nine chapters collected in this book illustrate different facets of transitivity and of their reflexes in the valency patterns of verbs, such as to offer a wide perspective on the ways in which the encoding of transitivity-related features can vary over time, and can be either more stable or more prone to change depending on various factors, which range from language contact, the interaction with language-specific preferential patterns to phonological changes.

References

Aldai, Gontzal & Søren Wichmann. 2018. Statistical observations on hierarchies of transitivity. *Folia Linguistica* 52 (2). 249–281.
Bhaskararao, Peri & Karumuri Subbarao (eds.). 2004. *Non-nominative subjects*. Amsterdam & Philadelphia: John Benjamins.
Chomsky, Noam A. 1965. *Aspects of the theory of syntax*. Cambridge, MA: MIT Press.
Comrie, Bernard. 2006. Transitivity pairs, markedness, and diachronic stability. *Linguistics* 44 (2). 303–318.
Croft, William. 2012. *Verbs. Aspect and clausal structure*. Oxford: Oxford University Press.
Gelderen, Elly van. 2011. Valency changes in the history of English. *Journal of Historical Linguistics* 1 (1). 106–143.
Goldberg, Adele E. 1995. *Constructions: A Construction Grammar approach to argument structure*. Chicago: Chicago University Press.
Goldberg, Adele. 2006. *Constructions at work: The nature of generalization in language*. Oxford: Oxford University Press.
Grebe, Paul. 1959. *Grammatik der deutschen Gegenwartssprache*. (Duden). Mannheim: Bibliographisches Institut.
Grossman, Eitan & Alena Witzlack-Makarevich. 2019. Valency and transitivity in contact: An overview. *Journal of Language Contact* 12. 1–26.
Grünthal, Riho & Johanna Nichols. 2016. Transitivizing-detransitivizing typology and language family history. *Lingua Posnaniensis* 58 (2). 11–31.
Haspelmath, Martin & Iren Hartmann. 2015. Comparing verbal valency across languages. In Andrej Malchukov & Bernard Comrie (eds.), *Valency classes in the world's languages*, 41–71. Berlin & New York: Mouton de Gruyter.
Haspelmath, Martin. 1993. More on the typology of inchoative/causative verb alternations. In Bernard Comrie & Maria Polinsky (eds.), *Causatives and transitivity*, 87–120. Amsterdam & Philadelphia: John Benjamins.
Haspelmath, Martin. 2015. Transitivity prominence. In Andrej Malchukov & Bernard Comrie (eds.), *Valency classes in the world's languages*, 131–147. Berlin & New York: Mouton de Gruyter.
Hopper, Paul & Sandra Thompson. 1980. Transitivity in grammar and discourse. *Language* 56. 251–299.
Levin, Beth & Malka Rappaport Hovav. 2005. *Argument realization*. Cambridge: Cambridge University Press.
Luraghi, Silvia. 2012. Basic valency orientation and the middle voice in Hittite. *Studies in Language* 36 (1). 1–32.
Luraghi, Silvia. 2019. Basic valency orientation, the anticausative alternation, and voice in PIE. In Melanie Malzahn (ed.), *Akten der 16th Fachtagung der Indogermanischen Gesellschaft*, 259–274. Wiesbaden: Reichert.
Luraghi, Silvia. 2020. *Experiential verbs in Homeric Greek. A constructional approach*. Leiden: Brill.

Malchukov, Andrej & Bernard Comrie (eds.) 2015. *Valency classes in the world's languages*. Berlin & New York: Mouton De Gruyter.

Malchukov, Andrej. 2005. Case pattern splits, verb types and construction competition. In Mengistu Amberber and Helen de Hoop (eds.), *Competition and variation in natural languages: The case for case*, 73–118. Amsterdam: Elsevier.

Malchukov, Andrej. 2006. Transitivity parameters and transitivity alternations. In: Leonid Kulikov, Andrej Malchukov & Peter de Swart (eds.), *Case, valency and transitivity*, 175–190. Amsterdam & Philadelphia: John Benjamins.

Malchukov, Andrej. 2015. Valency classes and alternations: parameters of variation. In Andrej Malchukov & Bernard Comrie (eds.), *Valency classes in the world's languages*, 73–130. Berlin & New York: Mouton de Gruyter.

Mel'čuk, Igor' Aleksandrovič. 1974. *Opyt teorii lingvističeskix modelej "smysl-tekst": semantika, sintaksis* [Essay of a theory of "meaning-text" linguistic models: semantics, syntax]. Moskva: Nauka.

Nau, Nicole & Jurgis Pakerys. 2016. Transitivity pairs in Baltic: Between Finnic and Slavic. *Lingua Posnaniensis* 58 (2). 83–126.

Næss, Åshild. 2007. *Prototypical transitivity*. Amsterdam & Philadelphia: John Benjamins.

Nedjalkov, Vladimir P. & Georgij Sil'nitsky. 1973. The typology of morphological and lexical causatives. In Ferenc Kiefer (ed.), *Trends in Soviet theoretical linguistics*, 1–32. Dordrecht: Springer.

Nichols, Johanna, David A. Peterson & Jonathan Barnes. 2004. Transitivising and detransitivising languages. *Linguistic Typology* 8 (2). 149–211.

Nichols, Johanna. 2017. Realization of the causative alternation: revised wordlist and examples. https://www.academia.edu/34318209/Realization_of_the_causative_alternation_Revised_wordlist_and_examples (accessed on 1st October 2020).

Ottósson, Kjartan. 2008. The Old Nordic middle voice in the pre-literary period: Questions of grammaticalization and cliticisation. In Folke Josephson & Ingmar Söhrman (eds.), *Interdependence of diachronic and synchronic analyses* (Studies in Language Companion Series 103), 185–219. Amsterdam & Philadelphia: John Benjamins.

Ottósson, Kjartan. 2013. The anticausative and related categories in the Old Germanic languages. In Folke Josephson & Ingmar Söhrman (eds.), *Diachronic and typological perspectives on verbs*, 329–382. Amsterdam & Philadelphia: John Benjamins.

Plank, Frans & Aditi Lahiri. 2015. Microscopic and macroscopic typology: Basic valence orientation, more pertinacious than meets the naked eye. *Linguistic Typology* 19 (1). 1–54.

Quirk, Randolph, Sidney Greenbaum, Geoffrey Leech & Jan Svartvik. 1985. *A comprehensive grammar of the English language*. London: Longman.

Sausa, Eleonora. 2016. Basic valency orientation in Homeric Greek. *Folia Linguistica Historica* 37. 205–238.

Stefanowitsch Anatol and Thomas Herbst. 2011. Argument Structure – Valency and/or Constructions? *Zeitschrift für Anglistik und Amerikanistik* 59 (4). 315–316

Tesnière, Lucien. 1959. *Eléments de syntaxe structural*. Paris: Klincksieck.

Tsunoda, Tasaku. 1985. Remarks on transitivity. *Journal of Linguistics* 21. 385–396.

Tsunoda, Tasaku. 2015. The hierarchy of two-place predicates: its limitations and uses. In Andrej Malchukov and Bernard Comrie (eds.), *Valency classes in the world's languages*, 1597–1625. Berlin & New York: Mouton de Gruyter.

Verhoeven, Elisabeth. 2007. *Experiential constructions in Yucatec Maya*. Amsterdam & Philadelphia: John Benjamins.

Eitan Grossman
Transitivity, diachrony, and language contact

Abstract: Transitivity is often analyzed from the point of view of the formal and functional factors that shape morphosyntax. The contribution of language contact is not often highlighted. This article surveys some evidence for considering language contact in shaping the morphosyntax of transitivity-related phenomena, and proposes that the source of broad areal patterns should be sought in low-level processes of contact-induced change, such as pattern replication, contact-induced grammaticalization, and matter replication of constructional elements of transitivity encoding. Such patterns may call into question the search for purely functional explanations of transitivity encoding.

Keywords: language contact, transitivity, valency

1 Introduction

In contrast to a traditional view of transitivity as the property of having a direct object, studies of transitivity since Hopper and Thompson (1980), Tsunoda (1981, 1985), and Givón (1985) have characterized transitivity as semantic in nature, multifactorial (involving multiple parameters, such as agentivity and affectedness), and gradient (i.e. a clause can be said to be more or less transitive). The core observation in this research tradition is that the higher the semantic transitivity of an event, the more likely it is that it will be expressed or coded with the morphosyntactic properties associated with transitivity, or what Haspelmath calls transitivity encoding (Haspelmath 2015).[1] These morphosyntactic properties are typically related to valence, i.e. case-marking (or 'flagging'), but others, such as argument indexation, valency- and transitivity-changing constructions, and more, have been discussed as well. Moreover, the set of factors that is known

---

[1] Interestingly, Haspelmath (2015) makes it clear that his conception of transitivity is not semantic in nature, but rather morphosyntactic, and suggests that this is the case for earlier studies such as Tsunoda (1985) as well.

Eitan Grossman, Hebrew University of Jerusalem, e-mail: eitan.grossman@mail.huji.ac.il

to determine the morphosyntactic properties associated with transitivity has expanded. For example, a recent overview of Differential Argument Marking (Witzlack-Makarevich and Seržant 2018) lists numerous properties as relevant for morphosyntax, whether inherent properties of arguments, such as person, animacy, uniqueness, discreteness, and number; or non-inherent properties of arguments, such as definiteness and specificity or information structure status; or event-related semantic properties of arguments, such as agentivity, affectedness, and resultativity; or properties of clauses, such as TAM values, clause type, or polarity.

These properties have often been arranged in hierarchies that are intended to capture facts about transitivity in and across languages, such as the potentiality of agency hierarchy (Dixon 1979), the empathy hierarchy (DeLancey 1981), and the prominence hierarchy (Aissen 1999), just to name a few. A particularly well-known one is Tsunoda's (1981, 1985) implicational transitivity hierarchy, reassessed in Malchukov (2005, 2015), Wichmann (2016) and Aldai and Wichmann (2018), which on the basis of inherent verbal semantics predicts the likelihood that a verbal predicate will occur in a language's transitive construction or to have transitivity encoding. For example, verbs that describe an event involving a direct effect on a patient (e.g. translation equivalents of 'hit' or 'shoot') are predicted to be more likely to occur in a transitive construction than verbs describing a perception event (e.g. translation equivalents of 'see' or 'hear').

Importantly, these synchronic hierarchies – and the properties that govern them – have commonly been thought to influence the diachronic pathways through which morphosyntactic coding means change. For example, some synchronic accounts of transitivity focus on information structure: topical P arguments ('direct objects') trigger extra marking to distinguish them from A arguments ('subjects') or to index their salient information-structural properties; another scenario claims that P arguments may be marked in contexts of topic-shift (Dalrymple and Nikolaeva 2011; Iemmolo 2010). The same properties have been invoked in diachronic accounts of the development of Differential Object Marking in unrelated languages, such as Chichewa (Downing 2018), Spanish (Melis 2018), and Khoe languages (McGregor 2018). Similarly, synchronic animacy or definiteness hierarchies have been invoked to explain diachronic change in various languages, e.g. Hindi (Montaut 2018). All of these studies share the assumption that synchronic hierarchies reflect the diachronic motivations and mechanisms that created them, conceivably because both the synchronic hierarchies and the diachronic processes reflect the same cognitive and communicative biases that constrain language use and thereby shape language change.

All of the above are what Bickel (2015, 2017) has called 'functional' factors or triggers. Functional triggers are biases that affect the probability that a linguistic property will evolve in a particular way. These can be cognitive biases, such as processing preferences, or communicative biases of the sort that lead to frequency effects. Theories based on such functional triggers are called functional theories (Bickel 2015).

But is that all there is to it? On the contrary: there is much – and diverse – evidence that 'event-based' factors or triggers contribute to shaping the mapping of transitivity, seen in semantic terms, to morphosyntactic properties[2] of clauses, in and across languages. Event-based triggers are the historically contingent facts of human history that bring speakers of different languages into new linguistic, social, and geographical environments, and are prominently implicated in many accounts of language contact (Bickel 2017). In other words, it seems that language contact may play a substantial role in determining the cross-linguistic distributions of the morphosyntactic properties associated with transitivity.

Functional theories and event-based theories have often been seen as competing explanations. For example, Bickel (2015) notes that it has been observed that overt case marking that distinguishes A from P in transitive clauses correlates with V-final order. This has been explained with reference to processing, a functional theory. On the other hand, it has been proposed that the frequency of case marking in Eurasia is the result of contact-based diffusion, an event-based theory. In other words, there are two competing theories, both of which are consistent with the data.

Using the Family Bias method (Bickel 2013), which investigates diachronic trends within and across language families, Bickel (2015) found there is indeed a bias in families towards case marking if word order is V-final, which may support a processing explanation. But there is also a bias in families towards case marking if the family is in Eurasia, which may support an event-based theory. These effects are statistically independent, which points to the conclusion that language contact plausibly enhanced an existing functional bias. In other words, functional and event-based accounts need not be mutually exclusive. Moreover, and importantly in the present context, functional accounts without event-based accounts – without language contact – do not capture the whole picture.

Even more suggestive of the importance of event-based triggers is the insight that the very functional factors that might bias language change might play out differently across areas and genealogical units. For example, consider Sin-

---

[2] For a variety of reasons, this assumption has come under fire. In particular, it has been argued that functional factors may not easily be read directly off of typological distributions, a point made by Greenberg (1978), Dryer (1989), Maslova (2000) Harris (2008), Bickel, Witzlack-Makarevich and Zakharko (2015), Cristofaro (2013, 2014, 2019), Grossman (2016), Grossman, Jacques and Antonov (2018) and Grossman and Polis (2018), among others.

nemäki's (2014) typological study of Differential Object Marking. Languages with Differential Object Marking – or split-P systems – are found in many parts of the world. However, the areal patterning of the systems reveals an interesting insight: while animacy effects are found all over the globe, definiteness- or specificity-based systems are concentrated in the Old World, particularly in Africa.

In other words, the very semantic and discourse-related properties that splits are allegedly based on may themselves show areal patterning, which means that even if there are universal factors that bias language change, their effects may show up differentially in ways that can be retrieved. Another reading of this situation is that some cross-linguistically prominent patterns might not have strong functional motivations at all, but may have diffused throughout languages due to the largely contingent historical events that brought populations into and out of contact and to the sociolinguistic features of these contact situations that facilitated or inhibited the diffusion of particular properties. This has been shown convincingly for differential argument marking (in particular split-A and split-P systems) by Bickel, Witzlack-Makarevich and Zakharko (2015), who provide evidence against the universality of referential scales, arguing instead that the empirical frequency of differential argument marking is largely the result of historical diffusion events. Another possibility is that at least some of the morphosyntactic properties commonly associated with transitivity are diachronically stable, in which case one would expect to find genealogical signals such that family- or genus-level preferences are visible.

The goal of the present article is to survey some evidence that event-based triggers – essentially, language contact – should be taken into account when considering the factors that shape the morphosyntax of transitivity-related phenomena in human languages. The structure of the article is as follows. In Section 2, I present evidence that transitivity-related phenomena show large-scale areal signals that point to the role of event-based triggers. In Section 3, I discuss some lower-level processes of language contact that may shape transitivity-related phenomena. Section 4 concludes this paper.

2 Areal signals and event-based triggers

Typological investigations of transitivity-related phenomena have consistently produced evidence for functional factors, but, importantly in this context, for event-based triggers as well. In this section, I focus on basic valence orientation or transitivity prominence, which is essentially the extent to which verbal predicates in a given language make use of transitive encoding (Haspelmath 2015). This is often operationalized on the basis of lists of verb meanings as a basis for comparison, and individual verbs or verb pairs in particular languages are coded for a variety of morphosyntactic properties with respect to which languages can vary (Malchukov 2015). Prominent features that have been tested cross-linguistically include derivational relationships between causal/noncausal verb pairs involving meanings like 'break' or 'dry' (see Haspelmath 1993, 2011; Nichols, Peterson and Barnes 2004; Haspelmath et al. 2014) and valency frames, which itself include case-marking patterns or flags and argument indexing on verbs (Haspelmath 2015). Transitivity prominence intersects with proposed semantically-based hierarchies (Tsunoda 1985; Malchukov 2005), in that such hierarchies predict that transitivity encoding might vary across languages, in terms of the number of predicates that are coded as transitive, but the list of verbal predicates should occupy a contiguous space on the hierarchy.

Semantically-based hierarchies have fared well, broadly speaking, in these studies; unsurprisingly, translation equivalents of 'break,' 'hit,' and 'kill' generally receive transitive encoding across samples of languages, while equivalents of 'die' and 'be dry' never do. Predictably, there is more variance with respect to the translation equivalents of 'see,' 'meet,' and 'like,' which are often treated as transitive in particular languages, but are also often found in a construction other than the transitive. Another angle on this is provided in Haspelmath et al. (2014), who argue that purely semantic accounts of derivational relationships between causal/noncausal verb pairs are bettered by communication-based accounts involving frequency. Overall, functional theories of transitivity hierarchies generally make good cross-linguistic predictions.

In contrast, such theories have little to say about why a particular language might have a higher or lower transitivity prominence. This gap is filled, to some extent, by considerations of language contact, as witnessed by areal signals. A first example is Haspelmath (1993), whose sample was mostly Eurasian, and who finds a European preference for anticausatives or detransitivization. In other words, in a select list of verb pairs, there was a European areal preference for treating transitive verbs as basic and intransitives as derived. Evidence is found from a West-East split within geographically diffused families, mainly Indo-European.

Nichols, Peterson and Barnes (2004), again looking at transitivity prominence ('basic valence orientation') in a global sample, identify many areal signals. For just a few examples, lability is preferred in Europe and dispreferred in the Americas and in the Pacific Rim. Transitivization is generally preferred worldwide, and dispreferred only in Europe (replicating the findings of Haspelmath 1993). Detransitivization is strongly dispreferred in north Asia and is preferred in Central America. Equipollent marking is preferred in Central America and western North America, and is dispreferred in Africa.

Say (2014) is probably the most detailed study of transitivity prominence and related phenomena in a single area. On the basis of 130 bivalent predicates in a dense sample of 57 Northern Eurasian languages, Say investigated the extent to which phylogenetic distance and geographical distance predict the extent to which languages are similar or dissimilar in terms of transitivity. Say found that overall, structural distance measures correlate positively with geographical and genetic distances. In particular, transitivity prominence shows areal effects at a sub-continental degree of granularity, with a preference for transitivity peaking in Central Western Europe and in the Far East, and a preference for intransitivity peaking in the Caucasus and in Eastern Europe.

Furthermore, it was found that genus-level genealogical units are relatively homogenous with respect to transitivity prominence, but there were no significant family-size effects, with lots of diversity in Uralic and Indo-European. In terms of the similarity between languages with respect to whether individual verbs – e.g. the translation equivalents of meanings like 'win' and 'see' – are transitive or intransitive, Say found significant genealogical signals at genus and family levels. In fact, verb hierarchies in Eurasia appear to be family-specific, e.g. experience predicates in Nakh-Daghestanian tend to be intransitive, as do contact predicates in Uralic. As Say points out, this genealogical signal is strange if verb hierarchies of transitivity prominence are universal.

Say concludes that valency patterns of individual verbs change relatively quickly and are easily transferable in language contact. However, languages are relatively stable in terms of those semantic features that are relevant for the assignment of the [+/−] transitivity values to individual verbs. Finally, transitivity hierarchies of verb meanings can be family-specific. Taken together, the results of these studies point to a certain amount of diachronic stability in transmission of some aspects of transitivity, as well as some likelihood to change due to chance, inherent functional biases, or language contact. Interestingly, in areas with relatively little phylogenetic diversity or in which long-term multilingualism has led to convergence in transitivity profiles, there is actually quite little opportunity for additional contact-induced change, unless new languages with different profiles enter the area. This may be the case for large swaths of Eurasia, to which some late-expanding and socio-politically dominant languages, like Russian, are relative latecomers: in such cases, there is a renewed opportunity for contact-induced change.

Summarizing this section, despite the predominance of functional theories related to transitivity phenomena, areal effects are, so to speak, all over the place. Moreover, there is some preliminary information about the relative diachronic stability of transitivity phenomena within families, at least for some areas. These facts should lead us to reconsider purely functional theories of what shapes transitivity phenomena.

3 From macro to micro: lower-level contact processes

How, then, do these areal patterns emerge? The answer will probably involve some combination of (i) functional factors, e.g. inherent semantics and usage biases; (ii) inheritance; (iii) language contact; (iv) by-roads (e.g. side effects of other changes); and (v) chance. This section focuses on low-level processes of contact-induced change that potentially scale up to areal and macro-areal patterns. In particular, this section discusses some mechanisms of contact-induced change that can shape morphosyntactic properties of constructions related to transitivity. There is still no comprehensive survey of the role of contact in shaping transitivity-related phenomena, although there is a lot of data to be gleaned from individual language descriptions and the literature on language contact.[3]

One type of contact-induced change involves changes in the number of and assignment principles for valency classes. In Kartvelian, for example, the case-marking of core arguments is generally determined by predicate class and the tense-aspect values of the clause (Haig 2015). In Laz, which has been heavily influenced by Turkish, the tense-aspect based valency split has been lost, while the predicate-based split has been retained. In the Ardeşen dialect of Laz, however, the marking of core arguments has been even more radically restructured on the basis of Turkish, such that core arguments are unmarked by case. Interestingly, this includes the R argument of ditransitive clauses. This is unlike Turkish, which uses the same case marker for both goals and R arguments. Haig (2015) points out that the Ardeşen Laz of Turkish-Laz bilinguals living in Ankara replicate the Turkish pattern, extending the Goal case marker -*ša* to R arguments of ditransitives. Such developments, which plausibly result from calquing, pattern replication (Matras and Sakel 2019), or metatypy (Ross 2015) naturally have consequences for the type of coding properties that are explored in language-specific and typological studies of transitivity. Another example of pattern replication is found in Lithuanian Romani, where erstwhile monovalent verbs may occur with a detransitivizing marker, copying the Slavic structure (Tenser 2005).

Another way that language contact can impact transitivity encoding is through substrate influence. This is particularly visible in creoles, where valency patterns consistently come from substrates rather than lexifiers (Michaelis 2019). This is illustrated by Haitian Creole, a French-lexifier creole (1), in which 'rain'

---

[3] Interestingly, the studies in Malchukov and Comrie (2015) have almost nothing to say about language contact. However, a special issue of the *Journal of Language Contact* (Grossman, Witzlack-Makarevich and Seržant 2019) was recently devoted to this topic.

predicates pattern like substrate languages, e.g. Fongbe (2), rather than like the lexifier.⁴

(1) Haitian Creole (French-lexifier creole, Caribbean; Fattier 2013)
    lapli   a   pral   tonbe   talè
    rain   DEF   FUT.go   fall   soon
    'It will rain very soon.'

(2) Fongbe (Kwa, Benin; Lefebvre and Brousseau 2002: 245)
    jí   jà
    rain   fall
    'It is raining.'

To the extent that this is the case, creole valency and transitivity patterns are thus not independent from those of their substrate languages, and thus do not provide independent evidence for functional theories.

Not all contact-induced changes in this domain are simply calquing. It is well known that language contact can play an indirect role in shaping transitivity-related phenomena via contact-induced grammaticalization (Heine and Kuteva 2005). In such cases, the particular developmental pathway of an inherited construction in one language is biased by the presence of a model from another language.

Examples of the grammaticalization of transitivity-related phenomena are fairly common, in particular in the domain of valency- and transitivity-changing constructions. A well-known case is the reshaping of the inherited Pennsylvania German passive construction in a number of ways, including the replacement of the agent-marking preposition *vun* by *bei*, as well as a change in linear order such that the *bei*-phrase is outside of the discontinuous verb (Burridge 2006). Other examples that have been proposed include Hup, a Nadahup language, which developed a passive construction similar to that found in East Tucanoan languages with which Hup has been in contact, but which is not found in other language from the family (Epps 2006). The Mapudungun reflexive construction may have developed an anticausative function due to contact with Spanish (Zúñiga 2015). Arkadiev (2020) describes a case in which Abaza copies an inverse construction from Kabardian. Norman (1982) and Chappell (2006) point out that Northern Sinitic varieties differ from southern varieties in having grammatical-

---

4 Glossing conventions are according to the Leipzig Glossing Rules. Abbreviations not found in the Leipzig list are ADD – additive, DETR – detransitivizer, DIR – directional, ILL – illative, RUS – Russian loan word.

ized a causative construction from the verbs meaning 'make' and 'let', a difference which they attribute to Manchu superstrate influence.

Of course, as noted in Section 2, large-scale areal signals may point to contact-triggered spreads of constructions associated with transitivity. For example, Bickel, Witzlack-Makarevich and Zakharko (2015) show that split-A and split-P systems show strong areal patterning, with split systems especially prominent in some parts of Eurasia and in the Sahul macro-area. In fact, the authors argue convincingly that there is little evidence for the universal referential scales often assumed to bias language change, claiming instead that 'differential case marking on A and P is first and foremost a pattern prone to diffusion' (Bickel, Witzlack-Makarevich and Zakharko 2015: 40).

We now turn from pattern-replication and contact-induced grammaticalization to some types of contact-induced change related to matter replication (Matras and Sakel 2019). In some cases, the case-marking patterns of arguments in a language is changed due to the replication of an overt flag. For example, some Quechuan varieties, such as Ulcumayo Quechua and Lamas Kechwa, borrow the Spanish accusative marker *a*, often in the same conditions that trigger Spanish overt accusative marking, i.e. [+specificity] (Sanchez 2011). Interestingly, the Spanish-origin accusative marker co-occurs with the inherited Quechuan accusative suffix -*ta*, as in (3) and (4).

(3) Ulcumayo Quechua (Quechuan, Peru; Sanchez 2011)
 Algo gati-pu-n a un niñu-ta
 dog follow-DIR-3SG ACC a boy-ACC
 'The dog follows a boy.'

(4) Lamas Kechwa (Quechuan, Peru; Sanchez 2011)
 kawa-yka-n a ese niñu-ta
 look-PROG-3SG ACC that boy-ACC
 '(S/he) is looking at that boy.'

Matter replication of case markers is documented in several Kiranti languages, which have a dative marker -*lai*, e.g. Bantawa (Doornebal 2009), Puma (Bickel et al. 2019); Camling, Athpare and Thulung (Ebert 1994), generally agreed to be borrowed from Nepali. In some languages, it participates in a Differential Object Marking system, marking P arguments.

However, the borrowing of case markers is far less common than the borrowing of verbs (Wichmann and Wohlgemuth 2008), which can itself lead to considerable contact-induced change in the domain of transitivity. This is because verbs in different languages have a range of morphosyntactic properties. These properties are language-specific and may vary between the donor language and the target language. In a situation of borrowing it is possible that a borrowed verb will acquire only some of these properties but not the others.

In some cases, this does not present any special complications. For example, Jacques (2019) shows that Japhug (Burmo-Qiangic) massively borrowed verbs from Tibetan (Bodic). Whereas Japhug can index up to two arguments on the verb and employs direct/inverse marking, Tibetan has no indexing whatsoever. Verbs borrowed from Tibetic languages in Japhug were borrowed mainly by 'direct insertion' in Wichmann and Wohlgemuth's (2008) terms, i.e. they were immediately available for the Japhug grammar without any morphological or syntactic adaptation and receive the same kind of indexing as inherited Japhug verbs with comparable semantics.

In contrast, borrowed verbs may have to be assigned to a valency class or transitivity pattern in the borrowing language. Even when languages are similar in terms of the morphosyntactic properties associated with their transitivity systems, there are often subtle but important differences. For example, Jacques (2019) shows that Japhug and Tibetan both have ergative-absolutive alignment in their transitive constructions, and loan verbs are often easily copied from one transitive construction to another. However, Tibetan has a richer case system than Japhug, and its core arguments are often marked by the dative case. Tibetan-origin verbs that have a dative-marked core argument in the donor language are integrated into Japhug valency patterns in a variety of ways, often depending on the semantic role of the argument in question. In other cases, Tibetan bivalent intransitive verbs are sometimes copied into the Japhug transitive construction.

In Michif, a mixed language whose verbal system derives from Plains Cree (Algonquian), there are numerous French- and English-origin verbs, while its nominal system derives from French. Michif verbs belong to one of four morphological classes, depending on the transitivity or intransitivity of the verb and the animacy of its S or P argument. This property of the transitivity system of Michif is completely different from the transitivity systems of the donor languages. Antonov (2019) finds that the majority of loan verbs are assigned to the verb class regularly indexing the single animate argument (the so-called Animate Intransitive class). Though for the most part this assignment is straightforwardly semantically based, there are exceptions: some source-language transitive verbs were integrated into the Animate Intransitive class, which regularly indexes the sole animate argument and not both arguments.

Arkhangelskij and Usacheva (2017) show that Russian verbs can be borrowed into Udmurt (Uralic) with detransitivizing morphology, i.e. the sux *–s'a*, even though Udmurt has a comparable construction involving the suffix *-isk*. Russian loan verbs are usually integrated into the Beserman dialect of Udmurt via a light verb strategy (Wichmann and Wohlgemuth 2008; Wohlgemuth 2009). Interestingly, there is some variation within Udmurt as to whether the light verb itself bears detransitivitizing morphology in such cases, as seen in (5) and (6).

(5) Udmurt (Uralic; Arkhangelskij and Usacheva 2017)
 fotograrovat's'a   kar-isk-i-z=no   korka
 take.pictures.REFL:RUS   do-DETR-PST-3SG=ADD   house.ILL
 pir-i-z
 enter-PST-3SG
 '[The guy] took picture of himself and went into the house.'

(6) Udmurt (Uralic Arkhangelskij and Usacheva 2017)
 fotograrovat's'a   kar-o
 take.pictures.REFL:RUS   do-PRS.3PL
 'They are taking pictures of themselves.'

Arkhangelskiy and Usacheva (2017) show that the presence or absence of the detransitivizer does not depend on the choice of lexical verb, the grammatical properties of the light verb, or the particular function of the detransitivizer in a given context. Rather, this feature shows areal patterning, such that the omission of the detransitivizer characterizes the areas in which Udmurt is especially influenced by the Turkic languages Bashkir and (possibly) Tatar. These languages, which also use the light verb strategy to integrate Russian loan verbs, consistently show omission of detransitivizers in comparable contexts.

Incorporation, which is often associated with detransitivization, is also interesting in light of loan verb integration. For example, loan verbs cannot incorporate nominals in Coptic (Grossman 2019), but loan nominals can be incorporated in native verb stems. Due to the massive influx of Greek loan verbs in Coptic, this means that the relative number of verbs that can incorporate nominals has drastically shrunk. In Japhug (Jacques 2019), on the other hand, both the verbal and the nominal parts of the incorporation construction can be of Tibetan origin. Furthermore, a native nominal can be incorporated into a Tibetan-origin verb. However, there are no documented cases of a native verb incorporating a Tibetan-origin nominal, which is precisely the situation allowed in Coptic.

The effects of loan verbs on transitivity encoding in the borrowing language can be substantial. For example, as noted above, Coptic borrowed hundreds of verbs from Greek. While the number of arguments for each verb in Greek was generally carried over into Coptic, Greek-origin verbs could not be fully integrated into the native transitivity patterns of Coptic (Grossman 2019); beyond being unable to incorporate nominals, they did not allow P indexing. On the other hand, Greek-origin verbs did occur with native valency patterns, including the transitive case frame. The result of this mass borrowing, therefore, was to substantially increase the class of bivalent verbs that did not allow the incorporation or indexing of P arguments. Seen from another perspective, contact-induced changed greatly expanded a grammatical transitivity split, based on the source language of verbs.

Not only can loan verbs be integrated in complex ways into native valency patterns, they can carry donor-language valency patterns over into the target language. This is the case in Middle English, which copied Old French verbs (e.g. *plaire* > *plesen* 'to please') together with their valency patterns, notably the dative-marking of the experiencer argument (in contrast to the native pattern). Interestingly, this valency pattern spread to native verbs with similar lexical meanings, such as *quemen* and *liken* (Trips and Stein 2019).

However, beyond the basic morphosyntactic means by which loan verbs are integrated into a native morphosyntax (Wichmann and Wohlgemuth 2008; Wohlgemuth 2009), we still know extremely little about the integration of loan verbs with respect to most phenomena associated with transitivity. That means, beyond the inherent interest for language contact research, that verb borrowing itself might play a hitherto unacknowledged role in the transitivity hierarchies discussed in Section 1. In particular, they might contribute to the dependence of such hierarchies not only on genealogical stability (e.g. the family-specific hierarchies found by Say 2014) or on areal convergence due to pattern-replication (e.g. the area-specific hierarchies found by Bickel, Witzlack-Makarevich and Zakharko 2015), but also to extensive matter replication.

4 Conclusions

In this survey, I have suggested that the functional factors that govern synchronic distributions of transitivity encoding, and by assumption the diachronic evolution of transitivity encoding, are likely to be unable to tell the whole story. Rather, at least some aspects of transitivity encoding are apparently diachronically stable at varying phylogenetic depths. Moreover, and at the heart of this paper, 'event-based' factors that lead to language contact, seem to play a large role in diverse domains related to transitivity. This is most clearly visible in large-scale areal effects visible in typological studies, on the one hand, and individual case-studies of particular contact situations, on the other.

The central proposal made here is that lower-level processes of contact-induced change may scale up to visible areal effects. These processes may include pattern replication (from substrate, adstrate and superstrate languages), contact-induced grammaticalization, matter replication of constructional elements related to transitivity, and loan verbs and their integration into native transitivity patterns. Contact-related changes are likely to interact with functional factors in a wide variety of ways, whether by enhancing or reducing existing biases, by leading to the diffusion of otherwise rare or dispreferred structures (as has been suggested for Differential Object Marking), and more.

Due to the extreme paucity of empirically-based generalizations about the effects of language contact on transitivity encoding, it is difficult to sketch a broader picture than that presented here. However, some avenues of research may be particularly promising. One such avenue is suggested by Nichols (2018), who has proposed a theory according to which a preference for causativization – i.e. a situation in which a language has a preference for intransitive base verbs and derived transitives – is an attractor state ("any state that is more easily or more often entered or acquired than departed or lost"). The situation in which this possibility and its diffusion is favored by a particular sociolinguistic context she calls 'symbiosis' ("where languages mingle in speech"). Symbiosis, in turn, is favored by certain demographic, sociocultural, and environmental factors she calls frontier conditions, with evidence from northern Eurasia, the Caucasus, North and Central America, and the Pacific. This amounts to a testable hypothesis about the interaction of functional and event-based triggers in the domain of transitivity phenomena. It is hypotheses of this sort that might bridge the gap between broad areal patterns observed in typological research, individual case-studies of language contact, and the sociolinguistic and demographic factors that are generally considered crucial for explaining the results of language contact.

In conclusion, this survey is intended to provide an alternative view on phenomena traditionally attributed to functional factors, and to suggest that synchronic distributions are not necessarily evidence for the diachronic processes that led to them. In a sense, this is similar to proposals made by Cristofaro (2013, 2014, 2019), who argues that synchronic distributions can be the result of multiple and diverse developmental pathways, which need not be motivated by a single overarching functional factor. In contrast to Cristofaro's perspective, however, I suggest that genealogical and areal signals in the patterning of transitivity encoding do not only call into question the need for overarching functional explanations, but rather point to the plausibility of an important – and still poorly understood – role played by genealogical stability, on the one hand, and contact-induced change, on the other.

References

Aissen, Judith. 1999. Markedness and subject choice in Optimality Theory. *Natural Language and Linguistic Theory* 17. 673–711.

Aldai, Gontzal & Søren Wichmann. 2018. Statistical observations on hierarchies of transitivity. *Folia Linguistica* 52 (2). 249–281.

Antonov, Anton. 2019. Loan verb integration in Michif. *Journal of Language Contact* 12 (1). 27–51.

Arkadiev, Peter M. 2020. Borrowing non-canonical inverse between Kabardian and Abaza. Talk presented at 19th International Morphology Meeting, Vienna, 6–8 February.

Arkhangelskij, Timofey & Maria Usacheva. 2017. Spontaneous Russian verbal borrowings in Udmurt. Talk presented at Contact-Driven Multilingual Practices, University of Helsinki, 1 June.

Bickel, Balthasar. 2013. Distributional biases in language families. In Balthasar Bickel, Lenore A. Genoble, David A. Peterson & Alan Timberlake (eds.), *Language typology and historical contingency*, 415–444. Amsterdam & Philadelphia: John Benjamins.

Bickel, Balthasar. 2015. Distributional typology: Statistical inquiries into the dynamics of linguistic diversity. In Bernd Heine & Heiko Narrog (eds.), *The Oxford handbook of linguistic analysis*, 2nd edn. 901–923. Oxford: Oxford University Press.

Bickel, Balthasar. 2017. Areas and universals. In Raymond Hickey (ed.), *The Cambridge handbook of areal linguistics*, 40–54. Cambridge: Cambridge University Press.

Bickel, Balthasar, Martin Gaenszle, Arjun Rai, Prem Dhoj Rai, Shree Kumar Rai, Vishnu S. Rai & Narayan P Sharma (Gautam). 2019. Two ways of suspending object agreement in Puma: Between incorporation, antipassivization, and optional agreement. *Himalayan Linguistics* 7. 1–18.

Bickel, Balthasar, Alena Witzlack-Makarevich & Taras Zakharko. 2015. Typological evidence against universal effects of referential scales on case alignment. In Ina Bornkessel-Schlesewsky, Andrej L. Malchukov & Marc Richards (eds.), *Scales and hierarchies: A cross-disciplinary perspective*, 7–43. Berlin & New York: Mouton de Gruyter.

Burridge, Kathryn. 2006. Language contact and convergence in Pennsylvania German. In R. M. W. Dixon & Alexandra Y. Aikhenvald (eds.), *Grammars in contact. A cross-linguistic typology*, 179–200. Oxford: Oxford University Press.

Chappell, Hilary. 2006. Language contact and areal diffusion in Sinitic languages. In Alexandra Aikhenvald & R.M.W. Dixon (eds.), *Areal diffusion and genetic inheritance: Problems for typology and genetic affiliation*, 328–357. Oxford: Oxford University Press.

Cristofaro, Sonia. 2013. The referential hierarchy: Reviewing the evidence in diachronic perspective. In Dik Bakker & Martin Haspelmath (eds.), *Languages across boundaries: Studies in the memory of Anna Siewierska*, 69–93. Berlin & New York: Mouton de Gruyter.

Cristofaro, Sonia. 2014. Competing motivation models and diachrony: What evidence for what motivations? In Brian MacWhinney, Andrej L. Malchukov & Edith A. Moravcsik (eds.), *Competing motivations in grammar and usage*, 282–298. Oxford: Oxford University Press.

Cristofaro, Sonia. 2019. Taking diachronic evidence seriously: Result-oriented vs. source-oriented explanations of typological universals. In Karsten Schmidtke-Bode, Natalia Levshina, Susanne Maria Michaelis & Ilja A. Seržant (eds.), *Explanation in typology: Diachronic sources, functional motivations and the nature of the evidence*, 25–46. Berlin: Language Science Press.

Dalrymple, Mary & Irina Nikolaeva. 2011. *Objects and information structure*. Cambridge: Cambridge University Press.

DeLancey, Scott. 1981. An interpretation of split ergativity and related patterns. *Language* 57 (3). 557–626.
Dixon, R. M. W. 1979. Ergativity. *Language* 55 (1). 59–138.
Doornebal, Marius Albert. 2009. *A grammar of Bantawa: Grammar, paradigm tables, glossary and texts of a Rai language of Eastern Nepal*. Leiden: Leiden University dissertation.
Downing, Laura J. 2018. Differential object marking in Chichewa. In Alena Witzlack-Makarevich & Ilja A. Seržant (eds.), *Diachrony of differential argument marking*, 41–67. Berlin: Language Science Press.
Dryer, Matthew S. 1989. Large linguistic areas and language sampling. *Studies in Language* 13 (2). 257–292.
Ebert, Karen. 1994. *The structure of Kiranti languages*. Zurich: ASAS-Verlag.
Epps, Patience. 2006. The Vaupes melting pot: Tukanoan influence on Hup. In R. M. W. Dixon & Alexandra Y. Aikhenvald (eds.), *Grammars in contact. A cross-linguistic typology*, 267–289. Oxford: Oxford University Press.
Fattier, Dominique. 2013. Haitian Creole structure dataset. In Susanne Maria Michaelis, Philippe Maurer, Martin Haspelmath, and Magnus Huber (eds.), *Atlas of Pidgin and Creole Language Structures Online*. Leipzig: Max Planck Institute for Evolutionary Anthropology. http://apics-online.info/ (accessed June 7, 2016).
Givón, Talmy. 1985. Ergative morphology and transitivity gradients in Newari. In Frans Plank (ed.), *Relational typology*, 89–107. Berlin & New York: Mouton de Gruyter.
Greenberg, Joseph H. 1978. Diachrony, synchrony and language universals. In Joseph H. Greenberg, Charles A. Ferguson & Edith A. Moravcsik (eds.), *Universals of human language. Volume 1: Method and theory*, 61–92. Stanford: Stanford University Press.
Grossman, Eitan. 2016. From rarum to rarissimum: An unexpected zero person marker. *Linguistic Typology* 20 (1). 1–23.
Grossman, Eitan. 2019. Language-specific transitivities in contact: The case of Coptic. *Journal of Language Contact* 12 (1). 89–115.
Grossman, Eitan, Guillaume Jacques & Anton Antonov. 2018. A crosslinguistic rarity in synchrony and diachrony: Adverbial subordinator prefixes exist. *STUF – Language Typology and Universals* 71 (4). 513–538.
Grossman, Eitan & Stephane Polis. 2018. Swimming against the typological tide or paddling along with language change? Dispreferred structures and diachronic biases in affix ordering. *Journal of Historical Linguistics* 8 (3). 388–443.
Grossman, Eitan, Alena Witzlack-Makarevich & Ilja A. Seržant. 2019. *Valency and transitivity in contact*. Special issue of *Journal of Language Contact*.
Haig, Geoffrey. 2015. Linguistic diffusion in present-day East Anatolia: From top to bottom. In Alexandra Aikhenvald & R.M.W. Dixon (eds.), *Areal diffusion and genetic inheritance: Problems in comparative linguistics*, 195–224. Oxford: Oxford University Press.
Harris, Alice. 2008. On the explanation of typologically unusual structures. In Jeff Good (ed.), *Linguistic universals and language change*, 54–76. Oxford: Oxford University Press.
Haspelmath, Martin. 1993. More on the typology of inchoative/causative verb alternations. In Bernard Comrie & Maria Polinsky (eds.), *Causatives and transitivity*, 87–121. Amsterdam & Philadelphia: John Benjamins.
Haspelmath, Martin. 2011. On S, A, P, T, and R as comparative concepts for alignment typology. *Linguistic Typology* 15 (3). 535–567.

Haspelmath, Martin. 2015. Transitivity prominence. In Andrej L. Malchukov & Bernard Comrie (eds.), *Valency classes in the world's languages*, 131–148. Berlin & New York: Mouton de Gruyter.

Haspelmath, Martin, Andreea Calude, Michael Spagnol, Heiko Narrog & Elif Bamyaci. 2014. Coding causal-noncausal verb alternations: A form-frequency correspondence explanation. *Journal of Linguistics* 50. 587–625.

Heine, Bernd & Tania Kuteva. 2005. *Language contact and grammatical change*. Cambridge: Cambridge University Press.

Hopper, Paul J. & Sandra A. Thompson. 1980. Transitivity in grammar and discourse. *Language* 56 (2). 251–299.

Iemmolo, Giorgio. 2010. Topicality and differential object marking evidence from Romance and beyond. *Studies in Language* 34. 239–272.

Jacques, Guillaume. 2019. Verbal valency and Japhug / Tibetan language contact. *Journal of Language Contact* 12 (1). 116–140.

Lefebvre Claire & Brousseau Anne-Marie. 2002. *A Grammar of Fongbe*. Berlin: Mouton de Gruyter.

Malchukov, Andrej L. 2005. Case pattern splits, verb types, and construction competition. In Mengistu Amberber & Helen de Hoop (eds.), *Competition and variation in natural languages: The case for case*, 73–118. Amsterdam: Elsevier. Amsterdam: Elsevier.

Malchukov, Andrej L. 2015. Valency classes and alternations: Parameters of variation. In Andrej L. Malchukov & Bernard Comrie (eds.), *Valency classes in the world's languages*, 73–130. Berlin & New York: Mouton de Gruyter.

Malchukov, Andrej L. & Bernard Comrie (eds.). 2015. *Valency classes in the world's languages*. 2 Vols. Berlin & New York: Mouton de Gruyter.

Maslova, Elena. 2000. A dynamic approach to the verification of distributional universals. *Linguistic Typology* 4. 307–333.

Matras, Yaron & Jeanette Sakel. 2019. Investigating the mechanisms of pattern replication in language convergence. *Studies in Language* 31 (4). 829–865.

McGregor, William. 2018. Emergence of optional accusative case marking in Khoe languages. In Alena Witzlack-Makarevich & Ilja A. Seržant (eds.), *Diachrony of differential argument marking*, 243–279. Berlin: Language Science Press.

Melis, Chantal. 2018. Spanish indexing DOM, topicality, and the case hierarchy. In Alena Witzlack-Makarevich & Ilja A. Seržant (eds.), *Diachrony of differential argument marking*, 97–128. Berlin: Language Science Press.

Michaelis, Susanne Maria. 2019. World-wide comparative evidence for calquing of valency patterns in creoles. *Journal of Language Contact* 12 (1). 191–231.

Montaut, Annie. 2018. The rise of differential object marking in Hindi and related languages. In Alena Witzlack-Makarevich & Ilja A. Seržant (eds.), *Diachrony of differential argument marking*, 281–313. Berlin: Language Science Press, 281–313.

Nichols, Johanna. 2018. Non-linguistic conditions for causativization as a linguistic attractor. *Frontiers in Psychology* 8. 2356.

Nichols, Johanna, David Peterson & Jonathan Barnes. 2004. Transitivizing and detransitivizing languages. *Linguistic Typology* 8. 149–211.

Norman, Jerry. 1982. Four notes on Chinese-Altaic linguistic contacts. *Tsinghua Journal of Chinese Studies* 14 (1–2). 243–247.

Ross, Malcolm D. 2015. Contact-induced change and the comparative method: Cases from Papua New Guinea. In Mark Durie Malcolm D. Ross (ed.), *The comparative method reviewed: Regularity and irregularity in language change*. Oxford: Oxford University Press, 180–217.
Sanchez, Liliana. 2011. Convergence in syntax/morphology mapping strategies: Evidence from Quechua-Spanish code mixing. *Lingua* 122. 511–528.
Say, Sergey. 2014. Bivalent verb classes in the languages of Europe. A quantitative typological study. *Language Dynamics and Change* 4 (1). 116–166.
Sinnemäki, Kaius. 2014. A typological perspective on differential object marking. *Linguistics* 52 (2). 281–313.
Tenser, Anton. 2005. *Lithuanian Romani*. Munich: Lincom.
Trips, Carola & Achim Stein. 2019. Contact-induced changes in the argument structure of Middle English verbs on the model of Old French. *Journal of Language Contact* 12 (1). 232–267.
Tsunoda, Tasaku. 1981. Split case-marking patterns in verb-types and tense/aspect/mood. *Linguistics* 19 (5–6). 389–438.
Tsunoda, Tasaku. 1985. Remarks on transitivity. *Journal of Linguistics* 21 (2). 385–396.
Wichmann, Søren. 2016. Quantitative tests of implicational verb hierarchies. In Taro Kageyama & Wesley M. Jacobsen (eds.), *Transitivity and valency alternations: Studies on Japanese and beyond*, 423–444. Berlin & New York: Mouton de Gruyter.
Wichmann, Søren & Jan Wohlgemuth. 2008. Loan verbs in a typological perspective. In Thomas Stolz, Dik Bakker & Rosa Salas Palomo (eds.), *Aspects of language contact: New theoretical, methodological and empirical findings with special focus on romancisation processes*, 89–121. Berlin & New York: Mouton de Gruyter.
Witzlack-Makarevich, Alena & Ilja A. Seržant. 2018. Differential argument marking: Patterns of variation. In Alena Witzlack-Makarevich & Ilja A. Seržant (eds.), *Diachrony of differential argument marking*, 1–40. Berlin: Language Science Press.
Wohlgemuth, Jan. 2009. *A typology of verbal borrowings*. Berlin & New York: Mouton de Gruyter.
Zúñiga, Fernando. 2015. Valency classes in Mapudungun. In Andrej L. Malchukov & Bernard Comrie (eds.), *Valency classes in the world's languages*, 1516–1543. Berlin & New York: Mouton de Gruyter.

Chiara Zanchi and Matteo Tarsi
Valency patterns and alternations in Gothic

Abstract: This paper investigates Gothic valency patterns and alternations applying the methodology of the ValPaL project. Our data consists of 87 verb meanings based on those in the ValPaL corpus, which we supplemented due to gaps in coverage. Valency alternations are divided into uncoded and coded patterns. The uncoded group includes partitive, null object, external possessor, cognate/kindred object, applicative, (marginally) causal : non causal, and (marginally) reflexive alternations. The coded group comprises the applicative, passive, causal : noncausal, reflexive, and reciprocal alternations. The nature of the Gothic corpus (extension, genre, and nature of the text) influenced the results: some constructions were less frequently attested than expected; genre influenced the frequency of some verbal usages; some marginally attested constructions are owed to the Greek translational source. Most remarkably, we showed that: (i) in respect to the debated issue regarding the interpretation of Gothic passives, these can be employed to express noncausal situations; (ii) within the causal : noncausal alternation, whereas the causal domain is tied to *ja*-suffixation, the noncausal domain can be expressed by a variety of means, including *na*-verbs. Our results confirmed Ottósson's (2013) view that the noncausal domain was systematized at a later stage than the causal one.

Keywords: Gothic, ValPaL, valency patterns, valency alternations, basic valency orientation

1 Introduction

The study of transitivity-related formations and constructions has long been an established subfield of Indo-European (IE) studies, not least with regard to Germanic (e.g. Egge 1887; Karsten 1911; Sundén 1913; Bökenkrüger 1924; Hermodsson 1952; Annerholm 1956; Bammesberger 1965; Krämer 1976; Joseph 1981; Suzuki 1989; Riecke 1996; García García 2005; Ottósson 2008). Recently, this line of research has intersected with typologically-oriented approaches to transitivity phenomena such as those investigating valency classes, valency alternations, and basic valency orientation (Nichols, Peterson and Barnes

---

Chiara Zanchi, University of Pavia, e-mail: chiara.zanchi01@unipv.it
Matteo Tarsi, University of Iceland, matteo.tarsi@nordiska.uu.se

 Open Access. © 2021 Chiara Zanchi and Matteo Tarsi, published by De Gruyter. [CC BY-NC-ND] This work is licensed under the Creative Commons Attribution-NonCommercial-NoDerivatives 4.0 International License.
https://doi.org/10.1515/9783110755657-003

2004; Malchukov and Comrie 2015; Hellan, Malchukov and Cennamo 2017). In particular, the Germanic evidence for the so-called anticausative alternation, its diachrony, and its implications for the reconstruction of Proto-Germanic (PGmc) and of Proto-Indo-European (PIE) basic valency orientation has recently received much attention (Ottósson 2008, 2013 on Old Nordic and Old Germanic in general; Cennamo, Eythórsson and Barðdal 2015 on Latin and Old Norse-Icelandic; Plank and Lahiri 2015 on German; as for other Indo-European branches, cf. Kulikov 2009 on Indo-Aryan; Luraghi 2012 on Hittite, Luraghi 2019 on Indo-European in general; Holvoet and Nau 2015 on Baltic; Sausa 2016 on Homeric Greek).

This paper constitutes a further contribution to this field. In it, we apply the ValPaL method (Hartmann, Haspelmath and Taylor 2013; Malchukov and Comrie 2015). The paper is structured as follows. Section 2 describes our methods: in it, we briefly describe the Gothic language and its sources and introduce the ValPaL approach. In Section 3, we review current relevant literature focusing on Gothic sentence structure and we present Gothic valency classes. Sections 4 and 5 are devoted to the description and analysis of coded and uncoded argument structure alternations in Gothic. In Section 6, we summarize our findings.[1]

2 Methodological remarks

2.1 The Gothic corpus

Within Germanic, Gothic belongs to the Eastern branch, now completely extinct. Other members of this branch are Burgundian, Vandalic, and a variety of Gothic, the so-called Crimean Gothic, recorded around the middle of the 16th century by Ogier Ghislain de Busbecq, ambassador of Ferdinand I (Holy Roman Emperor 1556–1564) to Constantinople. In comparison to the other East Germanic languages, which are only fragmentarily attested, Gothic is relatively well preserved and thus qualifies as a corpus language, i.e. one on which we may rely on a small, yet rea-

---

[1] The first data collection for this research was conducted by Caterina Saracco in 2016, while she was working at the Department of Humanities of the University of Pavia within the framework of the project *Transitivity and Argument Structure in Flux* (2015 PRIN call, grant no. 20159M7X5P). In the present study, that data sample was substantially enlarged. We thank two anonymous reviewers for their insightful comments. Needless to say, all remaining errors are ours. Although the two authors jointly wrote and edited this paper, it should be noted for academic purposes that Chiara Zanchi is responsible for Sections 1, 4, 5, and 6, and Matteo Tarsi for Sections 2 and 3.

sonably-sized, textual corpus. The chief source for Gothic is a fourth-century translation of the Bible, traditionally attributed to the Gothic bishop Wulfila, whose main manuscript witness, the *Codex Argenteus*, dates from the sixth century. A number of fragments and glosses are also preserved, mostly of biblical content (chiefly the *codices Carolinus, Ambrosiani, Taurinensis, Gissensis, Bononiensis, Gotica Parisina, Gotica Vindoboniensia, Gotica Veronensia, Fragmentum Spirense*). Some runic inscriptions have also been identified as Gothic, e.g. the spearhead of Kovel (3rd c., **tilarids** 'target rider'). It is generally acknowledged that Wulfila was fluent in Latin and, most crucially, Greek, which was the chief linguistic source for the translation.

The putative role of Wulfila as the only translator of the Bible is disputed (Miller 2019: 8). Most likely, the translation was a collective work, possibly conducted under the bishop's guidance (Falluomini 2008: 252). For the sake of brevity, we will refer to the author(s) of the translation by using the bishop's name, Wulfila.

The text of the Gothic Bible reflects a number of methodological criteria to which Wulfila adhered in the translation: (a) virtual one-to-one correspondence of translational equivalents, (b) word-to-word translation from Greek, and (c) replication of the Greek word order (Piras 2007: 62). Exceptions to these methodological principles are, of course, attested. The reasons for striving to adhere so closely to the Greek model were both ideological and practical. On the one hand, adherence was called for to preserve faithfulness to God's word as transmitted in the translational source; on the other hand, Greek as a literary language offered a reliable and prestigious model to follow. Unfortunately, but unsurprisingly, the Greek source text of the Gothic Bible is lost (Falluomini 2008). Streitberg (2000[1908]) attempted an artificial reconstruction of it, based on the Greek manuscripts belonging to the so-called "Byzantine class". It is also acknowledged that Wulfila must have had access to a Latin source, for influences from Latin are particularly evident in some portions of the Gothic text (e.g. in the Gospel of Luke, Friedrichsen 1939: 194–196, 242).

Because of the translational nature of the Gothic Bible, the question of whether this text constitutes a reliable source for Gothic morphosyntax has long been debated (cf. Keidan 2005: 49–50). The generally accepted view considers the Gothic Bible to be a faithful word-by-word, interlinear translation of the Greek source text (Yoshioka 1986: 219; Metlen 1993: 548; Ratkus 2020: 6 with references). An older less rigid interpretation of the correspondences between Greek text and Gothic translation instead dared to ascribe them to common genealogical origin, as Curme (1911) and Rice (1932) do. It seems, however, undisputable that the Gothic Bible closely adheres to its source text. Such generally conceded common ground, however, does not prevent scholars from disputing the interpretation of certain phenomena (see most recently Ratkus 2020 *contra* Kleyner 2019 on the value of the Gothic synthetic passive and cf. on this issue below).

To further complicate the matter, as with every dead language, Gothic, too, suffers from gaps in coverage, due to accidents of manuscript transmission. Hence, we find ourselves faced with major chasms in our understanding that must somehow be bridged (Joseph and Janda 2003: 19). Consequently, any apparent deficit in the corpus does not straightforwardly correspond to an actual lack in the grammar or in the lexicon of Gothic, as one has to reckon with extralinguistic factors, which often play a perceptible role in the shaping of a text (Zanchi 2019: 33–35).

Bearing these caveats in mind, we carried out our investigation of valency patterns in Gothic. At the same time, we constantly kept an eye on the Greek source text which sometimes provided insights, as well as on the two modern Germanic languages contained in the ValPaL database, German and Icelandic.

2.2 The ValPaL method and its applicability to a corpus language

The ValPaL project carried out a crosslinguistic investigation of argument structure properties of verbs belonging to different valency classes (Malchukov and Comrie 2015: 27–130 for full documentation). Before this project, argument structure properties of different verb classes were already being studied within different theoretical frameworks, such as Case Grammar, Role and Reference Grammar, and Lexical Decomposition Grammar (e.g. Apresjan 1969; Lehmann 1991; Dixon 1991, 2005; Levin 1993; Jones 1994; Levin and Rappaport Hovav 2005).

In the ValPaL project, valency classes are understood as groups of verbs with similar morphosyntactic properties, i.e. coding patterns and argument structure alternations. Hence, the classification of verbs into valency classes is morphosyntactically based but is nevertheless correlated with semantic verb classes (Levin 1993). The ValPaL verb selection singled out 80 core verb meanings included in the online database, such as SEE, GO, and KILL, and subsequently identified the semantically most fitting basic verb within the 36 languages included in the project. Additional verb meanings were included for specific languages, up to the total of 162 verb meanings represented in the database today. In the project, which focuses on modern languages only, the basicness of verbal lemmas to express the selected meanings was evaluated by experts (frequently native speakers) of each project language. The coding frames representing flagging, indexing, and word order were stored in a database for each verb meaning as instantiated by each one of the selected languages, together with the coding frames for each argument structure, i.e. the coded and uncoded alternations that the verbs allow for. Coded alternations are those that are marked on the verb by an affix, a clitic, or an auxiliary, whereas uncoded alternations are not marked in these ways.

Thus, for example, the meaning LIVE (in the sense 'live, dwell') is expressed by the Italian basic verb *abitare*, assigned the coding frame "1 > V.subj[1] (> 2)", "S > V.subj.[S]" > *in* L" (1), in which the > symbol indicates word order, the square brackets show indexing, and the S and L indicate the Subject and the Locative argument types respectively.[2] This verb allows for the uncoded transitive alternation (2), as well as for the coded impersonal reflexive (3), causative, and (marginally) passive alternations (examples and glosses are adapted from Cennamo and Fabrizio 2013). Examples (1)–(3) show the basic usage of this verb and one instance of the uncoded and coded alternations it attests to.[3]

(1) S > V.subj.[S]" > *in* L
    Mario **abita** in campagna
    M. live.PRS.3SG in countryside
    'Mario lives in the countryside.'

(2) Transitive alternation (uncoded)
    La famiglia **abita** una villa abbandonata
    DET.F family(F) live.PRS.3SG INDF.F country_house(F) abandoned.F
    'The family lives in an abandoned country house.'

(3) Impersonal reflexive (coded)[4]
    Lì si **abita** ancora in vecchi casali
    there REFL live.PRS.3SG still in old.PL farmhouse.PL
    'There, one still lives/we/you/they (INDF) live in old farmhouses.'

---

[2] Besides S and L roles, A, P, I, and X argument types are also recorded in the ValPaL, which stand for Agent and Patient of transitive verbs such as *break*, Instrument of verbs such as *cut*, and X for all other roles. We do not use the ValPaL coding frame throughout the paper, but we do use small caps to indicate ValPaL core verb meanings. Verb frequencies are put in round brackets: e.g. SEND *sandjan* (32x).
[3] Glosses follow the Leipzig Glossing Rules (https://www.eva.mpg.de/lingua/resources/glossing-rules.php) with some adjustments: on verbs, mood is specified only if not indicative and voice is indicated only if not active. Likewise, on nouns, number is omitted if singular and gender is only included when needed to show agreement. The following language-specific glosses are added to the Leipzig Glossing Rules repertoire: OPT = optative, PRET = preterite.
[4] This terminology is taken from Cennammo and Fabrizio (2013) and thoroughly explained in the discussion of example (3) below.

In (1), the locative second argument is expressed by a prepositional phrase headed by the preposition *in* 'in, into'. In (2), the locative argument is promoted from peripheral to core argument position: this is an uncoded applicative alternation in Cennamo's (2015) terms. Example (3) shows an impersonal alternation of the verb *abitare* 'live', in which the S argument is suppressed. The alternation here is coded with the reflexive marker *si* (on this alternation, cf. Cennamo and Fabrizio 2013 with references therein at the following link: http://valpal.info/languages/italian/alternations/3133700559).

Applying the ValPaL method to a corpus language such as Gothic was no trivial task. As we could not rely on native speakers' judgements to assess the basicness of competing verbs for any given core meaning, we had to resort to other morphological, frequency, and historical criteria (on this issue, see also the contributions by Inglese and by Roma in this volume). We regarded as more basic verbal lemmas showing the simplest morphological structure (e.g. GO *gaggan* with respect to all its preverbed variants, e.g. *at-gaggan* 'approach', *af-gaggan* 'go away', *afar-gaggan* 'follow', etc.). If a certain verb is underived but sparingly attested, we considered as basic the derived verb, provided that its number of attestations was significantly higher (e.g LIKE *leikan* 1x vs. *ga-leikan* 20x). If two competing verbal lemmas have a comparable degree of morphological complexity, we included the more frequent one in our study: e.g. EAT *matjan* (90x) vs. *itan* (4x). In the case of EAT *matjan* vs. *itan*, however, we also monitored the behavior of *itan*, as its reflexes represent the basic verb for eating in many modern Germanic languages (cf. e.g. Engl. *eat* and Germ. *essen*) and it allows for interesting comparisons with its preverbed variants (cf. Section 4.1). In cases in which none of these criteria applied, we selected more than one verb (e.g. BE HUNGRY *gredon* 1x and *huggrjan* 2x). In cases of imperfective verbs with a perfective counterpart prefixed with *ga-*, we usually took into account both aspectual variants, especially if neither lemma is very frequent (e.g. DRESS *wasjan* 7x and *ga-wasjan* 15x). To compensate some gaps in coverage (BE A HUNTER, BLINK, BOIL, COUGH, FEEL COLD, HUG, PLAY, SMELL), still in accordance with the ValPaL methodology for data collection, other verbs were added with comparable meaning and/or lexical aspect, especially if they allowed for the inclusion of new patterns.

For these reasons, the verb meanings included in this investigation do not entirely overlap with the canonical verb meanings of the ValPaL (Malchukov and Comrie 2015: 28–29). The overall selection included 87 Gothic verbs, displayed in Table 1, which manifested in 3,447 occurrences, extracted by crosschecking the digitalized text of the Gothic Gospels available at the PROIEL project and Wulfila project websites.[5]

Table 1: The ValPaL verb meanings in the Gothic corpus.

Verb meaning	Gothic basic lemma	Frequency	In ValPaL
ASK FOR	bidjan	130	yes
BE DRY	ga-staurknan	1	yes
BE HUNGRY (1)	gredon	1	yes
BE HUNGRY (2)	huggrjan	2	yes
BE SAD	gaurjan (gaurs wairþan)	4	yes
BEAT (1)	slahan	10	yes
BEAT (2)	bliggwan	5	yes
BREAK (1)	ga-brikan	8	yes
BREAK (2)	us-bruk-nan	3	yes
BRING	briggan	34	yes
BUILD	timrjan	7	yes
BURN (1)	tundnan	1	yes
BURN (2)	tandjan	2	yes
CARRY	bairan	44	yes
CLIMB	steigan	1	yes
COVER/HIDE (1)	huljan	2	yes
COVER/HIDE (1)	ga-huljan	7	yes
CRY	gretan / greitan	28	no
CUT	maitan	1	yes
DIE (1)	ga-dauþnan	28	yes
DIE (2)	ga-swiltan	42	yes
DIG	graban	2	yes
DRESS (1)	wasjan	7	yes
DRESS (2)	ga-wasjan	15	yes
DRINK (1)	drigkan	42	no
DRINK (2)	dragkjan	5	no

---

5 PROIEL Project: http://foni.uio.no:3000/sources/11 (accessed 28 November 2020); Wulfila Project: http://www.wulfila.be (accessed 28 November 2020).

Table 1 (continued)

Verb meaning	Gothic basic lemma	Frequency	In ValPaL
EAT (1)	matjan	90	yes
EAT (1)	itan	4	yes
FALL (1)	ga-driusan	24	no
FALL (1)	ga-drausjan	4	no
FEAR	ogan	46	yes
FEEL PAIN	winnan	48	yes
FILL (1)	fullnan	3	yes
FILL (2)	fulljan	4	yes
FOLLOW	laistjan	48	yes
FRIGHTEN	ogjan	1	yes
GIVE	giban	129	yes
GO	gaggan	201	yes
GRIND	malan	1	yes
HEAR	hausjan	106	yes
HELP	hilpan	4	yes
HIDE	ga-filhan	5	yes
JUMP	laikan	3	yes
KILL (1)	dauþjan	1	yes
KILL (2)	ga-dauþjan	1	yes
KILL (3)	af-dauþjan	5	yes
KNOW (1)	kunnan	90	yes
KNOW (2)	kannjan	7	yes
LAUGH	hlahjan	1	yes
LEAVE	bi-leiþan	26	yes
LIGHT	liuhtjan	4	no
LIGHTEN (1)	lauhatjan	1	yes
LIGHTEN (2)	ga-liuhtjan	2	yes
LIKE (1)	leikan	2	yes
LIKE (2)	ga-leikan	20	yes
LIVE (1)	liban	56	yes
LIVE (2)	bauan	14	yes
LOAD	af-hlaþan	1	yes

Table 1 (continued)

Verb meaning	Gothic basic lemma	Frequency	In ValPaL
LOOK AT	*in-saihvan*	12	yes
MEET	*ga-motjan*	11	yes
NAME	*namnjan*	11	yes
POUR	*giutan*	6	yes
PUT (1)	*lagjan*	28	yes
PUT (2)	*ga-lagjan*	27	yes
PUT (3) < MAKE SIT	*satjan*	9	yes
RAIN	*rignjan*	2	yes
ROLL (1)	*af-walwjan*	2	yes
ROLL (2)	*walwison*	1	yes
RUN	*rinnan*	14	yes
SAY	*qiþan*	1129	yes
SCREAM	*hropjan*	29	yes
SEARCH FOR	*sokjan*	73	yes
SEE	*saihvan*	102	yes
SEND	*sandjan*	32	yes
SHAVE	*skaban* (only PASS and PTCP.PRF.PASS)	2	yes
SHOUT AT (1)	*wopjan*	17	yes
SHOUT AT (1)	*sakan*	4	yes
SHOW	*at-augjan*	22	yes
SING	*siggwan*	5	yes
SINK (1)	*sigqan*	2	yes
SINK (2)	*sigqjan*	1	yes
SIT	*sitan*	33	yes
SIT DOWN	*ga-sitan*	11	yes
STEAL	*hlifan*	6	yes
TAKE	*niman*	195	yes
TALK	*rodjan*	135	yes
TEACH, LEARN	*laisjan (sik)*	61	yes
TEAR	*tahjan*	6	yes
TELL	*us-spillon*	2	yes

Table 1 (continued)

Verb meaning	Gothic basic lemma	Frequency	In ValPaL
THINK	hugjan	13	yes
THROW	wairpan	12	yes
TIE	ga-bindan	18	yes
TOUCH	at-tekan	21	yes
WASH	þwahan	5	yes
WIPE	bi-swairban	4	yes
	TOTAL	3,447	

The valency patterns and coded and uncoded alternations allowed for by these verbs are described in Sections 3–5. The full lists of verbs included in each valency class and featuring each alternation are shown in Tables 3–5 in Appendix A.1, together with a number of additional examples in Appendix A.2. The full database containing the data for the analysis is available on-line at https://su-lab.unipv.it/tasf/.

3 Gothic basic sentence structure and valency classes

3.1 Basic sentence structure in Gothic

In this section, we briefly introduce the basics of Gothic sentence structure, marking of grammatical relations, to the extent that it is useful for the purposes of the paper, as well as the background of the Gothic causal : noncausal alternation (discussed in Section 5).

Gothic nouns have four cases: nominative, accusative, genitive, and dative. Cases can serve a variety of syntactic and semantic functions, the latter also being encoded by diverse PPs (Kuryłowicz 1964: 31–32, 179–206; Hewson 2006). As in other Indo-European languages, the nominative occurs in S/A arguments in prototypical transitive constructions in which the participants, traditionally called 'subjects' in IE studies, trigger agreement with the verb. The accusative case is taken by P arguments in prototypical transitive constructions, in which it usually plays the role of patient. It can additionally carry out other functions unrelated to grammatical relations, such as allative and perlative roles (Thomason

2006: 82–83; Miller 2019: 109). The genitive has both adnominal and adverbial functions. Semantically, it is primarily used to convey partitive meanings, but it can also indicate spatial functions (Thomason 2006: 83). Syntactically, the dative is used to encode indirect objects, i.e. third arguments of ditransitives. Semantically, it encompasses a variety of additional roles besides recipients (Thomason 2006: 84–85; Miller 2019: 133).

As part of Germanic, Gothic features two main conjugational systems: strong, with seven classes, and weak, with four classes (Miller 2019: 178–205). Apart from strong verbs, in which present and preterite stems are formed by means of ablaut alternation, two classes of weak verbs, i.e. those forming preterite stems by means of a dental suffix, are focused on in this paper: the weak 1 and the weak 4 classes. The weak 1 class comprises the so-called *ja*-verbs, i.e. (chiefly deverbal) verbs derived through a causative *ja*-suffix (< PIE *é-i̯e/o-*; on other types of formation continued in the same verbal class, see Harðarson 2017: 935–936). Deadjectival *ja*-verbs also exist with factitive meaning, i.e. 'cause to have the quality described by the adjectival base', e.g. *fulljan* 'to fill' (⇐ *fulls* 'full') (Miller 2019: 193, 206). The weak 4 class, which is only preserved as distinct in Gothic, comprises verbs derived by means of a nasal suffix, hence the name *na*-verbs. These verbs are chiefly inchoative in meaning (also labelled anticausative, fientive, or nonagentive). Verbs of this class are either denominal and deadjectival (e.g. *fullnan* 'to get filled'), or deverbal (e.g. *tundnan* 'to burn', cf. *tandjan* 'to kindle') (see below in this section; Miller 2019: 193, 206 with references therein; cf. also West 1980; Suzuki 1989; Schwerdt 2001; Ferraresi 2005: 111–117; Ottósson 2008, 2013; Katz 2016; Rousseau 2016: 237–243).

The PIE middle voice is only reflected to a significant extent in the Gothic synthetic passive, which is restricted to the present indicative and optative (on the Gothic periphrastic passives, see below in this section). In the other old Germanic languages, the middle voice of PIE heritage was lost completely as a morphological category, and remnants of it are no more than linguistic fossils: e.g. OIcel. *heiti* (IND.PRS.1SG of *heita* 'to be called'), OE *hātte* (IND.PRS.1/3SG of *hātan* 'to be called') (cf. Cennamo, Eythórsson and Barðdal 2015: 678 on Old Norse). In past tenses, Gothic also developed an analytic passive (for accounts of its development, cf. Lühr 2008: 327; Drinka 2011), constructed with the auxiliaries *wisan* 'be' and *wairþan* 'become'. The analytic passive eventually came to be used in the present tense, thus competing with the synthetic one (Miller 2019: 519; see Section 5.1). Both Gothic passives have traditionally been interpreted as true passives: they allegedly do not allow "middle" noncausal, intransitive, and reflexive readings (cf. Section 5 for counterexamples).⁶ Furthermore, the Gothic reflexive marker *sik* 'self' is said to not yet have fully developed as a strategy to encode the noncausal domain, which is definitely a later development in Germanic. However, Gothic was "in the process of replacing the Indo-European mediopassive forms with nonargument reflexive formations" (Ferraresi 2005: 109–123) and attests to constructions with the reflexive *sik* employed as a noncausal element in the causal : noncausal alternation, to indicate inchoative and spontaneous events (Miller 2019: 393–395 with examples, in which the reflexive construction with *sik* is used to translate Greek passive forms; see also Cennamo, Eythórsson and Barðdal 2015: 678–679).

Hence, Gothic is said to mostly resort to the opposition between *ja*-causatives and *na*-verbs to encode the causal : noncausal alternation (e.g. *fulljan* 'to fill' : *fullnan* 'to get filled'). Given that the causal and the noncausal members of the alternation are equally marked morphologically, Gothic can be said to instantiate the equipollent strategy in terms of basic valency orientation (Nichols, Peterson and Barnes 2004). However, from a diachronic standpoint, this picture of Gothic as an equipollent language could shift slightly, depending on how the functions and dating of *na*-verbs are accounted for with respect to those of *ja*-causatives. According to some scholars (e.g. West 1980; Suzuki 1989; Schwerdt 2001; Ringe 2006; Lazzeroni 2009; Cennamo, Eythórsson and Barðdal 2015), *na*-verbs are inchoatives, indicating change of state events, and represent a more ancient category than *ja*-verbs, in that *na*-verbs derive inchoatives not only from transitives but also from adjectives, participles, and intransitives.

An alternative argument was made by Ottósson (2013). He suggested that *na*-verbs fundamentally indicate noncausal, spontaneous events (and not inchoatives), and that they represent a later PGmc development than *ja*-causatives, as the latter do not form causatives exclusively from *na*-verbs, but also from other verb classes, such as inactive verbs that are semantically noncausal (e.g. *ganisan* 'be healed, be saved' vs. *ganas-jan* 'save (someone)'). Thus, Ottósson argues, the development of *na*-verbs should be viewed in a wider context in which the development of the reflexive middles in other Germanic sub-branches also finds

---

6 As an anonymous reviewer suggested, we opted to use the terms 'causal' vs. 'noncausal' for the semantically related verb pairs of the type FRIGHTEN : FEAR, AMUSE : LAUGH, DROP : FALL, and then to use the terms 'labile', 'anticausative', 'causative' and so on for particular morphosyntactic coding relationships (see, e.g. Haspelmath et al. 2014). With verbs used in the noncausal domain, the P-argument of the corresponding transitive verb of the causal domain occurs as the sole argument and triggers agreement.

a place: specifically, a wider tendency to systematize the relationship between a transitive verb and its intransitive counterpart.[7]

3.2 Gothic valency patterns

In this section, we offer an overview of Gothic valency patterns. The patterns are described in order of increasing valency slots, starting with the so-called impersonal verbs in Gothic and extending to three-place verbs. The verbs were grouped in valency classes based on their most frequent attested patterns of occurrence; in order to classify argument structure constructions, coding properties, specifically, case marking and agreement, and passivization were taken into account.

3.2.1 The so-called impersonal verbs

This class of verbs comprises weather verbs and verbs featuring an accusative experiencer (cf. Table 3 in Appendix A.1). Weather verbs are crosslinguistically zero-valent. However, the Gothic lemma for RAIN, *rignjan*, may feature a dative subject construction:

(4) rignida **swibla** jah **funin** us himina
    rain.PRET.3SG brimstone.DAT and fire.DAT from sky.DAT
    '(But the same day that Lot went out of Sodom) it rained brimstone and fire from heaven, (and destroyed them all).' (Lk 17:29)[8]

The datives *swibla* 'brimstone' and *funin* 'fire' refer to the substances that rain from heaven. They are better understood as instruments that are made to fall by an omitted agent, i.e, God (see also Rousseau 2012: 192; Miller 2019: 139) for the following reasons. (i) It is usual for Gothic to feature dative instruments with physical transfer verbs and verbs of caused motion, as is *rignjan* in this context.

---

[7] On the antiquity of *ja*-verbs as a causative strategy, note that relics of *ja*-formations can be found in Old English, although Modern English predominantly exhibits lability (van Gelderen 2011; García García 2020).
[8] To the Gothic examples, we added the Greek source text and, whenever relevant, the corresponding Latin passages.

(ii) The comparison with the sole other occurrence of *rignjan* in the Gothic Bible (5) also points to a causal reading.⁹

(5) | unte | sunnon | seina | **urranneiþ** | ana | ubilans |
| --- | --- | --- | --- | --- | --- |
| for | sun.ACC | POSS.ACC | make_rise.PRS.3SG | on | evil.ACC.PL |
| jah | godans | jah | **rigneiþ** | ana | garaihtans |
| and | good.ACC.PL | and | rain.PRS.3SG | on | just.ACC.PL |
| jah | | ana | inwindans | | |
| and | | on | unjust.ACC.PL | | |

'(For he made his sun to rise on the evil and on the good), and made it rain on the just and on the unjust.' (Mt 5:45)

As the passage in (5) includes the verb *ur-rannjan* 'make rise', it undoubtedly indicates that God initiates the described natural phenomena (see Miller 2019: 111, who speaks of a "causative feature"). Thus, in both passages, *rignjan* has a causal usage.¹⁰ (iii) The corresponding Greek verb *brékhō* means 'wet, make wet, make it rain (ACT)' and 'get wet (MID)'. It is used with an explicit subject, God, in the Greek New Testament (e.g. in *Ex.* 9:23, 16:24) and does not allow for impersonal usage. Other Gothic weather verbs, such as LIGHTEN *lauhatjan*, also take a subject, which however does not refer to any supernatural entity but has kindred semantics and sometimes is cognate with the weather verb.

Cross-linguistically, verbs with experiencer participants are often impersonal and experiencers feature a different encoding from the canonical one for S/A arguments, i.e. the nominative case (Malchukov and Siewierska 2011; on accusative highest-ranking arguments, see also Fedriani 2014: 124–126; Wiemer and Bjarnadóttir 2014: 303– 305). Germanic languages constitute no exception in this respect: experiencers often receive a marker different from the nominative case, especially with verbs of liking and of negative experience (Viti 2017; on Gothic verbs for LIKE, cf. Section 3.2.3 below). Our sample includes two such verbs, traditionally labelled 'impersonal' in Gothic grammars, both conveying the meaning BE HUNGRY *huggrjan* and *gredon*, which are constructed impersonally and take the accusative of experiencer (see Appendix A.2.1 for examples).

---

9 For a discussion of a similar construction in Baltic and Slavic languages, see Holvoet and Nau (2014: 318, 334) and Lavine (2016).
10 This verb is a denominative like other members of the weak 1 class of verbs, e.g. *namnjan* 'name', *domjan* 'judge' and has no inherent causative meaning. The origin of these verbs is different from that of *ja*-causatives. In fact, this verbal class subsumes four different types of formation (see in detail Harðarson 2017: 935–936).

3.2.2 One-place verbs

The nominative subject (NomSubj) construction is canonical for Gothic one-place verbs (see Table 3 in Appendix A.1). From our sample, the verbs that feature this construction can be grouped into two categories: (i) activity verbs and (ii) verbs with noncausal semantics and also, often, derivational anticausative morphology (cf. Section 5.2). We include here an example with the activity verb LAUGH *hlahjan*.

(6) | wai | izwis, | jus | **hlahjandans** | | nu, | unte |
| --- | --- | --- | --- | --- | --- | --- |
| PTC | 2PL.DAT | 2PL.NOM | laugh.PTCP.PRS.NOM.PL | | now | because |
| gaunon | jah | gretan | duginnid | | | |
| lament.INF | and | cry.INF | begin.PRS.2PL | | | |

'Woe to those laughing now, for you will mourn and weep.' (Lk 6:25)

In the passage in (6), the verb occurs in the present participle and agrees with the nominative second person plural pronoun *jus*.

In addition, the bodily sensation verb FEEL PAIN *winnan* (48x) can be regarded as a one-place verb. It is usually constructed with an accusative object, which is mostly represented by a neuter (plural) adjective with an adverbial value and only rarely (3x) by another noun with kindred meaning (see examples in Appendix A.2.1). Hence, given the limited type of second arguments *winnan* can take, there are reasons to regard it as fundamentally intransitive, allowing for the insertion of an object with kindred semantics (cf. Section 4.5).

3.2.3 Two-place verbs

As is canonical in other IE languages, two-place verbs mostly instantiate the nominative-accusative (NomAcc) construction. In our sample, Gothic verbs occurring in NomAcc are the following (see Table 3 in Appendix A.1):
(i) Prototypically transitive verbs, i.e. verbs that denote events in which a volitional agent causes a change of state or position upon a non-volitional patient (on transitivity as a scalar notion, cf. the seminal paper by Hopper and Thompson 1980; for a more recent account on the inherent meaning of verbal constructions, cf. Croft 2012). In this group, consumption verbs of eating and drinking encode the partitive alternation (Section 4.1).
(ii) Derivationally causative verbs with *ja*-suffix (Section 5.2).
(iii) Transitive verbs that express non-prototypically transitive events, i.e. events in which there is no change of state and/or the affectedness of the patient-

like participant and/or the volitionality of the agent-like participant is lower or absent.
(iv) Experiential verbs of bodily sensations, cognition, and emotion, which take a nominative experiencer and an accusative stimulus.

Verbs of groups (iii) and (iv) denote less prototypically transitive events than group (i) and (ii) verbs. This is shown by the fact that the former ones feature high degrees of construal variability. As for experiential verbs, we have already seen in Section 3.2.1 a four-member group of verbs, traditionally labeled 'impersonal', which take an accusative experiencer. Below in this section we explore the behavior of LIKE *leikan* and *ga-leikan*, which instantiate the DatNom construction. In Section 4, we further discuss some verbs in groups (iii) and (iv) that instantiate other alternations.

Among the ValPaL verb meanings, the only verbs featuring the NomGen construction are FILL *fullnan* and HELP *hilpan* (see Table 3 in Appendix A.1 and examples in Appendix A.2.1). Gothic grammars (e.g. Wright 1910: 184; Miller 2019: 132) cite additional verbs instantiating the NomGen construction: *brūk-jan* 'use', *fraihnan* 'ask', *gaírn-jan* 'long for', *ga-þarban* 'abstain from', *luston* 'desire', and *niutan* 'enjoy'. These are verbs whose second arguments do not undergo a change of state and feature a low degree of affectedness, either because they are "verbs of intent" (on which, cf. e.g. Kiparsky 1998) or because their second argument is positively and not negatively affected by the described event (on the higher degree of affectedness undergone by maleficiary-like participants with respect to beneficiary-like ones, see Luraghi and Zanchi 2018). Given that in Gothic, in the same way as in other ancient IE languages, the genitive case and/or genitive PPs also have partitive functions (Miller 2019: 113 with references), the genitive case with these non-prototypically transitive verbs can be motivated by a low or reduced degree of affectedness of the second participant. A small group of ditransitive verbs, discussed in Section 3.2.4, also take genitive third participants.

Verbs taking a dative second participant are extensively described e.g. in Köhler (1864: 12–17, 20–35), Piper (1874: 1–22, 26–29), Balg (1891: 243–256), Winkler (1896: 4–18, 30–41; 97–107), and Delbrück (1907: 190–191). Among the ValPaL verb meanings, verbs of "social interaction" (Luraghi 2020a) and communication verbs instantiate the NomDat construction, crucially, with animate second arguments (cf. also *ana-biudan* 'command', *andbahtjan* 'serve', *and-hafjan* 'answer', *ga-motjan* 'meet', *kukjan* 'kiss', and *uf-hausjan* 'heed, obey', cited in Wright 1910: 184). In addition, the verb TOUCH *at-tekan* features the NomDat construction and typically describes situations in which Jesus heals the infirm by touching, i.e. by laying his hands upon the suffering people, who are conceived of as recipients/

beneficiaries. Thus, the dative second argument refers to humans with this verb as well (on the dative with *at-tekan*, see also Bernhardt 1888: 76–77).

The link between PIE dative and animacy is well-documented (Luraghi 2003: 39–40): the prepositionless dative consistently tends to encode typically animate participants in IE languages, such as recipients, beneficiaries, maleficiaries, and addressees (this is the so-called "destinative dative" in Hettrich's 2007 terms). Thus, the dative case is frequently employed in those textual contexts in which verbs involve a second animate participant. Certainly, the aforementioned ValPaL verbs can be accounted for in this way.

The verb LEAVE *bi-leiþan* (26x) also tends to select the NomDat construction, as in the following passage (7):

(7) jah   bileiþiþ   þaim   lambam   jah   þliuhiþ
    and   leave.PRS.3SG   DEM.DAT.PL   sheep.DAT.PL   and   flee.PRS.3SG
    '(The hired servant, being not the shepherd, whose own the sheep are not, sees the wolf coming) and leaves [lit. pass around] the sheep and flees.' (Jn 10:12)

Miller (2019: 157) lists *bi-leiþan* among verbs that feature "arbitrary case variability" between the dative and the accusative. This compound verb contains the preverb *bi-* 'around', which, as a preposition, can take the accusative and the dative case (Miller 2019: 240), and a motion verb, specifically PGmc *līþan* 'go (by), pass' < PIE *leit-* 'go (forth/down)' (cf. *af-leiþan* 'go away' and *inn-ga-leiþan* 'go to'). Thus, the compound *bi-leiþan* literally means 'pass around', lexicalizes as 'leave' (similarly to the Eng. particle verb *pass over* and Germ. *über-gehen*), and as such becomes a transitive verb taking a dative/accusative second argument, owing to the applicative function of the preverb *bi-* (Section 4.6). Possibly, the making of the compound verb was still ongoing in the period of translation of the Gospels, which could explain constructional variability.

The DatNom construction is employed with two experiential verbs, LIKE *leikan* (8) and its perfective counterpart *ga-leikan* (Mk 6:22). With these verbs, the animate experiencer is expressed in the dative case, whereas the animate or inanimate stimulus gets the nominative case and syntactically functions as a subject triggering verb agreement (see the relative clause in example [8]).

(8) unte   ik   þatei   leikaiþ   imma   tauja
    for   1SG.NOM   REL.NOM.N   please.PRS.3SG   3SG.DAT   do.PRS.1SG
    sinteino
    always
    '... for I always do what pleases him.' (Jn 8:29)

Other than the example in (8), the sole other occurrence of the verb (9) includes an additional accusative indicating an area/topic participant (relational accusative), regarded as an object in Ferraresi (2005: 64–66) and Miller (2019: 164). However, this accusative is an indefinite neuter adjective and is best analyzed as an adverbial dependent and not as a fully-fledged accusative argument taken by *leikan* (on the status of neuter singular and plural objects in Ancient Greek, see Luraghi and Zanchi 2018: 31). This construction is a word-by-word translation of the corresponding Greek passage, in which a neuter plural accusative also occurs (*pánta*).

(9) swaswe   ik   allaim   all   leika
    as   1SG.NOM   INDF.DAT.PL   INDF.ACC   please.PRS.1SG
    '... as I please all men in all'. (1Cor 10:33) [Gk. *kathṑs kagṑ* **pánta** *pâsin aréskō*]

The last type of two-place verbs takes argumental PPs: these comprise motion verbs taking goal or path participants and location and posture verbs taking a goal or locative participant (see Table 3 in Appendix A.1). Here, we exemplify this usage with LIVE *bauan*, as it interestingly instantiates an uncoded applicative alternation, discussed in Section 4.6:

(10) wait   auk þatei ni   bauiþ   in mis   ... þiuþ
     know.PRS.1SG   PTC that NEG   live.PRS.3SG in 1SG.DAT   good.NOM
     'For I know that the good does not live in me.' (Rom 7:18)
     [Gk. *oîda gàr hóti ouk oikeî en emoí ... agathón*; Lat. *scio enim quia non habitat in me ... bonum*]

A perception verb from our sample, LOOK AT *in-saihvan*, is also constructed with a PP *du*+DAT stimulus (and another perception verb, *at-saihvan* 'look at', although not in our sample, also behaves this way; see example (55) in Appendix A.2.1). Several factors might yield this effect: first, verbs of seeing/looking at are similar to motion verbs, in that eyes and sight also can be directed toward or away from something (Zanchi 2019: 129, 253). In this sense, stimuli can be conceptualized as goals or recipients toward which sight is turned. Second, the degree of affectedness of the stimulus participant is very low: no change of state or position is undergone by the stimuli, and the mere act of directing sight toward a stimulus does not even require that it actually be seen (Levin 1995: 187).

Finally, the verb THINK *hugjan* can take subordinate clauses (NomObj construction), retaining its basic meaning (Phil 2:2; Mt 5:17). Otherwise, it takes different PPs, with which it acquires different semantics: with *afar*+DAT it means 'trust in' (Mk 10:24), whereas with *waila*+DAT 'agree with' (Mt 5:25).

3.2.4 Three-place verbs

According to Malchukov, Haspelmath and Comrie (2010: 2), ditransitive constructions are constructions "consisting of a (ditransitive) verb, an agent argument (A), a recipient-like argument (R), and a theme argument (T)." Gothic ditransitive verbs take the accusative case and additional dative, genitive, or accusative arguments (cf. Ferraresi 2005: 63–65; Rousseau 2016: 262–267, 276–279; Miller 2019: 161–163).

The main types of double object verbs in Gothic take the NomAccDat and the NomDatAcc constructions. These are regarded as representing two different verb classes by Ferraresi (2005), allegedly due to the different respective order of the second and third participants. However, as Gothic word order is too free to establish clear functional differences between the two, we will analyze them together (cf. Miller 2019: 161–163).

The prototypically ditransitive physical transfer verb GIVE *giban* instantiates the NomAccDat construction in Gothic, as is typical of other ancient IE languages, which invariably show indirect alignment (in Malchukov, Haspelmath and Comrie's 2010 terms).

(11) *gibai   izai   afstassais   bokos*
     give.OPT.PRS.3SG 3SG.DAT.F   divorce.GEN   letter.ACC.PL
     '(It has been said: whosoever shall put away his wife,) let him give her a writing of divorcement.' (Mt 5:31)

Other verbs of physical transfer take the NomAccDat construction with human destinations, which are construed as recipients or beneficiaries. The verb THROW *wairpan* usually takes a PP encoding the goal but can be also used as a ditransitive with a dative recipient. Other physical transfer verbs can be also seen as ditransitives, in that they are always used with third prepositional arguments expressing goal or recipient-like participants (see Table 3 in Appendix A.1).

By a metaphorical extension according to which a transfer of knowledge can be understood as a physical transfer, verbs of communication and verbs of teaching can take the AccDat construction as well. The knowledge transfer verb SEARCH FOR *sokjan* behaves similarly; it means 'ask someone (R) for something (T)' if used with a T-accusative and a R-PP expressed by *du*+DAT. Note that in (12) below, the preverbed verb *miþ-sokjan* also occurs, which takes a R-dative (and implies an omitted indefinite accusative T-participant):

(12) jah   dugunnun   miþsokjan   imma   sokjandans
    and   begin.PRET.3PL   question.INF   3SG.DAT   ask_for.PTCP.PRS.NOM.PL
    du   imma   taikn   us   himina
    to   3SG.DAT   sign.ACC   from   heaven.DAT
    '(And the Pharisees came forth,) and began to question with him, seeking of him a sign from heaven.' (Mk 8:11)

Although the most typical Gothic verb of teaching, *laisjan*, takes the AccAcc construction in Gothic, (on which see below in this Section), the NomAccDat pattern seems to be well-established with teaching verbs: this pattern is illustrated, for example, by *and-bindan*, which means both 'unfasten, untie' and 'expound, explain'. Only in the latter sense, however, does it instantiate the NomAccDat construction (Mk 4:34).

The ditransitive verbs discussed thus far all show indirect alignment, where the T-participant gets the accusative encoding of patients of transitive verbs, canonical for both Gothic and IE in general. Ditransitives featuring the NomAcc-Gen construction instantiate secundative (Malchukov, Haspelmath and Comrie 2010) alignment, in which the R-participant is encoded in the accusative. From our sample, two verbs feature the NomAccGen construction: FILL *fulljan* and ASK FOR *bidjan* (cf. also Ferraresi 2005: 75; Miller 2019: 170). The former is a physical transfer verb, constructed with the R-participant in the accusative case and the T-participant in the genitive case:

(13) guþ   lubainais   fulljai   izwis   allaizos
     God.NOM   hope.GEN   fill.PRS.OPT.3SG   2PL.ACC   INDF.GEN
     fahedais
     joy.GEN
     'The God of hope fill you with all joy.' (Rom 15:13)
     [Gk. *ho dè theòs tês elpídos plērôsai humâs pásēs kharâs*]

The Gothic genitive also displays partitive properties, so the T-participant in genitive with *fulljan* (and with its anticausative counterpart *fullnan*) can be explained as a partitive genitive. It is highly improbable that this construction is a calque from the Greek source text. In fact, although the same construction is instantiated in the Greek verb *pleróō*, it is also paralleled in all three branches of Germanic, i.e. besides Gothic, West and North Germanic (OHG *fullen*, OIcel. *fylla*). The authenticity of this construction in Gothic is moreover confirmed by the occurrence of *ufar-fulljan* (+GEN) in 2Cor 7:4, which corresponds to Greek *huper-perisséuomai* (+DAT). Had the Gothic construction been calqued from Greek, one would only expect to see the dative case in 2Cor 7:4.

However, this construction is not retained in the subsequent modern Germanic languages: German *füllen* and Icelandic *fylla* take an instrumental dative or PP, respectively.

The latter verb featuring the NomAccGen construction, ASK FOR *bidjan* (e.g. Jn 14:14), is a verb of knowledge transfer and of intent (in Kiparsky's 1998 terms). Other verbs with kindred semantics behave similarly: *fraihnan* 'ask' and *beidan* 'wait' (neither included in the ValPaL verb meanings). Thus, the NomAccGen pattern with verbs of cognitive transfer and of intent is not rare, even within the relatively small Gothic corpus.

We conclude this section by discussing the few Gothic ditransitive verbs that feature the NomAccAcc construction exhibiting neutral alignment (Malchukov, Haspelmath and Comrie 2010; cf. Table 3 in Appendix A.1). One such verb is, again, ASK FOR *bidjan* (e.g. Jn 11:22): with this verb, however, the double accusative construction seems to be marginal, as the T-participant is always encoded by a neuter indefinite pronoun (on the status neuter objects with NomAccAcc constructions, cf. Luraghi and Zanchi 2018: 31; see also Section 3.2.3). The Gothic verb for TEACH *laisjan* also takes two accusatives (cf. example (44)), as is common for verbs of teaching in other IE languages (García García 2003; Hock 2014; Luraghi and Zanchi 2018). This fact is understandable, given that these verbs often contain causative derivational morphology, as in Ancient Greek (Luraghi and Zanchi 2018) and that they constitute the most typical cognitive transfer verbs (Haspelmath 2015: 19). In Gothic, *laisjan* also has causative morphology: it is a *ja*-causative beside the preterite-present *lais* 'I know' (the infinitive **lisan* is not attested) and, thus, literally means 'cause to know' (cf. similarly, the couple *kunnan* 'know' and *kannjan* 'cause to know'). Last, the NomAccAcc construction is featured in a group of Gothic verbs that can take a predicative complement (cf. also Wright 1910: 183 and Miller 2019: 168–170).

4 Gothic uncoded alternations

In this section we describe and analyze Gothic uncoded alternations, i.e. those which are not marked morphologically on the verb (cf. Section 2.2).

4.1 The partitive alternation

As anticipated in Section 3.2.3, a number of Gothic verbs that take accusative second arguments can alternate with second arguments in the partitive genitive (for recent accounts of the partitive genitive in Gothic, cf. Leiss 2007;

Miller 2019: 124–125; on the partitive genitive in Ancient Greek, cf. Napoli 2010; Conti and Luraghi 2014; see also Seržant 2014 on Russian and Seržant 2015 on Circum-Baltic languages; on partitives in general, cf. Luraghi and Huumo 2014 with references). The partitive genitive indicates partial affectedness, referring either to parts of specific entities or to an indefinite quantity of a non-specific mass entity (Conti and Luraghi 2014: 446). In our sample, it is used with consumption verbs, such as EAT *matjan* (14), *itan* (15), and DRINK *drigkan* (1Cor 11:28), and corresponds in Greek to a PP with *ek*+GEN or *apó*+GEN.

The partitive genitive is used to indicate a partial quantity of bread in (14) and of specific crumbs in (15). Notably, the verb *itan*, exemplified in (15), is never used with accusative objects but only with partitive genitive ones or indefinite null objects. By contrast, the compound verb *fra-itan* 'devour', which has an associated telic meaning, only allows for accusative objects (16).

(14) ak   þatei   matideduþ   þize   hlaibe
     but   that   eat.PRET.2PL DEM.GEN.PL bread.GEN.PL
     '... but because you ate of the loaves (and you were filled).' (Jn 6:26)

(15) jah   gairnida   saþ   itan   drauhsno
     and   desire.PRET.3SG   full.ACC.N   eat.INF   crumb.GEN.PL
     'And desiring to be fed with the crumbs (which fell from the rich man's table).' (Lk 16:21)

(16) saei   fret   þein   swes   miþ
     REL.NOM   devour.PRET.3SG   POSS.2SG.ACC property.ACC   with
     kalkjom
     prostitute.DAT.PL
     '(But when this son of yours came,) who devoured your living with prostitutes.' (Lk 15:30)

The partitive alternation also features in verbs of giving and taking, such as TAKE *niman* and GIVE *giban* (see Appendix A.2.2 for additional examples). Notably, partitive second arguments can be passivized: in (17), in which GIVE *giban* is used in the passive voice, the partitive genitive occurs as a first argument, thus confirming the fact that genitive partitives are not bound to any specific syntactic function in the sentence (on this feature of Greek partitives, cf. Conti and Luraghi 2014; Seržant 2014 and 2015).

(17) jabai gibaidau kunja þamma taikne
    if   give.OPT.3SG.PASS generation.DAT DEM.DAT sign.GEN.PL
    '(Why doth this generation seek after a sign? Verily I say to you) if only signs would be given to this generation.' (Mk 8:12)

With TAKE *niman*, the partitive function is encoded once through a PP *us*+DAT, possibly calqued from Greek *ek*+GEN:[11]

(18) unte [us meinamma]ᵢ nimiþ   jah gateihiþ   Øᵢ izwis
    for from POSS.1SG.DAT take.PRS.3SG and show.PRS.3SG   2PL.DAT
    'For he shall take of mine and show (it) to you.' (Jn 16:14)
    [Gk. *hóti **ek toû emoû** lḗmpsetai kaì anaggeleî humîn*]

The *us*+DAT PP in (18) could also indicate the source from which something is taken; however, the partitive reading for this PP is more likely, as the referent partly affected by the act of taking is also referred to via a null anaphor, as a dependent of the coordinated verb *ga-teihan* 'show'.

4.2 Other case alternations

Two-place verbs taking optional dative instruments, such as DRESS *wasjan*, also allow for an alternative construction in which the instrument receives accusative encoding (Miller 2019: 140). Similarly, THROW *wairpan* allows for an alternation between the accusative and the dative of the instrument thrown (cf. Mk 1:16 with the accusative vs. Mk 12:4 with the dative; see also Miller 2019: 157). Hewson (2006: 278) argues that *wairpan* takes the instrumental dative, and Miller adds that the accusative indicates instrument only when *wairpan* is used in a figurative sense. This semantic explanation is not convincing (see example (59) in Appendix A.2.2), but, at any rate, the AccDat alternation is not surprising, as similar verbs behave the same way in other ancient IE languages, as, for example, the Ancient Greek equivalent of this verb, *bállō*, also alternates between these two constructions, even in Homeric Greek (Sausa 2015).[12] Finally, in a single occur-

---

[11] In example (18), we added an empty set symbol to signal the null referential object and to co-reference it with the previously mentioned participant to which it refers. Needless to say, the position of such null object in the sentence cannot be reconstructed, and thus the position of the empty set symbol does not imply any location assumption on our part.

[12] In a class of semantically similar Latin verbs, the AccDat and AccAbl constructions alternate (cf. Luraghi and Zanchi 2019 with references). In Latin, the PIE instrumental merged with the

rence containing the communication verb SING *siggwan*, the accusative of the theme is omitted, whereas the addressee is expressed by a dative.

Two Gothic verbs, LEAVE *bi-leiþan* and HEAR *hausjan*, employ three alternate constructions: NomAcc, NomDat, and NomGen. The verb *bi-leiþan* is fundamentally a NomDat verb (Section 3.2.3). Occasionally, it can instantiate the NomAcc construction and the NomGen construction, the latter in negative contexts only (the so-called genitive of negation, on which see Bucci 2020), and be construed as a ditransitive verb. In contrast, the distribution of the three constructions with *hausjan* seems to be motivated by characteristics of the stimulus, i.e. (lack of) animacy, and of the experiencer, i.e. (lack of) active involvement in the perception event (cf. Miller 2019: 162).

Second participants encoded by prepositionless cases can alternate with second participant PPs. This happens with a number of verbs instantiating the NomAcc construction that denote events characterized by no change of state and a low degree of affectedness of the patients.

A single prototypically transitive verb, BEAT *slahan*, can be constructed with a PP:

(19) ak   sloh   in   brusts   seinos
     but   beat.PRET.3SG   in   breast(F).ACC.PL   POSS.3SG.ACC.PL.F
     '(And the publican, standing afar off, would not lift up so much as his eyes unto heaven,) but smote upon his own breast.' (Lk 18:13)

On the one hand, in (19) the NomPP construction may trigger an imperfective, and a thus less transitive reading of the type 'the publican repeatedly beat upon his own breast' (on the well-established link between perfectivity and transitivity, cf. Hopper and Thompson 1980). On the other hand, *slahan* could simply be construed with a goal participant, as happens in (20):

(20) jabai   hvas   izwis   in   andawleizn   slahiþ
     if   INDF.NOM   2PL.ACC   in   face.ACC   beat.PRS.3SG
     '... if a man beats you on the face.' (2Cor 11:20)[13]

---

ablative and not with the dative as in Gothic and Ancient Greek. Hence, the Latin AccDat vs. AccAbl alternation presents exactly the same kind of phenomenon as the alternation we see with *wairpan* and *bállō*.

13 In (20), *izwis* is morphologically ambiguous in that it could be either accusative or dative. However, the verb *slahan* usually takes the accusative of the person, and thus the accusative interpretation is more compelling.

Here, the direct object in the accusative expresses the inalienable possessor of the body part that is beaten, encoded by a PP. In the reflexive context in (19), the possessor is instead encoded through a reflexive possessive adjective agreeing with the possessum.

As we have discussed in Section 3.2.3 and 3.2.4, FILL *fullnan* is one of the few Gothic transitive verbs instantiating the NomGen construction, and its causative *ja*-counterpart *fulljan* is one of the rare ditransitives featuring the AccGen construction (on -*na*-/-*ja*-verb pairs, cf. Section 3.1 and 5.2). The verb *fullnan* arguably calques the corresponding Greek construction in the following passage, where it takes a PP with *in*+DAT (Codex Ambrosianus A) or *du*+DAT (Codex Ambrosianus B) instead of a prepositionless genitive:

(21) ei   fulnaiþ$_A$/fullnaiþ$_B$ in$_A$/du$_B$ allai   fullon   gudis
      if   fill.OPT.PRS.2PL   in/to   INDF.DAT   fullness.DAT   God.GEN
      '... that you might be filled until all the fulness of God.' (Eph 3:19)
      [Gk. *hína plērōthête **eis pân tò plḗrōma** toû theoû*]

One explanation for this unusual Gothic construction could be as follows: the Greek PP with *eis*+ACC does not mean 'you might be filled *with* the fullness of God' but rather 'you might be filled (with God's breadth, length, depth, and height, all previously mentioned) *up to* the fullness of God'. In New Testament Greek, instruments are not usually encoded by *eis*+ACC, but rather by prepositionless datives, *en*+DAT, *ek*/*apó*+GEN, *diá*+GEN, *epí*+GEN/DAT, and *katá*+ACC (Thomason 2006: 51). Thus, Wulfila did not employ two PPs to encode the usual second genitive arguments taken by the verb *fullnan*, but instead correctly interpreted Greek *eis*+ACC as a goal participant and translated it accordingly.

With the experiential verb *ga-leikan*, the NomDat is the most frequent construction (14 out of 20 occurrences; Section 3.2.3). However, the syntax of the verb changes completely when the past passive participle is used as an adjective translating either forms of the Greek verb *eudokéō* 'regard as good, be pleased by something' (Mk 1:11, Lk 3:22) or the Greek adjective *euarestón* 'pleased' (Lk 10:21, Col 3:20, Rom 12:2). In these contexts, the nominative case encodes the experiencer, whereas the stimuli are expressed by PPs with *in*+DAT, possibly calqued from Greek, which features a very similar PP with *en*+DAT. Furthermore, this verb also permits an impersonal usage: the predicate is inflected in the third person singular, the experiencer is encoded in the dative, and the stimuli are expressed by the PP *in*+DAT.

Ditransitive verbs of physical or knowledge transfer typically feature indirect alignment with the NomAccDat construction (cf. Section 3.2.4). Occasionally, however, R-participants can be encoded by prepositional goal or recipient participants.

4.3 Object insertion and object omission

The verb LIGHT *liuhtjan*, which specifically means 'emit light', occurs four times in the Gospels, where it is mostly (3x) used as an intransitive emission verb. In a single passage (22), *liuhtjan* takes a human second participant, which is conceptualized as an animate goal or recipient of emitted light:

(22) jah   liuteiþ   allaim   þaim   in   þamma   garda
     and   light.PRS.3sg   INDF.DAT.PL   DEM.DAT.PL   in   DEM.DAT house.DAT
     'And it (a candle) gives light to all those in this house.' (Mt 5:15)

Several two- and three-place Gothic verbs can be construed with omitted objects. In this respect, a distinction should be made between intransitive events and referential null objects. In the former case, several two-place and three-place verbs are often construed as activities and thus encode intransitive events characterized by indefinite null objects. Their frequency is arguably tied to the text genre of the Gothic corpus: Gospels contain many passages that express universally valid moral principles or prophecies, which are likely to include indefinite null objects (the optionality of indefinite objects is discussed in Levin 1993: 33, among others), as in (23):

(23) saei   hlefi,   þanaseiþs   ni   hlifai
     REL.NOM   steal.OPT.PRET.3SG   again   NEG   steal.OPT.PRS.3SG
     'The one who stole will no longer steal.' (Eph 4:28)

In addition, the argument status of locative second participants with motion and location/posture verbs is notoriously controversial (see e.g. Levin and Rappaport Hovav 1995: 1–21; Sausa 2015: 20), and indeed these participants can be omitted.

Referential null objects are known to be allowed and selected in ancient IE languages under certain syntactic, pragmatic, and stylistic conditions: specifically, with coordinated verbs and clauses, conjunct participles, and yes/no questions (cf. e.g. Luraghi 2004; Keydana and Luraghi 2012; Inglese, Rizzo and Pflugmacher 2019). In this respect Gothic is no exception and allows for referential null objects with ditransitive and transitive verbs. A single verb, CLIMB *steigan*, is attested only with a null referential object in our corpus.

4.4 The external possessor alternation

In Gothic, inalienable possessors can be encoded by genitive modifiers holding a syntactic dependency relation with the possessum. This construction is exemplified in (24) with TOUCH *at-tekan*.

(24) jah   attaitok   handau   izos
    and   touch.PRET.3SG   hand.DAT   3SG.GEN.F
    'And he touched her hand, (and the fever left her).' (Mt 8:15)

With other verbs from our sample, an alternative construction is allowed, in which the inalienable possessor is expressed by a syntactically independent noun phrase inflected in the dative case, traditionally called *dativus sympatheticus*, 'dative of affection' or 'dative of interest'. In accordance with more recent literature on the topic (e.g. Payne and Barshi 1999), we label this construction 'external possessor construction', due to the syntactic independency of the dative possessor from its possessum (on external possessor construction in IE languages, cf. Luraghi 2020b with references). The construction is shown in (25):

(25) jah   weihaim   fotuns   þwohi
    and   saint.DAT.PL   foot.ACC.PL   wash.OPT.PRET.3SG
    '... if she has washed the saints' feet.' (1Tim 5:10ab) [Gk. *ei **hagíōn** pódas ènipsen*]

According to Miller (2019: 144–146), the Gothic dative of inalienable possession is most typical with highly affected possessors. Similar explanations have been given in the typological literature on the matter (cited e.g. in Luraghi 2020b), which also highlights the fact that this construction is preferably selected with first and second person possessors with respect to other types of noun phrases.

However, our data sample, small though it is, points toward a more intricate picture in Gothic (and in any case, even the examples cited in Miller [2019: 145] point to a pattern that cannot be easily discerned). To begin with, examples (24) and (25) contain third person possessors, so apparently no difference can be detected based on the occurrence of first, second, and other participant types. In addition, in example (24), Jesus is performing a miracle by 'touching' an infirm, who certainly will be highly and positively affected by Jesus' hands. By contrast, example (25), which contains an external possessor construction, describes a situation in which the possessors, the saints, are certainly less affected by having their feet washed than the possessor in example (24) by being healed. Notably, also, the syntactic marking of the external possessor in (25) seems to be genuinely Gothic, as the corresponding Greek text has a genitive adnominal possessor (*hagíōn* 'of saints'). What can be inferred is that, in (24), the dative external possessor is not used to avoid the occurrence of a double dative construction (cf. also example (26) in Section 4.5, whose dative internal object can be similarly accounted for).

4.5 The cognate/kindred object alternation

Gothic is generally acknowledged to avoid cognate (i.e. etymologically related to the verbs that take them) and kindred (i.e. semantically similar to the verbs that take them) objects (Wolfe 2006: 210–211; Miller 2019: 109–110). However, these arguments are relatively well-represented in our small sample, where we do find usually intransitive, monotransitive, and ditransitive verbs that allow for the insertion of cognate and kindred objects. These objects can occur in the accusative or in the dative case. In particular, dative cognate objects are quite unusual in the framework of IE languages (Horrocks and Stavrou 2010).

For example, the verb FEAR *ogan* allows for both accusative and dative cognate objects:

(26) jah   ohtedun   sis   agis   mikil
     and   fear.PRET.3PL   REFL.DAT.PL   fear.ACC   great.ACC
     'And they feared a great fear.' (Mk 4:41)

(27) jah   ohtedun   agisa   mikilamma
     and   fear.PRET   fear.DAT   great.DAT
     'And they feared with a great fear.' (Lk 2:9) [Gk. *kaì* **ephobḗthēsan** *phóbon mègan*]

Examples (26) and (27) are very similar and indeed translate the same Greek expression, containing a passive aorist of the verb *phobéō* 'fear' taking a prepositionless relational accusative.[14] The difference between the two Gothic examples is that, in (26), the noncausal meaning of *ogan* 'fear', which is opposed to the causal *ja*-verb *ogjan* 'frighten' (cf. Section 5.2), is strengthened by the reflexive dative pronoun *sis*, which is lacking in (27). The dative reflexive pronoun expresses the subject experiencer's involvement and occurs commonly with this

---

[14] As an anonymous reviewer pointed out, similar constructions are known to be very prominent in Semitic languages and are also likely to appear in Bible translations of various sorts.

verb (cf. Section 5.3). The occurrence of a dative reflexive participant seems to prevent the occurrence of another prepositionless dative participant, which thus gets accusative encoding instead. Again (see Section 4.4), a construction with a double dative is avoided.

4.6 The applicative alternation

Crosslinguistically, applicatives are overt verbal morphemes that "allow the coding of a thematically peripheral argument or adjunct as a core-object argument" (Peterson 2007: 1). In her account of Italian valency patterns and alternations, Cennamo (2015: 437–438) describes the same pattern for the Italian equivalent of LIVE *abitare*, shown in examples (1) and (2). The Gothic equivalent, *bauan*, behaves the same way. Its usage with a prepositional locative participant encoded by *in*+DAT is shown in example (10), whereas its transitive usage is exemplified below:

(28) jah   liuhaþ   bauiþ   unatgaht
      and   light(N).ACC   live.PRS.3SG   unapproachable.ACC.N
      'And (he) dwells (in) unapproachable light' (1Tim 6:16)
      [Gk. *phôs oikôn aprósiton*; Lat. *lucem inhabitans inaccessibilem*]

Both examples (10) and (28) contain metaphoric locative participants, and thus the alternation does not seem to arise from an opposition between literal and metaphorical interpretations of the second argument taken by *bauan*. The corresponding Greek verb *oikéō* allows for the same Acc PP alternation, in that it takes an accusative locative participant as well as a prepositional phrase with *en*+DAT. In the Greek passage corresponding to (28), *oikéō* is used transitively, whereas in (10) *oikéō* takes *en*+DAT. In the Latin Vulgate, we also find a direct object construction with *inhabitans lucem* in the passage corresponding to (28), in which, however, the verb is compounded with the preverb *in-*. In (10), on the other hand, *non habitat in me* occurs, i.e. with the simplex verb taking the expected PP. The Gothic text thus represents a word-by-word translation in this case.

The applicative alternation can also be coded in Gothic (coded alternations are thoroughly discussed in Section 5). One of the Gothic verbs of our sample features the so-called *be*-alternation, known for Germanic languages and described by Haspelmath and Baumann (2013) for the ValPaL core meanings: the activity simplex verb LAUGH *hlahjan* (see example (6)), with the addition of the preverb *bi-* (literally) 'around' (cf. Section 3.2.3), results in the transitive compound *bi-hlahjan*, which takes accusative stimuli, as in (29).

(29) jah   bi-hlohun   ina
     and   around-laugh.PRET.3PL   3SG.ACC
     'They laughed at him.' (Mk 5:40; cf. also Mt 9:24, Lk 8:53)

Once again, this verb is similar to its Italian equivalent, *ridere*, which also takes a PP with *di* indicating the area semantic role (in e.g. Luraghi's 2003 terms), but a direct object if preverbed with *de-*. The accusative stimulus of *hlahjan* can also be passivized (Lk 6:21; on the applicative functions of IE preverbs, cf. Zanchi 2019: 65–67).

5 Gothic coded alternations

In this section, we deal with Gothic coded alternations, those which are overtly marked on the verb (cf. Section 2.2).

5.1 The passive alternation

Gothic is the sole member of the Germanic family that preserves, only in the present tense, continuants of the PIE mediopassive, which, however, in the overwhelming majority of cases is to be interpreted as a passive (Section 3.1). Hence, Gothic is the only Germanic language which displays a synthetic passive (on the loss of PIE mediopassive in Old Norse, cf. e.g. Cennamo, Eythórsson and Barðdal 2015: 678). However, in a handful of cases, it is still debatable whether nonpassive "middle" readings of the Gothic passive are possible (on this issue, cf. some examples below, Section 5.2, and the abundant references cited in Kleyner 2019 and Ratkus 2020).

In our corpus, a number of verbs attest to synthetic passive forms (cf. Table 5 in Appendix A.1). The verbs DRESS *ga-wasjan* (30) and KILL *af-dauþjan* (31) are discussed by Kleyner (2019) and Ratkus (2020). Kleyner (2019) favors a nonpassive interpretation, whereas Ratkus (2020) strongly argues for a passive reading. The passages in question are displayed below:

(30) *þanuþ~þan   þata   diwano   gawasjada*
     so.when   DEM.NOM   die.PTCP.PRF.PASS.NOM   dress.PRS.3SG.PASS
     unsdiwanein
     immortality.DAT
     'So when this mortal will be dressed with immortality . . . ' (1Cor 15:54a)

(31) saei   ubil   qiþai   attin   seinamma
     DEM.NOM   evil.ACC   say.OPT.3SG   father(M).DAT   POSS.DAT.M
     aiþþau   aiþein   seinai,   dauþau   afdauþjaidau
     or   mother(f).DAT POSS.DAT.F   death.DAT   kill.OPT.3SG.PASS
     '(He) who speaks evil to his father or to his mother, shall be killed by death.'
     (Mk 7:10)[15] [Gk. *ho kakologôn patéra ḕ mētéra thanátōi **teleutátō**]

In (30), the passive *gawasjada* could have a reflexive rather than a passive interpretation. However, God is here conceived to be the unexpressed intentional agent performing the miracles reported, i.e. transforming men into light and dressing them with immortality at the time of The Rapture (see also Ratkus 2019: 123–124; D'Agostino 2019: 41–42). Similarly, in (31), the passive form *afdauþjaidau* suggests a true passive reading: being put to death is described as a punishment inflicted by intentional agents. In other words, by using the passive form of the causal verb *af-dauþjan* and not its noncausal counterpart *af-dauþnan* (cf. Section 5.2), death is not construed as a spontaneous event, but rather as the consequence of a deliberate crime punishable by death (*contra* Kleyner 2019: 117; Ratkus 2020: 9–11). Note that the Gothic translation partially calques the Greek text in that *dauþau* is not required in Gothic, in which the verb itself means 'die', whereas the corresponding dative noun *thanátōi* is required in the Greek text, where the verbal form *teleutátō* from *teleutáō* means more generally 'bring to pass, accomplish, finish, make an end'.

As analytic passives can be used both in the present and the past tenses, this construction is thought to be in the process of expanding its domain at the expense of the synthetic form (Miller 2019: 2017; Ratkus 2020). Analytic passives can be constructed with the auxiliaries *wisan* 'be' or *wairþan* 'become', the former indicating an "entailed-state resultative" and the latter expressing "an attained-state resultative" (Katz 2016: 206; see also Kotin 1997; Pagliarulo 2008; Miller 2019: 216–219).

The verbs from our corpus that allow for the analytic passive alternation are in Table 5 in Appendix A.1. Here, we limit the discussion to two passages with analytic passives that may be susceptible to nonpassive interpretations:

---

15 Cf. also Rom 7:4, which contains an analytic passive of the same verb and in which the same idea of inflicted death is quite clearly conveyed.

(32) nu   fagino,   ni   unte gauridai
      now   rejoice.PRS.1SG NEG   as   sadden.PTCP.PRF.PASS.NOM.PL
      wesuþ   ak   unte gauridai   wesuþ
      be.PRET.2PL   but   as   sadden.PTCP.PRF.PASS.NOM.PL be.PRET.2PL
      du idreigai
      to repentance.DAT
      'Now I rejoice, not that you were grieved, but that you were grieved into repentance.' (2Cor 7:9)

(33) iþ   biþe gabauran   ist   barn   ni
      but   as   carry.PTCP.PRF.PASS.NOM.N   be.PRS.3SG   child.NOM NEG
      þanaseiþs ni   gaman   þizos   aglons
      longer   NEG   remember.PRS.3SG DEM.GEN   anguish.GEN
      '[The woman has pain when she is giving birth, because her hour has come;] but when the child is brought (to life), she remembers the tribulation no longer.' (Jn 16:21)

The context of (32) points toward a passive reading: the agent is clearly the writer of the letter to which reference is made in the text; in the passage just above (32), the same writer states: *unte jabai gaurida izwis in bokom* 'even if I made you sad with my letter' (2Cor 7:8). The writer also points out that his act of saddening his addressee had both good intentions and outcomes. Similarly, in (33), the passive form of *ga-bairan* has a passive value, as the agent, i.e. the woman who delivers the child, plays a prominent role in the overall context and is the main topic of this whole passage; she also returns to be the subject of the subsequent apodosis.

With ditransitive verbs or verbs that allow for ditransitive usages (Section 3.2.4), the participant that receives the accusative encoding, be it a T- or a R-participant, is invariably passivized. On the other hand, the dative participants, if expressed, remain as such. With verbs instantiating the double accusative construction, such as NAME *namnjan*, the non-predicative accusative is passivized, whereas the predicative accusative can be expressed (Lk 7:11) or omitted. With TEACH *laisjan*, the person who receives the instruction is passivized, while the thing that is taught is omitted (Jn 6:45).

The passive alternation can also be left uncoded with infinitives: these forms are said to be underspecified for voice (Miller 2019: 219–221). In object control structures, the passive reading is instead accounted for as a translational effect (Joseph 1981: 368; Harbert 2007: 331; see Table 4 in Appendix A.1 and example (60) in Appendix A.2.3).

(34) warþ   þan   gaswiltan   þamma   unledin   jah
     become.PRET.3SG PTC die.INF   DEM.DAT poor.DAT and
     briggan fram aggilum   in barma   Abrahamis
     bring.INF by   angel.DAT.PL   in bosom.DAT A.GEN
     'It happened to the poor to die and to be brought by the angels in Abraham's bosom'. (Lk 16:22)

In (34), the impersonal form *warþ* takes a dative participant, designating the maleficiary to whom the mentioned events happened, and two active infinitives. The former infinitive regularly indicates the noncausal event of dying, whereas the latter must be interpreted as a passive, to which a passive agent expressed by a PP with *fram*+DAT is further added.

5.2 The causal : noncausal alternation

Concerning the causal : noncausal alternation, a clear scenario emerges from our data, in which the causal member of the alternation is almost always expressed by *ja*-verbs, whereas the noncausal member seems to be encoded in a much less homogeneous way. This distribution lends support to Ottóson's (2013) suggestion that *ja*-causatives may be older than *na*-anticausatives, which are a later PGmc development occurring within the broader loss of the PIE inflectional middle.

Table 2 summarizes the Gothic causal : noncausal alternation as evidenced from ValPaL core verb meanings, displaying together the *ja*-verbs with causal meanings, their noncausal counterparts, and the strategies through which the alternation is expressed.[16]

Table 2: The causal : noncausal alternation in Gothic ValPaL verbs.

ValPaL verb meaning	Causal member	Noncausal member	Coding strategy
BREAK	brikan	us-bruk-nan	strong 4 vs. -na- + ablaut
BURN	tand-jan	tund-nan	-ja- vs. -na- + ablaut

---

16 To capture the highest number of attested causal : noncausal alternations, verbs with different preverbs must be paired owing to the inherent limitations of the Gothic corpus (Section 2.2). The fact that the causal and the noncausal members display different preverbs does not make the comparison problematic.

Table 2 (continued)

ValPaL verb meaning	Causal member	Noncausal member	Coding strategy
DRINK	*dragk-jan*	*drigkan*	*-ja-* + ablaut
	drigkan	analytic passive	Passive
FALL	*ga-draus-jan*	*ga-driusan*	*-ja-* + ablaut
FILL	*full-jan*	*full-nan*	*-ja-* vs. *-na-*
		synthetic passive	*-ja-* vs. passive
FRIGHTEN, FEAR	*og-jan*	*ogan* (*sik*)	*-ja-* vs. (reflexive)
GIVE	*giban*	synthetic passive (*at-giban*)[17]	Passive
GO	*letan gaggan*	*gaggan*	Periphrastic construction
HIDE	*letan ga-filhan*	*ga-filhan*	Periphrastic construction
KILL, DIE	*ga-dauþ-jan*	*ga-dauþ-nan*	*-ja-* vs. *-na-*
KNOW	*kann-jan*	*kunnan*	*-ja-* + ablaut
LIVE	*taujan liban*	*liban*	Periphrastic construction
MAKE SAD, GET SAD	*gaur-jan*	synthetic passive	*-ja-* vs. synthetic passive
MAKE SAD, BE SAD		*gaurs wairþan*	*-ja-* vs. adjective + copula
ROLL	*af-walw-jan*	*walwison*	*-ja-* vs. weak 2[18]
SINK	*sigq-jan*	*sigq-an*	*-ja-*
PUT, SIT	*sat-jan*[19]	*sitan*	*-ja-* + ablaut
PUT	*lag-jan*	*ligan*	*-ja-* + ablaut
SHOW	*at-augjan*	analytic passive	*-ja-* vs. passive
		at-augjan sik	*-ja-* vs. reflexive
		at-augjan	*-ja-* vs. uncoded
TEACH, KNOW	*lais-jan*	*lais* (**lisan*)	*-ja-* + ablaut
TEACH, LEARN		*laisjan sik*	*-ja-* vs. reflexive

As shown in Table 2, the causal members of the alternation are almost exclusively lexicalized by a *ja*-verb. The only exception to this generalization is the couple *brikan* vs. **bruk-nan*, in which the alternation is encoded through the

---

17 Cf. fn. 16.
18 The causative **walw-jan* (which only occurs with preverbs) allegedly constitutes a more ancient formation than *walwison* (PIE **wel-w-*, cf. Lat. *volvō*), in light of its parallels in Old English (*wielwan*, *wælwian*). The causative **walw-jan* is primary, whereas *walwison* represents a secondary denominative formation on PGmc **walwiz* (Lehmann 1986: s.v. **af-walwjan*).
19 This *ja*-causative is often used without any objects in the sense of 'plant' (Lk 17:28).

ablaut, and it is the noncausal member that is overtly marked via the *na*-suffix. The couple *brikan* – *bruk-nan parallels OIcel. *brjóta* – *brotna*, in which the latter verb is formed from the past participle of the former *brotinn*. This kind of *na*-verb formation is only attested in Gothic and Old Norse. The causal domain is also marginally expressed by two periphrastic constructions, which are limited to three verbal lemmas totaling five occurrences. The former construction contains the verb *letan* 'let' (35), whereas the latter includes the verb *taujan* 'do' (36).

(35) **letiþ** þo barna gaggan du mis
 let.PRS.2PL DEM.ACC.PL child.ACC.PL go.INF to 1SG.DAT
 'Let the children come to me.' (Mk 10:14) [Gk. *áphete tà paidía érkhesthai prós me*]

(36) ahma ist saei **liban taujiþ**
 spirit.NOM be.PRS.3SG REL.NOM live.INF do.PRS.3SG
 'It is the spirit that makes alive.' (Jn 6:63) [Gk. *tò pneûmá estin tò **zōipoioûn***]

In (35), an analogous form of the Gothic verb *letan* 'let' translates an imperative form of the Greek verb *aphíēmi* 'send away' (*áphete*). This construction is labelled as factitive by Cennamo (2015: 448–451), who describes it for the Italian verb *lasciare* 'let', and is obviously used in English as well (cf. the translation of (35)). In (36), the construction with *liban taujan* 'cause to live' seems to be no more than an *ad hoc* solution for translating the Greek compound *zōi-poiéō* '(literally) alive-make'.

The noncausal domain can be encoded by various markers, i.e. a *na*-verb, a class 2 weak verb, a synthetic passive, an analytic passive, a reflexive, or it may be left uncoded (42). As discussed in Section 5.1, whether the synthetic passive can also have nonpassive readings continues to be disputed. The controversy has been brought back in the spotlight by two very recent papers, which maintain opposite positions on the matter: Kleyner (2019) believes that a few Gothic synthetic passives can be used to encode the noncausal members in a causal : noncausal alternation, whereas Ratkus (2020) argues strongly against Kleyner's (2019) interpretation. In our view, both the synthetic and the analytic passives suggest noncausal readings in a handful of passages from our corpus, which are reported in the following.

(37) iþ jabai in matis broþar þeins
 but if in food.GEN brother.NOM POSS.2SG.NOM
 gaurjada
 make_sad.PRS.3SG.PASS
 'But if your brother gets upset because of your food.' (Rom 14:15)

(38) jah   ahmins   weihis   gafulljada
    and   spirit.GEN   holy.GEN   fill.PRS.3SG.PASS
    '(For he shall be great in the sight of the Lord and shall drink neither wine nor strong drink;) and he shall be full of the Holy Ghost (even from his mother's womb).' (Lk 1:15)

(39) þanuh   biþe   atgibada   akran
    but   when   give.PRS.3SG.PASS   fruit.NOM
    'But when the fruit is ready . . . ' (Mk 4:29)
    [Gk. *hótan dè paradoî ho karpós*; Lat. *et cum se produxerit fructus*]

(40) jaþ~þatei   ataugids   ist   Kefin,   jah
    and that   show.PTCP.PRF.PASS.NOM   be.PRS.3SG   C..DAT   and
    afar   þata   þaim   ainlibim
    after   DEM.ACC.N   DEM.DAT.PL   eleven.DAT.PL
    ' . . . and that he appeared to Cephas, and after that to the eleven.'
    (1Cor 15:5, see also Mk 9:4, 16:12S, 1Tim 3:16a)

In (37), there is no clear intentional agent that brings about the event of becoming sad, which is encoded by a synthetic passive of *gaurjan* 'make sad'. Instead, a cause that triggers the event is overtly expressed in the passage by a PP with *in*+GEN.[20] Similarly, in (38), it is not clear whether the event of being filled or being full is construed as brought about by an agent (i.e. God, in this case) and as having a dynamic temporal development, or whether being full with the Holy Spirit should be better understood as a timeless state that Jesus experiences from the very beginning of his existence. In neither case, however, is a proper passive reading compelling. The passage in (39) is highly disputed (Kleyner 2019: 115–117; Ratkus 2020: 7–8). It contains a compound of *giban*, occurring in a synthetic passive form and possibly bearing a nonpassive value. This Gothic passive form translates a Greek active aorist subjunctive *paradoî* (from *paradídōmi* 'give beside'). The passage is paralleled in Latin by an active future perfect indicative *produxerit* (from *producō* 'produce'), accompanied by a reflexive pronoun *se*. Thus, a Gothic passive construction with a nominative subject retains the word order of Greek and Latin. These languages differ from Gothic, however, in that they permit two active constructions to occur with verbs indicating spontaneous events. The reading of the event being conceived of as spontaneous emerges clearly from the Latin text, in which a reflexive pronoun *se* is also added (D'Agostino 2019: 52–53).

---

20 As noted in Section 5.1, this passage should be compared with (32).

Indeed, it is difficult to think of an entity that could play the agent's role in this context, especially as in the previous passage it is said that *silbo auk airþa akran bairiþ* 'for the earth itself bears fruit'. Therefore, the synthetic passive is most convincingly interpreted as expressing a spontaneous event. In (40), an analytic passive form of *at-augjan* 'show' is clearly employed to describe Jesus who appears directly to his disciples, and not Jesus who is shown to his disciples by some entity. A passive reading is not satisfying for this passage, which either indicates a spontaneous event (see also Miller 2019: 216, who simply states that the passive of *at-augjan* is used with the meaning of 'appear'). This noncausal interpretation is also strengthened by the fact that this verb also means 'appear' if used with a reflexive pronoun (cf. Miller 2019: 394–396 for Gothic reflexives with "anticausative" and "inchoative" functions in his terms):

(41) sumai   þan   qeþun   <þatei>   Helias
     INDF.NOM.PL then   say.PRET.3PL that   H..NOM
     ataugida   sik
     show.PRET.3SG REFL.ACC
     'Others said that Elijah had appeared.' (Lk 9:8)

Surprisingly, with *at-augjan*, such a noncausal reading can also be uncoded (Section 5.3):

(42) bi   spedistin þan anakumbjandam   þaim
     by   last.DAT   PTC recline.PTCP.PRS.DAT.PL DEM.DAT.PL
     ainlibim   ataugida
     eleven.DAT.PL   show.PRET.3SG
     'Afterward he appeared unto the eleven as they sat down for a meal.' (Mk 16:14)

In (42), the Gothic active form *ataugida* is employed to denote the same noncausal event of appearing as in (40).[21]

In addition, in two passages the analytic passive of DRINK *drigkan* is used to translate the Greek verb *methú(sk)ō* 'get/be drunk' and denotes noncausal events:

---

[21] The reflexive pronoun does not occur in the previous context, as it does e.g. in (46).

(43) jah þaiei drugkanai wairþand,
and REL.NOM.PL drink.PTCP.PRF.PASS.NOM.PL become.PRS.3PL
nahts drugkanai wairþand
night.GEN drink.PTCP.PRF.PASS.NOM.PL become.PRS.3PL
'And those who get drunk get drunk overnight.' (1Thess 5:7;
see also 1Cor 11:21)

A reflexive of first or second person pronoun (Section 5.3) is obligatorily employed with TEACH *laisjan* (44) to mean LEARN *(ga-)laisjan sik* (45). As mentioned in Section 3.2.4, *laisjan* is a causative verb beside the preterite-present *lais* 'I know', thus originally meaning 'cause to know' → 'teach' (see Miller 2019: 294).

(44) Jah laisida ins in gajukom manag
And teach.PRET.3SG DEM.ACC.PL in parable.DAT.PL much.ACC.N
'And he taught them many things by parables.' (Mk 4:2)

(45) ik galaisida mik in þaimei im
1SG.NOM teach.PRET.1SG REFL.ACC in REL.DAT.PL be.PRS.1sg
ganohiþs wisan
satisfy.PTCP.PRF.PASS.NOM be.INF
'I learned to be satisfied in whatever circumstances I am in.' (Phil 4:11)

5.3 The reflexive and the reciprocal alternation

The reflexive alternation is encoded by the reflexive pronoun *sik* or *sik silba* with the third person, whereas it is expressed by the addition of a first or a second person pronoun in the respective persons (Wright 1910; cf. example (45) above and verbs in Table 5 of Appendix A.1):

(46) unte jabai ni huljai sik qino skabaidau
for if NEG cover.OPT.3SG REFL.ACC woman.NOM shave.OPT.3SG
iþ jabai agl ist qinon du kapillon
but if shameful.NOM.N be.PRS.3SG woman.DAT to cut_hair.INF
aiþþau skaban, gahuljai
or shave.INF cover.OPT.3SG
'For if a woman does not cover herself, also let her be shorn. And if it is disgraceful to a woman to be shorn or to be shaven, she should cover (herself).' (1Cor 11:6)

In (46), the reflexive alternation in the first protasis is regularly expressed by the reflexive pronoun in the accusative. In the second apodosis, however, the reflexive meaning is implied but does not receive any overt marker. This may well be a case of referential null object; however, other Gothic verbs allow for an uncoded reflexive alternation.

Three verbs from our corpus can denote reflexive situations without the overt occurrence of the reflexive pronoun (see Table 4 in Appendix A.1). They all translate Greek middle aorists, as shown in (47):

(47) gagg   þwahan   in   swumsl   Siloamis... galaiþ   jah
     go.IMP.2SG wash.INF in   pool.ACC S..GEN   go.PRET.3SG and
     afþwoh   jah   qam   saihvands
     wash.PRET.3SG   and   come.PRET.3SG   see.PTCP.PRS.NOM
     '"Go and wash in the pool of Siloam." ... He went there and washed and came back seeing.' (Jn 9:7) [Gk. húpage nípsai ... apêlthen oûn kaì enípsato, kaì êlthen blépōn]

In (47), the simplex and the compound verbs þwahan and af-þwahan are used in active forms but describe reflexive situations. One might argue that the reflexive usage for the first active infinitive þwahan is motivated by the fact that these forms may be underspecified for voice (Section 5.1). However, this explanation is not possible for the preterite of af-þwahan. In the ValPaL database, this same alternation is called "understood reflexive object" alternation and is attested for WASH and DRESS and other verbs denoting "caring for the body" (http://valpal.info/languages/english/alternations/3532288527).

The reciprocal alternation is almost exclusively encoded by the reflexive pronoun sik (or its equivalent first and second person pronouns) accompanied by the adverb misso 'mutually' (Wright 1910: 189; Miller 2019: 392–394):

(48) jah   jus   skuluþ   izwis   misso   þwahan
     and   2PL.NOM   should.PRS.2PL   2PL.DAT   mutually wash.INF
     fotuns
     foot.ACC.PL
     'And you should mutually wash your feet.' (Jn 13:14)

In (48), the reciprocants (izwis misso) take the dative case and play the role of external possessors (on which see Section 4.4).

In a single passage, reciprocity is encoded via a bipartite construction of the polyptotic type (cf. Nedjalkov 2007: 154–157 and Evans 2008: 46 on this terminology): anþar-NOM anþar-ACC. This construction (49) is instantiated by the verb BUILD timrjan, which acquires the metaphorical interpretation of 'morally edify one another'.

(49) inuh   þis   þrafsteiþ   izwis   misso   jah
      for   DEM.GEN   comfort.PRS.2PL   2PL.DAT   mutually   and
      timrjaiþ   ainhvarjizuh   anþar   anþarana
      build.OPT.PRS.2PL   each_and_every.NOM   another:NOM   another.ACC
      'Because of that, you comfort yourselves mutually, and you should – each
      and every one – edify one another.' (1Thess 5:11)

6 Conclusions

In this paper, we applied the ValPaL methodology to study valency patterns and alternations of 87 Gothic verbs. After providing a short overview of Gothic sentence structure, we detailed the syntactic and semantic properties of Gothic impersonal, one-, two-, and three-place verbs. We then described and analyzed Gothic uncoded and coded alternations. In terms of uncoded alternations, the verbs of our sample attest to the partitive, null object, external possessor, cognate/kindred object, applicative, causal : noncausal (marginal), and reflexive alternations (marginal), as well as a number of other case alternations that have parallels in other ancient IE languages. Regarding the coded alternations, we discussed the applicative, passive, causal : noncausal, reflexive, and reciprocal alternations.

In carrying out the analysis, we faced a number of methodological challenges, due to the nature of the Gothic corpus. In particular, we observed that (i) some constructions (e.g. NomGen and NomDat) occur less frequently than they might be expected to due to the ValPaL verb selection; (ii) some verbal usages (i.e. the frequent absolute usage of transitive verbs and the causal reading associated with the weather verb *rignjan*) are tied to textual genre and the view of the world of which the Gospels are an expression; (iii) a number of verbal constructions (e.g. periphrastic construction to encode the causal member in the causal : noncausal alternation) can be ascribed to the adherence to the Greek text as the chief translational source. To address these issues diligently, not only did we keep a constant eye on the Greek text, but we also consistently integrated our data with those contained in reference grammars.

We showed that a systematic corpus analysis, conducted within a solid typological framework, is useful for shedding light on still-debated and intricate issues pertaining to Gothic syntax, and Gothic passive constructions in particular. Our data suggests that both synthetic and analytic Gothic passives can occasionally be used to express noncausal situations. Moreover, we showed that the reflexive alternation, too, is at times employed to express noncausal event types.

Moreover, our data showed that, while the noncausal domain in the causal : noncausal alternation can be encoded by a variety of means (*na*-verbs, class 2 weak verbs, passives, the reflexive pronoun), the causal domain, in contrast, is tightly restricted to *ja*-verbs beyond two poorly-attested periphrastic constructions calqued from Greek. We argue that this data supports Ottósson's (2013) view according to which the encoding of noncausal domain was systematized at a later stage than was the causal domain. This scenario may be well framed within larger Indo-European picture, in which the loss of PIE inflectional middle arguably contributed to the emergence of an array of new noncausal formations, which underwent a systematization later than Gothic allows us to observe.

List of abbreviations

(Not in the Leipzig Glossig Rules)

A	agent
Engl.	English
Eph	*Letter to the Ephesians*
Ex.	*Exodus*
Germ.	German
Gk.	Greek (New Testament Greek)
IE	Indo-European
Jn	*John's Gospel*
Lat.	Latin (of Jerome's *Vulgate*)
Lk	*Luke's Gospel*
Mk	*Mark's Gospel*
Mt	*Matthew's Gospel*
OE	Old English
OIcel.	Old Icelandic
OPT	optative
PGmc	Proto-Germanic
Phil	*Letter of Paul to the Philippians*
PIE	Proto-Indo-European
PRET	preterite
R	Recipient
Rom	*Letter to the Romans*
S	subject
T	Theme
1Cor	*First Letter to the Corinthians*
1Thess	*First Letter to the Thessalonians*
1Tim	*First Letter to Timothy*
2Cor	*Second Letter to the Corinthians*

References

Annerholm, Hjalmar. 1956. *Studier över de inkoativa verben på na(n)* [Studies on the inchoative *na(n)*-verbs]. Lund: Carl Bloms Boktryckeri.

Apresjan, Jurij D. 1969. *Èksperimental'noe issledovanie russkogo glagola* [Experimental study of the Russian verb]. Moskva: Nauka.

Balg, Gerhard Hubert. 1891. *The First Germanic Bible: Translated from the Greek by the Gothic Bishop Wulfila in the Fourth Century: And the other remains of the Gothic language.* New York: Westermann; London: Truebner; Halle an der Saale: Niemeyer.

Bammesberger, Alfred. 1965. *Deverbative jan-Verba des Altenglischen*. Munich: Mikrokopie.

Bernhardt, Ernst. 1888. Zur gotischen Casuslehre. *Beiträge zur deutschen Philologie* 11. 71–82.

Bökenkrüger, Wilhelm. 1924. *Das reflexive Verb im Althochdeutschen*. Giessen: Münchow.

Bucci, Giacomo. 2020. Genitive of negation in Gothic. *Amsterdamer Beiträge zur älteren Germanistik* 80(1/2). 76–107.

Cennamo, Michela. 2015. Valency patterns in Italian. In Andrej Malchukov & Bernard Comrie (eds.), *Valency classes in the world's languages*, 417–481. Berlin & New York: Mouton de Gruyter.

Cennamo, Michela & Claudia Fabrizio. 2013. Italian valency patterns. In Iren Hartmann, Martin Haspelmath & Bradley Taylor (eds.), *Valency Patterns Leipzig*. Leipzig: Max Planck Institute for Evolutionary Anthropology. http://ValPaL.info/languages/italian (accessed 16 May 2020).

Cennamo, Michela, Thórhallur Eythórsson & Jóhanna Barðdal. 2015. Semantic and (morpho) syntactic constraints on anticausativization: Evidence from Latin and Old Norse-Icelandic. *Linguistics* 53 (4). 677–729.

Conti, Luz & Silvia Luraghi. 2014. The Ancient Greek partitive genitive in typological perspective. In Silvia Luraghi & Tuomas Huumo (eds.), *Partitive cases and related categories*, 443–476. Berlin & New York: Mouton de Gruyter.

Croft, William. 2012. *Verbs: Aspect and causal structure*. Oxford: Oxford University Press.

Curme, George O. 1911. Is the Gothic bible Gothic? *Journal of English and German Philology* 10. 151–190, 335–377.

Delbrück, Berthold. 1907. *Synkretismus: Ein Beitrag zur germanischen Kasuslehre*. Strasbourg: Trübner.

Dixon, Robert M. W. 1991. *A new approach to English grammar, on semantic principles*. Oxford: Clarendon Press.

Dixon, Robert M. W. 2005. *A semantic approach to English grammar*. Oxford: Oxford University Press.

D'Agostino, Giulia. 2019. *The semantics and uses of the Gothic medio-passive*. Pavia: Università di Pavia MA thesis.

Drinka, Bridget. 2011. The sacral stamp of Greek: Periphrastic constructions in the New Testament translations of Latin, Gothic, and Old Church Slavonic. In Eirik Welo (ed.), *Indo-European syntax and pragmatics: Contrastive approaches*, 41–73. Oslo: University of Oslo.

Egge, Albert E. 1887. Inchoative or *n*-verbs in Gothic, Etc. *The American Journal of Philology* 7. 38–45.

Evans, Nicholas. 2008. Reciprocal constructions: Towards a structural typology. In Ekkehard König & Volker Gast (eds.), *Reciprocals and reflexives: Theoretical and cross-linguistic explorations*, 33–103. Berlin & New York: Mouton de Gruyter.

Falluomini, Carla. 2008. Il testo gotico nella tradizione biblica. In Vittoria Dolcetti Corazza & Renato Gendre (eds.), *Intorno alla Bibbia gotica, Atti del VII Seminario avanzato in Filologia Germanica*, 249–288. Alessandria: Edizioni dell'Orso.

Fedriani, Chiara. 2014. *Experiential predicates in Latin*. Leiden: Brill.
Ferraresi, Gisella. 2005. *Word order and phrase structure in Gothic*. Leuven: Peeters.
Friedrichsen, George W. S. 1939. *The Gothic version of the Epistles: A study of its style and textual history*. Oxford: OUP.
García García, Luisa. 2003. Valenzstruktur der gotischen Kausativa. *Sprachwissenschaft* 2 (4). 373–394.
García García, Luisa. 2005. *Germanische Kausativbildung: Die deverbalen jan-Verben im Gotischen*. Göttingen: Vandenhoeck & Ruprecht.
García García, Luisa. 2020. The basic valency orientation of Old English and the causative *ja*-formation: a synchronic and diachronic approach. *English Language and Linguistics* 24 (1). 1–25.
Gelderen, Elly van. 2011. Valency changes in the history of English. *Journal of Historical Linguistics* 1 (1). 106–143.
Harbert, Wayne. 2007. *The Germanic Languages*. Cambridge: CUP.
Harðarson, Jón A. 2017. The morphology of Germanic. In Jared Klein, Brian D. Joseph & Matthias Fritz (eds.), *Handbook of comparative and historical Indo-European linguistics*, 913–954. Berlin & New York: Mouton de Gruyter.
Hartmann, Iren & Martin Haspelmath & Bradley Taylor (eds.) 2013. *Valency patterns Leipzig*. Leipzig: Max Planck Institute for Evolutionary Anthropology. (Available online at http://valpal.info, accessed 23 March 2021).
Haspelmath, Martin. 2015. Ditransitive constructions. *Annual Review of Linguistics* 1. 19–41.
Haspelmath, Martin & Luisa Baumann. 2013. German Valency Patterns. In Iren Hartmann, Martin Haspelmath & Bradley Taylor (eds.), *Valency Patterns Leipzig*. Leipzig: Max Planck Institute for Evolutionary Anthropology. http://ValPaL.info/languages/italian (accessed 29 May 2020).
Haspelmath, Martin, Andreea S. Calude, Michael Spagnol, Heiko Narrog & Elif Bamyac. 2014. Coding causal-noncausal verb alternations: A form-frequency correspondence explanation. *Journal of Linguistics* 50 (3). 587–625.
Hellan, Lars, Andrej Malchukov & Michela Cennamo (eds.). 2017. *Contrastive studies in verbal valency*. Amsterdam & Philadelphia: John Benjamins.
Hermodsson, Lars. 1952. *Reflexive und intransitive Verba im älteren Westgermanischen*. Uppsala: Almqvist & Wiksell.
Hettrich, Heinrich. 2007. *Materialien zu einer Kasussyntax des Rgveda*. Würzburg: Universität Würzburg Institut für Altertumswissenschaft.
Hewson, John. 2006. From Ancient to Modern Germanic. In John Hewson & Vit Bubenik (eds.), *From case to adposition: The development of configurational syntax in Indo-European Languages*, 274–303. Amsterdam & Philadelphia: John Benjamins.
Hock, Hans H. 2014. Some notes on Indo-European double direct-object constructions. In Alfred Bammesberger, Olav Hackstein & Sabine Ziegler (eds.), *Von Fall zu Fall: Studien zur indogermanischen Syntax*, 151–164. Göttingen: Vandenhoeck & Ruprecht.
Holvoet, Axel & Nicole Nau (eds.). 2014. *Grammatical relations and their non-canonical encoding in Baltic*. Amsterdam & Philadelphia: John Benjamins.
Holvoet, Axel & Nicole Nau (eds.). 2015. *Voice and argument structure in Baltic*. Amsterdam & Philadelphia: John Benjamins.
Hopper, Paul J. & Sandra Thompson. 1980. Transitivity in grammar and discourse. *Language* 56. 251–299.
Horrocks, Geoffrey & Melita Stavrou. 2010. Morphological aspect and the function and distribution of cognate objects across languages. In Malka Rappaport Hovav, Edit Doron & Ivy Sichel (eds.), *Lexical semantics, syntax, and event structure*, 284–308. Oxford: OUP.

Inglese, Guglielmo, Giuseppe Rizzo & Miriam Pflugmacher. 2019. Definite referential null objects in Old Hittite. A corpus study. *Indogermanische Forschungen* 124 (1). 137–170.
Jones, Douglas (ed.). 1994. Working papers and projects on verb class alternations in Bangla, German, English, and Korean. *MIT AI Memo* 1517.
Joseph, Brian D. 1981. On the so-called 'Passive' use of the Gothic active infinitive. *Journal of English and Germanic Philology* 80. 369–379.
Joseph, Brian D. & Richard D. Janda (eds.). 2003. *The handbook of historical linguistics*. Oxford: Blackwell.
Karsten, Torsten E. 1911. Zur Kenntnis der inchoativen Aktionsart im Deutschen II: Denominative ē-Verba mit intransitiv-inchoativer (bezw. perfektiv-ingressiver) Funktion. *Neuphilologische Mitteilungen* 1 (2). 1–11.
Katz, R. Moses Jr. 2016. *The resultative in Gothic*. Athens, GA: University of Georgia PhD dissertation.
Keidan, Artemij. 2005. Il gotico di Wulfila: tra diacronia e retorica. *AIΩN Linguistica* 23. 49–105.
Keydana, Götz & Silvia Luraghi. 2012. Definite referential null objects in Vedic Sanskrit and Ancient Greek. *Acta Linguistica Hafniensia* 44 (2). 116–128.
Kiparsky, Paul. 1998. Partitive case and aspect. In Miriam Butt & Wilhelm Geuder (eds.), *The projection of arguments: Lexical and compositional factors*, 265–307. Stanford: CSLI Publications.
Kleyner, Svetlana. 2019. Changed in translation: Greek actives become Gothic passives. *Transactions of the philological society* 117 (1). 112–131. https://doi.org/10.1111/1467-968X.12149 (accessed 1 October 2020).
Köhler, Artur. 1864. *Über den syntaktischen Gebrauch des Dativs im Gotischen*. Ph.D. dissertation, Georg-Augusts-Universität zu Göttingen. Published *Germania* 11: 261–305 (1866).
Kotin, Michail L. 1997. Die analytischen Formen und Fügungen im deutschen Verbalsystem: Herausbildung und Status (unter Berücksichtigung des Gotischen). *Sprachwissenschaft* 22 (4). 479–500.
Krämer, Peter. 1976. Die inchoative Verbalkategorie des Alt- und Frühmittelhochdeutschen. In Helmut Birkhan (ed.) *Festgabe für Otto Höfler zum 75. Geburtstag*, 409–428. Wien: W. Braumüller.
Kulikov, Leonid. 2009. Valency-changing categories in Indo-Aryan and Indo-European: A diachronic typological portrait of Vedic Sanskrit. In Anju Saxena & Åke Viberg (eds.), *Multilingualism*, 75–92. Uppsala: Uppsala Universitet.
Kuryłowicz, Jerzy. 1964. *The inflectional categories of Indo-European*. Heidelberg: Winter.
Lavine, James E. 2016. Variable argument realization in Lithuanian impersonals. In Axel Holvoet & Nicole Nau (eds.), *Argument realization in Baltic*, 107–136. Amsterdam & Philadelphia: John Benjamins.
Lehmann, Christian. 1991. Predicate classes and PARTICIPATION. In Hansjakob Seiler & Waldfried Premper (eds.), *Partizipation: das sprachliche Erfassen von Sachverhalten*, 183–239. Tübingen: Narr.
Lazzeroni, Romano. 2009. Causativi e transitivi indoeuropei: fra comparazione e tipologia. *Studi e Saggi Linguistici* 57. 7–23.
Leiss, Elisabeth. 2007. Covert patterns of definiteness / indefiniteness and aspectuality in Old Icelandic, Gothic, and Old High German. In Elisabeth Stark, Elisabeth Leiss & Werner Abraham (eds.), *Nominal determination: Typology, context constraints, and historical emergence*, 73–102. Amsterdam & Philadelphia: John Benjamins.

Levin, Beth. 1993. *English verb classes and alternations*. Chicago: University of Chicago Press.
Levin, Beth. 1995a. Approaches to lexical semantic representation. In Donald E. Walker, Antonio Zampolli and Nicoletta Calzolari, (eds.), *Automating the lexicon I: Research and practice in a multilingual environment*, 53–91 Oxford: Oxford University Press.
Levin, Beth & Malka Rappaport Hovav. 1995. *Unaccusativity: At the syntax-lexical semantics interface*. Cambridge, MA: The MIT Press.
Levin, Beth & Malka Rappaport Hovav. 2005. *Argument realization*. Cambridge: Cambridge University Press.
Lühr, Rosemarie. 2008. Loss and emergence of grammatical categories. *Sprachwissenschaft* 33 (3). 317–349.
Luraghi, Silvia. 2003. *On the meaning of prepositions and cases*. Amsterdam & Philadelphia: John Benjamins.
Luraghi, Silvia. 2004. Null objects in Latin and Greek and the relevance of linguistic typology for language reconstruction. In Karlene Jones-Bley, Martin E. Huld, Angela Della Volpe & Miriam Robbins Dexter (eds.), *Proceedings of the 15th Annual UCLA Indo-European conference*, 234–256. Washington DC: Institute for the Study of Man.
Luraghi, Silvia. 2012. Basic valency orientation and the middle voice in Hittite. *Studies in Language* 36 (1). 1–32.
Luraghi, Silvia. 2019. Basic valency orientation, the anticausative alternation, and voice in PIE. In Melanie Malzahn (ed.), *Akten der 16th Fachtagung der Indogermanischen Gesellschaft*, 259–274. Wiesbaden: Reichert.
Luraghi, Silvia. 2020a. *Experiential verbs in Homeric Greek: A constructional approach*. Leiden: Brill.
Luraghi, Silvia. 2020b. External possessor constructions in Indo-European. In Jóhanna Barðdal, Spike Gildea & Eugenio R. Lujan Martines (eds.), *Reconstructing syntax*, 162–196. Leiden: Brill.
Luraghi, Silvia & Tuomas Huumo. 2014. *Partitive cases and related categories*. Berlin & New York: Mouton de Gruyter.
Luraghi, Silvia & Chiara Zanchi. 2018. Double accusative constructions and ditransitives in Ancient Greek. In Agnes Korn & Andrej Malchukov (eds.), *Ditransitive Constructions in a Cross-Linguistic Perspective*, 25–47. Wiesbaden: Reichert.
Luraghi, Silvia & Chiara Zanchi. 2019. A constructionist approach to argument structure alternation: a corpus-based study on Latin verbs taking AccAbl and AccDat constructions. Paper presented at the *20th International Colloquium on Latin Linguistics*, Universidad de Las Palmas de Gran Canaria, 17–21 June.
Malchukov, Andrej, Martin Haspelmath & Bernard Comrie. 2010. Ditransitive constructions: a typological overview. In Andrej Malchukov, Martin Haspelmath & Bernard Comrie (eds.), *Studies in ditransitive constructions. A comparative handbook*, 1–64. Berlin & New York: Mouton de Gruyter.
Malchukov, Andrej & Bernard Comrie (eds.). 2015. *Valency classes in the world's languages*. Berlin & New York: Mouton de Gruyter.
Malchukov, Andrej & Anna Siewierska (eds.). 2011. *Impersonal constructions: A cross-linguistic perspective*. Amsterdam & Philadelphia: John Benjamins.
Metlen, Michael. 1993. What a Greek interlinear of the Gothic Bible text can teach us. *Journal of English and German Philology* 32 (4). 530–548.
Miller, Gary D. 2019. *The Oxford Gothic grammar*. Oxford: OUP.
Napoli, Maria. 2010. The case for the partitive case: The contribution of Ancient Greek. *Transactions of the Philological Society* 108 (1). 15–40.

Nedjalkov, Vladimir P. 2007. Encoding of the reciprocal meaning. In Vladimir P. Nedjalkov, Emma Š. Geniušene & Zlatka Guentchéva (eds.), *Reciprocal constructions*, 147–208. Amsterdam & Philadelphia: John Benjamins.

Nichols, Johanna, David A. Peterson & Jonathan Barnes. 2004. Transitivising and detransitivising languages. *Linguistic Typology* 8 (2). 149–211.

Ottósson, Kjartan. 2008. The Old Nordic middle voice in the pre-literary period: Questions of grammaticalization and cliticisation. In Folke Josephson & Ingmar Söhrman (eds.), *Interdependence of Diachronic and Synchronic Analyses*, 185–219. Amsterdam & Philadelphia: John Benjamins.

Ottósson, Kjartan. 2013. The anticausative and related categories in the Old Germanic languages. In Folke Josephson & Ingmar Söhrman (eds.), *Diachronic and typological perspectives on verbs*, 329–382. Amsterdam & Philadelphia: John Benjamins.

Pagliarulo, Giuseppe. 2008. Innovazione e conservazione nel passivo gotico. In Vittoria Dolcetti Corazza & Renato Gendre (eds.), *Intorno alla Bibbia gotica, Atti del VII Seminario avanzato in Filologia Germanica*, 329–339. Alessandria: Edizioni dell'Orso.

Payne, Doris L. & Immanuel Barshi. 1999. *External possessions*. Amsterdam & Philadelphia: John Benjamins.

Peterson, David A. 2007. *Applicative constructions*. Oxford: OUP.

Piper, Paul. 1874. *Ueber den Gebrauch des Dativs im Ulfilas, Heliand und Otfried*. Altona: Meyer.

Piras, Antonio. 2007. *Manuale di gotico. Avviamento alla lettura della versione gotica del Nuovo Testamento*. Roma: Herder.

Plank, Frans & Aditi Lahiri. 2015. Microscopic and macroscopic typology: Basic valence orientation, more pertinacious than meets the naked eye. *Linguistic Typology* 19 (1). 1–54.

Ratkus, Artūras. 2019. The stylistic uses of Gothic passive constructions. *Vertimo studijos* 12. 116–137.

Ratkus, Artūras. 2020. The (non-)existence of the middle voice in Gothic: in search of a mirage. *Transaction of the Philological Society* 118 (2). 263–303. https://doi.org/10.1111/1467-968X.12190 (accessed 1 October 2020).

Rice, Allan L. 1932. *Gothic prepositional compounds in their relation to the Greek originals*. Philadelphia, PA: University of Pennsylvania PhD dissertation.

Riecke, Jörg. 1996. *Die schwachen jan-Verben des Althochdeutschen. Ein Gliederungsversuch*. Göttingen: Vandenhoeck & Ruprecht.

Ringe, Don. 2006. *From Proto-Indo-European to Proto-Germanic (A linguistic history of English 1)*. Oxford: OUP.

Rousseau, André. 2012. *Grammaire explicative du gotique (Skeireins razdos Gutþiudos)*. Paris: L'Harmattan.

Rousseau, André. 2016. *Gotica: Études sur la langue gotique*. Paris: Champion.

Sausa, Eleonora. 2015. *Argument structure constructions in Homeric Greek. A study on bivalent verbs*. Pavia: Università di Pavia PhD dissertation.

Sausa, Eleonora. 2016. Basic valency orientation in Homeric Greek. *Folia Linguistica Historica* 37. 205–238.

Schwerdt, Judith. 2001. Zur Bedeutung des -nan-Suffixes der gotischen schwachen Verben. *Beiträge zur Geschichte der deutschen Sprache und Literatur* 123. 175–210.

Seržant, Ilja A. 2014. The Independent Partitive Genitive in North Russian. In Ilja A. Seržant & Björn Wiemer (eds.), *Contemporary approaches to dialectology: The area of North, Northwest Russian and Belarusian vernaculars*, 270–329. Bergen: John Grieg AS.

Seržant, Ilja A. 2015. Independent partitive as a Circum-Baltic isogloss. *Journal Language Contact* 8. 341–418.

Streitberg, Wilhelm. 2000 [1908]. *Die gotische Bibel*. Winter: Heidelberg.
Sundén, Karl F. 1913. Are Old English intransitive-inchoative ō-verbs originally ai-verbs? In *Minnesskrift af forna lärjungar tillägnad Professor Axel Erdmann på hans sjuttioårsdag den 6 febr. 1913*, 282–312. Uppsala: Almqvist & Wiksell.
Suzuki, Seiichi. 1989. *The morphosyntax of detransitive suffixes -þ- and -n- in Gothic. A synchronic and diachronic study*. New York: Peter Lang.
Thomason, Olga. 2006. *Prepositional systems in Biblical Greek, Gothic, Classical Armenian, and Old Church Slavic*. Athens, GA: University of Georgia PhD dissertation.
ValPaL project. http://ValPaL.info/about/database (accessed 1 October 2020).
Viti, Carlotta. 2017. Semantic and cognitive factors of argument marking in ancient Indo-European languages. *Diachronica* 34 (3). 368–419.
Yoshioka, Jiro. 1986. The influence of the Latin version of the Bible on the Gothic version in the case of prepositions. *Journal of Indo-European Studies* 14 (3–4). 219–229.
West, Jonathan. 1980. Die Semantik der vierten Klasse des gotischen schwachen Verbums. *Zeitschrift für deutsche Philologie* 99 (1). 403–410.
Wiemer, Björn & Valgerður Bjarnadóttir. 2014. On the non-canonical marking of the highest-ranking argument in Lithuanian and Icelandic. In Axel Hovloet & Nicole Nau (eds.), *Grammatical relations and their non-canonical encoding*, 301–361. Amsterdam & Philadelphia: John Benjamins.
Winkler, Heinrich. 1896. *Germanische Casussyntax*. Berlin: Dümmler.
Wolfe, Brendan N. 2006. Figurae etymologicae in Gothic. *Oxford University Working Papers in Linguistics, Philology & Phonetics* 11. 207–2014.
Wright, Joseph. 1910. *Grammar of the Gothic language*. Oxford: Clarendon Press.
Zanchi, Chiara. 2019. *Multiple preverbs in ancient Indo-European languages. A comparative study on Vedic, Homeric Greek, Old Church Slavic, and Old Irish*. Tübingen: Narr.

A.1 Tables

Table 3: Gothic valency classes and verbs that instantiate them.

VALENCY CLASS	Verb type	Verb lemmas
Zero-place verbs		
	weather verbs	RAIN *rignjan*
One-place verbs		
Accusative experiencer	experiential verbs	BE HUNGRY *huggrjan, gredon*
NomSbj	activity verbs	CRY *gretan/greitan*
		JUMP *laikan*
		LAUGH *hlahjan*
		LIVE *liban*
		RUN *rinnan*
		SCREAM *hropjan*
		THINK *hugjan*

Table 3 (continued)

VALENCY CLASS	Verb type	Verb lemmas
	emission verbs	LIGHT *liuhtjan* LIGHTEN *lauhatjan*
	noncausal verbs	BE DRY *ga-staurknan* BREAK *us-bruknan* BURN *tundnan* DIE *ga-swiltan, ga-dauþ-nan* FALL *ga-driusan* ROLL *walwison* SINK *sigq-an*
	experiential verbs	FEEL PAIN *winnan*
two-place verbs		
NomAcc	prototypically transitive verbs	BEAT *slahan, bliggwan* BREAK *ga-brikan* BUILD *timrjan* CARRY *bairam* CUT *maitan*
		DRINK *drigkan* EAT *matjan* TAKE *niman* TEAR *tahjan* TIE *ga-bindan* THROW *wairpan*
	causative *ja*-verbs	MAKE SAD *gaurjan* BURN *tandjan* KILL *dauþjan, af-dauþjan*
	non-prototypically transitive verbs	COVER/HIDE *huljan* DRESS *wasjan, ga-wasjan* FOLLOW *laistjan* HIDE *ga-filhan* LIGHTEN *ga-liuhtjan* SEARCH FOR *sokjan* SHOUT AT *wopjan* SING *siggwan* WASH *þwahan* WIPE *bi-swairban*
	experiential verbs	FEAR *ogan* FEEL PAIN *winnan* HEAR *hausjan* KNOW *kunnan* SEE *saihvan*

Table 3 (continued)

VALENCY CLASS	Verb type	Verb lemmas
NomGen	non-prototypically transitive verbs	FILL *fullnan* HELP *hilpan*
NomDat	verbs of "social interaction" (+animacy)	MEET *ga-motjan* TOUCH *at-tekan*
	communication verbs	SHOUT AT *sakan* TELL *us-spillon*
	non-prototypically transitive verbs	LEAVE *bi-leiþan*
DatNom	experiential verbs	LIKE *leikan, ga-leikan*
NomPP	motion verbs	GO *gaggan*
	posture/location verbs	LIVE *bauan* SIT *sitan* SIT DOWN *ga-sitan*
	experiential verbs	LOOK AT *in-saihvan*
NomObj	experiential verbs	THINK *hugjan*
Three-place verbs		
NomAccDat	physical transfer verbs	GIVE *giban* PUT *lagjan, ga-lagjan* THROW *wairpan*
	knowledge transfer verbs	SAY *qiþan* TELL *spillon* TALK *rodjan* KNOW *kannjan* 'make know' SHOW *at-augjan*
NomAccPP	physical transfer verbs	POUR *giutan* SEND *sandjan*
	knowledge transfer verbs	SEARCH FOR *sokjan*
NomAccGen	physical transfer verbs	FILL *fulljan*
	knowledge transfer verbs	ASK FOR *bidjan*
NomAccAcc	knowledge transfer verbs	TEACH *laisjan*
	verbs with a predicative complement	BRING *briggan* GIVE *giban* KNOW *kunnan* LEAVE *bi-leiþan* NAME *namnjan* PUT *ga-lagjan* SAY *qiþan* SEE *saihvan*

Table 4: Gothic uncoded alternations and verbal types and lemmas that instantiate them.

TYPE OF ALTERNATION	VERB TYPE	VERB LEMMAS
Partitive		
	consumption verbs	EAT *matjan, itan* DRINK *drigkan*
	verbs of giving and taking	GIVE *giban* TAKE *niman*
NomAcc / NomDat		
	verbs with dative instruments	DRESS *wasjan* THROW *wairpan*
	communication verbs	SING *siggwan*
NomAcc / NomDat / NomGen		
	non-prototypically transitive verbs	LEAVE *bi-leiþan*
	experiential verbs	HEAR *hausjan*
NomAcc / NomPP		
	non-prototypically transitive verbs	FOLLOW *laistjan* SEE *saihvan* SHOUT AT *wopjan*
	prototypically transitive verb (imperfective reading)	BEAT *slahan*
NomDat / NomPP		
	experiential verbs	LIKE *ga-leikan*
	physical transfer verbs	GIVE *giban* PUT *lagjan, ga-lagjan*
	knowledge transfer verbs	SAY *qiþan* TALK *rodjan*
Object insertion		
	emission verb	LIGHT *liuhtjan*

Table 4 (continued)

Type of alternation	Verb type	Verb lemmas
Null object		
indefinite	two-place verbs construed as activities	BUILD *timrjan*
		DIG *graban*
		EAT *matjan*
		FEAR *ogan*
		FEEL PAIN *winnan*
		FOLLOW *laistjan*
		GRIND *malan*
		HIT *bliggwan*
		KNOW *kunnan*
		LIGHTEN *lauhatjan*
		LOOK AT *in-saihvan*
		SEE *saihvan*
		SHOUT AT *wopjan, sakan*
		SING *siggwan*
		STEAL *hlifan*
		TELL *us-spillon*
		TEAR *tahjan*
		ASK FOR *bidjan*
	three-place verbs construed as activites	GIVE *giban*
		NAME *namnjan*
		PUT *lagjan*
		SAY *qiþan*
		TALK *rodjan*
		TAKE *niman*
		TEACH *laisjan*
	motion verbs	GO *gaggan*
	location/posture verbs	SIT *sitan*
		SIT DOWN *ga-sitan*
referential	two-place verbs	MAKE SAD *gaurjan*
		BREAK *ga-brikan*
		DRESS *wasjan*
		FOLLOW *laistjan*
		LIKE *ga-leikan*
		LOOK AT *in-saihvan*
		SEARCH FOR *sokjan*
		TEAR *tahjan*
		THROW *wairpan*
		WIPE *bi-swairban*

Table 4 (continued)

TYPE OF ALTERNATION	VERB TYPE	VERB LEMMAS
	ditransitive	BRING *briggan* FILL *fulljan* PUT *ga-lagjan*
External possessor		
	verbs of putting	PUT *lagjan, ga-lagjan*
	verbs of washing	WASH *þwahan*
Cognate/kindred object		
NomAcc	one-place verbs	GO *gaggan*
	three-place verbs	TEACH *laisjan*
NomDat	one-place verbs	DIE *ga-swiltan* SCREAM *uf-hropjan*
	two-place verbs	KILL *af-daupjan*
NomAcc-NomDat	experiential verbs	FEAR *ogan*
Applicative		
	location verbs	LIVE *bauan*
Passive infinitive		
	two-place verbs	BRING *briggan* HIDE *filhan* SEE *saihvan* SHAVE *skaban*
Causal : noncausal		
	ja-verbs	SHOW *at-augjan*
	experiential verbs	FEAR *ogan (sik)*
Understood reflexive		
	caring for the body verbs	DRESS *wasjan, ga-wasjan* WASH *þwahan*

Table 5: Gothic coded alternations and verbal types and lemmas that instantiate them.

TYPE OF ALTERNATION	VERB TYPE	VERB LEMMAS
Applicative		
	activity verbs	LAUGH *hlahjan*
	motion verbs	LEAVE *bi-leiþan*

Table 5 (continued)

TYPE OF ALTERNATION	VERB TYPE	VERB LEMMAS
Passive		
synthetic	two-place verbs	BUILD *timrjan* FALL *ga-drausjan* SING *siggwan* DRESS *ga-wasjan* KILL *af-dauþjan*
analytic with *wisan*	two-place verbs	MAKE SAD *gaurjan* BREAK *ga-brikan* CARRY *bairan* DRINK *dragkjan* KNOW *kunnan* TIE *ga-bindan*
analytic with *wairþan*	two-place verbs	COVER/HIDE *ga-huljan* HIDE *ga-filhan* KILL *ga-dauþjan*
with three-place verbs	NomAccDat, NomAccGen construction (Acc is passivized)	DRESS *wasjan, ga-wasjan* DRINK *dragkjan* 'make drink' GIVE *giban* KNOW *kannjan* 'make know' LOAD *af-hlaþan* PUT *ga-lagjan* SAY *qiþan* TALK *rodjan*
	NomAccAcc (R passivized)	TEACH *laisjan*
	NomAccAcc (non-predicative passivized)	NAME *namnjan*
Causal : noncausal		
Causal member		
periphrastic causatives	one-place verbs	GO *gaggan* LIVE *liban*
	two-place verbs	HIDE *ga-filhan*
inflectional class	strong 4 verbs	BREAK *brikan*

Table 5 (continued)

TYPE OF ALTERNATION	VERB TYPE	VERB LEMMAS
derivation	*ja*-verbs	BURN *tandjan* DRINK *dringkjan* FALL *ga-drausjan* FILL *fulljan* FRIGHTEN *ogjan* KILL *ga-dauþ-jan* KNOW *kannjan* MAKE SAD *gaurjan* ROLL *af-walwjan* SINK *sigqjan* PUT *lagjan* SHOW *at-augjan* SIT *satjan* TEACH *laisjan*
Noncausal member		
inflectional class	weak 2 verbs	ROLL *walwison*
derivation	*na*-verbs	BREAK *us-bruknan* BURN *tundnan* DIE *ga-dauþ-nan*
	ablaut verbs	DRINK *dringkan* FALL *ga-driusan* KNOW *kunnan, lais* PUT *ligan* SIT *sitan*
passives	two-place verbs	DRINK *dringkan*
	three-place verbs	GIVE *giban*
	ja-verbs	FILL *fulljan* MAKE SAD *gaurjan* SHOW *at-augjan*
reflexive	experiential verbs	FEAR *ogan (sik)*
	ja-verbs	LEARN *laisjan sik* SHOW *at-augjan sik*

Table 5 (continued)

Type of alternation	Verb type	Verb lemmas
Reflexive alternation		
	two-place verbs	COVER/HIDE *huljan*
		DRESS *ga-wasjan*
		HIDE *ga-filhan*
		HIT *bliggwan*
		SAY *qiþan*
		TALK *rodjan*
		THROW *wairpan*
Reciprocal alternation		
sik misso	communication verbs	SAY *qiþan*
		SHOUT AT *wopjan*
	two-place verbs	SEE *saihvan*
		WASH *þwahan*
polyptotic construction	two-place verbs	BUILD *timrjan*

A.2 Additional examples

A.2.1 Additional examples to Section 3.2.1

BE HUNGRY *gredon*

(50) *jabai* **gredo** *fijand þeinana*
 if be_hungry.OPT.3SG enemy.ACC POSS.2SG
 'If your enemy is hungry ... ' (Rom 12:20) [Gk. *allà eàn* **peinâi** *ho ekhthrós sou*]

FEEL PAIN *winnan*

(51) *ei* **manag winnai** *jah frakunþs*
 that big.ACC suffer.OPT.PRS.3SG and reject.PTCP.PRF.PASS.NOM
 wairþai
 become.OPT.PRS.3SG
 ' ... that he should suffer greatly and be rejected.' (Mk 9:12)

(52) ei   hveh   **wrakja**   galgins   Xristaus   ni
     that only   persecution.ACC   cross.GEN X..GEN   NEG
     winnaina
     suffer.OPT.PRS.3PL
     '... only that they might not suffer the persecution of the cross of Christ.'
     (Gal 6:12; see also 2Tim 3:12; 1Thes 3:4)

LIKE *ga-leikan*

(53) in   þizei   mis   **galeikaiþ**   in   siukeim,
     in   REL.GEN.   1SG.DAT   please.PRS.3SG   in   infirmity.DAT.PL
     in   anamahtim,   in   nauþim,   in
     in   reproach.DAT.PL   in   necessity.DAT.PL   in
     wrekeim,   in   þreihslam   faur   Xristu
     persecution.DAT.PL   in   distress.DAT.PL   for   X..ACC
     'Therefore, I take pleasure in infirmities, in reproaches, in necessities, in persecutions, in distresses for Christ's sake.' (2Cor 12:10)
     [Gk. diò **eudokô** en astheneíais, en húbresin, en anágkais, en diōgmoîs kaì stenokhōríais hupèr kristoû]

HELP *hilpan*

(54) **hilp**   meinaizos   ungalaubeinais
     help.IMP.2SG   POSS.1SG.GEN   unbelief.GEN
     'Help you my unbelief!' (Mk 9:24)

LOOK AT *in-saihvan*

(55) **insaihvands**   du   himina
     look_at.PTCP.PRS.NOM   to   sky.DAT
     '(Then he took the five loaves and the two fish, and) looking (up) in the direction of heaven, he blessed them.' (Lk 9:16)

PUT *ga-lagjan*

(56) jah   bedun   ina   ei   **lagidedi**   imma
     and   ask.PRET.3PL   3SG.ACC   that   put.OPT.PRET.3SG   3SG.DAT
     handau
     hand.ACC.PL
     'And they beseech him to put his hand upon him' (Mk 7:32; see also 1Tim 5:22)

SHOW *at-augjan*
(57) **ataugida**   imma   allans   þiudinassuns
    show.PRET.3SG 3SG.DAT INDF.ACC.PL kingdom.ACC.PL
    '(And the devil...) showed him all the kingdoms of the world in a moment of time.' (Lk 4:5)

A.2.2 Additional examples to Section 4

GIVE *giban*
(58) ei   akranis   þis   weinagardis   **gebeina**   imma.
    that fruit.GEN DEM.GEN vineyard.GEN give.OPT.PRET.3PL 3SG.DAT
    '...that they should give him of the fruit of the vineyard.' (Lk 20:10)

THROW *wairpan*
(59) **wairpandans**   nati   in   marein
    throw.PTCP.PRS.ACC.PL net.ACC in   see.ACC
    '(Now as he walked by the sea of Galilee, he saw Simon and Andrew his brother) casting a net into the sea: (for they were fishers).' (Mk 1:16)

A.2.3 Additional examples to Section 5

SEE *saihvan*
(60) Atsaihviþ   armaion   izwara   ni   taujan
    beware.IMP.2PL charity.ACC 2PL.GEN NEG do.INF
    in   andwairþja   manne   du   **saihvan** im
    in   face.DAT   man.GEN.PL   to   see.INF   3PL.DAT
    'And beware not to do your righteousness before men in order to be seen by them' (Mt 6:1)

Elisa Roma
Valency Patterns of Old Irish verbs: finite and non-finite syntax

Abstract: This paper compares argument marking of finite and non-finite forms (verbal nouns) of 26 Old Irish verbs, focusing on the relationship of transitive coding patterns of finite forms with the mapping of the argument in the genitive case with non-finite forms. The collection of argument structures is cast in the framework of the Leipzig Valency Patterns Project (Hartmann, Haspelmath, and Taylor 2013, Malchukov and Comrie 2015). The paper argues that, although most genitive arguments with transitive verbs express the microrole which corresponds to the second argument (the P-argument), this is not a strict rule, and some verbal nouns of transitive verbs clearly allow the first argument (the A-argument) to surface in the genitive. It is claimed that there is a correlation between the likelihood for finite forms to occur with an accusative argument and the likelihood for the genitive argument of non-finite forms to correspond to the P-argument. This likelihood is measured through a transitivity index that tries to supply a criterion that substitutes acceptability judgments, which are unavailable for past varieties. Each verb's index can be calculated and each verb can consequently be accommodated in the resulting transitivity scale. Finally, the scale ranking Old Irish verbs according to the transitivity index is compared with cross-linguistic hierarchies of transitivity which have been put forward in the literature.

Keywords: Old Irish, valency patterns, transitivity, argument marking, verbal nouns, non-finite syntax

1 Introduction

This paper focuses on the relationship between case-marking of arguments with finite and non-finite forms in the Old Irish Glosses and on its correlation with transitivity. Old Irish is a member of the Celtic branch of the Indo-European family,

---

Acknowledgments: I owe to my co-editor and to two anonymous reviewers many comments and suggestions that encouraged me to expand and improve an earlier version of this paper. I am also grateful to the audience of my presentations at the conference The Shaping of Transitivity and Argument Structure (Pavia, 26–28 October 2018) and at the XVIth International Congress of Celtic Studies (Bangor, 22–26 July 2019) for useful questions and observations.

Elisa Roma, University of Pavia, elisa.roma@unipv.it

∂ Open Access. © 2021 Elisa Roma, published by De Gruyter. [CC BY-NC-ND] This work is licensed under the Creative Commons Attribution-NonCommercial-NoDerivatives 4.0 International License.
https://doi.org/10.1515/9783110755657-004

and the earliest Celtic language for which extant record allows a full grammatical description. Among the sources for this stage of the language, which, broadly stated, covers the 8th and 9th centuries, the collections of anonymous glosses on Latin texts which have been taken into account for this study (see Section 2.2) represent the most important contemporary documents.

The comparison of case-marking with finite and non-finite forms presented here relies on the results of a full collection of the argument structures attested in the Glosses for 26 verbs. The data collection was cast in the general framework of the Leipzig Valency Patterns Project (Hartmann, Haspelmath and Taylor 2013; Malchukov and Comrie 2015, henceforth ValPaL). Verbs were chosen and argument structures were classified applying the ValPaL format, in order to grant representativity of different valency patterns and to allow comparison. The main aim of the enquiry, however, is not to give valency patterns for a set of meanings, supplying form-meaning pairs, as in ValPaL, but rather to classify attested patterns for a set of predicates and to compare the patterns with finite and non-finite forms, given that the patterns with non-finite forms have been claimed to correlate with transitivity (see Section 4).

The paper is organized as follows: Section 2 provides some background on argument marking in Old Irish and presents the framework for data-collection and the dataset; Section 3 dwells on word order issues related to argument marking in Old Irish; Section 4 compares the valency patterns of finite and non-finite forms in the dataset and discusses them on the background of the transitivity distinction, on which previous literature on Old Irish is based; Section 5 focuses on the conditions of occurrence of less frequent patterns and Section 6 introduces a measure of transitivity, the transitivity index, which fits in with the distribution of argument marking with non-finite forms better than a simple transitive vs. intransitive opposition, and briefly compares the scale resulting from this index to cross-linguistic transitivity hierarchies. Section 7 summarizes the results.

2 Background description and outline of data collection

2.1 Argument marking in Old Irish

Old Irish has nominal case inflection. Two cases, nominative and accusative, code verbal arguments with finite forms, while the others (dative, genitive and vocative) do not. The genitive is an adnominal case, while the dative is a prepositional case, which occurs prepositionless only in a few not strictly argumental phrases (standard of comparison after comparative adjectives, mostly petrified temporal/modal adverbials). The accusative is also a prepositional case.

Verbal arguments, therefore, may be expressed by nominals in the nominative and accusative case or by prepositional phrases, selected by the verb. Prepositions select nominal case and fuse with pronouns, giving what are usually called inflected or conjugated prepositions. Verbs obligatorily agree in person and number with a nominal nominative argument but pronominal subjects are expressed only through verbal person endings, which can refer, i.e. they have full referential function – they behave as pro-indexes in Haspelmath's (2013) classification. Given that free pronouns cannot occur as verbal arguments (Thurneysen 1946: 254; Roma 2000), and in fact have been classified as extra-clausal constituents (García Castillero 2013; see Haspelmath 2013: 206), non-prepositional pronominal arguments may only be expressed through bound morphemes on the verbal complex: verb inflection, which combines tense, mood and person, and so-called infixed/suffixed object pronouns. Person and number distinctions for all kinds of pronominal indexes are common ones in Indo-European languages (three persons, two numbers). An example with three free-standing arguments is given in (1), an example with three pronominal, bound arguments in (2).[1]

(1) na=taibred   cách   uáib   bréic   imm=alaile
     NEG.IMP=give.IMP.3SG each.NOM   from.2PL   falsehood.ACC   around=other.ACC
     'let not anyone of you deceive another'
     (Wb 27b12)

---

[1] Examples are quoted according to the diplomatic edition of the Old Irish Glosses (Stokes and Strachan 1901-03, with emendations in Griffith 2013 and Bauer 2015). Morphological glosses conform to the conventions of the Leipzig Glossing Rules. In particular, note that two rather infrequent symbols are employed here: angle brackets for infixed morphemes, both in the glossed example and in the interlinear gloss (left-peripheral infix, Rule 9), and backslash for initial consonant mutations, in the interlinear gloss (Rule 4D). In the original manuscripts various kinds of clitics and other bound morphemes are usually written together with their host, but sometimes they are written separately (cp. *la dia* in 12.b and 12.d). When this is so in the printed edition, the quoted text is left as such and no symbol is inserted to separate the morphemes, since such symbols in the object language allow the reader to match morpheme and morphological gloss, but do not represent a fully-fledged morphological analysis. Conventionally, however, conjunctions which affect verb stress and inflection have been detached through the symbol separating affixes, while conjunctions which do not trigger stress and inflection changes have been detached by the symbol for clitics. Translations begin with case letters only when the quoted example represents the beginning of a gloss in the manuscript. Abbreviations not listed in the Rules are: COMPV = comparative, HAB = habitual, IMPF = imperfect (habitual past), SUB= subordinate clause, VN = verbal noun.

(2) d<a>ratsat   form=sa
    <3SG.OBJ.N>give.PRF.3PL on.1SG=1SG
    'they have inflicted it upon me'
    (Ml 73b17)

The difference between the two sets of verbal indexes, i.e. subject and object indexes, is that personal endings (subject indexes) cannot be omitted, as they are fused together with tense and mood inflection, so that 3rd person forms regularly co-occur with nominal arguments, while affixed pronouns (object indexes) are generally in complementary distribution with nominal objects, and may co-occur with a nominal object very rarely (see Griffith 2015 and Roma 2018 about the degree of co-occurrence of indexes and nominal arguments).[2] The different syntactic status of direct arguments (subjects and objects) as opposed to prepositional arguments and non-arguments emerges from the following behaviors: as stated above, pronominal direct arguments must be coded through bound morphemes on the verbal complex, in contrast with bound morphemes on prepositions; relative clauses on subjects and objects are marked differently, possibly through a verbal form with relative ending;[3] only direct arguments enter in coding alternations with the passive, while other arguments preserve the same marking in both diatheses (see 4.a and 4.b below).

---

[2] Griffith (2011, 2015) has argued that person inflection and object indexes (infixes and suffixes) in Old Irish are not pronominal arguments but agreement affixes, and that so-called emphatic particles or *notae augentes* (cf. e.g. 3sg. -*som* in (18), cp. 1sg. -*sa* in 2 and 6.b) are pronominal arguments instead, despite the fact that they are optional, similarly to free subject pronouns in pro-drop languages like Italian. The reason why I cannot subscribe to this view is that it is based on assumptions that are in contrast with the framework adopted here (Haspelmath 2013; Kibrik 2019). These assumptions are: that bound morphemes are in principle less likely to code arguments and to refer than stressed and clitic pronouns; that if verb inflection and argument phrases may co-occur only one of them, rather than their combination, codes the argument; that verb inflection in so-called pro-drop languages implies a co-referent null controller (*pro*). Since these assumptions have been discussed by Haspemath (2013), I need not repeat his criticisms here. Note that the pronominal enclitics which are assumed to be arguments in Griffith's analysis are not case-marked: they can attach to any kind of lexical host, provided that it contains a person index (verb inflection or pronominal affix on verbs, possessive proclitic with nouns, pronominal affix with prepositions). Therefore, differently from nominal arguments, their syntactic function only depends on the bound morphemes themselves, with which they must always co-occur.

[3] I cannot dwell here on the intricacies of Old Irish relativization strategies, but I refer the reader to the description in Roma (2007: 246-257) and to the clear summary in Stifter (2009: 106-107). What is relevant here is that some strategies are allowed only for subjects and objects (i.e. non-prepositional arguments).

Passive verb inflection includes Number distinctions (sg. vs. pl.), but not Person distinctions. So while nominal subjects (i.e. promoted objects) bear nominative case and are cross-indexed on passive verbal forms, 1st and 2nd person subjects must be expressed only by the same forms as object affixes, cp. (3.a) and (3.b).[4] In Old Irish passive forms may also occur without any direct argument: (4.a) and (4.b) are examples of this strategy, which removes both the nominative and the accusative argument, while admitting only prepositional arguments. In that case, the passive singular inflectional ending does not represent bound anaphora.

(3) a. *ni-derlaichta   a=pecdæ   doib*
    NEG-forgive.PRF.PASS.PL their=sin.NOM.PL to.3PL
    'Their sins have not been forgiven them'
    (Wb 33b8)

(3) b. *co<t>oscaigther*
    <2SG.OBJ>move.SBJV.PASS.SG
    'May you be moved'
    (Ml 55b3)

(4) a. *is=i=ndeseircc   et   spirut   rigthir   cuccuib*
    COP.PRS.3SG=in=love.DAT and   spirit.DAT go.FUT.PASS.SG   towards.2PL
    'it is in love and spirit that one will go to you' (lit. 'will be gone towards you')
    (Wb 9a23)

---

4 I merge the two constructions in (3.a) and (3.b) together, i.e. passive with number agreement and passive with infixed pronoun, rather than grouping (3.b) with (4.a) and (4.b), because in the Old Irish Glosses they represent clear matches with regard to valency patterns, i.e. they are an instance of coding split in the ValPaL framework (Haspelmath and Hartmann 2015: 57-78; a similar view is put forward for Old Irish in García Castillero 2015; see Section 4 for the effects of this criterion). However, "impersonal passive" is frequently used for (3.b), since the pronominal argument belongs to the object morphemes set. Graver (2011), for instance, terms the three kinds of passive constructions exemplified by (3.a), (3.b) and (4.a) "canonical passive", "impersonal passive" and "active subject impersonal" respectively, and rather groups the last two together, i.e. the pattern in (3.b) together with (4.a). It is not clear to me whether the construction in (4.b) would be classified by Graver as impersonal passive or active subject impersonal.

(4) b. co=frisaccat   ón   dílgud   doib
        that=hope.PRS.3PL DEM.ACC.N forgive.VN.ACC to.3PL
        amal   durolged   dian=aithrib
        as   forgive.PRF.PASS.SG   to.their=father.DAT.PL
        'So that they hope for that, for forgiveness to them, as their fathers
        had been forgiven' (lit. 'had been forgiven to their fathers')
        (Ml 124a2)

Basic word order is VSO, and the initial position of the predicate is rigid (see Lash 2020 and Section 3 below).

Non-finite forms, so-called verbal nouns,[5] behave syntactically as nouns and inflect for case, but not for voice and tense. Their rection is nominal, which means that their overt direct arguments are genitive modifiers (see Section 4 and 5 for argument linking in non-finite clauses). Pronominal arguments are expressed by bound forms (indexes) on the verbal noun: these genitive pronominal indexes are a set of proclitic forms (e.g. *a* in *tri-a-forcital* in 6.a below), which trigger initial consonant mutations on the following noun and fuse with some preceding prepositions (Thurneysen 1946: 158, § 250; 276, § 438; 445, § 720). Although their rection is nominal, verbal nouns in Old Irish clearly behave as non-finite counterparts of predicates, similarly to infinitives in other Indo-European languages, and involve the same semantic microroles as the corresponding finite predicates. Constructions with verbal nouns could therefore be considered instances of coded alternations within the ValPaL framework, although they are not valency-changing or diathetic operations in the first place. The relationship between finite and non-finite counterparts emerges from the following evidence:

a. recurrent instances like (5), where the verbal noun construction *cen tabairt anman trén fríu* 'without adding substantives to them' is clearly a non-finite counterpart to the finite clause *nitabarr ainm trén fríu* 'a substantive is not added to them'

---

[5] The other non-finite verbal forms of Old Irish, i.e. the participle of necessity or gerundive and the past passive participle, are in fact used in finite clauses (with a copular form) or as noun modifiers within NPs (Thurneysen 1946: 441-444, §§ 714-719). These forms do not involve a specific case-marking of arguments, although they are passive in meaning (e.g. *tabarthi* 'to be given', *tabarthae* 'given'), but they were not included in this study because they are very rare: for the verbs reckoned here, there are only 12 occurrences of the participle of necessity and 3 of the past participle in Wb, Ml and Sg altogether.

b. a clearly verbal construction where the verbal noun is governed by the preposition *do* 'to' and one of its direct arguments, mostly the object,[6] precedes it and receives case-marking from the matrix clause -viz. *pianaib* in (6.a) and *indois anechtir* in (6.b) (see Stüber 2009b; Sanfelici 2014, 2015)
c. a specific argument flagging of the A-argument[7] of verbal nouns with the preposition *do*, exemplified below (*do dia* in example (7), see (35.a-b) in Section 6, cf. (15.d)).

Note, however, that the construction in (6) is an emergent one in the Old Irish Glosses and occurs in a minority of the instances of verbal nouns considered in this study (54/868, 6.22%).

(5) *ni-tabarr   ainm   trén   friu   .i.*
    NEG-give.PRS.PASS.SG noun.NOM strong.NOM at.3PL id est
    foragab   duaid inna   anman   adiecta
    leave.PRF.3SG David the.ACC.PL noun.ACC.PL adjectival.ACC.PL
    cen   tabairt   anman   trén   friu
    without give.VN.ACC noun.GEN.PL strong.GEN.PL at.3PL
    'a substantive is not added to them, that is, David left the adjectives without adding substantives to them'
    (Ml 30a9)

(6) a. *indi   chomallaite   timnae   ndae*
       DEM.NOM.PL REL\fulfill.PRS.REL.3PL commandment.ACC God.GEN.SG
       tri-a=forcital   doib ⁊   ní
       through-its=teach.VN.ACC to.3PL and NEG.COP.PRS.3SG
       ar=pianaib   du=thabairt   forru
       for=punishment.DAT.PL to=give.VN.DAT on.3PL.ACC
       'those who fulfill the commandment of God through its teaching to them and it's not because punishments are inflicted on them (they fulfill it)'
       (Ml 114b7)

---

6 The direct argument preceding the verbal noun is the object in 51 out of 54 occurrences of this construction with the verbal nouns examined in this study. Since all the instances with a raised subject (Wb 13c18, 16d12, Ml 39d3) have a pronominal, bound direct object, I suggest that the preposed argument may be the subject when the object is either absent or pronominal (and the subject is not, see 6.b and Section 5; cp. Stüber 2009b: 9, 108).
7 I use this expression here in the same sense and with the same non-commitment to semantic implications as in ValPaL (Database Questionnaire Manual, fn. 6, Malchukov and al. 2015: 29, table 1; Haspelmath 2015: 137).

(6) b. *ansu   lium=sa   ind=oís   anechtir*
       difficult.COMPV by.1SG=1SG   the=people.NOM   outland
       dia=fius
       to.its=know.VN.DAT
       'It is more grievous to me that the outland folk would know it'
       (Wb 16d12) (Wb 16d12)

In sum, Old Irish verbal nouns correspond to the nominal pole in Lehmann's (1998: 200) continuum of sententiality (no mood, tense, aspect, diathesis; subject possibly in oblique slot; nominal government; dispensability of subject; combinability with adpositions and case affixes), except that they allow independent (nominal) polarity distinctions, with the nominal negator *cen* (see (5) above and (15.a) below), in addition to the negative bound morpheme *neph-*, as in (7) below.

(7) *tri=neph-thabart   do   dia   fortachtae   doib*
    through=NEG-give.VN.ACC   to   God.DAT   help.VN.GEN   to.3PL
    'Through God's not giving help to them'
    (Ml 54b22)

A sketch illustrating the basic distribution of argument marking in Old Irish is given in Table 1. For the purposes of this study, nominal (free-standing) and pronominal (bound) distributional equivalents are treated alike, but Section 5 will deal with some specific behaviors of pronominal indexes which emerge from the data.

Table 1: Sketch of argument marking in Old Irish.

	SUBJECT (nominative)	OBJECT (accusative)	PREPOSITIONAL ARGUMENT (dative/accusative)	NON-PREPOSITIONAL ARGUMENT OF VN (genitive)
nouns (free-standing)	nominative case (+ cross-reference on verb)	accusative case	(preposition +) dative/accusative case	genitive case
pronouns (bound)	person endings on verb (obligatory mood+tense+person inflection)	affixal morphemes on verb (infixed/suffixed pronouns)	affixal morphemes on prepositions (inflected prepositions)	possessive proclitics set

2.2 The framework and the dataset

Most of the verbs chosen for inquiry are included in the ValPaL Project list of 70 core meanings (Malchukov et al. 2015: 28–29) or in its extension to 80 meanings in the online Database, but a few were selected because of their frequency and relevance in the Old Irish available corpora. To select each verb, the following procedure was followed. The author's intuitions about the Old Irish counterpart matching each verb meaning in ValPaL was checked by entering the English form into the Advanced Search function in the online dictionary e-DIL, and selecting the option "definition", i.e. the basic meaning of a lexical entry. The results of this enquiry allowed a preliminary survey of verbs and verbal nouns which are attested in the existing contemporary Old Irish sources, the three major corpora of Glosses (Stokes and Strachan 1901–1903, see below for details), and could thus be included for data collection. Many verbs and meanings were abandoned at this stage for lack or scarcity of occurrences, in particular of non-finite forms (e.g. 'rain', 'laugh', 'be hungry', 'search for'), especially in cases where finite forms or the verbal noun are attested in only one of the three major corpora of Glosses (e.g. 'eat'). In case of doubt, more than one verb belonging to the same semantic field was included (e.g. ro·finnadar and ad·gnin for 'know', do·beir and do·indnaig for 'give',[8] ad·gladathar and labraithir for 'talk'). Sometimes substitutes were chosen, e.g. caraid 'love' for 'like', ad·cobra 'desire' for predicates expressing feelings in general, whose counterparts in Old Irish are usually copular predicates and do not have a corresponding non-finite form. Still in agreement with the ValPaL procedure for data collection (Database Questionnaire Manual § 9.3), a few verbs were then added, because of their frequency in the Old Irish Glosses, because they allowed to include new patterns or because they showed a balanced number of occurrences in the three sources used for this study (do·fich 'punish', do·luigi 'forgive', do·icc 'come', do·ruimnethar 'forget', fris·gair 'answer', ad·rími 'count', con·oscaigi 'move').

The patterns were extracted from existing databases and dictionaries of the Old Irish Glosses (Stokes and Strachan 1901–1903): Kavanagh (2001) for the Würzburg Glosses on the Pauline Epistles (henceforth Wb), Bauer (2015) for the St. Gall Glosses on Priscian (henceforth Sg), and Griffith (2013) for the Milan Glosses on a Commentary on the Psalms (henceforth Ml).

---

[8] The addition of do·indnaig was also suggested by the fact that do·beir enters in many constructions with nouns and verbal nouns as a light verb (e.g. do·beir aithis for 'put reproch on').

Glosses consisting of a single verb form and translating a single Latin word were not taken into account for the purposes of this study. An example of this kind of gloss is (8):

(8) *adgladathar* (Ml 74a8, glossing *quasi ipse profeta iam doctus {.i. dauid} adloquitur*)

In (8) *adgladathar* 'addresses' directly translates the Latin word *adloquitur* 'speaks to', and has therefore not been taken into account, although the form shows obligatory coding of A ([speaker]) through the verb's inflectional ending (3sg. present indicative), as all finite forms in Old Irish.

Table 2 reports the 26 verbs reckoned, listed roughly according to their overall frequency (finite + non-finite forms), in decreasing order, in the Old Irish texts taken into account here. Since non-finite verbal forms in Old Irish are abstract nouns (Thurneysen 1946: 444–455; Stüber 2017), traditionally Verbal Nouns, their separate lexical entry is also given. Overall occurrences are given in brackets; these include single gloss translations such as (8), and, for verbal nouns, instances of plural forms and forms preceded by the the article, which have not been taken into account to survey valency patterns (see Section 4).

Table 2: List of verbs reckoned.

Verb		Verbal Noun (eDIL lexical entry)		Verb meaning	in ValPaL
as·beir[9]	(478)	*epert*	(75)	say	yes
do·beir	(403)	*tabart*	(113)	give	yes
gaibid	(198)	*gabál*	(23)	take	yes
téit	(134)	*techt/dul*	(56+14)	go	yes
do·fich	(23)	*dígal*	(170)	punish, avenge	no
ro·finnadar	(107)	*fi(u)s*	(31)	find out, know	yes
beirid	(86)	*breth*	(36)	carry, bring	yes
do·adbat	(81)	*taidbsiu*	(33)	show	yes
as·indet	(48)	*aisndís*	(63)	tell	yes

---

[9] The raised dot symbol <·> used when giving a citation verbal form is the standard way, used in Thurneysen (1946), to separate the unstressed part of the verbal complex from the stressed syllable, which immediately follows it. The citation form for Old Irish verbs is 3sg. present indicative, which is given here and throughout the paper.

Table 2 (continued)

Verb		Verbal Noun (eDIL lexical entry)		Verb meaning	in ValPaL
for·tét	(19)	fortacht	(85)	help	yes
caraid	(37)	serc	(62)	love	no
guidid	(64)	guide	(25)	ask for, pray	yes
for·cain	(46)	forcetal	(42)	teach	yes
do·luigi	(40)	dílgud	(40)	forgive	no
ad·cobra	(24)	accobar	(42)	desire	no
do·indnaig	(35)	tindnacol	(26)	bestow	no
ad·rími	(34)	áram	(25)	count	no
do·icc	(46)	tíchtu	(12)	come	no
con·oscaigi	(26)	cumscugud	(28)	move, change	no
do·moinethar	(42)	toimtiu	(10)	think	yes
ad·cí	(47)	aicsiu	(4)	see	yes
labraithir	(23)	labrad	(24)	talk, speak	yes
ad·gládathar	(13)	accaldam	(14)	talk to, address	yes
fris·gair	(2)	frecrae	(19)	answer	no
do·ruimnethar	(8)	dermat	(5)	forget	no
ad·gnin	(8)	aithne	(4)	know, recognize	yes

The main criteria for the classification of argument structures are coding properties, that is case-marking, adpositions and agreement. Among behavioral properties (as defined in the ValPaL Database manual, § 7.1), only the passive alternation has been taken into account in a systematic way for this study, while relativization strategies associated with direct vs. adpositional arguments have been considered only when interpreting the data (see Section 5). In the ValPaL framework word order is considered a coding property only in the absence of other coding properties, but although Old Irish displays case-marking, adpositions and agreement, and in non-finite clauses case-marking and adpositions combine with rigid word order, the relative order of arguments has been taken into account in the data collection, in order to find out whether position might be considered a behavioral property, as recently argued by Le Mair et al. (2017). Note, however, that the symbol "greater than" which separates constituents in the valency patterns given in the paper is not meant to imply that word order is syntactically significant, as in ValPaL.

Before presenting the data, it should be noted that the criterion for argumenthood in ValPaL (Database Questionnaire Manual, § 7.1; Haspelmath and Hartmann 2015: 49), and in general criteria for argumenthood, cannot easily be applied to a language which does not have speakers any more, since they involve grammaticality judgments. Moreover, the phrase detachment test suggested in the Leipzig project, which gives grammatical results only for non-arguments (contrast 9.a with 9.b), is even less reliable for Old Irish, since Old Irish happens to use forms of the lexical verb as responsives and more generally as anaphoric verbal forms (with a default pronominal neuter object, see Roma 2018), as in (10). In other words, any verb form, possibly with a default non-referring neuter object, may occur as a substitute to the verb phrase, in a reduced or possibly different valency frame, similarly to English *do*: corresponding to (9.a) and (9.b), one would expect something like "I wrote and I wrote a letter" and "I wrote a letter and I wrote it with a pen" (and also, with a verb that does not govern a direct object, "I answered to him and I answered it yesterday").[10]

(9) a. *I wrote and I did a letter*

(9) b. *I wrote a letter and I did it with a pen*

(10) do\<sn\>ic-fa   cobir   cid   mall
       \<3PL.OBJ\>come-FUT.3SG help.NOM though.COP.SBJV.3SG slow
       bith   maith immurgu intain   do\<nd\>icc-fa
       COP.FUT.3SG good however the.time \<REL\3SG.N.OBJ\>come-FUT.3SG
       'help will come to them though it be slow: it will, however, be good when it will come'
       (Wb5c5)

Therefore, the criteria for inclusion in the argument frames were rather semantic and broad, designed to capture all possible alternations. The configurations gathered are simplified versions of the ValPaL database coding frames, combining basic coding sets and semantic roles (microroles). A simplified and partial list of coding frames is given in (11) for both finite (11.a) and non-finite (11.b) forms of *for·cain* 'teach'. For each frame, the figure on the left provides the number

---

10 In a sense, this construction could be considered an instance of a valency slot filled at the syntactic level but not corresponding to a semantic participant (Lehmann 2015: 1553). It is however impossible to ascertain how systematic it was.

of instances in the corpus; 1, 2, 3 in the frames correspond to arguments, as in ValPaL.

(11) a. Coding frames of *for·cain* 'teach'
    11 V.subj[1] > 1-nom [teacher] > 2-acc [taught thing]
    9 V.subj[1] > 1-nom [teacher] > 2-acc [taught person]
    4 V.subj[1] > 1-nom [teacher] > 2-acc [taught thing] > *do*+3-dat [taught person]
    4 V.subj[1] > 1-nom [teacher]
    1 V.subj[1] > 1-nom [teacher] > 2-CL [taught thing][11]
    1 V.subj[1] > 1-nom [teacher] > 2-LATacc [taught thing]
    1 V.subj[1] > 1-nom [teacher] > 2-LATCL [taught thing]
    2 passive V.subj[1] > 1-nom [taught thing]
    2 passive V.subj[1] > 1-nom [taught person]

(11) b. Coding frames of *forcetal* 'teaching'
    10 2-gen [taught person]
    7 1-gen [teacher][12]
    1 2-gen [taught thing]
    1 1-gen [teacher] > *do*+3-dat [taught person]
    1 2-gen [taught thing] > *do*+3-dat [taught person]
    1 *la*+1-acc [teacher]

The valency patterns attested in the corpus for each verb and their frequency are taken as evidence for possible coding frames. As stated above, however, the aim of the enquiry is to classify attested patterns for a set of predicates, rather than supplying valency patterns for a set of meanings, as in ValPaL. The frames attested with finite forms have been compared with those attested with non-finite forms, which, in contrast to finite verb forms, are not inflected for voice (passive).

---

11 CL = clausal argument (finite clause), LAT = Latin form governed by the Old Irish verb. Code switching and code mixing are frequent in the glosses (cf. Bisagni 2013-2014) and when a Latin case-form or prepositional phrase parallels an Old Irish argument it has been included in the collection.
12 One doubtful example has been included here, namely Ml 114d14 *a forcital ade dano* 'his/its teaching then'. Although *a* is classified as objective genitive by Griffith (2013), the expression corresponds to *pastorali disciplina* in the Latin text and is therefore likely to belong here ('instruction by the shepherd').

3 Word order

Before focusing on the main topic of this paper, i.e. the relationship between the coding of direct arguments in finite and non-finite clauses, I'll tackle briefly an issue on which the classification of valency frames sheds light, namely the role of word order in Old Irish syntactic configuration. The brief discussion in this Section is not meant to address the order of arguments in general, however, but only to ground the syntactic analysis presented in the following Sections, which does not take into account word order directly.

Quantitative data allow, in fact, to test the view put forward by Le Mair et al. (2017), who claim that prepositional arguments immediately following some copular predicates in Old Irish[13] are oblique subjects, despite the fact that the verb form agrees with a nominative argument. Le Mair et al. (2017) argue that since what follows the verb is predominantly the subject in a sample of clauses from Wb with transitive verbs, what follows the verb must regularly be the subject and immediate postverbal position is a behavioral property of subjects in Old Irish. As a consequence, prepositional arguments immediately following these copular predicates are viewed as non-canonically marked subjects. If so, one could expect that these prepositional arguments frequently accompanied the corresponding non-finite forms, and could correspondingly behave similarly to subjects with non-finite forms. Unfortunately, the predicates mentioned by Le Mair et al. (2017) are copular predicates, which do not really have a non-finite counterpart.

However, on the basis of the data surveyed for this study it can be shown that immediate postverbal position of prepositional arguments is frequent in the Old Irish Glosses whatever the predicate and whatever the argument frame, all the more so given that nominative arguments are frequently non-overt (so-called zero anaphora, which in the case of Old Irish should rather be termed bound anaphora, see Section 2.1). It is therefore hard to maintain that immediate postverbal position is a behavioral property of subjects, or for that matter of any other argument.

I will illustrate this by comparing the relevant orders attested with a predicate assumed to involve a non-canonical, i.e. prepositional, subject, namely *is maith la* 'is good for', with the orders attested with a verb selecting three arguments, namely *do·luigi* 'forgive'. The frames and word orders for *is maith la* are reported

---

[13] Le Mair et al. (2017) take into account "combinations of the copula with a predicative noun or adjective" (2017: 116). From the Appendix one may further assume that the prepositional arguments surveyed are only those with *do* 'to, for' and with *la* 'with, by, according to'.

in (12.a), the frames and word orders for *do·luigi do* in (13.a).[14] Examples of some attested patterns for each predicate are given in (12.b-e) and (13.b-e) respectively.

(12) a. *is maith* basic coding frame: 1-nom [liked thing/person] > *la*+2-acc [liker] '2 likes 1'
    3 instances   predicate > *la*+2-acc (zero anaphora, 12.b)
    3 instances   predicate > 1-nom > *la*+2 (subject clitic *són*, 12.c)
    10 instances 1-[liked thing] > relative predicate > *la*+2-acc (12.d)
    14 instances *la*+2-acc > 1-nom (inflected preposition and overt nominative argument, 12.e)

(12) b. *mad   maid   la   dia*
if.COP.SBJV.3SG good.NOM by God.ACC
'If it is good for God'
(Wb 14a11)

(12) c. *is   ferr   són   les=som*
COP.PRS.3SG good.COMPV that.NOM by.3SG.M=3SG.M
'that is better for him'
(Wb 6b10)

(12) d. *is=ed   as   maith   la=dia*
COP.PRS.3SG=DEM.NOM.N COP.PRS.REL good.NOM by=God.ACC
'this is what is good for God'
(Ml 130b8)

(12) e. *is=maith   les   á=fir-lugae*
COP.PRS.3SG=good.NOM by.3SG.M the=true-oath.NOM
nothongad   cách . . .
REL\swear.IMPF.3SG everyone.NOM
'good for him is the true-oath that everyone used to swear . . . '
(Ml 36a20)

(13) a. *do·luigi* basic coding frame: 1-nom [forgiver] > 2-acc [forgiven deed] > *do*+3-dat [forgiven person]
    3 instances   predicate > *do*+3-dat (pronominal index, no accusative argument, 13.b)

---

14 Both predicates, *is maith* and *do·luigi*, occur without the prepositional argument considered here, but only instances with this argument are listed in (12.a) and (13.a).

3 instances   predicate > *do*+3-dat > 2-acc (pronominal index/zero anaphora, 13.c)
2 instances   predicate > 1-nom > *do*+3-dat > 2-acc (overt nominative argument, inflected preposition, 13.d)
1 instance   predicate > 2-acc > *do*+3-dat (zero anaphora)
1 instance   predicate+2-acc > *do*+3-dat (pronominal index, infixed pronoun)
1 instance   predicate+2-acc > 1-nom > *do*+3-dat (overt nominative argument, infixed pronoun)
4 instances   passive predicate > *do*+3-dat (zero anaphora or no direct argument, see 4.b)
3 instances   passive predicate > 1-nom > *do*+2-dat (overt nominative argument, see 3.a)
2 instances   passive predicate > *do*+3-dat > 1-nom (overt nominative argument, inflected preposition, 13.e, see 15.c)

(13) b. *dílgid   dó*
       forgive.IMP.2PL   to.3SG.M
       'forgive him'
       (Wb 14d21)

(13) c. *cia   dulogae   doib   an=uili*
       although   forgive.SBJV.2SG to.3PL   their=all.ACC.PL
       torgabala
       transgression.ACC.PL
       'Although you forgive them all their transgressions'
       (Ml 138b7)

(13) d. *dulug-fa   dia   dam   mu   pecthu*
       forgive-FUT.3SG   God.NOM   to.1SG   my   sin.ACC.PL
       'God will forgive me my sins'
       (Ml 58c18)

(13) e. *intain   duluigter   dun   ar=pecthi*
       the.time   REL\forgive.PASS.PRS.PL   to.1PL   our=sin.NOM.PL
       'when our sins are forgiven us'
       (Ml 32c15)

If one looks at the order attested with *is maith la* 'like', what immediately follows the predicate is invariably the prepositional argument with *la* rather than the argument in the nominative case (13/16); the only nominative form that occurs before the prepositional argument is the demonstrative clitic subject *són* (in 3 instances out of 30).[15] Nevertheless, the same position is shared by prepositional arguments with the other predicate, *do·luigi*, for which subjecthood of the nominative argument, semantically the forgiver (or the forgiven deed with the passive), has not been questioned: in 14 out of 20 cases the prepositional argument flagged with *do* immediately follows the verb form of *do·luigi*.

More generally, the data suggest that the position of prepositional arguments is not syntactically significant, but points rather to factors such as givenness, topicality and animacy. This is prompted by two symptoms. The first one is the frequency with which prepositional pronominal arguments, which in Old Irish surface as inflected prepositions (see Table 1), precede an overt direct argument: 14/17 for *is maith la*, 6/9 for *do·luigi do*. This preferred order[16] is confirmed by the occurrence of minimal pairs such as (14.a) vs. (14.b), in two close glosses:

(14) a. *duberat   an=anman   for-na   tire*
       give.PRS.3PL their=name.ACC.PL on-the.ACC.PL land.ACC.PL
       'they give their names to the lands'
       (Ml 69a11)

(14) b. *duberat   forru   an=anman*
       give.PRS.3PL on.3PL.ACC   their=name.ACC.PL
       'they give them their names'
       (Ml 69a13)

While in (14.a), where both the accusative object and the prepositional argument are full NPs, the accusative argument precedes the prepositional argument, in (14.b), where the prepositional argument is a pronoun, the inflected preposition precedes the direct object in the accusative.

The second symptom is control, a typical behavioral property. Control properties of prepositional arguments of main clauses on the arguments of non-finite clauses depend on the predicate (Stüber 2007–08: 140–148). The prepositional argument of *is maith la* is no exception, that is, it does not trigger obligatory control in contrast to other arguments. Compare (15.a, b, c, d and e). The preposi-

---

15 This 3rd person pronominal clitic is case-marked and enjoys a certain degree of positional freedom, as compared to the so-called emphatic particles expressing the subject, that can appear only after the first stressed word (the predicate). See Griffith (2011: 71-72) for a clear presentation of the paradigm and the properties of this form.
16 Note that inflected prepositions are stressed words and may also occur clause-finally.

tional arguments *dúibsi* in (15.a), *lat* in (15.b), with *is maith*, *dosom* in (15.c), with *do·luigi*, control complement clause subjects, while *limsa* in (15.d) and *lasin* in (15.e), again with *is maith*, do not. Note that while the copular predicate in (15.b, d, e) is *is maith la* 'is good according to X, X likes', the copular predicate in (15.a) is *is maith do* 'is good for X, X should'.

(15) a. ní   maid   dúib=si   didiu   cen
        NEG.COP.PRS.3SG good.NOM   to.2PL=2PL   then   without
        dílgud
        forgive.VN.ACC
        'it is not good for you, then, not to forgive'
        (Wb 14d19)

(15) b. rubu   ferr   lat   comaitecht
        COP.PRF.3SG good.COMPV   by.2SG   favor.VN.NOM
        du   assaraib   indaas   dun=ni
        to   Assyrians.DAT than   to.1PL=1PL
        'it was better for you to favor the Assyrians rather than us'
        (Ml 72b18)

(15) c. ara-nderlaigthe   do=som   pecad   techtae
        that-forgive.SBJV.PST.PASS.SG   to.3SG=3SG sin.NOM   go.VN.GEN
        dochum   bersabae
        towards   Bathsheba.GEN
        'that the sin of going to Bathsheba might be forgiven him'
        (Ml 32c17)

(15) d. ar=ropad   maith   lim=sa   labrad
        for=COP.COND.3SG   good.NOM   by.1SG=1SG   speak.VN.NOM
        il-belre   dúib=si
        many-tongue.GEN.PL   to.2PL=2PL
        'for I would like you to speak many tongues'
        (Wb 12c29)

(15) e. lasin   rubu   maith   an=anad
        by.whom   COP.PRF.3SG   good.NOM   their=remain.VN.NOM
        isin=doiri
        in.the=captivity
        'to whom it was good to remain in the Captivity'
        (Ml 131d11)

The data from valency patterns in a sense complement the data and hypotheses discussed by Lash (2020), who argues that the position of so-called late subjects (subjects not immediately following the verb) in Old Irish depends on information structure factors, on the one hand, since the position immediately following the verb is associated with given/old information, and on the other hand on atypical transitivity.[17]

4 Case marking with finite vs. non finite forms

This Section addresses the main focus of this paper, the relationship between finite and non-finite syntax and its correlation with transitivity. The standard view is that a genitive argument with non-finite forms of transitive verbs is nearly always objective, i.e. it codes the argument which, with finite active forms, is flagged by the accusative case.

So Thurneysen's reference grammar (1946: 158, § 250) states: "a genitive (or possessive pronoun [. . .]) qualifying an abstract noun which functions as verbal noun of a transitive verb, and is still felt as such, is nearly always objective". More recently, Stüber (2007–8: 137; cf. Stüber 2009: 33–34, fn. 22) supports a similar view: "Bei Verbalnomina zu transitiven Verben bezeichnet ein beigefügter Genitiv immer das Object, ein Genitivus subjectivus ist daher nur bei intransitiven Verben überhaupt möglich." [With verbal nouns of transitive verbs, an appended genitive always expresses the object, therefore a subjective genitive is generally possible only with intransitive verbs].

These sources do not give an explicit definition of "transitive verb", but, applying the traditional distinction, it may be assumed that verbs which in Old Irish govern a direct accusative argument can be classified as transitive verbs. This criterion happens to give the same results as Haspelmath's (2015: 136) definition: a given verb in a given language is transitive if it has two participants that are coded like the two main arguments of the prototypical transitive verb 'break'. However, the behavior of genitive arguments with non-finite forms does not match this transitive-intransitive distinction even considering only the restricted set of verbs under inquiry here, as I will show through the data in Tables 3, 4 and 5.

---

[17] I cannot deal here with the details of the fine-grained analysis in Lash (2020). It is important to stress, however, that in Lash (2020) transitivity as a factor correlating with constituent order is viewed rather as a property of clauses, than of predicates, and corresponds to what in the framework adopted here may be termed prototypical two-place transitive coding frame (which excludes passive clauses, for example).

Table 3 groups verbs whose finite forms occur with a direct second argument (accusative case) more than 80% of instances, and whose non-finite forms turned out to govern a genitive argument always corresponding to the one in accusative with finite forms ("objective genitive"). Table 4 groups verbs whose finite forms occur with an accusative argument less than 50% of instances, and whose non-finite forms mostly govern a genitive argument corresponding to the nominative with finite forms ("subjective genitive"). Table 5 groups verbs whose finite forms occur with an accusative argument in at least 50% of instances but whose non-finite forms can also govern a genitive argument corresponding to the nominative with finite forms, as with the verbs in Table 4. It is claimed here that verbs that behave like those in Table 5 show a lower degree of transitivity than verbs that behave like those in Table 3, and that verbs that behave like those in Table 4, traditionally classified as "intransitive", show the lowest degree of transitivity (see Section 6).

In each Table the figures in the second columns on the left are the number of occurrences in the corpus of finite forms with an accusative argument, out of all occurrences of active finite forms. The attested microroles of the accusative argument are given in square brackets.

The third columns give the number of passive occurrences with the same participant coded on the verb, either through number agreement with an NP in the nominative, zero anaphora (3rd persons), or by a pronominal bound morpheme, the so-called infixed pronoun (1st and 2nd person direct arguments with the passive can only be coded as objects; see Section 2.1, (3.a) and (3.b)). Both constructions correlate with accusative rection (2nd columns) and have been considered here indicators of transitivity.[18] However, as mentioned in Section 2.1, passive forms in Old Irish may also occur without any direct argument, as in (4.a) and (4.b). This strategy, which removes both the nominative and the accusative argument, while admitting only adpositional arguments, does not correlate with accusative rection in the active and can on the contrary be considered as an indicator of lower transitivity. Occurrences of this "non-promotional"[19] passive have been added in the third column with the traditional label "impersonal" ("I").

---

18 See footnotes 4 and 17 for alternative analyses in the literature.
19 Note that "non-promotional" here strictly refers to morpho-syntactic promotion (i.e. from accusative to nominative, and/or with bound person markers on the verb; see Section 2.1 and footnote 4), not to pragmatic promotion. I claim on the contrary that adpositional arguments, although maintaining the same morpho-syntactic flagging as with with active forms, are pragmatically promoted through this direct argument removing strategy, but I cannot pursue this issue here. Anyhow, the stance I adopted for the analysis is that the occurrence of the passive alternation in Old Irish is related both to the coding pattern (transitivity value) and to the func-

In the fourth columns are reported the figures for genitives corresponding to the accusative argument (2-arg) vs. the nominative argument (1-arg) with the verbal nouns, out of all the occurrences with a genitive argument. Note that occurrences of the verbal nouns without any genitive argument are not included in Tables 3, 4 and 5, but they have been taken into account for this study (see Section 6, comments on Table 8), while instances where the verbal nouns occur in the plural, and/or preceded by the definite article and not accompanied any further argument were excluded. Plural forms and forms preceded by the article might be viewed as fully nominal occurrences (which have referential rather than predicative use), although it must be stressed that most constructions of verbal nouns in Old Irish do not support this distinction (with the exception of the construction in (6.a, b), which is clearly predicative, see Stüber 2009a); see anyhow Section 5 on verbal nouns with possessives.

Table 3: "Well-behaved", fully transitive verbs (> 80% with accusative arguments).

VERB	FINITE ACTIVE FORMS with accusative/ total of finite active forms	FINITE PASSIVE FORMS	NON-FINITE FORMS 2-gen=accusative argument/ total with genitive
do·beir 'give'	283/287 [gift/put thing]	115	*tabart* 2-gen 83/83
gaibid 'take'	94/100 [taken/recited thing/person]	56+ 36 anticausative	*gabál* 2-gen 14/14
ro·finnadar 'find out/ know'	60/64 [known person/ thing][20]	5	*fius* 2-gen 20/20
beirid 'bring'	48/52 [brought/referred thing/person]	34	*breth* 2-gen 21/21
guidid 'ask for, pray'	47/53, 29 [asked thing] ≈ 18 [askee][21]	3 [asked thing]	*guide* 2-gen 12/12, 11 [askee], 1 [asked thing]
do·adbat 'show'	39/40 [shown thing][22]	24	*taidbsiu* 2-gen 24/24

---

tion of the alternation, so that an attempt has been made to trace a line between the two factors (see Malchukov 2015: 106-107 about the relative importance of the two factors in determining the compatibility and likelihood of the alternations).

20 38 clausal arguments have been excluded. Finite complement clauses are not included in Tables 3, 4 and 5, although they occupy the accusative argument slot, since they don't provide evidence for case marking, which is the criterion adopted here, as in ValPaL (see Haspelmath and Hartmann 2015: 56). The number of clausal arguments for each verb (active + passive) is given in the footnotes.
21 2 clausal arguments have been excluded.
22 13 clausal arguments have been excluded.

Table 3 (continued)

VERB	FINITE ACTIVE FORMS with accusative/ total of finite active forms	FINITE PASSIVE FORMS	NON-FINITE FORMS 2-gen=accusative argument/ total with genitive
ad·cí 'see'	24/27 [seen person/ thing][23]	11	aicsiu 2-gen 2/2
ad·rími 'count'	21/21 [counted thing]	3	áram 2-gen 5/5
do·indnaig 'bestow'	19/19 [gift]	15	tindnacol 2-gen 17/17
ad·cobra 'desire'	15/15 [desired thing][24]	1	accobur 2-gen 7/7
con·oscaigi 'move'	9/9 [moved/changed thing]	15	cumscugud 2-gen 16/16
do·ruimnethar 'forget'	6/6 [forgotten person/ thing]	–	dermat 2-gen 4/4
ad·gnin 'recognize'	5/5 [recognized thing/ person]	3	aithne 2-gen 2/2
ad·gládathar 'address'	2/2 [addressee]	–	accaldam 2-gen 7/7

Table 4: Doubtfully or weakly transitive verbs (< 50% with accusative arguments).

VERB	FINITE ACTIVE FORMS with accusative/ total of finite active forms	FINITE PASSIVE FORMS	NON-FINITE FORMS 2-gen=accusative arg, 1-gen=nominative arg/ total with genitive
téit 'go'	15/130, 12 [goal] ≈ 3 [route]	(3 l)	techt 1-gen 14/17, 2-gen 3/17 dul 2-gen 3/3
do·icc 'come'	18/45 [goal]	–	tichtu 1-gen 7/10, 2-gen 3/10
fris·gair 'answer'	0/2	–	frecrae 1-gen 3/4, 2-gen 1/4?[25]

---

[23] 2 clausal arguments have been excluded.
[24] 2 clausal arguments have been excluded.
[25] See the discussion below on (18), a doubtful example.

Table 5: Transitive verbs (> 50% with accusative arguments) with genitives corresponding to either the accusative or the nominative argument.

VERB	FINITE ACTIVE FORMS with accusative/ total of finite active forms	FINITE PASSIVE FORMS	NON-FINITE FORMS 2-gen=accusative arg, 1-gen=nominative arg/ total with genitive
as·beir 'say'	239/243 [said content][26]	79	*epert* 2-gen 17/19, 1-gen 2/19
caraid 'love'	28/29 [loved person/thing]	2	*serc*[27] 2-gen 17/23, 1-gen 6/23
for·cain 'teach'	25/29, 16 [taught thing] ≈ 9 [taught person][28]	2 [taught thing], 2 [taught person]	*forcetal* 2-gen 12/20 (10 [taught person]), 1-gen 8/20
do·luigi 'forgive'	16/24 [forgiven deed]	7 [forgiven deed][29] (+3 l)	*dílgud* 2-gen 16/19, 1-gen 3/19
as·indet 'tell'	14/20 [said content][30]	1	*aisndís* 2-gen 5/7, 1-gen 2/7
do·moinethar 'think'	15/17 [thought thing][31]	1	*toimtiu* 2-gen 0/1, 1-gen 1/1 [thinker][32]
labraithir 'speak'	13/23, 10 [spoken content] ≈ 3 [spoken language]	–	*labrad* 2-gen 10/14 (9 [spoken language]), 1-gen 4/10
do·fich 'avenge'	6/12, 4 [punished deed] ≈ 2 [beneficiary]	4 [beneficiary], 3 [punished deed] (+2 l)[33]	*dígal* 2-gen 14/19 (11 punished deed] ≈ 3 [beneficiary]), 1-gen 5/19
for·tét 'help'	8/10 [helpee]	–	*fortacht* 1-gen 28/39, 2-gen 11/39

---

26 131 clausal arguments (finite clauses) and 24 quotations (utterance arguments in ValPaL, see Haspelmath and Hartmann 2015: 56) have been excluded.
27 The instances include 5 occurrences of the compound *deserc*, corresponding to Latin *charitas*, since in the Ml and Sg databases they are grouped under the same headword. See Section 6 about Wb 18b21 (example (33)).
28 2 clausal arguments have been excluded.
29 1 clausal argument has been excluded.
30 3 clausal arguments have been excluded.
31 18 clausal arguments have been excluded.
32 6 out of 7 occurrences of this verbal noun have a clausal argument.
33 I refer to Roma (2020) for a detailed analysis of the argument frames of the verb *do·fich*.

With verbs like *beirid* 'bring' or *gaibid* 'take' the genitive accompanying the respective verbal nouns invariably corresponds to the accusative argument (the brought thing or person and the taken thing or person respectively). This regular pattern of transitive verbs is found for 14 verbs (the verbs in Table 3) out of the 26 taken into account for this study. With the verb *gaibid*, the 36 instances of the peculiar construction which I have labelled "anticausative" are instances of the so-called nasalizing relative clauses with a neuter object petrified in the perfect form (*rondgab*, cf. Thurneysen 1946: 267, § 424), literally 'which has found it(self)', meaning 'to be (in a certain way, position)', similarly to English *to find oneself*, French *se trouver*, Italian *trovarsi*, but with a petrified singular neuter object pronoun. An example is given in (16).

(16) amal   ru<nd>gabsat   isind   eclais
     as   <REL\3SG.N.OBJ>find.PRF.3PL in.the church.DAT
    'as they are in the Church'
    (Ml 64c5)

Sansò (2018) has shown that lexical restrictions on antipassives are cross-linguistically more common than lexical restrictions on passives. The construction exemplified in (16) would be an instance of an extreme lexical restriction on an anticausative construction (with a single verb, *gaibid*) and I view its occurrence as a further indicator of transitivity besides canonical passives (3.a, b).

Among verbs that occur less than 50% of instances with an accusative argument (Table 4), the preference for the non-finite argument in the genitive to correspond to the subject is clear for *fris·gair* 'answer'. This verb is however attested only in a couple of examples in finite form, and formal ambiguities of the form *a* with the verbal noun, which in principle can be a sg. or pl. possessive or even the definite article,[34] do not allow to exclude the possibility of having a genitive corresponding to the second argument, representing either the addressee or the question. An ambiguous example is reported in (17), while (18) contains the only instance where the genitive argument could in fact be the second argument. Nevertheless, in most cases, the second argument with *frecrae* is coded by

---

34 The distinction between these forms is regularly committed to initial mutations on the head noun (lenition after sg. masc./neut. possessive, nasalization after pl. possessive and nom./acc. sg. neuter article, no mutation after sg. fem. possessive), but unfortunately mutations are not regularly spelt on <f>; lenition may be marked, through phonological spelling (omission of the consonant) or by a superscribed dot, but these practices are not consistent (Thurneysen 1946: 142, § 231.7). In (18), the form *a* cannot be the article because of *adi*, a genitive clitic that can only occur in combination with a possessive (Thurneysen 1946: 304, § 481).

a prepositional phrase, *do*+dative (10 instances),[35] as in the two occurrences of finite forms, and not by a genitive phrase.

(17) *iss=ed   inso   a=frecrae   .i. quod rl.*
     is=3SG.N that   the/its=answer
     'That's the answer, that is *quod* etc.' (or 'its answer', i.e. 'the answer to it'?)
     (Sg 200a10)

(18) *na-nní   asbertis=(s)om   fris=(s)om   ˥   dugnitis*
     any-thing.NOM   say.IMPF.3PL=3PL   to.3SG.M=3SG.M   and do.IMPF.3PL
     ba   ed   a=frecrae=adi
     COP.PST.3SG   DEM.NOM.N   his/its/their=answer=3SG/PL
     les=(s)om   apud mé oratio rl.
     by.3SG.M=3SG.M
     'Whatever they used to say to him and to do, that was the answer to it/them by him, *apud me oratio* etc.' (or, rather, 'that was his answer according to him')[36]
     (Ml 62c13)

With verbs traditionally labeled in the literature as intransitives, such as motion verbs, the situation is even less clearcut. With finite forms the verbs *do·icc* 'come' and *téit* 'go' can govern the accusative, although in a minority of instances, and accordingly the genitive arguments with verbal nouns mainly but not exclusively code the argument corresponding to the (nominative) subject (note, however, the different behavior of the two verbal nouns of *téit*, i.e. *techt* vs. the suppletive stem *dul*, whose genitive argument is invariably the goal). Griffith and Lash (2018: 108) suggest the working definition that if the accusative argument is not a patient/theme, but e.g. a locative, the verb is not transitive: in order for a verb to be transitive, the direct object in the accusative "must be a theme, not any other theta-role." If so, the accusative goals of the verbs *téit* and *do·icc* would not suffice to classify these verbs as transitive.

---

35 To these, 2 instances with a Latin dative should be added (Wb 3a3, Wb 13a13).
36 Both Stokes and Strachan (1901-3) and Griffith (2013) translate 'to them', which would imply that the genitive pronoun expresses the addressee, but I assume that the indefinite neuter form *nanní* could also in principle be the antecedent of the pronominal form *a* with clitic *adi* ('the answer to that'), and, besides, that this pronominal form may have the pronoun in *fris* as its antecedent, i.e. it may code the answerer ('his answer according to him', where 'his' and 'him' are not co-referential and refer to the psalmist and the commentator respectively). My preference goes to the last interpretation.

Nevertheless, even excluding motion verbs, a general transitive vs. intransitive opposition is not sufficient to predict the role of the genitive argument with the verbal noun, as the remaining 9 verbs show (Table 5).

With the verbal nouns of *for·tét* 'help', *for·cain* 'teach', *do·fich* 'punish/avenge', *as·indet* 'tell, declare', *labraithir* 'speak, talk', *caraid* 'love', less frequently *do·luigi* 'forgive' and *as·beir* 'say', so-called subjective genitive arguments clearly do occur. Some of these verbs may govern accusative arguments with different semantic roles, as the data in Table 5 show. For example, the uncoded alternation in (19.a-b) is attested for *for·cain* 'teach' (see 11.a), the uncoded alternation in (20.a-c) for *do·fich* 'punish/avenge':

(19) a. V.subj[1] > 1-nom [teacher] > 2-acc [taught thing]
V.subj[1] > 1-nom [teacher] > 2-acc [taught thing] > *do*+3-dat [taught person]

(19) b. V.subj[1] > 1-nom [teacher] > 2-acc [taught person]

(20) a. V.subj[1] > 1-nom [punisher] > 2-acc [punished deed]
(> *for*+3-acc [punished person])

(20) b. V.subj[1] > 1-nom [punisher] > 2-acc [beneficiary]
(> *for*+3-acc [punished person])

(20) c. V.subj[1] > 1-nom [punisher] > *tar cenn*+2-gen [beneficiary]
V.subj[1] > 1-nom [punisher] > *tar ési*+2-gen [punished deed][37]

However, while the alternation of microroles for objects is reflected in the alternation of genitives with verbal nouns, which may correspond to the same semantic microroles, the occurrences of genitives corresponding to the first argument do not correlate with semantic shifts related to polysemy of the verb or due to different argument frames. For example, subjective genitives with *forcetal* 'teaching', *fortacht* 'help', *dígal* 'punishment/vengeance', do not trigger any semantic shift or consistent valency change. Usually, if the genitive with the verbal noun flags the first argument, the second argument is omitted (elliptical, generic or

---

[37] The prepositions *tar cenn* 'on behalf of' and *tar ési* 'behind' are complex prepositions made up of the preposition *tar* 'across, over' and a noun in the accusative (*cenn* 'head' and *éis* 'trace'); their complement was originally an adnominal complement and that is why it bears the genitive case.

controlled by the main predicate), as in (21.a, b and c) respectively, similarly to what happens to the first argument when the genitive flags the second argument, as in (22). See however the discussion in Section 5 on these and similar examples.

(21) a. *amal   du<n>gniat   doini   ón*
     as   <REL\3SG.OBJ.N>do.PRS.3PL[38] men.NOM   DEM.ACC.N
     .i.   air ni   bi   firian   án=digal=ade
     id est for NEG   COP.PRS.HAB.3SG just their=punish.VN.NOM=3PL
     'as men do (that), that is because their punishment (how they punish) is not just'
     (Ml 128d3)

(21) b. *cumscugud   du   diglae   dín   són*
     move.VN.NOM your punish.VN.GEN   from.1PL DEM.NOM.N
     'The removal of your punishment from us'
     (Ml 105d7)

(21) c. *ma-ní   eroimet   a=forcital*
     if-NEG   receive.SBJV.3PL his=teach.VN.ACC
     'if they don't receive his teaching'
     (Ml 30d13)

(22) *ar=loure=ni   do=precept   et   forcitul*
     our=sufficiency.NOM=1PL to=preach.VN.DAT and teach.VN.DAT
     cáich
     everyone.GEN
     'Our sufficiency to preach and instruct everyone'
     (Wb 15a14)

On the other hand, some of the invariably transitive verbs in Table 3 are among the most frequent verbs in Old Irish, are highly polysemous and occur with various argument frames, although the macrorole of the accusative argument belongs to the same class: for example *gaibid* may mean 'take', 'begin' or 'recite' (a psalm); *beirid* 'bring (an object)' or 'refer (an expression)'; *do·beir*

---

[38] I interpret this form as *dundgniat*, with neuter infixed pronoun <d> co-referencing *ón* (Thurneysen 1946: 303, § 479) and relative nasalization <n> (Thurneysen 1946: 259, § 413; 316, § 497), in the construction exemplified in (5), and this is why <n> is analysed as an infixed morpheme. The alternative analysis (*n* as a simple relative marker) would not bear on the issue discussed here.

'give' occurs as a light verb in a variety of constructions (e.g. *do·beir fortacht do* 'give help to', *do·beir indithim i/fri* 'give attention in/towards', *do·beir dígail for* 'give punishment on', *do·beir ainm do/for* 'give a name to/on', *do·beir aithis for* 'give reproach on').

It could be argued that causative meaning of the verb, i.e. the presence of [CAUSE] as a semantic feature of verb semantics, might be associated with a higher likelihood of a second argument genitive with the verbal noun (and with a high transitivity index as proposed below in Section 6, Table 8), since this condition applies to many of the verbs in Table 3 (*do·indnaig* 'bestow', *do·beir* 'give', *gaibid* 'take', *beirid* 'bring', *do·adbat* 'show', *con·oscaigi* 'move'); see Lehmann (2015: 1569–1671, Table 6) on so-called agentive situation types. This semantic feature would in turn be related on the one hand to prevalent trivalent coding frames, and on the other hand to the possibility of anticausative uncoded alternations with non-finite forms, in the absence of voice ('the giving of something' = 'the fact that (someone) gives something' or 'that something is given'; 'someone's movement' = 'the fact that someone is moved' or 'moves'; see Lehmann 2015: 1571–1577 about the asymmetry of valency alternations with different types of transitive verbs). However, the relationship with causativity is not straightforward, given that *for·cain* 'teach' should group with causatives while *ad·cí* 'see' should not.

To sum up, the data in Tables 3, 4 and 5 show that verbs which are mostly accompanied by an accusative argument in finite clauses (i.e. they occur with a direct object the vast majority of instances, more than 80% of cases) invariably display objective genitives with non-finite forms. This can be tested in particular looking at verbs with high token frequency such as for example *do·beir* 'give', *gaibid* 'take', *beirid* 'bring'. Subjective genitives may not be ruled out in these cases, however (see for instance *as·beir* 'say', which in finite clauses occurs with a direct object in 98% of instances), but, if they occur, the prediction is that the genitive must be pronominal and animate, or very high in the animacy hierarchy. Less frequent patterns such as these are dealt with in Section 5, while Section 6 illustrates the transitivity scale that emerges from the data in Tables 3, 4 and 5.

5 Restrictions

It turns out in fact that there are restrictions on the kind of accusative and genitive arguments which may occur with finite and non-finite forms respectively.

An accusative argument with weakly or not fully transitive verbs (that occur with a direct object less than 80% of instances) is very likely to be a pronominal object (infixed pronoun), and/or to have a human referent, or to appear as the head of a direct, i.e. non prepositional, relative clause (e.g. 'the place I go', 'the person I teach'), or to undergo lexical restrictions. Table 6 reports the figures for infixed pronouns, referents high in the animacy hierarchy,[39] relativized objects and a few lexical items recurrently found with motion verbs. Note that the conditions in columns 2 and 3 often occur simultaneously (for example in case of 1st and 2nd person pronouns), the conditions in columns 3 and 4, 4 and 5 may occur simultaneously. Examples for each type are given in (23), (24), (25), (26).

(23) for<dub>cechna
 <2PL.OBJ.REL>teach.FUT.3SG
 'who will teach you'[40]
 (Wb 9a16)

(24) ní-ticed   scís   mo=chnamai
 NEG-come.IMPF.3SG   weariness.NOM   my=bone.ACC.PL
 'Weariness did not use to come to my bones'
 (Ml 41d9)

(25) is=sain   aní   forchanat   et   dogniat
 is=different   DEM.NOM.N   REL\teach.PRS.3PL and   REL\do.PRS.3PL
 'What they teach and what they do is different'
 (Wb 28c16)

(26) tiagait   báas   nanapaig
 go.PRS.3PL   death.ACC   premature.ACC
 'They go to premature death'
 (Wb 11d12)

---

[39] What is meant here is the animacy hierarchy proper (Comrie 1989, ch. 9; see Dahl and Fraurud 1996), but, regarding the upper part of the hierarchy, it is further assumed that referents including the speaker and the addressee are high in animacy (as commonly held in the literature, see Lehmann 2015: 1555), that día ('God'), not usually included in the hierarchy, ranks higher than humans, that referents of expressions such as mo chnamai 'my bones' in (24) are high in animacy.

[40] Glossing Latin qui uos commonefaciat (1 Cor. IV, 17).

Table 6: Types of accusative arguments with weakly (<50%) or not fully transitive (<80%) verbs.

	pronominal object (infixed pronoun)	hightly animate referent	head of relative clause	recurrent object (lexical restrictions)
for·cain 'teach'	7/9 [taught person], 1/16 [taught thing]	6/9[41]	12/16 [taught thing],	1/25[42]
for·tét 'help'	4/8	8/8	3/8	
do·icc 'come'	17/18	15/18		
téit 'go'	3/15	0/15	8/15	7/15[43]
do·fich 'avenge'[44]	2/2	2/2		
labraithir 'speak'	3/10 [spoken content], 1/3 [spoken language]		4/13	2/13[45]

---

41 For *for·cain* only instances where the accusative argument is the taught person have been taken into account here, assuming that [taught thing] and [taught person] represent different macroroles.

42 This is an instance of the so-called *figura etymologica,* a construction where the object of the verb is its verbal noun (lit. 'teach a teaching'), namely Wb 8c3 in (i), where the object is the head of a relative clause:

i. ni=forcital óisa foirbthi forchanim dúib
   NEG.COP.PRS.3SG=teach.VN.NOM people.GEN perfect.GEN REL\teach.PRS.1SG to.2PL
   'it is not the teaching of perfect folk I teach to you'

This instance has been taken into account here because the same internal argument also occurs with the passive in what looks like an extremely rare ditransitive construction, Wb 3b23 in (ii):

ii. a=forcital for<ndob>canar
    ART=teach.VN.NOM <REL\2PL.OBJ>teach.PRS.PASS.SG
    'the teaching that you are taught'

(ii) is the only instance of such a construction with the verbs analyzed for this study, but a similar instance occurs at Wb 19a6 *iscúrsagad rondcúrsagusa* lit. 'it is a reprimand I reprimanded him', where the cleft structure is clearly a predicate focalization strategy (García Castillero 2014: 65).

43 The recurrent objects are *bás* 'death' (3), *leth* 'part' (3), *martre* 'martyrdom' (1). In 3 occurrences out of 7 the object is also the head of a relative clause.

44 For *do·fich* only the instances where the accusative argument is the beneficiary have been taken into account in Table 5. In the remaining 4 instances where an accusative argument surfaces, the object represents the punished deed and is inanimate (see comments on Table 5 in Section 5). Note that both roles, i.e. beneficiary and punished deed, can be flagged with a (complex) preposition with this verb, namely *tar cenn* 'on behalf' for the beneficiary (2 instances; 7 instances with the verbal noun) and *tar ési* 'behind, after' for the punished deed (1 instance; 7 instances with the verbal noun), see Roma (2020).

Note that different columns in Table 6 are relevant for different verbs, since with *labraithir* 'speak, talk' the object is always inanimate, with motion verbs like *téit* 'go' and *do·icc* 'come' the goal is mostly inanimate and flagged by a preposition, while with *for·cain* 'teach' and *do·fich* 'punish' the direct object is mostly inanimate ([taught thing] and [punished deed], respectively), and with *for·tét* 'help' the direct object is always animate (see Tables 4 and 5).

Similarly, a genitive argument which corresponds to the first argument with transitive verbs (more than 50% of active finite forms with an accusative argument), and conversely to the second with weakly transitive verbs, is almost invariably a pronominal argument (a possessive, i.e. a pronominal genitive which is proclitic to the nominal host), or at any rate it is very high in the animacy hierarchy, or it belongs to a restricted class of lexical items. Table 7 reports the figures for possessives, for the genitive *dé* 'of God' and for the same lexical elements in Table 6. Examples for each type are given in (27), (28), (29).

(27) ma=adced   torbe   inna=thecht
     if=see.SBJV.2PL advantage.ACC   in.3SG.GEN=N\go.VN.DAT
     'If you should see profit in going to it'
     (Wb 11b22)

(28) fortacht   dé   duib
     help.VN.NOM   God.GEN   to.2PL
     'God's help to you'
     (Ml 68a15)

(29) am=irlam   techte   martre   cach=dia
     COP.PRS.1SG=ready   go.VN.GEN   martyrdom.GEN   every=day.ACC
     'I am ready to go to martyrdom every day'
     (Wb 13c8)

---

45 The recurrent object is *ilbélre* 'many languages'. With the verbal noun *labrad*, in 9 out of 10 instances the object is the same (*ilbélre*) and in 1/10 a possessive. Therefore, although the genitive complementing *labrad* is predominantly the object (which is why these examples do not feature in Table 7), it could be said that similar restrictions (in particular lexical restrictions) hold for the direct objects of *labraithir* and for the genitives complementing its verbal noun.

Table 7: Types of less frequent genitive arguments with non-finite forms (1st argument of transitive verbs, 2nd argument of weakly transitive verbs).

	pronominal argument (possessive)	highly animate referent: *dé* 'of God'	lexical restrictions
serc 'love'	3/6	2/6[46]	
epert 'say'	3/3		
aisndís 'tell'	2/2		
forcetal 'teach'	5/8		
fortacht 'help'	11/28	15/28	
dílgud 'forgive'	1/3	2/3	
dígal 'avenge'	3/5	1/5[47]	
labrad 'speak'	2/4		
toimtiu 'think'	1/1		
tíchtu 'come'	2/3		
techt 'go'	1/3		2/3
frecrae 'answer'	1/1?[48]		

The semantic role of the accusative argument with finite forms seems on the other hand to be less relevant for its mapping onto the genitive with non-finite forms: it is difficult for example to classify the object arguments of *gaibid* 'take' or 'recite', *do·adbat* 'show' and *ad·cobra* 'desire' as semantically closer to each other rather than to the object of *as·indet* 'tell', *for·cain* 'teach' or *caraid* 'love', respectively. This again is in contrast with hypotheses which would classify transitive verbs according to the semantic role of the object, such as Griffith and Lash's suggestion (2018) mentioned above in Section 4, rather than relying, more generally, on verb semantics and argument structure (Lehmann 2015). Anyhow, this is the inescapable conclusion if one wants to maintain that there is a correlation between transitivity and the semantic role of the genitive argument with non-finite forms.

A proviso should be made at this point concerning the function of pronominal arguments in general, and in particular of possessives with verbal nouns. As

---

[46] In the remaining occurrence out of 6, which features the compound *deserc* (see footnote 27), the genitive coding the [lover] is *in spirto* 'of the (holy) Spirit' (Wb 5d18).
[47] In the remaining occurrence out of 5, the genitive coding the [punisher] is *ind aingil* 'of the angel' (Ml 77d16).
[48] See example (18).

noted above in Section 2.2, pronominal neuter objects (affixal pronouns) might occur with any verb in verb-phrase anaphora, as in example (10). However, the occurrences in verbal anaphora constructions has limited bearing on the ratio of occurrences with an accusative arguments (the data in the second columns of Tables 3, 4 and 5), since there are only 8 occurrences altogether with the verbs considered here.[49] It has also very limited bearing on the frequency of pronominal affixes (the data in the second column in Table 6), since, as noted above, these are mainly instances with animate referents and therefore non-neuter infixes.

On the other hand, possessives in Old Irish are determiners, which means that they might trigger referential function and shift to concrete meaning of verbal nouns (Thurneysen 1946: 445). A clear example of this use is (30), which was excluded from the dataset together with all cases of semantic shifts involving changes in semantic features.

(30) .i. numerus .i. is=an=áram=di
           COP.PRS.3SG=their=count.VN.NOM=3PL
   'numerus, that is, it's their number'
   (Ml 18d3)

This behavior as determiners, however, holds for nominal genitives too, because definite genitive noun phrases trigger definiteness of the whole NP and, like possessives, are generally in complementary distribution with the head-noun's definite article, despite their position on the right of the head (Thurneysen 1946: 295–6, §470; Ó Gealbháin 1991; see Roma 2009 and 2014 for details).

This poses a problem for the classification of some instances with pronominal genitives (possessives). For example in (31) below the context forces a referential interpretation of *toimtiu*, i.e. 'what you think' rather than '(the fact) that you think/thought/have thought/are thought (etc.).'

(31) íar   far=toimtin=si
     after your=think.VN.DAT=2PL
   'according to your thought'
   (Wb 20a14)

---

[49] 2 with *do·icc*, 1 each with *téit, ad·rími, as·beir, ad·gnin, do·beir, ro·finnadar*. The loci and the reasons why these are so classified can be found in Roma (2018, examples 11, 12.a, 12.b, 13.c, 17, 19, 20, 23).

Therefore, it cannot be ruled out that verbal nouns with definite genitive modifiers (in particular, so-called subjective genitives in Table 5) lean towards referential interpretation and that some of the instances included in Table 7 should be viewed as fully referential noun phrases. It is important to stress, however, that this ambiguity is inherent in Old Irish syntax, it may be triggered by any kind of definite genitive modifier, and does not impinge on the correspondence between the valency patterns of finite forms and verbal nouns: see Bisang (2016) on the relationship between finiteness, nominalization and information structure.[50] Less frequent genitives (as per Table 7 and fourth columns of Tables 4 and 5) are not confined to nominal concrete senses of verbal nouns. Counterexamples are (27), (29) above and (32) below. Note that translations with nominal vs. verbal forms are not reliable cues in this connection.

(32)   *aní*   *rogéni*   *ho=gnimaib*
       DEM.N.NOM   REL\do.PRF.3SG   from=deed.DAT.PL
       á=epert   *asrobrad=són*   *ho=briathraib*
       his=say.VN.NOM   say.PRF.PASS.SG=DEM.NOM.N   from=word.DAT.PL
       'what he had done in deeds, his saying (to say) that it had been said in words'
       (Ml 31b24)

6 Transitivity index

Bearing this in mind, I get back to the correlation between transitivity and argument marking with non-finite forms. I propose to illustrate this correlation through a transitivity scale, based on a transitivity index which combines frequency and kind of passivization with the likelihood to co-occur with an accusative argument. Table 8 reports this transitivity scale, where the index is simply the ratio of accusative arguments and promotional passives out of all occurrences (data in the second and third columns in Tables 3, 4 and 5). The index for each verb is therefore calculated as follows:

---

[50] Recall that plural verbal nouns and verbal nouns with an article have been excluded from the occurrences reckoned here, although they replicate the same valency patterns as the singular with no article. Their inclusion would increase the number of genitives corresponding to the first argument.

number of occurrences accompanied by an object argument + number of occurrences of the canonical passive construction/ total number of occurrences

Examples:
index for *as·beir* 'say'   index for *téit* 'go'
239+90/243+90 = 0.987   15/130+3 = 0.112

The closest the index is to 1, the highest ratio, the higher the degree of transitivity. This scale reflects quite closely the likelihood of governing a genitive argument which corresponds to the direct object, and conversely to the subject, in Old Irish. This likelihood is reflected in the index for verbal nouns, that is the ratio of second and first argument genitives (third and fourth columns in Table 8 below, based on the data in the fourth columns of Tables 3, 4 and 5). The bold lines in Table 8 are meant to separate groups of verbs according to the broad classification reflected in Tables 3, 5 and 4 respectively, i.e. "well-behaved" fully transitive verbs, transitive verbs which may combine with genitives coding the first argument, and doubtfully or weakly transitive verbs. If the basic distinction transitive/intransitive applied as claimed in the literature (see Section 4), one would expect a clear polarization, such as, ideally, the highest index (1) for finite forms and, above all, for non-finite forms of transitive verbs, and the lowest (0) for both finite and non-finite forms of intransitive verbs.

Table 8: Transitivity scale based on transitivity indexes (frequency of accusative arguments and passives and frequency of genitives with verbal nouns corresponding to accusative arguments).

TRANSITIVITY INDEX (finite form)	VERBS	TRANSITIVITY INDEX (non-finite form)	VERBAL NOUNS
1	*ad·gládathar* 'address', *ad·gnin* 'recognize', *ad·cobra* 'desire', *ad·rími* 'count', *do·indnaig* 'bestow', *do·adbat* 'show', *do·ruimnethar* 'forget', *con·oscaigi* 'move'	1	accaldam, accobur, áram, cumscugud, dermat, taidbsiu, tindnacol, dul
0.99	*do·beir* 'give'	1	tabart
0.96	*gaibid* 'take'	1	gabál
0.95	*beirid* 'bring'	1	breth
0.94	*ro·finnadar* 'know'	1	fius

Table 8 (continued)

TRANSITIVITY INDEX (finite form)	VERBS	TRANSITIVITY INDEX (non-finite form)	VERBAL NOUNS
0.92	ad·cí 'see'	1	aicsiu
0.89	guidid 'ask'	1	guide
0.98	as·beir 'say'	0.89	epert
0.96	caraid 'love'	0.73	serc
0.88	do·moinethar 'think'	0[51]	toimtiu
0.87	for·cain 'teach'	0.6	forcetal
0.8	for·tét 'help'	0.28	fortacht
0.71	as·indet 'tell'	0.71	aisndís
0.67	do·luigi 'forgive'	0.84	dílgud
0.61	do·fich 'punish/avenge'	0.73	dígal
0.56	labraithir 'speak, talk'	0.71	labrad
0.4	do·icc 'come'	0.3	tíchtu
0.11	téit 'go'	0.17	techt
0	fris·gair 'answer'	0 (0.25?)[52]	frecrae

The divergent position in the scale of non-finite forms of *for·cain* (0.60 vs. 0.87) and *for·tét* (0.28 vs. 0.8) is related to the restrictions shown above in Section 5, that is, to the fact that their most frequent accusative arguments are infixed pronouns or heads of relative clauses (8/9 [taught person] and 7/8 infixed or relative for *for·tét*, see Table 6) and that their genitival arguments are mostly pronominal or *dé* 'of God' (see Table 7). The opposite inconsistency for *do·luigi* and *do·fich* is due, on the other hand, to the general choice of excluding occurrences not accompanied by any genitive, but with an overt argument: out of 29 occurrences of the verbal noun *dílgud* with an overt argument, 19 are accompanied by a genitive argument, while 7 are accompanied only by *do*+3-dat [forgiven person], 2 by a prepositional phrase expressing the forgiver (*ó*+1-dat) and 1 by an adjectival modifier (*dílgud díadae* 'divine forgiveness'); out of 96 occurrences of the verbal noun *dígal* with an overt argument, only 19 have a genitive argu-

---

[51] Only a single example occurs with the genitive; see footnote 32.
[52] See Section 4 about the doubtful status of 1 out of 4 occurrences of genitive phrases with *frecrae* (example 18).

ment, while most of them (69) are accompanied only or at least by *for*+3-dat [punished person]. The verbs *do·luigi* and *do·fich* are basically three-place predicates, and the animate participants corresponding to the microroles [forgiven person] and [punished person] surface as prepositional arguments (*do*+dat and *for*+acc respectively), which cannot be coded by a genitive with the verbal noun (see Section 4). Similarly, the verbal noun *frecrae* 'answer' is mostly accompanied only by a prepositional argument (*do*+2-dat, either [addressee], 6 instances, or [question], 3 instances), as noted above in Section 4, and less frequently by a genitive (4 instances). The verbal noun *toimtiu* 'thinking' governs a genitive argument in only one instance and is mostly complemented by a clause. The relatively high proportion of second argument genitives with the verbal noun *labrad* 'speak' is biased by the occurrence of 9 identical instances in Wb of the expression *labrad ilbélre* 'speak many tongues' (see footnote 45).

The behavior of suppletive-stem verbal nouns, i.e. *serc* 'love' to *caraid* and *dul* 'go' to *téit*, is somewhat independent from the corresponding finite verb constructions. In fact *dul* shows the highest index while *téit* a very low index, and *serc* shows a lower index than *caraid*. Regarding *serc*, however, it should be noted that the figures in Tables 5, 7 and 8 include 5 instances out of 23 of the compound *deserc* (see footnote 27), and are based on the interpretation of Wb 18b21 given in (33) below.

(33) *serc   dǽ   dúib=si   et   far=serc=si   do=dia*
     love.VN.NOM God.GEN to.2PL=2PL and your=love=2PL to=God.DAT
     'God's love for you and your love for God'
     (Wb 18b21)

This interpretation is explicitly given by Kavanagh (2001: 789) and reflects Stokes and Strachan's (1901: 618) translation in the standard edition of this manuscript ('God's love to you and your love to God'), but is in contrast to Thurneysen's (1946: 158, § 250.1) and Stüber's (2009a: 10) analyses, which view the genitives as objective genitives ('love for God from you and love for you from God'). Both analyses are possible, in principle, since the Old Irish preposition *do* can have dative meaning, marking recipients and beneficiaries, as in (3.a), (4.b), (15.b, c), (28) and (34), but is also a regular way to flag the first argument of a verbal noun ('by'), as in (15.d) and (35.a, b) (see Section 2.1, example (7); Stüber 2009b; see Lehmann 1988: 197 on "dative" subjects with verbal nouns).

(34) *furóil   serce   ho=pool   doib=som*
     abundance.NOM   love.VN.GEN   from=Paul   to.3PL=3PL
     'the abundance of love from Paul to them'
     (Wb 14d30)

(35) a. *ar=fortacht=ni   du=dia*
       our=help=1PL   to=God.DAT
       'that God would help us'
       (Ml 106d2)

(35) b. *ebert   do   domine   and*
       say.VN.NOM   to.3SG.M   there
       'that he says *domine* ['O Lord'] there'
       (Ml 35c27)

My preference for the first interpretation is based on the one hand on 4 occurrences in the same text (Wb) of a construction of *serc* with the possessive expressing the [loved person] but the preposition *la* (which commonly flags experiencers), rather than *do*, flagging the [lover], as in (36). The preposition *do*, on the contrary, flags the loved person with *serc* in Wb 14d30, (34) above, and Wb 12b26 (*seircc immircidi do dia* 'suitable love for God').

(36) *ni=sí   ar=sercc   less*
     NEG.COP.PRS.3SG=3SG.F   our=love.VN.NOM(F)   by.3SG.M
     'Not so is the love for us by him'
     (Wb 4b16)

This interpretation in my view also agrees with the expectation that, according the usual structure of the Glosses under scrutiny, the first part of a comment is more likely to be a closer translation of the Latin than the following expansion, and therefore that in this case the first part should be a closer translation of *caritas Dei* in the Latin text that the Irish glosses over, i.e. *Gratia Domini nostri, Iesu Christi, et caritas Dei, et communicatio sancti Spiritus, sit cum omnibus uobís* (2 Cor. XIII, 13).

If Thurneysen's and Stüber's interpretation is chosen, however, the genitives in (33) express the [loved person] and *do* flags the first argument [lover], according to the pattern in (35); in that case, the figures in Tables 5 and 7 should be revised accordingly, yielding a higher index for *serc* in Table 8, namely 0.82. If, moreover, instances of the compound *deṡerc* are excluded, the resulting index is 0.94.

The transitivity scale that emerges from Table 8 reflects different degrees of transitivity of Old Irish verbs and can be viewed as a transitivity cline (Malchukov 2015: 79; Haspelmath 2015: 142–144). The transitivity index can be used to arrange any other verb in the cline and, more generally, to establish the position of an Old Irish predicate with respect to the transitivity scales that have been proposed in the literature. However, the scale in Table 8 cannot be directly compared with cross-linguistic transitivity hierarchies such as Tsunoda's (1985) and Malchukov's (2005), and even with Haspelmath's (2015: 143) transitivity-prominence ranking of verb meanings, although it can be viewed as a transitivity ranking of verbs in a single language. The reasons are manyfold. First of all, the correlation of transitivity with the cross-linguistic semantic scales is confirmed by the frequency of transitive valency frames associated with each meaning across languages (Haspelmath 2015: 142–144) and with verb classes in a given language (Malchukov 2015: 74–89), but it does not imply that, in a given language, each verb, i.e. an individual lexeme, representing a class of meanings, is more transitive, in the sense defined here, than the verbs corresponding to the meanings on its right (or above it) in the scale. Presumably, all the verbs in Tables 3 and 5, that is, all verbs that have a transitivity index ≥ 0.50, would be classified as "transitive" for the purposes of the transitivity scales that arrange verbs into semantic scales or maps. Secondly, the sample of verbs in the scale in Table 8 was selected in order to test the relationship between finite and non-finite syntax, given the available data, and not in order to be representative of the distribution of frames with two-place predicates (see Section 2.2). This goal excluded experiential predicates which in Old Irish are expressed by complex predicates that involve the copula and a nominal predicate,[53] such as for example *is maith la* 'like' (see Section 3). On the other hand, this criterion led to include many three-place predicates, which may not be part of the benchmark to measure transitive encoding (Tsunoda 2015; Aldai and Wichmann 2018).

Allowing for these provisos, it can be observed that the indexes for the 15 Old Irish verbs whose meanings also feature in Haspelmath's (2015: 143) transitivity ranking are similar to the percentage of transitively encoded verbs crosslinguistically according to ValPaL data, as shown in (37), with the notable exception of some *verba dicendi* (*as·beir, ad·gládathar, labraithir*) and of *do·moinethar* 'think'.

(37)
Verb meaning	Old Irish Transitivity index	Transitivity Prominence (ValPaL)
'show'	1	1
'take'	0.96	1
'give/bestow'	0.99/1	0.98
'bring'	0.99	0.95
'say'	0.98	0.41
'talk (addressee/message)'	1/0.56	0.40

---

53 See Haspelmath and Hartmann (2015: 58-59) on these kinds of counterparts in ValPaL.

'recognize/know'	1/0.94	0.88
'see'	0.92	0.93
'ask for'	0.89	0.95
'think'	0.88	0.52
'help'	0.8	0.78
'tell'	0.71	0.78
'go'	0.11	0.05

Concerning *verba dicendi*, the observations by Lehmann (2015: 1581–1583) about different selections of the participants involved in situations of communication apply (and, in fact, to the four participants considered by Lehmann, i.e. speaker, addressee, message and topic, the code (language) should also be added): *as·beir* selects the message content and allows the addition of addressee (*fri*+acc) and topic (*de*+dat), *ad·gládathar* selects the addressee, while *labraithir* allows the addition of either the message or the language (direct object) or of the topic (*de*+dat), but apparently not of the addressee.

7 Summary and conclusions

This paper has tried to flesh out the details of the relationship between transitivity and argument structure in finite and non-finite clauses in Old Irish. Using a sample of 26 verbs, it has been shown that, although the generally held view that genitive arguments with non-finite forms of transitive verbs regularly flag the object (the argument which in finite clauses is in the accusative case) is confirmed in the vast majority of cases, in a significant number of instances this is not the case. Non-finite forms of transitive verbs (verbs which in finite forms occur with an accusative argument in more than 50% of instances) may combine with a so-called subjective genitive, i.e. an argument in the genitive which corresponds to the first argument (the argument in the nominative with finite forms), if it is a pronoun and/or its referent is high in the animacy hierarchy. In sum, rather than a simple overlap with the transitive/intransitive opposition, it turns out that the higher the frequency with which finite forms of a verb occur with an accusative argument, the higher is the likelihood that the genitive with non-finite forms codes the object.

To measure this likelihood through the "object argument frequency", a transitivity index is proposed, the ratio of occurrences, out of all the occurrences in finite form of a verb, of finite active forms with a direct object (accusative argument), i.e. in the protypical transitive construction, and of passive constructions which remove the nominative argument but not the accusative argument, i.e. in the canonical passive constructions. This index is then compared to the parallel index which measures the likelihood for the genitive argument of non-finite forms to map the same participant that with finite active forms occurs in the accusative and with finite passive forms in the nominative. Any verb which is not included in the present survey could be arranged in the resulting "transitivity scale".

The transitivity index is a theoretically simple but useful criterion to highlight transitivity patterns and measure transitivity for past varieties, for which we cannot rely on acceptability judgments. However, it can be used only indirectly to construct a transitivity hierarchy of verb meanings along the lines of Tsunoda (1985), Malchukov (2005) and Haspelmath (2015), that is, a hierarchy or implicational scale of transitivity that ranks verb meanings.

Abbreviations

Texts
Ml   The Milan Glosses on the Psalms (Stokes and Strachan 1901–1903, vol. I, pp. 7–483; Griffith 2013)
Sg   The St. Gall Glosses on Priscian (Stokes and Strachan 1901–1903, vol. II, pp. 49–224; Bauer 2015)
Wb   The Würzburg Glosses on the Pauline Epistles (Stokes and Strachan 1901–1903, vol. I, pp. 499–712)

Grammatical Glosses (not included in the Leipzig Glossing Rules)
COMPV   comparative
HAB   habitual
IMPF   imperfect (habitual past)
SUB   subordinate clause
VN   verbal noun

References

Aldai, Gontzal & Søren Wichmann. 2018. Statistical observations on hierarchies of transitivity. *Folia Linguistica* 52 (2). 249–281.
Bauer, Bernhard. 2015. *The online database of the Old Irish Priscian Glosses*. (downloaded from http://www.univie.ac.at/indogermanistik/priscian/ 30 June 2016).
Bisagni, Jacopo. 2013–2014. Prolegomena to the study of code-switching in the Old Irish glosses. *Peritia* 24–25. 1–58.

Bisang, Walter. 2016. Finiteness, nominalization, and information structure: Convergence and divergence. In Claudine Chamoreau & Zarina Estrada-Fernández (eds.), *Finiteness and nominalization*, 13–41. Amsterdam & Philadelphia: John Benjamins.

Comrie, Bernard. 1989. *Language universals and linguistic typology*, 2nd edn. Oxford: Blackwell.

Dahl, Östen & Kari Fraurud. 1996. Animacy in grammar and discourse. In Thorstein Fretheim & Jeanette K. Gundel (eds.), *Reference and referent accessibility*, 47–64. Amsterdam & Philadelphia: John Benjamins.

eDIL 2019. *Electronic Dictionary of the Irish Language*, edited by Gregory Toner, Máire Ní Mhaonaigh, Sharon Arbuthnot, Marie-Luise Theuerkauf & Dagmar Wodtko (accessible from www.dil.ie 2019).

García Castillero, Carlos. 2013. Old Irish tonic pronouns as extraclausal constituents. *Ériu* 63. 1–39.

García Castillero, Carlos. 2014. De-adjectival preverbs in the Old Irish verbal complex: A synchronic and diachronic study. *Zeitschrift für Celtische Philologie* 61. 57–100.

García Castillero, Carlos. 2015. On the history and prehistory of the Old Irish passive ending *-ar*. *Indogermanische Forschungen* 120 (1). 115–151.

Graver, Jenny. 2011. The syntax and development of the Old Irish Autonomous Verb. In Andrew Carnie (ed.), *Formal Approaches to Celtic Linguistics*, 41–63. Newcastle upon Tyne: Cambridge Scholars.

Griffith, Aaron. 2011. Old Irish pronouns: Agreement affixes vs. clitic arguments. In Andrew Carnie (ed.), *Formal Approaches to Celtic Linguistics*, 65–93. Newcastle upon Tyne: Cambridge Scholars.

Griffith, Aaron. 2013. *Dictionary and database of the Old Irish Glosses in the Milan MS Ambr. C301 inf.* (downloaded from http://www.univie.ac.at/ indogermanistick/milan_glosses.htm (accessed 3 November 2013).

Griffith, Aaron. 2015. Degrees of agreement in Old Irish. In Jürg Fleischer, Elisabeth Rieken & Paul Widmer (eds.), *Agreement from a diachronic perspective*, 165–187. Berlin & New York: Mouton De Gruyter.

Griffith, Aaron & Lash, Elliott. 2018. Coordinate subjects, expletives and the EPP in Early Irish. *Journal of Celtic Linguistics* 19. 87–156.

Hartmann, Iren, Martin Haspelmath & Bradley Taylor (eds.). 2013. *Valency Patterns Leipzig*. Leipzig: Max Planck Institute for Evolutionary Anthropology. http://valpal.info (accessed 7 May 2018).

Haspelmath, Martin. 2013. Argument indexing: A conceptual framework for the syntactic status of bound person forms. In Dik Bakker & Martin Haspelmath (eds.), *Languages across boundaries: Studies in memory of Anna Siewierska*, 197–226. Berlin & New York: Mouton de Gruyter.

Haspelmath, Martin. 2015. Transitivity prominence. In Andrej Malchukov & Bernard Comrie (eds.), 131–147.

Haspelmath, Martin & Iren Hartmann. 2015. Comparing verbal valency across languages. In Andrej Malchukov and Bernard Comrie (eds.), 41–71.

Kavanagh, Séamus. 2001. *A lexicon of the Old Irish Glosses in the Würzburg manuscript of the Epistles of St. Paul*. Herausgegeben von Dagmar S. Wodtko. Wien: Österreichische Akademie der Wissenschaften.

Kibrik, Andrej A. 2019. Rethinking agreement: Cognition-to-form mapping. *Cognitive Linguistics* 30 (1). 37–83.

Lash, Elliott. 2020. Transitivity and subject position in Old Irish. *Transactions of the Philological Society* 118 (1). 94–140.

Lehmann, Christian. 1988. Towards a typology of clause linkage. In John Haiman & Sandra A. Thompson (eds.), *Clause combining in grammar and discourse*, 181–225. Amsterdam & Philadelphia: John Benjamins.

Lehmann, Christian. 2015. Situation types, valency frames and operations. In Andrej Malchukov & Bernard Comrie (eds.), 1547–1595.

Le Mair, Esther, Cynthia A. Johnson, Michael Frotscher, Thórhallur Eythórsson & Jóhanna Barðdal. 2017. Position as a behavioural property of subjects. *Indogermanische Forschungen* 122 (1). 111–142.

Malchukov, Andrej. 2005. Case pattern splits, verb types and construction competition. In Mengistu Amberber & Helen de Hoop (eds.), *Competition and variation in natural languages: The case for case*, 73–118. Amsterdam: Elsevier.

Malchukov, Andrej. 2015. Valency classes and alternations: Parameters of variation. In Andrej Malchukov & Bernard Comrie (eds.), 73–130.

Malchukov, Andrej & and the Leipzig Valency Classes Project team. 2015. Leipzig questionnaire on valency classes. In Andrej Malchukov & Bernard Comrie (eds.): 27–39.

Malchukov, Andrej & Bernard Comrie (eds.). 2015. *Valency classes in the world's languages*. 2 Vols. Berlin & New York, Mouton De Gruyter.

Ó Gealbháin, Séamas. 1991. The double article and related features of genitive syntax in Old Irish and Middle Welsh. *Celtica* 22. 119–144.

Roma, Elisa. 2000. How subject pronouns spread in Irish: A diachronic study and synchronic account of the third person + pronoun pattern. *Ériu* 51. 107–157.

Roma, Elisa. 2007. Relativisation strategies in Insular Celtic languages. History and contacts with English. In Paolo Ramat & Elisa Roma (eds.), *Europe and the Mediterranean as linguistic areas. Convergencies from a historical and typological perspective*, 245–288. Amsterdam & Philadelphia: John Benjamins.

Roma, Elisa. 2009. How many definiteness markers per NP in Old Irish? Evidence from the Würzburg Glosses. In Stefan Zimmer (ed.), *Kelten am Rhein, Akten des dreizehnten Internationalen Keltologiekongresses/Proceedings of the Thirteenth International Congress of Celtic Studies* (Bonn, 23–27 July 2007). Zweiter Teil. *Philologie. Sprachen und Literaturen*, 223–231. Mainz am Rhein: Philipp von Zabern.

Roma, Elisa. 2014. Old Irish Noun Phrases: Data from the Milan Glosses and a hypothesis for the origin of the single article constraint. In Elisa Roma & David Stifter (eds.), *Linguistic and Philogical Studies in Early Irish*, 131–176. Lewinston N.Y. & Lampeter: Edwin Mellen.

Roma, Elisa. 2018. Old Irish pronominal objects and their use in verbal pro-forms. In Raimund Karl & Katharina Möller (eds.). *Proceedings of the Second European Symposium in Celtic Studies* (Bangor, 31 July-3 August 2017), 7–19. Hagen: Curach Bhán.

Roma, Elisa. 2020. Constructions and polysemy of three Old Irish verbs. *Celtica* 32. 15–26.

Sanfelici, Emanuela. 2014. Thoughts on Old and Middle Irish verbal nouns: The type DP *do*VN. In Elisa Roma & David Stifter (eds.), *Linguistic and philological studies in Early Irish*, 177–201. Lewinston N.Y. & Lampeter: Edwin Mellen.

Sanfelici, Emanuela. 2015. *Le subordinate non-finite in antico e medio irlandese: il tipo DP do*NV. München: LINCOM.

Sansò, Andrea. 2018. Explaining the diversity of antipassives: Formal grammar vs. (diachronic) typology. *Language and Linguistic Compass* 12 (6). https://onlinelibrary.wiley.com/doi/10.1111/lnc3.12277 (accessed 19 June18).

Stifter, David. 2009. Early Irish. In Martin J. Ball & Nicole Müller (eds.), *The Celtic languages*, 2nd edn, 55–116. London: Routledge.

Stokes, Whitley & John Strachan. 1901–1903. *Thesaurus Palaeohibernicus*. 2 Vols. Cambridge: Cambridge University Press (Repr. 1987, Dublin, Dublin Institute for Advanced Studies).

Stüber, Karin. 2007–2008. Subjektskodierung bei infiniten Komplementen in Altirischen: Syntax, Semantik, Pragmatik. *Die Sprache* 47 (2). 135–162.

Stüber, Karin. 2009a. *Der altirische do-Infinitiv – eine verkannte Kategorie*. Bremen: Hempen Verlag.

Stüber, Karin. 2009b. Zur Subjektskodierung mit *do* 'zu, für' beim altirischen Verbalnomen. *Die Sprache* 48. 241–246.

Stüber, Karin. 2017. Subjects of non-finite adverbial clauses in the Old Irish biblical Glosses. In Erich Poppe, Karin Stüber & Paul Widmer (eds.), *Referential Properties and their Impact on the Syntax of Insular Celtic Languages*, 201–216. Münster: Nodus.

Thurneysen, Rudolf (1946). *A grammar of Old Irish*. Translated from the German by Daniel A. Binchy & Osborn Bergin. Dublin: Dublin Institute for Advanced Studies.

Tsunoda, Tasaku (1985). Remarks on transitivity. *Journal of Linguistics* 21. 385–396.

Tsunoda, Tasaku (2015). The hierarchy of two-place predicates: its limitations and uses. In Andrej Malchukov and Bernard Comrie (eds.), 1597–1625.

Guglielmo Inglese
Anticausativization and basic valency orientation in Latin

Abstract: This paper focuses on basic valency orientation in Latin, based on the typology laid out by Nichols, Peterson and Barnes (2004). The data analyzed shows that Latin does not feature a strong orientation in its basic valency, due to a widespread use of suppletion. Only with inanimate verbs can one detect a certain tendency for intransitivization via either verbal voice or the use of the reflexive pronoun *se*. Other more marginal strategies include the use of causative verbal compounds with *-facio* 'make' and lability. In this respect, the Latin data sharply contrasts with current reconstructions of Proto-Indo-European (PIE) as a transitivizing language, as well as with modern Romance languages, which make extensive use of intransitivization and lability. Such an intermediate position of Latin is historically explained as reflecting the convergence of different factors, chiefly the loss of the PIE causative morphology and the functional extension of the inherited mediopassive voice. Once put in a diachronic perspective, the Latin data provides unique insights on the dynamics, the direction, and the timing of the drift from transitivization to intransitivization that notoriously characterizes the Indo-European languages of Europe (Comrie 2006).

Keywords: Latin, basic valency orientation, (anti)causativization, transitivity, middle and reflexive

---

Acknowledgments: Earlier versions of this paper have been presented at the conference *The shaping of transitivity and argument structure: theoretical and empirical perspectives* (University of Pavia, 25–27 October 2018) and at the *20th International Colloquium on Latin Linguistics* (Universidad de Las Palmas de Gran Canaria, 17–21 June 2019). I would like to thank the audience at both conferences, as well as the volume's editors and two anonymous reviewers, for their insightful comments on the paper. All remaining shortcomings are, of course, my own. This research has been funded by the Italian Ministry of Education (PRIN 2015, grant no. 20159M7X5P_002) and by FWO Research Foundation Flanders (grant no. 12T5320N).

Guglielmo Inglese, KU Leuven, e-mail: guglielmo.inglese@kuleuven.be

∂ Open Access. © 2021 Guglielmo Inglese, published by De Gruyter. [CC BY-NC-ND] This work is licensed under the Creative Commons Attribution-NonCommercial-NoDerivatives 4.0 International License.
https://doi.org/10.1515/9783110755657-005

1 Introduction

Anticausativization can be defined as the grammatical alternation whereby languages encode events that are conceived as brought about by an external volitional entity (e.g. *the boy broke the vase*) as opposed to ones that come about spontaneously (e.g. *the vase broke*). Syntactically, the anticausative alternation often implies a transitivity shift: externally caused events are predominantly encoded by transitive verbs whereas their spontaneous counterpart is mostly intransitive.

Languages may resort to various means of encoding the anticausative alternation. Specifically, Nichols, Peterson and Barnes (2004) proposed that languages can be typologized based on whether they preferably lexicalize spontaneous events or externally caused ones as morphologically basic verbs. Such a preference goes under the name of basic valency orientation. Drawing from the observation of the behavior of 18 verb pairs in a sample of 80 languages, Nichols, Peterson and Barnes (2004) pointed out that languages feature either oriented or non-oriented strategies, i.e. they may show a preference towards either overt transitivization or intransitivization or they may be indeterminate or neutral as to the orientation of the lexicalization pattern, in cases in which none of the members of the verb pair can be derived from the other (see Section 2.2).

In recent years, the study of basic valency orientation has become a topic of interest in Indo-European (IE) linguistics. Beside the modern IE languages originally featured in Nichols, Peterson and Barnes (2004), studies focusing on ancient IE languages have appeared as well, including Sanskrit (Kulikov 2009), Hittite (Luraghi 2012), Gothic (Ottósson 2013), Old Norse (Cennamo, Eythórsson and Barðdal 2015), Proto-Germanic (Plank and Lahiri 2015), Homeric Greek (Sausa 2016), and Old English (García García 2019). Generalizing over the findings of these studies, one can conclude that ancient IE languages display a system in which a number of derivational transitivizing strategies coexisted alongside the use of the active vs. middle inflectional voice opposition. This situation can to some extent be reconstructed for Proto-Indo-European (PIE) (cf. Luraghi 2019).

In this paper, I will make the case that our understanding of basic valency orientation in ancient IE languages and in PIE can still be profitably enhanced by the study of Latin. The study of valency phenomena and (anti)causativization strategies is not new to Latin linguistics (e.g. Cennamo, Eythórsson and Barðdal 2015; Pinkster 2015: Chap. 5), but a more general account of how these strategies relate to one another in terms of valency orientation is still missing. This work is devoted to such an investigation.

The paper is organized as follows. Section 2 discusses the theoretical background of the work: besides an overview on anticausativization (Section 2), the study by Nichols, Peterson and Barnes (2004) is presented in some detail (Section 3). Section 4 features a summary of previous research on basic valency in ancient IE languages and the reconstruction of the PIE basic valency. In Section 5, I turn to discussing the Latin data. After a brief note on the material employed and the methodology (Section 5.1), I illustrate the different strategies detected in Latin (Section 5.2) and then proceed to an *interim* summary of the data, with a focus on the individuation of Latin's basic valency (Section 5.3). The findings of Section 5 are then discussed from a diachronic perspective in Section 6, where I address the historical position of Latin with respect to PIE and Romance languages. Section 7 offers a conclusive summary of the paper's findings.

2 The anticausative alternation: a definition

As compared to other valency changing operations such as the passive and the reflexive, the notion of anticausativization constitutes a relatively recent acquisition in linguistics (cf. Nedjalkov and Sil'nickij 1969; Haspelmath 1987; on the relationship between the anticausative alternation and other voice phenomena see Kulikov 2010, 2013; Zúñiga and Kittilä 2019). Over the past 50 years, anticausativization has enjoyed the linguists' interest, and valency alternations of this type have been explored both within formal (see *i.a.* Schäfer 2008; Alexiadou 2010; Alexiadou, Anagnostopoulou and Schäfer 2015 with references) and functional/typological frameworks (see *i.a.* Nedjalkov and Sil'nickij 1969; Haspelmath 1987, 1993, 2016; Nichols, Peterson and Barnes 2004; Levin and Rappaport Hovav 1995; Zúñiga and Kittilä 2019: 40–52).[1]

With the term anticausative, scholars essentially refer to "the intransitive use of a transitive verb where the original inanimate object/P argument, the Undergoer, occurs as subject" (Cennamo, Eythórsson and Barðdal 2015: 679). As a result, the Agent is removed from the verb's semantic valency (Kulikov 2013: 272) and

---

[1] Besides causative and anticausative (cf. Haspelmath 2016), verb pairs that undergo the (anti) causative alternations also go under the name of causative vs. inchoative (e.g. Borer 1991; Haspelmath 1993), induced vs. plain (Nichols, Peterson and Barnes 2004), causal vs. non-causal (Haspelmath *et al.* 2014), causative vs. non-causative (Grüntal and Nichols 2016). Note that the terms causative and anticausative have also been employed to refer to the overtly marked member of a morphological opposition (cf. Haspelmath 2016: 37). In this paper, I use these terms in the semantic sense, without any implication as to the morphological markedness of individual strategies.

the whole situation is presented as coming about spontaneously (Haspelmath 1993: 90). From a syntactic standpoint, anticausativization has been described as an intransitivizing strategy, as it entails a change in transitivity (see also Alexiadou, Anagnostopoulou and Schäfer 2015). Causative events typically feature an Agent and a Patient participants and are therefore prototypically transitive (Hopper and Thompson 1980; Næss 2007). By contrast, spontaneous events tend to be intransitive, as their event frame features one Patient participant only.

A textbook example of the semantics of the anticausative alternation is the use of the English verb *break*, as in (1a-b):

(1) a. *The boy **broke** the vase*   CAUSATIVE
    b. *The vase **broke***   ANTICAUSATIVE

There exists a number of well-known constraints on the classes of verbs that may participate in the anticausative alternation (see Cennamo, Eythórsson and Barðdal 2015: 680–681; Alexiadou, Anagnostopoulou and Schäfer 2015: 20–23, 52–56). Transitive verbs that cannot undergo anticausativization include (i) those featuring agent-oriented meaning components (Haspelmath 1987: 12), i.e. those verbs that lexicalize the manner component (Haspelmath 1993: 94; Levin and Rappaport Hovav 2005: 11; Rappaport Hovav and Levin 2010) and (ii) verbs that lexicalize a specified causer (Koontz-Garboden 2009: 80–86). In addition, languages show restrictions as to the aspectual classes of predicates that enter the anticausative alternation (Cennamo 2012; Cennamo, Eythórsson and Barðdal 2015), with telic change-of-state events constituting the core of anticausative verbs cross linguistically (Alexiadou, Anagnostopoulou and Schäfer 2015: 53).[2]

A number of useful syntactic tests have been devised, especially in formal frameworks, to individuate anticausative constructions and keep them distinct from closely related constructions such as passives (see Alexiadou, Anagnostopoulou and Schäfer 2015: 20–23, 36–44). Anticausatives cannot occur with Agent phrases (e.g. **the vase broke by the boy*) nor with agentive adverbs such as *deliberately*. On the other hand, they are compatible with the expression of the

---

[2] Anticausatives have often been equated with unaccusatives in Levin and Rappaport Hovav's (1995) terms (see e.g. Haspelmath 2016), on the ground that both types of verbs essentially refer to uncontrolled events undergone by an affected Patient. However, the two notions are not coextensive. The class of anticausatives only includes those verbs that that are opposed to a causative counterpart in a transitivity alternation, while on the contrary lexical unaccusatives may lack a corresponding causative counterpart (see further Alexiadou, Anagnostopoulou and Schäfer 2015: 80–96).

cause component, i.e. with *from*-phrases (e.g. *the ice melted from heat*), and they license adverbials that underscore the spontaneity of the process such as *by itself*. As discussed by Gianollo (2014: 980–981), these criteria also apply to anticausatives in Latin.

3 Basic valency between lexical typology and the anticausative alternation

Anticausativization was first explored by scholars interested in how verbal valency and argument structure can be manipulated. As such, it remains an essentially (morpho)syntactic notion. By contrast, the notion of basic valency as proposed by Nichols, Peterson and Barnes (2004) has been elaborated within the framework of lexical typology. Specifically, the main interest of Nichols, Peterson and Barnes (2004) is how languages pattern with respect to the lexicalization of semantically non-causative, i.e. plain, verbs as opposed to semantically causative (induced) ones (cf. Nedjalkov 1969; Nichols 1982; Haspelmath 1993; Nichols, Peterson and Barnes 2004; Comrie 2006; Cysouw 2010; see also Luraghi and Mertyris, this volume).

Nichols, Peterson and Barnes (2004) argue that languages show preferences for the lexicalization of either plain or induced verbs as morphologically more basic and can be accordingly assigned a basic valency orientation, i.e. the "valence orientation of their entire verbal lexicon" (Plank and Lahiri 2015: 3). The data for Nichols, Peterson and Barnes (2004) study consists in 18 verb pairs in a sample of 80 languages (see below on the criteria behind the data collection).[3] The meanings are selected to maximize semantic sparseness, and include both animate and inanimate verbs, that is, verbs that "have a varying degree of agency and volition on the part of an animate S/O" (Nichols, Peterson and Barnes 2004: 155), e.g. *eat* and *hide*, and verbs that can be understood as having "varying degrees of independence, resistance to force, etc. on the part of an inanimate S/O" (Nichols, Peterson and Barnes 2004: 156), e.g. *boil* and *break*.

The possible types of morphosyntactic correspondence within verb pairs are summarized in Table 1. I return in more detail to these correspondence types in Section 5 when discussing the Latin data.

---

[3] It should be remarked that Nichols, Peterson and Barnes (2004) is not simply a study on (anti)causativization strategies, since the verbs that they investigate do not entirely overlap with verbs that commonly undergo the anticausative alternation (cf. Haspelmath 1993) and include a number of verbs with animate S/O participants such as *eat* and *learn*.

Table 1: Types of correspondence (adapted from Nichols, Peterson and Barnes 2004: 159–160).

Language	Verb pair		Type of correspondence
	Plain	Induced	
Hittite	ze- 'cook (intr.)'	za-nu- 'cook (tr.)'	AUGMENTATION
Russian	serdit'-sja 'be/get angry'	serdit' 'make angry'	REDUCTION
Siberian Yupik	aghagh-nga- 'hang (intr.)'	aghagh-te- 'hang (tr.)'	DOUBLE DERIVATION
Hausa	yi dariya 'laugh'	ba dariya 'make laugh'	AUXILIARY CHANGE
Lai	ʔa-thin phaaŋ 'be afraid'	ʔa-thin phaʔn 'frighten'	ABLAUT
W. Armenian	var.i- 'burn' (intr.)	var.e- 'burn (tr.)'	CONJUGATION CLASS CHANGE
English	*die*	*kill*	SUPPLETION
English	*break*	*break*	LABILITY

Generalizing over their findings, Nichols, Peterson and Barnes (2004: 150) propose that "languages can be typologized into a few broad groups". The major distinction is that into oriented and non-oriented languages.

Oriented languages show a clear orientation in their basic valency. They can be distinguished into transitivizing and intransitivizing languages, based on whether they preferably lexicalize plain verbs as basic as compared to morphologically more complex induced ones (AUGMENTATION), or *vice versa* (REDUCTION). An example of a transitivizing language is Hittite, where one finds pairs such as plain *ze-* 'cook (intr.)' vs. induced *za-nu-* 'cook (tr.)'. By contrast, Russian constitutes a good instance of an intransitivizing language, since it features the extensive use of the intransitivizing reflexive marker *-sja*, as in e.g. plain *serdit'-sja* 'be(come) angry' vs. induced *serdit'* 'make angry'.

Non-oriented languages are characterized by the fact that none of the pair members is morphologically more complex (and derived) from the other. Non-oriented languages can be further divided into neutral and indeterminate ones. In neutral languages, both members of the pair equally feature an overt morphological exponent. In these languages, double derivation, auxiliary change, and ablaut are the preferred strategies. An example is Siberian Yupik, where the plain and the induced verbs are likewise marked with a dedicated derivational morpheme, e.g. *aghagh-nga-* 'hang (intr.)' and *aghagh-te-* 'hang (tr.)'. By contrast, in indeterminate languages both members of the pair are likewise unmarked. Strategies that fall within this group are suppletion, conjugation class change, and lability. The behavior of English *break* in (1) is a typical example of lability.

4 Basic valency orientation in ancient Indo-European languages

In recent years, the study of basic valency has become a topic of renewed interest in IE linguistics. The language sample employed by Nichols, Peterson and Barnes (2004) already included a number of modern IE languages. Based on this data, the authors detected a pattern of areal distribution, whereby modern western IE languages tend to be intransitivizing (e.g. Russian, Modern Greek, German; but see Plank and Lahiri 2015 for a reassessment of German), while modern eastern IE languages tend to be transitivizing (Hindi, West Armenian).

The picture has been further enriched by data from ancient IE languages. Studies that closely follow Nichols, Peterson and Barnes (2004) are Luraghi (2012) on Hittite and Sausa (2016) on Homeric Greek (see also Luraghi and Mertyris, this volume, on the development of basic valency in the history of Greek). These two languages offer a contrasting picture. According to Sausa (2016), Homeric Greek is largely intransitivizing, as it employs active vs. middle voice alternation for 11 out of the 18 verb pairs under examination, especially for inanimate verbs, e.g. active *kaí-ō* 'burn (tr.)' vs. middle *kaí-omai* 'burn (intr.)'. Voice alternation is also attested in Hittite as a possible strategy (Luraghi 2012), e.g. active *duwarn-i* 'break (tr.)' vs. middle *duwarna-ttari* 'break (intr.)', but it remains rather marginal as compared to the by far more frequent use of causative derivational morphology, e.g. *ze-* 'cook (intr.)' vs. *za-nu-* 'cook (tr.)'. As a result, Hittite can best be described as transitivizing.

If one broadens the observation to other ancient IE languages, it turns out that traces of transitivization can be singled out in several other branches. In Germanic, transitivization seems to be the most widespread and older pattern, and there are good reasons to reconstruct Proto-Germanic as transitivizing. As pointed out by Ottósson (2013), in Gothic causativization through the suffix *-ja-* is older than intransitivizing derivation through *-na-* (see also Zanchi and Tarsi, this volume). Transitivization remains a major trend in Modern German. As discussed by Plank and Lahiri (2015) ablauting verbs of the type *sitzen* 'sit' vs. *setzen* 'set' should be taken as instantiating a transitivization pattern. In Modern English lability is the predominant pattern. However, traces of an earlier causative pattern can still be detected in Old English, where one still finds *ja*-causatives, as in *rīsan* 'rise' vs. *rǣran* 'raise' (cf. van Gelderen 2011; García García 2019). Indo-Aryan languages also offer evidence for transitivizing suffixes (e.g. *-aya-*) being the most widespread pattern, with voice alternation playing a much more limited role (thus *i.a.* Lazzeroni 2004, 2009; Kulikov 2009).

More controversial is the reconstruction of the basic valency orientation of the proto-language. In an earlier paper, Nichols (1982) reconstructed PIE as mostly intransitivizing. The evidence from early IE languages surveyed in this section however shows that this view is untenable. In fact, the comparative data points towards a different scenario, in which transitivization via causative affixes was largely predominant with all verb types (see Covini 2017). Voice alternation, which at this stage may better be regarded as an indeterminate strategy of the conjugation class change type (see Luraghi and Mertyris, this volume, for discussion), played a marginal role with change-of-state verbs only (Comrie 2006: 315; Plank and Lahiri 2015; Luraghi 2019).

5 Basic valency orientation in Latin

In the ongoing debate on basic valency in (P)IE, Latin has virtually been given no attention. In Latin linguistics, there is already ample scholarship on the topics of valency (cf. Lehmann 2002), causativization (cf. Hoffmann 2016; Lehmann 2016; cf. also papers in Bortolussi and Lecaudé 2014) and anticausativization strategies (cf. Gianollo 2014; Cennamo, Eythórsson and Barðdal 2015; Pinkster 2015: Chap. 5). However, a comprehensive account of these different phenomena within the framework of basic valency orientation is still lacking. In the following sections, I apply the methodology laid out in Nichols, Peterson and Barnes (2004) to determine the basic valency of the Latin verbal lexicon and its orientation.

5.1 Data and methodology

The data for this study comes from 24 meanings selected based on the updated guidelines in Nichols (2017). Two are novelties as compared to the original study by Nichols, Peterson and Barnes (2004). First, six new meaning pairs are taken into account (animate: *run, wake up, fall asleep*; inanimate: *shine, shake, roar*). Second, plain verbs are distinguished into continuous and bounded. This is a coarse classification employed by Nichols (2017) to refer to actionality distinctions of verbs into atelic (stative/durative) and telic (change-of-state, achievements, punctual). This is an important methodological point, since aspectual differences were disregarded in the original study (Nichols, Peterson and Barnes 2004: 156–157). However, as discussed by Luraghi (2012; see also Cennamo, Eythórsson and Barðdal 2015), taking into account both atelic and telic plain verbs may shed light on aspectual constraints on the realization of the alternation. Following Nichols, Peterson and

Barnes (2004), I do not take into consideration analytic causative constructions, unless a causative periphrasis is the only way to express the induced member of a given verb pair (see Section 5.2.1). This means that analytic causative constructions, which are numerous and of different types in Latin, fall out of the scope of this study and will not be systematically discussed (see Simone and Cerbasi 2001; Brucale and Mocciaro 2016; Hoffman 2016: 45–60; Lehmann 2016).

Based on the meaning list in Nichols (2017), the Latin verb pairs under study have been manually retrieved from standard dictionaries (Lewis and Short 1879; Glare 2012; the selection is restricted to verbs attested in Early and Classical Latin sources).

Data selection poses a significant methodological challenge. In Nichols, Peterson and Barnes (2004), verbs pairs were either elicited from speakers or retrieved from dictionaries. Unfortunately, Latin being a dead language, speakers' intuition cannot be used to assess the basicness of nearly synonymous verbs for a given meaning slot. This is especially a problem in Latin, where there is an abundance of equally plausible basic lexemes, partly due to the much larger corpus size as compared to e.g. Hittite.

This is an issue because the choice of the basic verb for a given meaning slot is decisive in the individuation of the correspondence pattern, thereby affecting the overall assessment of the basic valency and its orientation. Let us consider two instructive examples. For the causative meaning 'kill', possible Latin candidates are the verbs *neco*, *occido*, *caedo*, and *interficio*. In this case, the choice does not influence the resulting correspondence type within the pair, since irrespective of the induced verb, the correspondence with plain *morior* 'die' is consistently one of suppletion. This is, however, not always the case. Consider the meaning 'fall'. For this pair, the induced slot is assigned to *demitto* 'let fall'. For the plain counterpart two options are available: if one opts for *cado* 'fall' the resulting correspondence is one of suppletion, whereas in case *demittor* 'fall' is selected (or reflexive *se demittere*, see below), the correspondence is one of reduction.

It is thus of paramount importance to develop a consistent set of criteria for the individuation of the basic verbs for each meaning slot. According to van Gelderen (2011) "the choice of the basic variant is subjective". However, this may result in a much too biased data selection. I believe that some more principled criteria can be combined to assess the basicness of individual lexemes (see similar remarks in Luraghi 2012; Sausa 2016; Zanchi and Tarsi, this volume). Possible criteria include frequency, morphological complexity, and the verbs' semantics.

Frequency may constitute a good indicator of basicness. For example, for the meaning 'laugh', *rideo* is preferred over *cachinno* on account of its much higher frequency (97 vs. 7 tokens, data from Delatte *et al.* 1981). The basic insight is that high frequency is a proxy for verbs' entrenchment in the speakers' lexicon as the default expression for a given meaning (e.g. Bybee 2007). Morphological complexity is also a helpful parameter, because simpler forms are often more basic than more complex (prefixed) ones. This is why, for instance, for 'fall' the plain simple verb *cado* is preferred to *de-cido* and *con-cido*. In addition, the verbs' lexical semantics is another important diagnostic criterion. Verbs that are primarily associated with a given meaning are preferred over those that express that meaning only secondarily and/or metaphorically. For example, *morior* 'die' is preferred to *obeo* 'go against > die', *doceo* 'teach' is preferred to *trado* 'transmit > teach', and *neco* 'kill' is preferred to *caedo* 'cut off > kill'. Verbs whose semantics is either too specific or too generic are also avoided. This is the case for verbs that lexicalize a more specific manner/instrument component, as e.g. *trucido* 'butcher', *manduco* 'chew', *coquo* 'cook', which are excluded in favor of less specific *neco* 'kill', *edo* 'eat', and *ferveo* 'boil', respectively. I have also avoided verbs that lexicalize much too generic events. On this premise, *quatio* is preferred to *agito* for 'shake' because the latter is also used with reference to more generic induced motion events and also in a metaphorical sense. Similar considerations hold for *luceo*, preferred over *fulgeo* for 'shine', because the latter is not restricted to denoting the emission of light but is more generally used to express brightness and visibility.

By carefully weighing in and combining these criteria, I have arrived at the individuation of the Latin verb pairs reported in Table 2. Verbs are divided into those with typically animate vs. inanimate S/Os.

Table 2: Latin verb pairs (based on Nichols 2017).

	ANIMATE S/O			
MEANING	**PLAIN (ATELIC)**[4]	**PLAIN (TELIC)**	**INDUCED**	**CORRESPONDENCE**
1 laugh	rideo	-	[risum moveo]	periphrasis
2 die, be dead	mortuus	morior	neco	suppletion
3 sit down, be sitting	sedeo	consīdo	pono	suppletion
4 eat (up)	edo	comedo	alo	suppletion
5 know, learn	scio	disco	doceo	suppletion
6 see, catch sight	video		monstro	suppletion
7 be(come) angry	irascor		irrito	suppletion
8 fear, get scared	metuo	horresco	terreo	suppletion

---

4 Note that some verbs may have both an atelic and a telic interpretation, e.g. *lateo* 'be hidden, go into hiding'. For some meanings, there is no finite verb form expressing the atelic spontaneous event: in this case the corresponding adjective (e.g. *siccus* 'dry') or resultative participle (e.g. *mortuus* 'dead', *casus* 'fallen') is given. See further Section 5.3.

Table 2 (contiuned)

MEANING	PLAIN (ATELIC)	PLAIN (TELIC)	INDUCED	CORRESPONDENCE
9 hide, go into hiding	lateo		celo	suppletion
19 awake, wake up	vigilo	expergiscor	excito (e somno)	suppletion
20 asleep, fall asleep	dormio	obdormi(sc)o	sopio	suppletion
21 run	curro	accurro	incito	suppletion
INANIMATE S/O				
10 (come to) boil	ferveo	fervesco	fervefacio	double der./aug.
11 burn, catch fire	ardeo	ardesco	uro	suppletion
12 be broken, break	fractus	frangor/se frangere	frango	voice/reduction[5]
13 be open, open	pateo	aperior/se aperire	aperio	voice/reduction
14 dry (up)	siccus	siccor	sicco	voice
15 be(come) straight	rectus	[corrigor]	corrigo	[voice]
16 hang	pendeo	-	(sus)pendo	suppletion[6]
17 turn over	versus	vertor/se verto	verto	voice/reduction
18 fall	casus	cado	demitto	suppletion
22 shine, light up	luceo	lucesco	accendo	suppletion
23 shake, tramble	tremo	tremesco (poetic)	quatio	suppletion
24 roar, rattle	(con)crepo		(con)crepo	lability

5.2 Latin verb pairs: types of correspondences

As the data in Table 2 shows, in Latin the verb pairs under scrutiny attest to different types of correspondence. In the reminder of this section, I will take a closer look at each correspondence type and its properties.

---

[5] On the reasons to treat reflexivization and voice alternation as occupying the same slot, e.g. *frangor/se frangere* 'break (intr.)' see Section 5.2.3.
[6] Historically, *pendo* 'weigh, hang' and *pendeo* 'be hanging' are derived from the same PIE root *(s)pend-* 'spin' (cf. de Vaan 2008 *s.v.*). The former reflects a simple thematic formation *(s)pend-e/o-* whereas the latter is formed through the addition of the stative suffix *-eh1-*, so that the two verbs belong to two different conjugation classes (cf. also *iacēre* 'lie' vs. *iacere* 'cast', *candēre* 'shine' vs. *ac-cendere* 'light up', Weiss 2011: 404). However, since conjugation class change is not a productive pattern of derivation in Latin, the correspondence between these two can be best regarded synchronically as one of suppletion (see more below in sec. 5.2.2), or better, as partial suppletion (cf. Nichols, Peterson and Barnes 2004: 159).

5.2.1 Verbal periphrases

In the case of verbal periphrases, there is no simple verb that lexicalizes the meaning at hand, and either the spontaneous or the causative event is encoded by an analytic construction. This type of correspondence is instantiated in my data only for the meaning 'laugh'. As shown in example (2a-b), the plain verb is the simple verb *rideo*, whereas the induced counterpart is expressed by the analytic construction *risum movere* 'move to laughter'.

(2) a. **risi**   te   hodie multum
    laugh.PST.1SG 2SG.ACC today much
    'I've laughed a good deal at you today.' (Plaut. *Stich.* 1, 3, 89)
  b. *est   plane   oratoris   **movere**   **risum***
     be.PRS.3SG clearly orator.GEN move.PRS.INF laughter.ACC
     'The orator is clearly allowed to move to laughter.' (Cic. *De Or.* 2, 236)

A preference for a periphrastic construction for the causative meaning 'make laugh' is unsurprising. The same pattern is also attested in Homeric Greek (*geláō* 'laugh' vs. *ephéēke gelásai* 'lead to laugh' [*Od.* 14.465], Sausa 2016: 216) and reflects a general tendency for the event of laughing to be more typically encoded as spontaneous (cf. Haspelmath 1993: 105). Since I follow here Nichols, Peterson and Barnes (2004) in considering only basic lexemes, the use of the periphrasis *risum movere* for 'make laugh' should not be strictly speaking included among possible correspondence types.

5.2.2 Suppletion

In suppletive pairs, both members of the verb pair are lexicalized by two different equally basic and unrelated lexemes (cf. Hoffmann 2016: 40–42, who speaks of lexical causatives for basic active verbs with causative semantics). The pattern is exemplified by the pair *morior* 'die' ~ *neco* 'kill', as in (3b), where the occurrence of the Cause *fame* 'of hunger' makes it particularly clear that in this context *neco* is used with the meaning 'let die'.

(3) a. *ut   fame   senatores   quinque **morerentur***
       so_that hunger.ABL senator.NOM.PL five   die.SBJV.IMPF.MID.3PL
       'So that five senators died of hunger.' (Cic. *Att.* 6, 1, 6)

b. qui   plebem   fame   **necaret**
    REL.NOM   people.ACC hunger.ABL   kill.SBJV.IMPF.3SG
    '(Who was the one) who would let people die of hunger.' (Cic. Q. Fr. 2, 3, 2)

It is worth noticing that with the meaning 'die' suppletion is a typologically widespread pattern (Haspelmath 1993: 106) and is also commonly attested in other ancient IE languages, including Hittite (*āk-ⁱ* 'die' vs. *kuen-ᶻⁱ* 'kill') and Ancient Greek (*thnḗskō* 'die' vs. *kteínō* 'kill'). As the data in Table 2 shows, Latin synchronically attests to a surprisingly high number of suppletive pairs, especially when compared to Hittite and Ancient Greek. However, as I discuss in Section 6, there is evidence that at least some of these pairs historically reflect an earlier transitivizing pattern.

5.2.3 Voice alternation and reduction

Besides suppletion, the second most frequent pattern is voice alternation/reduction. This is an essentially intransitivizing pattern, whereby the plain verb is derived from the induced one either by means of the active/middle voice alternation, by means of the so-called *r*-endings, or through the use of the reflexive pronoun *se* (see Flobert 1975; Feltenius 1977; Gianollo 2014; Cennamo, Eythórsson and Barðdal 2015; Pinkster 2015: Chap. 5). As an example of this pattern, consider the correspondence between induced transitive *vertit* 'turns (that side)' in (4) and plain intransitive *vertitur* 'turns' and *se vertunt* 'turned' in (5a) and (5b), respectively.

(4)   eam   partem (...) ad   speciem   **vertit**   nobis
      DEM.ACC   part.ACC   to   sight.ACC   turn.PRS.3SG   1PL.DAT
      '(The moon) turns that side to our sight.' (Lucr. 5, 724)

(5) a. **vertitur**   interea   caelum
        turn.PRS.MID.3SG   meanwhile   sky.NOM
        'In the meanwhile, the sky turns (westward).' (Verg. A. 2, 250)
    b. Pompeiani   **se**   **verterunt**   et   loco   cesserunt
        of_P.NOM.PL   REFL   turn.PST.3PL   and   place.ABL   leave.PST.3PL
        'The followers of Pompeo turned around and left the place.'
        (Caes. B. C. 3, 51)

As comparison between (5a) and (5b) shows, the *r*-inflection and reflexive *se* can be regarded as functionally equivalent strategies, as they both serve the purpose of deriving the plain counterpart from the basic induced verbs.

Morphologically, the use of the reflexive pronoun is clearly a reduction strategy, since the plain verb receives additional marking as compared to the basic induced one, as in the case of Russian *serdit'-sja* 'be/get angry' ~ *serdit'* 'make angry' in Table 1. The status of voice alternation is less straightforward. There is disagreement as to whether voice alternation in IE languages should be regarded either as an indeterminate or as a reduction strategy (cf. Luraghi 2019 with references). In some IE languages, such as Hittite, and possibly in PIE, voice alternation should be regarded as an indeterminate strategy, since the alternation between the active and the middle inflection essentially conforms to the pattern of conjugation class change as defined by Nichols, Peterson and Barnes (2004: 159) (thus convincingly Luraghi 2012, 2019). However, as discussed by Sausa (2016: 211–212) the notion of conjugation class change does not entirely fit the pattern of voice alternation of IE languages such as Ancient Greek, in which the middle voice can be regarded as a marked voice category and as instantiating an intransitivizing pattern (a similar point is made by Luraghi and Mertyris, this volume).

Similar considerations can profitably be extended to Latin and I regard the *r*-inflection as a reduction/intransitivization strategy for a number of reasons. Firstly, the *r*-inflection is overall systematically used for intransitivization in opposition to the active inflection, chiefly in passive function, to the effect that voice is fully integrated in the verbal paradigm as an inflectional category (cf. Clackson and Horrocks 2011: 25–26; Pinkster 2015: 236–258). Secondly, the *r*-inflection is also morphologically more complex than the active, since the inflectional set is phonologically heavier in most endings, e.g. *am-o* vs. *am-o-r*, *am-a-s* vs. *am-a-ris*, *am-a-t* vs. *am-a-tur*. Moreover, as also remarked by Nichols, Peterson and Barnes (2004: 175–176), the *r*-inflection presents a number of oddities (e.g. deponent and semi-deponent verbs) that make it less simple and regular than the active inflection. In this respect, the *r*-paradigm can be regarded as inflectionally marked as opposed to the unmarked active inflection (cf. Croft 2003: 92).

A closer look at the data reveals that reduction and voice alternation are also attested as marginal strategies for more verbs than the ones reported in Table 2. A few examples will serve to illustrate this point. For the meaning 'hide', besides *celo*, other possible candidates for the induced verb are also *abdo* and *condo*, which both attest to intransitivizing *se*-reflexive forms. For the induced verb *demitto* 'let fall', the most basic plain counterpart is the simple verb *cedo*. However, for this verb both intransitivizing *demittor* and *se demittere* are marginally attested. Similarly, transitive *uro* 'burn' is also paired with intransitivizing *uror*, which however shows a much narrower distribution (in terms of token frequency, see Delatte *et al.* 1981) as compared to simple *ardeo* 'burn (intr.)'. Intransitivization is not limited to basic induced verbs, but it is occasionally attested also for augmented induced verbs, as in the case of *sese fervefaciunt* in (6), which remains however isolated as compared to the much more frequent basic plain verb *ferveo* 'boil (intr.)'.

(6) *eaeps*e   **sese**   *patinae*   ***fervefaciunt***
    same.NOM.PL.F   REFL   dish(F).NOM.PL   make_boil.PRS.3PL
    'The very dishes become warm (by themselves).' (Plaut. *Ps.* 3, 2, 44)

When compared to induced verbs, both the *r*-inflection and reflexive *se* can be likewise characterized as intransitivizing strategies and are thus equivalent for the purpose of determining basic valency. This is not to say that the two are fully overlapping in their functional domain. As pointed out by several scholars, there exist a number of differences between the two, and specific motivations can be detected for the choice of one strategy over the other with individual verbs (see Gianollo 2014; Cennamo, Eythórsson and Barðdal 2015 for discussion with extensive references).

To begin with, the *r*-inflection and *se*-reflexives historically represent two different layers of intransitivization. Forms of the *r*-inflection constitute the older layer, as they ultimately continue the inherited PIE middle voice inflection (cf. Weiss 2011: 387–391). In Latin, the *r*-inflection shows a complex distribution. On the one hand, it is used in passive and anticausative function in the *infectum* system. On the other hand, it includes a number of deponents or *media tantum*, i.e. verbs that are inflected in the middle only (on these see esp. Gianollo 2005, 2010). The original function of the middle voice in PIE is a matter of ongoing debate, but there is a general consensus that anticausativization may have featured among the earliest functions, with the passive being fully developed in the daughter languages only (cf. Inglese 2020; Luraghi, Inglese and Kölligan forthc. with references).

The reflexive pronoun *se* is also of PIE inheritance, as it continues the **se-/ swe-* pronominal stem. Earlier accounts reconstruct a reflexive function for this form as early as in PIE (e.g. Brugmann and Delbrück 1893–1916). However, more recent studies have pointed out that the stem **se-* was possibly anaphoric to begin with, and that it only developed a reflexive function at a subsequent stage (cf. Mendoza 1984; Petit 1999; Puddu 2005, 2007; Dunkel 2014: 751–762; Viti 2015: 94–96 with references). Out of this core reflexive function, in Latin the pronoun *se* further developed an anticausative function, as a first step in its broader development as a general marker of intransitivization/unaccusativity in Romance languages (cf. Kemmer 1993; Cennamo 1993, 2016).

Also owing to their different origin, it is unsurprising that the *r*-inflection and *se*-reflexives do not entirely overlap in their distribution in Early and Classical Latin. As discussed by Cennamo, Eythórsson and Barðdal (2015), the two main parameters that account for the distribution of *r*-forms and *se*-reflexives are the verb's lexical aspect and the subject's agency. Concerning the former, *r*-forms are used in anticausative function with all verb classes that allow the alternation, including atelic verbs, e.g. *volvere* 'roll, flow' (note that this was unlikely the PIE situation, as the anticausative function of the middle was possibly in origin confined to spontaneous change-of-state events, cf. Luraghi 2012, 2019). *Se*-reflexives instead strongly prefer telic predicates. As to agency, *r*-forms are preferred when the subject participant lacks control over the event, while *se*-reflexives correlate with a certain degree of agency/control of the subject. This distinction can be neatly illustrated by comparing (5a) and (5b). In (5a), the middle form *vertitur* 'turns' refers to an uncontrolled event of physical motion undergone by the inanimate subject *caelum* 'sky', whereas in (5b) the form *se verterunt* 'they turned' clearly refers to a controlled event initiated by the animate participant *Pompeiani* 'the followers of Pompeo'. It must be stressed that these are tendencies at best, since *se*-reflexives in anticausative function can also occur with inanimate non-controlling subjects, as in the case of *patinae* 'dishes' in (6). Moreover, it should be added that the reflexive pattern in anticausative function is mostly confined to technical works. It only becomes widespread in other textual types in Late Latin (Cennamo, Eythórsson and Barðdal 2015: 686), when it also loses its connection with telic predicates (thus Gianollo 2014).

The distribution outlined so far is progressively altered in Late Latin, when the two constructions become fully equivalent. At this stage, one also witnesses the rise of labile verbs, owing to a general restructuring of the voice system that ultimately led to the rise of the Romance voice system (Gianollo 2014; Cennamo, Eythórsson and Barðdal 2015).

5.2.4 Augmentation and double derivation

The third pattern under analysis is noteworthy both in its synchronic status and in its diachronic background. In this case, the alternation concerns both verbal aspect and transitivity. Verbs that instantiate this pattern feature a threefold distinction between a basic plain stative verb, a plain change-of-state verb in *-sc-*, and an induced counterpart in *-facio*. This pattern is exemplified by the triplet *ferveo ~ fervesco ~ fervefacio* in (7):

(7) a. **fervit** aqua et **fervet**
boil.PRS.3SG water.NOM and boil.FUT.3SG
'The water is boiling and will boil.' (Lucil. *apud* Quint. 1, 6, 8)

b. *possent=ne   seriae   **fervescere***
   can.SBJV.IMPF.3PL=INT vessel.NOM.PL start_to_boil.PRS.INF
   '(And the cook asked) whether the vessels could start to boil.'
   (Plaut. *Capt.* 4, 4, 9)
c. *eodem   addito   et   oleum,   postea*
   DEM.DAT   add.IMP.FUT.3SG   also   oil.ACC   afterwards
   fervefacito
   make_boil.IMP.FUT.3SG
   'To this (mixture) one should also add oil, and then let (it) boil.'
   (Cato R. R. 156, 5)

In (7a), *fervit* 'boils' refers to a spontaneous atelic event of boiling and is used intransitively. Similarly, in (7b) *fervescere* is syntactically intransitive and indicates a non-causative event, but it contrasts with *fervit* in (7a) in its aspectual construal: whereas the former is atelic, the latter profiles a change-of-state ingressive event. The difference between (7a-b), signaled by the suffix *-sc-*, is thus mainly an aspectual one. Conversely, in (7c) the form *fervefacito* is used transitively (here with omission of a definite referential, anaphoric direct object) and indicates a causative event 'make/let boil'. Thus, while the difference between (7b) and (7c) is only one of transitivity, both verbs being telic, the difference between (7a) and (7c) is both one of transitivity and of telicity.

The pattern exemplified in (7a-c) enjoys a somewhat wider productivity than that emerging from Table 2, but still remains quantitatively marginal in the history of Latin (cf. Hahn 1947; Fruyt 2011: 783; Litta and Budassi 2020). As already remarked by Hahn (1947), the core of the verbs that instantiate the *fervefacio* pattern must be old, since one finds triplets such as *areo* 'be dry' ~ *aresco* 'dry up' ~ *arefacio* 'make dry' as early as in Cato's *De Agri Cultura* (2nd c. BC). Other meanings in Table 2 for which this pattern is attested as a less basic strategy are listed in (8):

(8) a. 'open' (13): *pateo* 'be open' ~ *patesco* 'open up' ~ *patefacio* 'open (tr.)'
    b. 'dry' (14): *areo* 'be dry' ~ *aresco* 'dry up' ~ *arefacio* 'make dry'
    c. 'shake' (23): *tremo* 'tremble' ~ *tremesco* 'start to shake' ~ *tremefacio* 'make tremble'
    d. 'awake' (19): *expergiscor* 'wake up' ~ *expergefacio* 'awaken'

From a purely synchronic standpoint, the tripartite pattern under discussion can be sketched as [V ~ V-*sco* ~ V-*facio*] ⇔ [PLAIN.ATELIC ~ PLAIN.TELIC ~ INDUCED]. Within this threefold pattern, the correspondence between V and V-*facio* is one of augmentation. By contrast, the correspondence between V-*sco* and V-*facio* is one of double derivation, because both the plain and the induced verbs are equally derived.

The Latin V ~ V-*sco* ~ V-*facio* system is ultimately a manifestation of a derivational pattern already in force in PIE, which is known as the Caland System. It involves a basic root out of which several related formations can be derived by means of specific suffixes, including adjectives, nouns, and stative/inceptive/factitive verbs (cf. Nussbaum 1976; Rau 2009, 2013; Dell'Oro 2015; Bozzone 2016). Semantically, roots that belong to the Caland System often indicate basic property concepts, including color, shape, temperature, physical state etc., and this is also the case of the verbs that enter the V ~ V-*sco* ~ V-*facio* pattern in Latin (cf. Fruyt 2001: 81–82). Patterns of derivation reflecting the Caland System are attested in other ancient IE languages, as in the case of Hittite *idalu-* 'evil', *idalaw-atar* 'evilness', *idalaw-ešš-* 'become evil', *idalaw-aḫḫ-* 'make evil'. In Latin, derivational families that can be traced back to the Caland System typically feature a basic stative-intransitive verb in -*ē*-, an inchoative counterpart in -*sc*-, a causative verb in -*facio*, an abstract noun in -*or*, and an adjective in -*idus* (cf. Schindler 1999; Rau 2009: esp. 114–115, 123–125 for Latin data; see Olsen 2003 for an alternative explanation of the adjectives in -*idus*). As an example of this pattern, consider the family of Latin *candidus* 'white' in Table 3 (abbreviations in parentheses refer to authors where the forms are first attested).

Table 3: The Caland system in Latin.

Adjective	Noun	Stative verb	Change-of-state verb	Causative verb
cand-idus 'white' (Pl.)	cand-or 'whiteness' (Naev.)	cand-eo, -ēre 'be white' (Enn.)	cand-ē-sco 'become white' (Lucr.)	cand-e-facio 'make white' (Plaut.) cand-idāre 'make white' (App.)

The morphological status as well as the prehistory of the V ~ V-*sco* ~ V-*facio* pattern are worth a more detailed discussion. To begin with, broadening the observation to other verbs that instantiate the pattern, the base plain verb can either be a radical formation, e.g. *trem-o* (~ *tremisco* ~ *tremefacio*) or a stative *ē*-verb, e.g. *are-o* 'be dry'. While radical formations are morphologically basic, the interpretation of the *ē*-type is less straightforward. In fact, intransitive stative *ē*-verbs of the second conjugation historically go back to a suffixed form, possibly in *-*eh_1-(ye/o)*- (cf. *i.a.* Mignot 1969; Watkins 1971; Jasanoff 2002–2003; Weiss 2011; Malzahn 2018 for details). Nevertheless, in spite of their derivational origin, stative *ē*-verbs do not constitute a productive verb forming strategy in Latin (Mignot 1969: 100) and their derivation is not always transparent. For example, *luceo* 'shine' is not synchronically derived from the noun *lūx* 'light', but both independently go back to PIE **leuk-* (Watkins 1971: 68–69). This means that for the purpose of assessing the correspondence type, *ē*-verbs can be considered as morphologically simple, in pair with truly basic radical formation of the *tremo*-type.[7]

The suffix *-sc-* can be considered a derivational morpheme on a synchronic level, as it enters a productive and transparent word formation rule (Budassi and Litta 2017). The affix is unanimously considered a continuant of the PIE present stem pluractional morpheme **-sḱe/o-* (see e.g. Berrettoni 1971; Jasanoff 2002–2003: 134–133; Oettinger 2017; on the PIE suffix see Inglese and Mattiola 2020 with references). As Haverling (2000) has shown, Latin *-sc-* displays a wide range of aspect-related functions (see also Berrettoni 1971). It suffices here to say that in Early Latin the suffix must also have been originally connected with the encoding of inceptive change-of-state events of the type *fervesco* 'start boiling' and was productively applied to numerous verbs. Only later, in Late Latin, did the suffix undergo a progressive semantic bleaching, so that newly created *sco*-verbs became functionally equivalent to their bases, e.g. *fumo* = *fumesco* 'emit smoke' (see Haverling 2000 for a full discussion).

Let us now turn to forms in *-facio*. As per Hahn (1947), Latin displays different types of complex verbal forms featuring the verb *facio* 'make' (see also Fruyt 2001).[8] Besides formations based on adverbs (e.g. *bene-facio* 'do well') and on

---

[7] For deadjectival verbs, a marginal correspondence pattern that synchronically belongs to CONJUGATION CLASS CHANGE is also attested (for other verbs that also feature this pattern see fn. 6). These are cases in which a plain stative verb of the 2nd conjugation is paired with an induced change-of-state verb of the 1st conjugation, as in e.g. *clarēre* 'be bright' vs. *clarare* 'make bright', both based on *clarus* 'bright'. This pattern historically reflects two different derivational strategies of PIE, which have become opaque in Latin. Again, stative verbs of the 2nd conjugation *-ēre* continue the PIE stative suffix **-eh$_1$-*, whereas induced verbs in *-are* reflect PIE factitive **-eh$_2$-*. Outcomes of **-eh$_2$-* can be observed as fully productive in Hittite factitive *aḫḫ*-verbs, e.g *newa-* 'new (adj.)' > *newaḫḫ-* 'renew' parallel to Latin *novāre* 'renew' (Kloekhorst 2008: 164), but in Italic this formation is archaic and recessive (Watkins 1971: 54–55).

[8] As is well known, verbs of the V-*facio* type are often paired with counterparts in *-fio*, e.g. *calefacio* ~ *calefio* (cf. Hahn 1947). Forms in *-fio* are often regarded as indicating the passive counterpart of *facio*-form. A passive interpretation is for instance clearly at play when the verb is employed in an imperative predication, which by definition implies the presence of an external controlling agent (cf. *abi intro ac jube huic aquam calefieri* 'go inside and order some water to be warmed up' [Plaut. *Epid.* 655]). However, *fio*-forms can also indicate spontaneous events, thereby providing the anticausative counterpart to *facio*-verbs, e.g. *faces calefiunt* 'the torches become warm' (*Auct. Her.* 3, 12, 21). In this respect, *fio*-forms are close in meaning to inchoative *sco*-forms (cf. Fruyt 2001: 83 fn. 6). Nevertheless, given their passive/anticausative polysemy, for the purpose of this paper I consider only *-ē(sc)-* forms as indicating the plain counterpart of *facio*-verbs.

genitives (e.g. *multi-facio* 'value highly'), the largest group consists of the combination of *-facio* with a verbal stem. This group includes (i) forms paired with stative intransitives *ē*-verbs (e.g. *caleo* 'be warm' ~ *calefacio* 'make warm'), (ii) forms based on and equivalent to causative transitive verbs (e.g. *quatio* = *quatefacio* 'shake'), (iii) forms pared with *sco*-verbs (e.g. *raresco* 'grow thin' ~ *rarefacio* 'make thin'), and finally (iv) forms based on 1st or 3rd conjugation verbs (e.g. *labo* 'fall' ~ *labefacio* 'make fall' and *tremo* 'shake' ~ *tremefacio* 'cause to shake'). Hahn (1947) already points out that among the group of deverbal *facio*-verbs, type (i), i.e. the *calefacio* type, is historically the oldest, and is well attested in Early Latin, whereas the other types constitute later innovations.[9]

The synchronic interpretation of the *calefacio* type has prompted a lively discussion. Specifically, even though scholars agree in describing verbs of the *calefacio* type as single lexemes (and not as multiword expressions), the status of the *-facio* component remains disputed. According to Fruyt (2001, 2011: 783–785), within this formation *-facio* behaves as a fully grammaticalized bound morpheme, i.e. an affix, while Brucale and Mocciaro (2016) suggest that *-facio* is better analyzed as the second member of a verbal compound. Indeed, the *calefacio* type shows a number of morphological oddities in contrast with other compound verb forms involving *facio* and verbal prefixes (see already Hahn 1947; Fruyt 2001). First, the radical vowel *-a-* does not undergo weakening, thus showing that the form fails to participate in the common Latin apophony pattern of the type *facio* ~ *inficio*. Secondly, the two members can also occur separately, and their order can even be reversed (in *tmesis*, e.g. *facit are* in Lucr. 6, 962). These two facts point to a rather shallow morphological link between the two components of the *calefacio* type. Nevertheless, traces of an increasing univerbation can be seen in the syncopated forms such as *calface* (Cic. *Fam.* 16, 18, 2). From a historical perspective, these facts suggest that the formation of the *calefacio* type, even though well attested since the earliest Latin sources, must be a comparatively late development within the PIE verbal system. In fact, there is agreement that the *calefacio* type must go back to some sort of periphrastic formation, with the two components eventually undergoing univerbation and *-facio* progressively developing into a derivational affix.[10]

---

9 Another type of causative construction involving *-facio* is the denominal pattern featuring the suffix *-fic-*, as in *aedi-fic-o* 'build'. This type is productive in Latin and unlike the *calefacio* type survives in Romance languages (see Brucale and Mocciaro 2016 for discussion).

10 Similar processes, whereby analytic constructions give rise to synthetic forms are not unknown in the Latin verbal system. Compare, among others, the possible emergence of the *ba*-imperfect and the *b*-future from earlier periphrastic construction involving the root $*b^huh_2$- 'be' (cf. Fruyt 2011: 758–760).

Also controversial is the interpretation of the first component in -e- that combines with -facio. From a synchronic standpoint, forms such as cale- cannot be described as autonomous lexemes, as they do not correspond to any finite form of the verb. At best, they can be analyzed as verbal stems. Concerning its origin, the cal-e- formant has been understood as reflecting either an old imperative (Hahn 1947) or an infinitive (Fruyt 2001, 2011: 783).

Alternatively, particularly interesting are attempts to view the -e- of cal-e-facio, as well as the suffix of simple stative verbs in -ē-, as the relic of an old instrumental noun in *-eh_1 (see chiefly Jasanoff 1978, 2002–2003). This reconstruction is based on comparison between the Latin calefacio/calefio type and the Indo-Aryan so-called cvī construction. The latter can be synchronically described as an analytic construction featuring a preverb in -ī issued from an a-stem noun/adjective combined with the verbs kr̥- 'make' (or dha- 'put') and bhū- 'be(come)', e.g. tīvra- 'strong' > tīvrī̆ kr̥-/bhū- 'make/become strong'. Without going into too much detail, according to proponents of this reconstruction, both the calefacio type and the cvī construction go back to a PIE construction that featured the instrumental of an abstract noun in *-eh_1 combined with the verbs *d^heh_1- 'put, make, do' and *b^huh_2- 'be' and meaning 'make something X, be(come) X', respectively (see Jasanoff 1978, 2002–2003; Schindler 1980; Ruijgh 2004; Balles 2009; Bozzone 2016 for slightly different accounts).[11] If this is correct, then even though the Latin calefacio type seems to have undergone univerbation at a later stage, this is not a recent Latin formation, as its roots go back to the protolanguage.[12]

---

[11] The morphological behavior of the calefacio type discussed earlier in this section makes it clear that the PIE construction ROOT-*eh_1 *d^heh_1-/*b^huh_2- 'be/make X' was not yet univerbated in the protolanguage, and possibly behaved as a periphrastic (anti)causative construction. Given its periphrastic nature, the existence of the ROOT-*eh_1*d^heh_1-/*b^huh_2- construction in the protolanguage does not challenge Luraghi's (2019) conclusion that PIE was largely transitivizing.

[12] In this respect, Brucale and Mocciaro's (2016: 285–286) observation that compounds in -fico represent an older formation as compared to the calefacio type should be taken with due care. As a matter of fact, the morphological evidence adduced by Brucale and Mocciaro (2016), chiefly the weak root vocalism -i- and the use of a connective vowel -i- (cf. laetus 'glad' > laet-i-fic-o 'make glad'), only shows that the -fico type univerbated at an earlier date, but the PIE pattern out of which the calefacio type originated is, as discussed, in all likelihood at least as old. Earlier univerbation of the -fico type is further supported by the fact that these verbs do not generally allow a passive/anticausative counterpart in -fio (see fn. 8)

5.2.5 Lability

Lability concerns those verbs that "can show valency alternation, i.e. change in syntactic pattern, with no formal change in the verb" (Kulikov and Lavidas 2014: 871; see also Letuchiy 2009; Creissels 2014). Lability that affects anticausative verbs also goes under the name of P-lability, i.e. patient preserving lability. Labile syntax in Latin has been extensively studied by Gianollo (2014), who has shown that the occasional labile use of anticausative verbs occurs already in Early Latin but gains ground as a widespread strategy only at later times.

From the perspective of basic valency, lability can be defined as an indeterminate pattern, since the plain and the induced verbs are encoded by the same form and are thus equally unmarked. Among the verb pairs in Table 2, this correspondence type is attested only once for the verb *(con)crepo* 'rattle', as shown in (9a-b), in which the likewise active basic forms *crepuit* and *crepant* are used to express the spontaneous event 'rattles' and the causative event 'make rattle', respectively.

(9) a. **crepuit** foris
    rattle.PST.3SG door.NOM
    'The door made a noise.' (Plaut. *Am.* 1, 2, 34)
   b. procul auxiliantia gentes aera
      afar helping.ACC.PL.N people.NOM.PL bronze(N).ACC.PL
      crepant
      rattle.PRS.3PL
      'Afar people make the bronze rattle in (her) help.' (Stat. *Th.* 6, 687)

Instances of lability are also attested for a few verbs other than *(con)crepo* 'rattle' in Table 2, including *aperio* (Plaut. *Pers.* 300), *sicco* (Cato *Agr.* 112.2), and *luceo* (Plaut. *Cas.* 118). Such a narrow distribution is perfectly in line with Gianollo's (2014: 966–970) observation that P-lability becomes increasingly common only in Late Latin (lability is also on the rise in Greek, see discussion in Luraghi and Mertyris, this volume).

It is worth remarking that some instances of lability are in fact the historical outcome of the conflation of different PIE formations that were fully differentiated in the protolanguage. A case in point is the verb *luceo* 'shine', whose syntax is exemplified in (10):

(10) a. luce **lucebat** aliena
       light.ABL shine.IMPF.3SG stranger.ABL
       '(The moon) was shining of a borrowed light' (Cic. *Rep.* 4 ,16, 15)

b. ***lucebis** facem*
   light.FUT.2SG torch.ACC
   'You will light a torch.' (Plaut. *Cas.* 118)

As comparison between (10a) and (10b) illustrates, the verb *luceo* can be used intransitively, as in (10a), or transitively, as in (10b). Taken at face value, this evidence points towards a synchronically labile use of the verb *luceo* on par with *crepo* in (9a-b). A more careful consideration of the diachrony of *luceo* reveals a more complex picture. In fact, the two usages of *luceo* can be traced back to two different formations. PIE featured two distinct derivational suffixes, the already mentioned stative suffix *-eh$_1$-, and the causative suffix *-éye/o-. In Latin, the two suffixes phonologically merged as -ē-, and verbs originally belonging to the two different formations equally ended up in the 2nd conjugation (Watkins 1971: 68–69; Weiss 2011: 403–404). Once the two formations fell together, this resulted in the gradual loss of ē-causatives of the type *moneo* 'remind, warn' as compared to the somewhat more productive ē-statives (cf. Fruyt 2011: 783 fn. 214). The labile pattern of *luceo* can thus be easily understood as the outcome of such a merger: *luceo$_1$* in (10a) is intransitive and atelic, and derives from the PIE stative verb **leuk-eh$_1$-* 'be shining', whereas *luceo$_2$* in (10b) is transitive and telic, and can be traced back to the PIE causative form **louk-éye-* 'make shine'.

5.3 Verb pairs and correspondences: a summary

In the previous sections, I have surveyed the different correspondence types attested in Latin for the encoding of transitivity alternations of the (anti)causative type. Drawing upon the observation of the behavior of the 24 verb pairs, we are now in the position to assess the basic valency of Latin and its orientation.

As the data in Table 2 shows, the prevalence of suppletion indicates that Latin is predominantly indeterminate for animate verbs. To put it differently, Latin basic valency is not strongly oriented towards either transitivization or intransitivization. Only with inanimate verbs does Latin show a minor tendency towards reduction/voice alternation. In this respect, Latin sharply contrasts with both Hittite, which, as discussed in Section 4, is strongly transitivizing, and with Ancient Greek, which features instead a substantial tendency towards intransitivization via voice alternation.

From the survey conducted in Section 5.2, it is remarkable that, with the exception of the limited use of *facio*-compounds, Latin lacks a productive pattern of formation of morphologically causative verbs (cf. Hoffmann 2016: 35; Lehmann 2016). Again, this fact is particularly striking if compared to the abundance of derivational verbal causative morphology attested in other ancient IE languages and that can be reconstructed for the protolanguage (cf. Covini 2017). As I discuss in the next section, this can be partly explained by the fact that causative strategies were regularly lost via sound changes in Latin. Note, however, that the lack of morphological causativization is consistent with the typological generalization proposed by Nichols, Peterson and Barnes (2004: 164) that within the same language, augmentation and suppletion tend to be mutually exclusive.

Let us turn now to discussing in more detail some notable aspects of the various strategies and of their mutual relationship.

In the first place, the verbs' lexical aspect plays a role in determining the choice of the correspondence pattern. Within the class of plain verbs, if one differentiates between the atelic and the telic variant, e.g. *be dry* vs. *dry up*, three patterns can be detected, based on whether the atelic situation is encoded by a stative verb (*sedeo* 'sit', *pateo* 'be open'), an adjective (*siccus* 'dry'), or a participle (*mortuus* 'dead'). If the plain atelic verb is a simple stative verb, its telic counterpart is often derived by means of two telicizing strategies, that is prefixation, e.g. *edo* 'eat' > *com-edo* 'eat up' (see Romagno 2003), or *-sc-*suffixation, e.g. *ardeo* 'burn' > *ardesco* 'catch fire'. Some verbs attest to the simultaneous use of both prefixation and *-sc-*suffixation, e.g. *dormio* 'sleep' > *ob-dormisco* 'fall asleep' (see Haverling 2000). By contrast, if the telic plain verb is a simple verb, e.g. *siccor* 'dry up', the atelic counterpart is expressed by a nominal form, i.e. an adjective, or by a non-finite verbal form, i.e. by a participle.

Aspect plays a role in predicting the choice of the correspondence type also between plain and induced verbs, depending on whether the telic or the atelic verb is more basic. If the plain atelic verb is a morphologically simple stative verb, the induced counterpart is either suppletive, e.g. *ardeo* 'burn (intr.)' vs. *uro* 'burn (tr.)', or a form in *-facio*, e.g. *ferveo* 'boil (intr.)' vs. *fervefacio* 'make boil'. By contrast, if the induced verb is basic, then the corresponding atelic event is preferably encoded via adjectives or participles, e.g. *frango* 'break' vs. *fractus* 'broken'.

Animacy is also a key factor in determining the distribution of different correspondence types. As we have seen, animate and inanimate verbs show a contrasting picture. In Latin, suppletion is virtually the only available strategy with animate verbs. Inanimate verbs show a more varied picture and besides suppletion also attest to double derivation, voice alternation, reduction, and lability. Such a split between animate and inanimate verbs is not at all exceptional (see Nichols, Peterson and Barnes 2004: 177). Specifically, the fact that reduction strategies are only attested with inanimate verbs complies with Nichols and associates' universal preferred lexicalization tendency, whereby languages preferably treat inanimate induced verbs as basic (Nichols, Peterson and Barnes 2004: 172).

Within the IE family, such a split has also been observed for Greek (Luraghi and Mertyris, this volume)

As I have already remarked in Section 5.2, it must be stressed that the choice of the verbs in Table 2 in part overshadows the fact that in Latin less basic strategies are also available for the lexicalization of some meanings. This observation bears two noteworthy methodological consequences. On the one hand, it shows once again that the choice of the verb pairs largely determines our understanding of the basic valency profile of a language, and that is it therefore of primary importance to have a sound methodology for the individuation of the verb pairs. On the other hand, the case of Latin offers a neat illustration of the limits of the basic valency approach as elaborated by Nichols, Peterson and Barnes (2004). As a matter of fact, while the very notion of basic valency is useful to grasp the general behavior of languages and to make meaningful large-scale cross-linguistic generalization, the assessment of a language's basic valency often implies an oversimplification of the actual facts of language. Indeed, besides the mainstream patterns which are taken into account in typologizing basic valency, languages often attest to a sizable number of minor alternative strategies. It is often the case that such a coexistence of different correspondence types reflects the historical layering of older and newer strategies.

6 Basic valency from PIE to Romance languages: a diachronic perspective

As I have discussed in Section 5, Early and Classical Latin texts offer a heterogeneous picture when it comes to the possible strategies for the encoding of the (anti)causative alternation. A closer look at the inventory of strategies available reveals that such synchronic variation reflects a historical layering of formations inherited from PIE and Latin innovations. In this section, I offer a historical perspective on the basic valency of Latin and elaborate in more detail on the position of Latin with respect to the basic valency of PIE and that of Romance languages.

To begin with, the basic valency of Latin can be compared with that of PIE. The main difference that can be detected between Latin and the basic valency reconstructed for PIE is the lack of transitivizing derivational morphology (see Section 4). Such a difference can probably be better understood as a consequence of the more general restructuring of the verbal system that took place between PIE and Italic and that also affects grammatical features other than the encoding of voice, such as aspect, tense, and mood (see Fortson 2010: 278–281; Clackson and Horrocks 2011: 18–26; Weiss 2011: Chap. 35–39 with further references).

On the one hand, the basic valency of Latin partly continues an inherited situation. This is clearly the case of the anticausative use of the middle inflection, which may be reconstructed for the protolanguage already (Luraghi 2019). Another archaic feature is the retention of formations that originally belonged to the Caland System. As discussed in Section 5.2.4, these include the pattern whereby a plain stative verb in *-ē-* < **-eh₁-* (and a plain change-of-state verb in *-sc-*) coexists alongside the induced counterpart in *-e-facio* (forms in *-facio* built on root verbs, e.g. *trem-o ~ trem-e-facio*, reflect in all likelihood a later extension).

On the other hand, one also detects a number of innovations. First, one observes an increasing opacization of erstwhile productive causativization strategies, which is mostly due to regular sound changes. Among formations that cease to be productive in Latin one counts nasal-infixed formations, e.g. *pando* 'make open' < PIE **pt-n(e)-h₂-*, **-éye-* causatives, e.g. *doceo* 'teach' < **dek̂-* 'accept', and **-eh₂-* factitives, e.g. *novāre* 'renew' < PIE **new-eh₂-* (cf. Covini 2017). In this respect, some verb pairs that synchronically display suppletion historically reflect a transitivization pattern. This is the case of the synchronically suppletive pair *pateo* 'be open' vs. *pando* 'open', which ultimately continue an opposition between the PIE plain stative stem **pth₂-h₁yé-* vs. the induced nasal infixed stem **pt-n(e)-h₂-* (cf. *LIV*² s.v. **peth₂.*¹, de Vaan 2008 s.v. *pando*). Some induced verbs in *-eo*, which synchronically must be analyzed as basic, hence as instantiating suppletion, also reflect earlier causativization strategies. Examples are *terreo* 'frighten', *sōpio* 'put to sleep', *doceo* 'teach < make accept', all originally featuring the PIE causative suffix **-éye/o-* (see Fruyt 2011: 782–783; Covini 2017 for details).

Besides the opacization of causative morphology, which ultimately leads to the expansion of the suppletive pattern, another innovation that contributes to reshaping the basic valency profile of Latin is the rise of *se*-reflexives. These expand out of their original reflexive function and start covering the range of functions previously associated with the inherited *r*-inflection, including the anticausative (Cennamo, Eythórsson and Barðdal 2015). This is an ongoing process of replacement of the old *r*-inflection that is only fully achieved in Romance languages. Notably, in this case we do not witness the rise of an entirely innovative pattern, but rather the formal renewal of an already existing pattern (cf. Reinöhl and Himmelman 2017).

Turning now to the subsequent development of Latin, a remarkable difference can be detected between the basic valency of Latin and that of Romance languages. In general, one observes a decay of suppletion, which is replaced by different strategies. In the first place, there are Romance languages that show a markedly intransitivizing profile. This is the case of Italian. Italian is mostly intransitivizing, as it uses *si*-reflexivization as the main intransitivizing strategies with most verbs, both animate and inanimate ones (on Italian see further Ježek 2003; Cennamo and Ježek 2011). In case *si*-reflexivization is not employed, the pattern is by preference a periphrastic one, with the use of the new *fare* 'make' + infinitive periphrastic causative formation typical of Romance languages for the induced verbs (cf. Simone and Cerbasi 2001). Similar considerations hold for French, which is regarded by Haspelmath (1993: 101) as predominantly intransitivizing. Different is the case of Portuguese, which is mostly indeterminate. However, unlike in Latin where indeterminacy is due to the diffusion of suppletion, indeterminacy of Portuguese is rather due to extensive lability (cf. Nichols, Peterson and Barnes 2004). Remarkably, both *se*-reflexivization and lability, which eventually take over in Romance languages, are only at the onset in Latin (on the development of the Latin reflexive in Romance languages see Cennamo 1993, 1998, 2016, 2020, this volume *i.a.*).

The time span covered by the development from PIE to Romance languages gives us a privileged viewpoint on the diachronic stability of basic valency. As Nichols, Peterson and Barnes (2004) remark, among those languages that show an oriented basic valency, transitivizing languages are cross-linguistically more common than intransitivizing ones. This means that the widespread intransitivizing pattern of the modern IE languages of Europe is a typologically marked phenomenon. As the historical evidence presented in this paper has shown, such a marked intransitivizing profile is clearly an innovation, since it is likely that PIE preferred transitivization as the basic means of encoding the (anti)causative alternation. The intransitivizing European pattern seems even more remarkable if one considers that basic valency has repeatedly been pointed out as being a relatively stable typological feature, especially when compared to other features more prone to change, such as e.g. word order or alignment (cf. Nichols 1992; Wichmann 2015). Therefore, the history from PIE to Romance languages "gives some indication of the time span needed by a language to develop this cross-linguistically marked pattern as its basic typological profile" (Comrie 2006: 316).

The Latin data analyzed in this paper shows an intermediate phase in this typologically unexpected shift and is of relevance to get a better perspective on the transitivizing > intransitivizing drift that occurred in some of the IE languages of Europe. As I have discussed, the intransitivizing profile of Romance languages finds its seeds already in Latin, in which intransitivization is an available strategy for a number of (inanimate verbs). The reason why intransitivization took over is in all likelihood to be sought in internal factors, viz. the loss of older causative morphology, which left open a functional gap for the inherited middle voice to extend in its anticausative function, and this was later renewed and eventually replaced by lability and *se*-reflexives (Gianollo 2014). The key role of the loss of causativization strategies in the development of a new basic valency profile is not exceptional: for instance, as discussed by van Gelderen

(2011), it was the decay of older transitivizing strategies that triggered the large-scale shift from transitivization to lability from Old English to Modern English (see also García García 2019; lability in English is the main pattern also due to the loss of the Indo-European reflexive pronoun in English, which was preserved and gave rise to reflexive middles in other Germanic languages such as German, see van Gelderen 2000: 28).

Given its typologically exceptional nature, it has been argued that the rise of reflexive anticausatives is to be considered an areal feature of the IE languages of Europe. As Comrie (2006: 316) puts it, we may be witnessing "an areally conditioned renewal of the semantics of the [PIE] middle voice by means of reflexive morphology." This scenario is in principle not at all unlikely. On the one hand, we now know that other typological 'quirks' of European languages, such as the otherwise typologically uncommon frequency of HAVE-perfects, most likely became established through extensive language contact in the region (see Drinka 2017 with references). On the other hand, language contact has been shown to be a major factor in the change of transitivity patterns in general (see Grossman, this volume).

Unfortunately, the details of the putative contact scenario behind the rise of reflexive anticausatives, and the consequent shift in the European languages' basic valency, remains to date unexplored. It is clear that the development of new anticausative reflexives displays different timing in different IE sub-groups in Europe. A preliminary survey may point towards Latin, and thus Romance languages, as a potential candidate for the source of reflexive intransitivization. As we have seen, Latin preserves the PIE middle and employs the reflexive pronoun in anticausative function since its earliest phase. In Gothic, anticausative reflexives are virtually unattested, and only develop in later stages of Germanic (cf. Ottósson 2013). The Slavic languages already attest to reflexives in anticausative functions in Old Church Slavonic (cf. Malicka-Kleparska 2016), but given the relatively late attestation one cannot rule out the possibility that these constitute a late development. All in all, if indeed language contact played a role in the large-scale drift in the basic valency of IE languages of Europe towards intransitivization, the data presented in this paper is at least suggestive that Latin may be the origin of this pattern. Indeed, in Latin the renewal of the PIE middle by means of reflexive morphology, as discussed by Comrie (2006), appears to have taken place at an earlier date. More research is needed to confirm the plausibility of this contact scenario. At any rate, this situation is compatible with the well-known leading role of Latin (and Romance varieties) in the spread of linguistic innovations among the IE languages of Europe, as in the case of the expansion of HAVE-perfects (cf. Drinka 2017).

7 Conclusions

In this paper, I have explored the basic valency orientation of Latin, based on the guidelines proposed by Nichols, Peterson and Barnes (2004) and Nichols (2017). With respect to the original study, the analysis of Latin has brought to light two important methodological considerations. Firstly, when dealing with an extinct language, there is a need to develop a sound methodology for the correct individuation of the verb pairs to be analyzed. Secondly, a closer observation of the Latin data reveals that the basic valency approach often leads to much too simplistic generalizations on the behavior of individual languages, which may feature several competing strategies for the encoding of anticausativization. Whereas it might blur the neat synchronic typological picture, such a variation is extremely insightful as to the historical layering of strategies of different dating and origin.

The analysis conducted in this paper was based on 24 verb pairs attested in Early and Classical Latin sources. Once properly individuated, these 24 verb pairs offer an interesting picture. Latin attests to a variety of strategies for the encoding of the anticausative alternation. Suppletion is by far the preferred strategy, but one also finds that other strategies are employed, including voice alternation, the reflexive pronoun *se*, verbal compounds in *-facio*, and lability. Overall, the extensive use of suppletion makes basic valency in Latin largely indeterminate, and only inanimate verbs show a certain proclivity towards intransitivization. These findings are at odds with the behavior of other ancient IE languages, which are predominantly oriented, as well as with modern Romance languages, which are mostly intransitivizing or make use of lability.

Such an intermediate position of Latin can be better understood if one considers the data from a diachronic perspective. As I have argued, the Latin situation historically results from the convergence of different factors. Among these, a key role is played by the loss of the PIE transitivizing morphology and by the extension of the functional domain of the inherited middle voice, eventually renewed by the more recent construction based on the reflexive pronoun *se*. These changes pave the way for the development of basic valency in Romance languages. Once dynamized in a historical perspective, the Latin data offers us unique insights for the understanding of the dynamics, the direction, and the timing of the typologically rare transitivizing-to-intransitivizing drift that took place in the IE languages of Europe (Comrie 2006). As I have argued, one cannot rule out the possibility that Latin has provided the model for the rise and diffusion of intransitivization as a widespread pattern across Europe.

Abbreviations

Examples are glossed following the *Leipzig Glossing Rules*. Other glosses include IMPF = imperfect, MID = middle voice.

Abbreviations for Latin authors and texts are the following:

A.	Aeneis,
Agr.	De Agri Cultura,
App.	Appuleius,
Auct. Her.	Auctor ad Herennium,
Am.	Amphitruo,
Att.	Epistulae ad Atticum,
B. C.	Bellum Civile,
Caes.	Caesar,
Capt.	Captivi,
Cas.	Casina,
Cic.	Cicero,
De Or.	De Oratore,
Enn.	Ennius,
Epid.	Epidicus,
Fam.	Epistulae ad Familiares,
Lucil.	Lucilius,
Lucr.	Lucretius, De Rerum Natura
Pers.	Persa,
Naev.	Naevius,
Plaut.	Plautus,
Ps.	Pseudolus,
Q. Fr.	Epistulae ad Q. Fratrem,
Quint.	Quintilianus, Institutiones Oratoriae
R. R.	De Re Rustica,
Rep.	De Re Publica,
Stat.	Statius,
Stich.	Stichus,
Th.	Thebais,
Verg.	Vergil

References

Alexiadou, Artemis. 2010. On the morpho-syntax of (anti-)causative verbs. In Malka Rappaport Hovav, Edit Doron & Ivy Sichel (eds.), *Syntax, lexical semantics and event structure*, 177–203. Oxford: Oxford University Press.

Alexiadou, Artemis, Elena Anagnostopoulou & Florian Schäfer. 2015. *External arguments in transitivity alternations: A layering approach*. Oxford: Oxford University Press.

Balles, Irene. 2009. The Old Indic *cvi* construction, the Caland system and the PIE adjective. In Jens E. Rasmussen & Thomas Olander (eds.), *Internal reconstruction in Indo-European: Methods, results, and problems: Section papers from the XVI International Conference on Historical Linguistics (Copenhagen, August 2003)*, 1–15. Copenhagen: Museum Tusculanum Press.

Berrettoni, Pierangiolo. 1971. Considerazioni sui verbi latini in *-scō*. *Studi e Saggi Linguistici* 11. 89–169.

Borer, Hagit. 1991. The causative–inchoative alternation: A case study in parallel morphology. *The Linguistic Review* 8. 119–158.

Bortolussi, Bernard & Peggy Lecaudé (eds.). 2014. *La causativité en latin*. Paris: L'Harmattan.

Bozzone, Chiara. 2016. The origin of the Caland System and the typology of adjectives. *Indo-European Linguistics* 4. 15–52.

Brucale, Luisa & Egle Mocciaro. 2016. Composizione verbale in latino: Il caso dei verbi in *-facio*, *-fico*. In Paolo Poccetti (ed.), *LATINITATIS RATIONES: Descriptive and historical accounts for the Latin language*, 279–297. Berlin & New York: Mouton De Gruyter.

Brugmann, Karl & Berthold Delbrück. 1893–1916. *Grundriss der vergleichenden Grammatik der indogermanischen Sprachen*. Strasbourg: Trübner.

Bybee, Joan L. 2007. *Frequency of use and the organization of language*. Oxford: Oxford University Press.

Budassi, Marco, & Eleonora Litta. 2017. In trouble with the rules: Theoretical issues raised by the insertion of *-sc-* verbs into word formation Latin. In Elenora Litta & Marco Passarotti (eds.), *Proceedings of the Workshop on Resources and Tools for Derivational Morphology (DeriMo)*, 15–26. Milan: Educatt.

Cennamo, Michela. 1993. *The reanalysis of reflexives: A diachronic perspective*. Napels: Liguori.

Cennamo, Michela. 1998. Late Latin pleonastic reflexives and the unaccusative hypothesis. *Transactions of the Philological Society* 97 (1). 103–150.

Cennamo, Michela. 2012. Aspectual constraints on the (anti)causative alternation in Old Italian. *Transactions of the Philological Society* 110 (3). 394–421.

Cennamo, Michela. 2016. Voice. In Adam Ledgeway & Martin Maiden (eds.), *The Oxford guide to Romance languages*, 967–980. Oxford: Oxford University Press.

Cennamo, Michela. 2020. The actualization of new voice patterns in Romance. In Bridget Drinka (ed.), *Historical linguistics 2017: Selected papers from the 23rd International Conference on Historical Linguistics, San Antonio, Texas, 31 July – 4 August 2017*, 109–142. Amsterdam & Philadelphia: John Benjamins.

Cennamo, Michela, Thórhallur Eythórsson & Jóhanna Barðdal. 2015. Semantic and (morpho) syntactic constraints on anticausativization: Evidence from Latin and Old Norse-Icelandic. *Linguistics* 53 (4). 677–729.

Cennamo, Michela & Elisabetta Ježek. 2011. The anticausative alternation in Italian: Constraints and variation. In Giovanna Massariello & Serena Dal Masi (eds.), *Le interfacce*, 809–823. Roma: Bulzoni.

Clackson, James & Geoffrey Horrocks. 2011. *The Blackwell history of the Latin language*. Oxford: Wiley-Blackwell.

Comrie, Bernard. 2006. Transitivity pairs, markedness, and diachronic stability. *Linguistics* 44 (2). 303–318.

Covini, Andrea Lorenzo. 2017. *Formazioni causative nelle lingue indoeuropee di più antica attestazione*. Università per Stranieri di Siena & Universität zu Köln PhD dissertation.

Creissels, Denis. 2014. P-lability and radical P-alignment. *Linguistics* 52 (4). 911–944.

Croft, William. 2003. *Typology and universal*, 2nd edn. Cambridge: Cambridge University Press.

Cysouw, Michael. 2010. Semantic maps as metrics on meaning. *Linguistic Discovery* 8. 70–95.
Delatte, Louis, Etienne Evrard, Suzanne Govaerts & Joseph Denooz. 1981. *Dictionnaire fréquentiel et index inverse de la langue latine*. Liège: LASLA.
Dell'Oro, Francesca. 2015. *Leggi, sistemi e leghe suffissali 'di Caland': Storia della questione 'Caland' come problema teorico della linguistica indoeuropea*. Innsbruck: Institut für Sprachwissenschaft.
Drinka, Bridget. 2017. *Language contact in Europe: The periphrastic perfect through history*. Cambridge: Cambridge University Press.
Dunkel, George E. 2014. *Lexikon der indogermanischen Partikeln und Pronominal-stämme. Band 2: Lexikon*. Heidelberg: Winter.
Feltenius, Leif. 1977. *Intransitivization in Latin*. Uppsala: Almqvist & Wiksell.
Flobert, Pierre. 1975. *Les verbs deponents latins des origines à Charlemagne*. Paris: Les Belles Lettres.
Fortson, Benjamin W. 2010. *Indo-European language and culture: An introduction*, 2nd edn. Chichester: Blackwell Wiley.
Fruyt, Michèle. 2001. Réflexions sur la notion de mot en latin: Les verbes du type *calefacio*. In Claude Moussy (ed.), *De lingua Latina novae quaestiones. Actes du Xe Colloque International de Linguistique Latine*, 81–94. Louvain: Peeters.
Fruyt, Michèle. 2011. Grammaticalization in Latin. In Philip Baldi & Pierluigi Cuzzolin (eds.), *New perspectives on historical Latin syntax. Volume 4: Complex sentences, grammaticalization, typology*, 661–848. Berlin & New York: Mouton de Gruyter.
García García, Luisa. 2019. The basic valency orientation of Old English and the causative *ja*-formation: A synchronic and diachronic approach. *English Language and Linguistics* 24. 1–25.
van Gelderen, Elly. 2000. *A history of English reflexive pronouns*. Amsterdam & Philadelphia: John Benjamins.
van Gelderen, Elly. 2011. Valency changes in the history of English. *Journal of Historical Linguistics* 1 (1). 106–143.
Gianollo, Chiara. 2005. Middle voice in Latin and the phenomenon of split intransitivity. In Gualtiero Calboli (ed.), *Latina Lingua! Proceedings of the 12th International Colloquium on Latin Linguistics (Bologna, June 9–14, 2003)*. Roma: Herder.
Gianollo, Chiara. 2010. I verbi deponenti latini e l'unità della flessione in -*r*. *Incontri Triestini di Filologia Classica* 8. 23–49.
Gianollo, Chiara. 2014. Labile verbs in Late Latin. *Linguistics* 52 (4). 945–1002.
Glare, Peter W. G. 2012. *The Oxford Latin dictionary*, 2nd edn. Oxford: Oxford University Press.
Grünthal, Riho & Johanna Nichols. 2016. Transitivizing-detransitivizing typology and language family history. *Lingua Posnaniensis* 58 (2). 11–31.
Hahn, Adelaide E. 1947. The Type *calefacio*. *Transactions and Proceedings of the American Philological Association* 78. 301–335.
Haspelmath, Martin. 1987. *Transitivity alternations of the anticausative type*. Köln: Universität zu Köln (Arbeitspapiere N.F. 5).
Haspelmath, Martin. 1993. More on the typology of the inchoative/causative verb alternations. In Bernard Comrie & Maria Polinsky (eds.), *Causatives and Transitivity*, 87–120. Amsterdam & Philadelphia: John Benjamins.
Haspelmath, Martin. 2016. Universals of causative and anticausative verb formation and the spontaneity scale. *Lingua Posnaniensis* 58 (2). 33–63.

Haspelmath, Martin, Andreea Calude, Michael Spagnol, Heiko Narrog & Elif Bamyacı. 2014. Coding causal-noncausal verb alternations: A form-frequency correspondence explanation. *Journal of linguistics* 50 (3). 587–625.

Haverling, Gerd. 2000. *On Sco-verbs, prefixes and semantic functions: A study in the development of prefixed and unprefixed verbs from early to Late Latin*. Göteborg: Acta Universitatis Gothoburgensis.

Hoffmann, Roland. 2016. On causativity in Latin. *Journal of Latin Linguistics* 15 (1). 33–71.

Hopper, Paul J. & Sandra A. Thompson. 1980. Transitivity in Grammar and Discourse. *Language* 56 (2). 251–299.

Inglese, Guglielmo. 2020. *The Hittite middle voice*. Leiden & Boston: Brill.

Inglese, Guglielmo & Simone Mattiola. 2020. Pluractionality in Hittite: a new look at the suffix -ške/a-. *Sprachtypologie und Universalienforschung (STUF)* 73 (2). 261–303.

Jasanoff, Jay H. 1978. *Stative and middle in Indo-European*. Innsbruck: Institut für Sprachwissenschaft.

Jasanoff, Jay H. 2002–2003. 'Stative' *-ē- revisited. *Die Sprache* 43. 127–170.

Ježek, Elisabetta. 2003. *Classi di verbi tra semantica e sintassi*. Pisa: Edizioni ETS.

Kemmer, Susanne. 1993. *The middle voice*. Amsterdam & Philadelphia: John Benjamins.

Koontz-Garboden, Andrew. 2009. Anticausativization. *Natural Language & Linguistic Theory* 27. 77–138.

Kulikov, Leonid. 2009. Valency-changing categories in Indo-Aryan and Indo-European: A diachronic typological portrait of Vedic Sanskrit. In Anju Saxena & Åke Viberg (eds.), *Multilingualism*, 75–92. Uppsala: Uppsala Universitet.

Kulikov, Leonid. 2010. Voice typology. In Jae Jung Song (ed.), *The Oxford handbook of linguistic typology*, 368–398. Oxford: Oxford University Press.

Kulikov, Leonid. 2013. Middle and reflexive. In Silvia Luraghi & Claudia Parodi (eds.), *The Bloomsbury companion to syntax*, 261–280. London, New Delhi, New York & Sydney: Bloomsbury.

Kulikov, Leonid & Nikolaos Lavidas (eds.). 2014. *Typology of labile verbs*. Special issue of *Linguistics* 52.

Lazzeroni, Romano. 2004. Inaccusatività indoeuropea e alternanza causativa vedica. *Archivio Glottologico Italiano* 89. 1–28.

Lazzeroni, Romano. 2009. Causativi e transitivi indoeuropei: Fra comparazione e tipologia. *Studi e Saggi Linguistici* 57. 7–23.

Lehmann, Christian. 2002. Latin valency in typological perspective. In A. M. Bolkestein, Caroline Kroon, Harm Pinkster, Wim Remmelink & Rodie Risselada (eds.), *Theory and description in Latin linguistics*, 183–204. Leiden: Brill.

Lehmann, Christian. 2016. Latin causativization in typological perspective. In Paolo Poccetti (ed.), *LATINITATIS RATIONES: Descriptive and historical accounts for the Latin language*, 918–943. Berlin & New York: Mouton De Gruyter.

Letuchiy, Alexander. 2009. Towards a typology of labile verbs: Lability vs. derivation. In Patience Epps & Alexandre Arkhipov (eds.), *New challenges in typology: Transcending the borders and refining the distinctions*, 223–244. Berlin & New York: Mouton de Gruyter.

Levin, Beth & Malka Rappaport Hovav. 1995. *Unaccusativity at the syntax-lexical semantics interface*. Cambridge (MA): MIT Press.

Levin, Beth & Malka Rappaport Hovav. 2005. *Argument realization*. Cambridge: Cambridge University Press.

Lewis, Charlton T. & Charles Short. 1879. *A Latin dictionary*. Oxford: Clarendon Press.

Litta, Eleonora & Marco Budassi. 2020. What we talk about when we talk about paradigms: Representing Latin word formation. In Jesús Fernández-Domínguez, Alexandra Bagasheva & Cristina Lara Clares (eds.), *Paradigmatic relations in word formation*, 128–163. Leiden & Boston: Brill.

Luraghi, Silvia. 2012. Basic valency orientation and the middle voice in Hittite. *Studies in Language* 36 (1). 1–32.

Luraghi, Silvia. 2019. Basic valency orientation, the anticausative alternation, and voice in PIE. In Melanie Malzahn (ed.), *Akten der 16th Fachtagung der Indogermanischen Gesellschaft*, 259–274. Wiesbaden: Reichert.

Luraghi, Silvia, Guglielmo Inglese & Daniel Kölligan. Forthcoming. The passive voice in ancient Indo-European languages: Inflection, derivation, periphrastic verb forms. *Folia Linguistica Historica*.

Malicka-Kleparska, Anna. 2016. Old Church Slavonic as a language with the middle voice morphology. *SKASE Journal of Theoretical Linguistics* 13 (2). Available at http://www.skase.sk/Volumes/JTL32 (accessed 1 October 2020).

Malzahn, Melanie. 2018. A short history of Latin presents in long -e-. In Dieter Gunkel, Stephanie W. Jamison, Angelo O. Mercado, Kazuhiko Yoshida (eds.), *Vina Diem Celebrent. Studies in Linguistics and Philology in Honor of Brent Vine*, 202–217. Ann Arbor: Beech Stave Press.

Mendoza, Julia. 1984. La reflexividad en indoeuropeo. In Alberto Berbabè (ed.), *Athlon: Satura grammatica in honorem Francisci R. Adrados*, Volume 1, 325–338. Madrid: Gredos.

Mignot, Xavier. 1969. *Les verbes dénominatifs latins*. Paris: Klincksieck.

Næss, Åshild. 2007. *Prototypical transitivity*. Amsterdam & Philadelphia: John Benjamins.

Nedjalkov, Vladimir P. 1969. Nekotorye verojatnostnye universalii v glagol'nom slovoobrazovanii [Some probabilistic universals in verb formation]. In Igor' F. Vardul' (ed.), *Jazykovye universalii i lingvističeskaja tipologija* [Linguistic universals and linguistic typology], 106–114. Moscow: Nauka.

Nedjalkov, Vladimir P. & Georgij G. Sil'nickij. 1969. Tipologija morfologičeskogo i leksičeskogo kauzativov [Typology of morphological and lexical causatives]. In Xolodovič, Aleksandr A. (ed.), *Tipologija kauzativnyx konstrukcij* [Typology of causative constructions], 20–60. Moskva: Nauka.

Nichols, Johanna. 1982. Ingush transitivization and detransitivization. *Berkley Linguistic Society* 8. 445–462.

Nichols, Johanna. 1992. *Linguistic diversity in space and time*. Chicago: The University of Chicago Press.

Nichols, Johanna. 2017. Realization of the causative alternation: Revised wordlist and examples. Available at https://www.academia.edu/34318209/Realization_of_the_causative_alternation_Revised_wordlist_and_examples (accessed 1 October 2020).

Nichols, Johanna, David Peterson & Jonathan Barnes. 2004. Transitivising and detransitivising languages. *Linguistic Typology* 8 (2). 149–211.

Nussbaum, Alan. 1976. *Caland's 'law' and the Caland System*. University of Harvard PhD dissertation.

Nussbaum, Alan. 1999. *Jocidus*. An account of the Latin adjectives in -idus. In Heiner Eichner & H. C. Luschutzky (eds.), *Compositione indogermanicae in memoriam Jochem Schindler*, 377–419. Prague: Enigma.

Oettinger, Norbert. 2017. Lateinisch *lūcēscit* aus *lūcēs-cit lūcē-scit*? Überlegungen zur indogermanischen Wortbildung. In Ivo Hajnal, Daniel Kölligan & Katharina Zipser (eds.),

Miscellanea Indogermanica. Festschrift für José Luis García Ramón zum 65. Geburststag, 593–602. Innsbruck: Institut für Sprachwissenschaft.

Olsen, Birgit Anette. 2003. Another account of the Latin adjectives in *-idus*. *Historische Sprachforschung* 116 (2). 234–275.

Ottósson, Kjartan. 2013. The anticausative and related categories in the Old Germanic languages. In Folke Josephson & Ingmar Söhrman (eds.), *Diachronic and typological perspectives on verbs*, 329–382. Amsterdam & Philadelphia: John Benjamins.

Petit, Daniel. 1999. *Sue- en grec ancien: la famille du pronom réfléchi. Linguistique grecque et comparaison indo-européenne*. Louvain: Peeters.

Pinkster, Harm. 2015. *The Oxford latin syntax*, Volume 1. Oxford: Oxford University Press.

Plank, Frans & Aditi Lahiri. 2015. Microscopic and macroscopic typology: Basic valence orientation, more pertinacious than meets the naked eye. *Linguistic Typology* 19 (1). 1–54.

Puddu, Nicoletta. 2005. *Riflessivi e intensificatori: Greco, latino e le altre lingue indoeuropee*. Pisa: ETS Edizioni.

Puddu, Nicoletta. 2007. Typology and historical linguistics: Some remarks on reflexives in ancient IE languages. In Matti Miestamo & Bernhard Wälchli (eds.), *New challenges in typology: Broadening the horizons and redefining the foundations*, 249–270. Berlin & New York: Mouton de Gruyter.

Rappaport Hovav, Malka & Beth Levin. 2010. Reflections on manner/result complementarity. In Malka Rappaport Hovav, Edit Doron & Ivy Sichel (eds.), *Syntax, lexical semantics and event*, 21–38. Oxford: Oxford University Press.

Rau, Jeremy. 2009. *Indo-european nominal morphology: The decads and the Caland system*. Innsbruck: Institut für Sprachwissenschaft.

Rau, Jeremy. 2013. Notes on stative verbal roots, the Caland system, and primary verbal morphology in Indo-Iranian and Indo-European. In Adam Cooper, Jeremy Rau & Michael Weiss (eds.), *Multi nominis grammaticus: Studies in classical and Indo-European linguistics in honor of Alan J. Nussbaum, on the occasion of his sixty-fifth birthday*, 255–273. Ann Arbor: Beech Stave Press.

Reinöhl, Uta & Nikolaus P. Himmelmann. 2017. Renewal: A figure of speech or a process sui generis? *Language* 93 (2). 381–413.

Romagno, Domenica. 2003. Azionalità e transitività: il caso dei preverbi latini. *Archivio Glottologico Italiano* 88 (2). 156–170.

Ruijgh, Cornelius J. 2004. The stative value of the PIE verbal suffix *-éh$_1$-. In J. H. W. Penney (ed.), *Indo-European perspectives: Studies in honour of Anna Morpurgo Davies*, 48–64. Oxford: Oxford University Press.

Sausa, Eleonora. 2016. Basic valency orientation in Homeric Greek. *Folia Linguistica Historica* 37. 205–238.

Schäfer, Florian Mathis. 2008. *The syntax of (anti-)causatives: External arguments in change-of-state contexts*. Amsterdam & Philadelphia: John Benjamins.

Schindler, Jochem. 1980. Zur Herkunft der altindischen *cvī*-Bildungen. In Manfred Mayrhofer, Martin Peters & Oskar E. Pfeiffer (eds.), *Lautgeschichte und Etymologie. Akten der VI. Fachtagung der Indogermanischen Gesellschaft*, 386–393. Wiesbaden: Reichert.

Simone, Raffaele & Donato Cerbasi. 2001. Types and diachronic evolution of Romance causative constructions. *Romanische Forschungen* 113 (3). 441–473.

de Vaan, Michiel. 2008. *Etymological dictionary of Latin and the other Italic languages*. Leiden & Boston: Brill.

Viti, Carlotta. 2015. *Variation und Wandel in der Syntax der alten indogermanischen Sprachen*. Tübingen: Narr.
Watkins, Calvert. 1971. Hittite and Indo-European studies: The denominative statives in *-ē-*. *Transaction of the Philological Society* 74. 67–74.
Weiss, Michael. 2011. *Outline of the historical and comparative grammar of Latin*. Ann Arbor: Beech Stave Press.
Wichmann, Søren. 2015. Diachronic stability and typology. In Claire Bowern & Bethwyn Evans (eds.), *Handbook of historical linguistics*, 212–224. London & New York: Routledge.
Zúñiga, Fernando & Seppo Kittilä. 2019. *Grammatical voice*. Cambridge: Cambridge University Press.

Silvia Luraghi and Dionysios Mertyris
Basic valency in diachrony: from Ancient to Modern Greek

Abstract: The paper discusses changes in the encoding of basic valency and valency alternation in Greek. At its earliest stage, Homeric Greek, valency alternation is most frequently encoded through voice, whereby the active voice encodes caused events and the middle encodes spontaneous ones. This pattern is almost exclusive with inanimate verbs, while one third of animate verbs show suppletion. In Modern Greek lability plays a relevant role for inanimate verbs, while suppletion increases its frequency among animate verbs. Diachronic evidence shows an extension of voice alternation in Classical Greek, while lability emerged at the end of the Classical age and developed in Middle Greek. Comparison of Ancient with Modern Greek points to the replacement of a detransitivizing strategy (voice opposition) through an undetermined one (lability), which is clear-cut with inanimate verbs, with animate verbs showing an increasingly marginal adherence to either pattern and a tendency toward suppletion.

Keywords: diachrony, basic valency, lability, middle voice, Greek

1 Introduction

Since Nichols, Peterson and Barnes (2004) proposed a typology of lexical, or basic, valency, language specific in-depth studies have multiplied. Recently, research on changes in basic valency in single languages and language families has also brought diachrony into the picture (e.g. van Gelderen 2011; Plank and Lahiri 2015; Grünthal and Nichols 2016; Grünthal et al. this volume). With this paper we aim to provide further evidence for possible diachronic trends of basic valency orientation with a detailed study of Greek over a time span of three millennia.

Note: The glosses follow the Leipzig glossing rules (https://www.eva.mpg.de/lingua/resources/glossing-rules.php). For the sake of simplification, we have omitted some categories: in particular, gender of nouns, pronouns and adjectives is never specified, nominal number is specified only when it is plural, and verbal mood is indicated only for non-indicative moods only. Concerning voice, we always gloss as mid all non-active forms. Active voice is not INDICATED, unless it is contrasted with mid (non-active) in the gloss.

Silvia Luraghi, University of Pavia, e-mail: silvia.luraghi@unipv.it
Dionysios Mertyris, Ulster University, e-mail: dionys84@gmail.com

In the framework of valency patterns and valency orientation, the Greek language is an ideal field of investigation not only on account of the extensive evidence stemming from such a long attested history, but also because, among the Indo-European languages, it is the only one that has preserved the inflectional middle voice inherited from Proto-Indo-European, hence providing unique evidence on the diachrony of voice systems as well. Hence, Greek offers evidence for changes in the function of the inflectional middle, which is involved in the (anti)causative alternation to varying extents at different language stages.

For the purposes of this paper, we follow the definition of grammatical voice in Zúñiga and Kittilä (2019: 4) that we quote below [emphasis added].

> GRAMMATICAL VOICE is defined here as a grammatical category whose values correspond to particular diatheses marked on the form of predicates. Diathesis refers to the number of semantic arguments involved in a state of affairs, to how they are involved in it, and to how they are assigned to GRs of varying salience and flexibility. *Voice refers to the way a specific diathesis is formally marked on functional or lexical verbs in the predicate complex.*

The paper is organized as follows. In Section 2 we provide some background on the notions of basic valency and valency orientation. The data from the earliest literary Greek source, the Homeric poems, are reviewed in Section 3. In Section 4 we survey the Modern Greek data, before proceeding to discussing changes attested in the long time span that separates the earliest from the modern stage in Section 5. In Section 6 we discuss the findings and draw some conclusions.

2 Basic valency

Events can be construed differently by speakers, depending, for example, on how many participants are brought into the frame that one wants to adopt taking a certain vantage point. This has consequences on the encoding of specific events. Among possible variables, what concerns us here is the possibility to depict a situation as happening spontaneously, as in (1), or as being brought about by some external entity, as in (2).

(1) *The windowpane broke.*

(2) *The boy broke the windowpane.*

In (1), the verb *break* is used intransitively: in terms of valency, the verb is monovalent. In (2), in turn, the verb is transitive, hence bivalent. Notably, in English with this specific verb pair the transitivity alternation is not marked morphologically: the verb *break* is said to be labile precisely because it can be used transitively and intransitively without overt marking. However, as is well known, languages behave differently in this respect: in Italian, for example, the verb *rompere* 'break (tr.)' needs overt marking to encode the intransitive meaning *rompersi* 'break (intr.)', as shown in (3) and (4).

(3) *Il vetro si è rotto.*
 ART glass REFL is broken
 'The glass broke.'

(4) *Il bambino ha rotto il vetro.*
 ART boy has broken the glass
 'The boy broke the glass.'

In (3) the verb form *si è rotto* features the reflexive clitic *si*, which, in such cases, indicates valency reduction and profiles the event as spontaneous. This is an example of the so-called reflexive middle, which is widespread in the Indo-European languages of Europe, including other Romance languages, Slavic languages, and several Germanic languages with the notable exception of English. Conversely, in (4) the verb form *ha rotto* is transitive and morphologically unmarked for valency.[1]

In other languages, it is the transitive meaning that requires overt marking, as in Jakarta Indonesian (examples from http://valpal.info/meanings/break), as shown in (5) and (6).

(5) *Gelasnya pecah.*
 gelas-nya pecah
 glass-ASSOC break
 'The glass broke.'

(6) *Dalan mecahin gelas.*
 Dalan m-(p)ecah-in gelas
 Dalan G.ACT-break-G.APPL glass
 'Dalan broke the glass.'

---

[1] Note further that in periphrastic verb forms such as *si è rotto* and *ha rotto* one also finds different auxiliaries: while the occurrence of the reflexive clitic triggers the use of the auxiliary *essere* 'be' typical of unaccusative verbs, transitive verbs all feature the auxiliary *avere* 'have', which also occurs with unergative verbs.

In (6) the transitive form *mecahin* features extra marking with respect to the basic intransitive form *pecah* with the addition of the activizing prefix *m-* and of the applicative suffix *-in*. This type of alternation is usually referred to as the (anti) causative alternation. It has received increasing attention since Nedyalkov and Sil'nitsky (1969, English translation 1973), see e.g. Haspelmath (1987, 1993).

In order to capture a language's propension toward overt marking of either transitive or intransitive verbs, or toward other types of encoding such as lability in English, Nichols, Peterson and Barnes (2004) worked out a typology of lexical valency. The authors view lexical (or basic) valency orientation of a language as its "preferred or predominant or most common form of lexicalization or valence-related derivation" (Nichols, Peterson and Barnes 2004: 150–151). By analyzing 18 verb pairs in a sample of 80 languages, they found evidence for several types of strategies for the encoding of basic valency. Types (a) and (b) below involve forms that are marked by the addition of morphological material:

(a) Transitivizing languages: basic form is intransitive; transitive form is morphologically more complex. Augmented correspondences; example: Jakarta Indonesian, see (5) and (6) (special case: the basic form is an adjective)
(b) Detransitivizing languages: basic form is transitive; intransitive form is morphologically more complex. Reduced correspondences; example: Italian, see (1) and (2)

Strategies grouped under (c) and (d) all have in common the fact that they do not involve the addition or deletion of any morphological material:

(c) Undetermined correspondence:
    – Suppletion; example: English *die/kill*
    – Ambivalent (labile); example: English *break/break*
    – Conjugation class change; example: Classical Armenian *bžške-* 'heal' *bžški-* 'be healed' (Luraghi, Inglese and Kölligan 2021)
(d) Neutral correspondence:
    – Ablaut (English *fall/fell*)
    – Double derivation (equipollent); example: Hittite *parganu-* 'make tall' from *parku-* 'tall' *maknu-* 'make numerous' from *mekki-* 'much' *parkuess-* 'become high' or *makkess-* 'become numerous' (see Luraghi 2012)
    – Auxiliary change; example: Italian *ho affondato* 'I sank (tr.)' *è affondato* 'it sank (intr.)'

Verbs are further divided into animate and inanimate, depending on whether they tend to take animate or inanimate S/O (S/O is defined as the subject of the intransitive member of the verb pair and the causee of the transitive member). According to Nichols, Peterson and Barnes (2004), this distinction should reflect a cross-linguistic tendency, especially visible in languages which do not have a clear orientation, to feature transitivizing strategies for inanimate verbs and detransitivizing ones for animate verbs.

Before turning to the verb pairs, a note on the use of the notion of 'transitivity' and related terms is in order. Nichols and her associates state that ""Transitive" and "intransitive" are used in their strict, non-scalar senses: a verb is transitive if it governs a direct object; it is intransitive if it has no object" (Nichols, Peterson and Barnes 2004: 150). This raises some problems with verbs such as 'eat' which frequently take a direct object across languages. Similarly, perception verbs such as 'see' are often transitive, as they are in English and Greek, and the same holds for the verb 'learn'. Concerning this last verb, Haspelmath (1993: 105) remarks that "learning may be regarded as an agentive event itself, and in many languages the verb 'learn' is even transitive." As we will see, this peculiarity of the verb 'teach' is reflected in the choice between different lexemes in Modern Greek (see Sections 4 and 5.3.1). This problem is acknowledged by Nichols and associates, who make clear that theirs "is a typology of A-affecting lexical valence orientation" (Nichols, Peterson and Barnes 2004: 150) and propose the terms plain vs. induced rather than intransitive vs. transitive: plain refers to verbs that indicate non-induced, mostly spontaneous events. We will conform to this terminology as well.

The verbs and verb pairs in Nichols, Peterson and Barnes (2004) have been supplemented by a number of proxies in Nichols (2007). See Table 1.

Table 1: Verb pairs for basic valency test.

PLAIN	INDUCED	PROXY
ANIMATE (HUMAN) SUBJECTS		
1 laugh	make laugh, amuse	cry
2 die	kill	
3 sit	seat, have sit, make sit	lie down; go to bed, put to bed
4 eat	feed, give food	drink, give to drink
5 learn	teach	understand, find out, grasp
6 see	show	
7 be(come) angry	anger	annoy(ed)
8 fear, be afraid	frighten, scare	
9 hide, go into hiding	hide, conceal	
INANIMATE SUBJECTS		
10 (come to) boil	(bring to) boil	cook
11 burn, catch fire	burn, set fire	be aflame; char
12 break	break	split, shatter, smash
13 open	open	close
14 dry	(make) dry	wet, clean; black, white

Table 1 (continued)

PLAIN	INDUCED	PROXY
15 be(come) straight	straighten	crooked, long, round, flat
16 hang	hang (up)	lean (incline), extend, project, protrude
17 turn over	turn over	turn, turn around, rotate, revolve, roll; shake, tremble; move; ascend, rise
18 fall	drop, let fall	fall down, fall over, etc.; sink

Nichols, Peterson and Barnes' (2004) distinction between animate and inanimate verbs can be matched by the spontaneity scale proposed in Haspelmath (1993), shown in Table 2, which ranks events according to the likelihood of happening spontaneously vs. being caused by some external entity.[2]

Table 2: The spontaneity scale.

1. boil	16. begin
2. freeze	17. spread
3. dry	18. roll
4. wake up	19. develop
5. go out/put out (fire)	20. get lost/lose
6. sink	21. rise/raise
7. learn/teach	22. improve
8. melt	23. rock
9. stop	24. connect
10. turn	25. change
11. dissolve	26. gather
12. burn	27. open
13. destroy	28. break
14. fill	29. close
15. finish	30. split

This scale was further refined based on data from ValPaL (Valency Patterns Leipzig http://valpal.info/, see Introduction to this volume), hence inducing degrees of spontaneity from actual data rather than based on intuition, and including verbs that do not normally show the anticausative alternation (Haspelmath 2016). Haspelmath argues that among intransitive, change-of-state verbs (unaccusative in Haspelmath's 2016 terminology; another frequently used term for such verbs is inchoative) one can make a distinction between automatic and costly. Automatic vs. costly events are defined as follows: "an automatic process is a process that is easily construed as occurring on its own, without any external energy input,

---

[2] We left out the pair die/kill, which, as noted by Letuchiy (2010: 239) "is considered to be unique among all transitive/intransitive pairs", as it turns out to be instantiated by suppletion in the great majority of languages, see further Haspelmath (1993) and below, Section 3.

such as 'melt', 'freeze', 'dry', 'wake up', 'sink', 'go out (fire)'. A costly process is a process that does not so easily occur on its own, but typically involves some energy input ("cost"), e.g. 'break (intr.)', 'split (intr.)', 'open (intr.)', 'close (intr.)', 'change (intr.)', 'gather (intr.)'." (Haspelmath 2016: 3). Following this approach, among verbs in Nichols, Peterson and Barnes' (2004) sample 'boil', 'burn', 'dry' and 'fall' belong into the automatic group, while other verbs belong into the costly one. We will return to this scale when discussing the distribution of labile verbs in Modern Greek (Section 6).

3 Ancient Greek

In this Section we discuss basic valency in Ancient Greek, focusing on the earliest literary source, the Homeric poems.[3] The Ancient Greek verb features a systematic distinction between an active and a middle voice. A sizable number of verbs can only be inflected in the active (*activa tantum*) or in the middle (*media tantum*) (see below in this section for percentages), all other verbs can in principle feature both voices.

Based on data in Sausa (2016), voice alternation is the most frequent strategy for inanimate verbs with few exceptions, while animate verbs show a wider range of variation. Let us consider verb pairs in Table 3 (adapted from Sausa 2016).

Table 3: Homeric Greek strategies for the encoding of valency alternation.

PLAIN	INDUCED	PLAIN	INDUCED	STRATEGY
ANIMATE VERBS				
1 laugh	make laugh	*geláō* (ACT)	*ephíēmi gelásai*	PERIPHRASIS
2 die	kill	*thnḗskō* (ACT)	*kteínō* (ACT)	SUPPLETION
3 sit	seat	*hêmai* (MID)	*hízō* (ACT)	SUPPLETION+VOICE
		hízomai (MID)		VOICE
		hízō (ACT)		LABILE ACTIVE
4 eat	feed	*esthíō* (ACT)	*bóskō* (ACT)	SUPPLETION
5 learn	teach	*édaon* (ACT)	*dédae* (ACT)	AUGMENTATION
		didáskomai (MID)	*didáskō* (ACT)	VOICE
6 see	show	*horáō* (ACT)	*deíknumi* (ACT)	SUPPLETION
7 get angry	anger	*kholóomai* (MID)	*kholóō* (ACT)	VOICE

---

[3] Homeric Greek (ca. 11th c. BCE) Classical Greek (5th-4th c. BCE); Hellenistic Koine (3rd c. BCE – 4th c. CE); Medieval Greek (5th-15th c. CE); Modern Greek (16th c. CE – today).

Table 3 (continued)

PLAIN	INDUCED	PLAIN	INDUCED	STRATEGY
8 fear	frighten	deídō (ACT)	deidíssomai (MID)	AUGMENTATION
9 hide	conceal	keúthomai (MID)	keúthō (ACT)	VOICE
INANIMATE VERBS				
10 boil	boil	zéō (ACT)	– –	
11 catch fire	burn, set fire	kaíomai (MID)	kaíō (ACT)	VOICE
12 break	break	rhḗgnumai (MID)	rhḗgnumi (ACT)	VOICE
13 open	open	oígnumai (MID)	oígō (ACT)	VOICE
14 dry	(make) dry	térsomai (MID)	tersaínō (ACT)	DOUBLE DERIVATION (+VOICE)
15 be straight	straighten	tanúomai (MID)	tanúō (ACT)	VOICE
16 hang	hang (up)	krémamai (MID)	kremánnumi (ACT)	VOICE
17 turn over	turn over	stréphomai (MID)	stréphō (ACT)	VOICE
18 fall	drop, let fall	píptō (ACT)	híēmi (ACT)	SUPPLETION

Among animate verbs, voice alternation, though the most frequent strategy, accounts for less than half of the verb pairs. With other verb pairs, a variety of strategies is attested. The verb *geláō* 'laugh' occurs once in the Homeric poems in a periphrasis with *ephíēmi* 'push', 'cause to'. Sausa (2016: 216 fn. 16) quotes Haspelmath's (1993: 105) remark, that views "the verb laugh [as] an extreme case . . . , which is so typically spontaneous that it is hardly ever expressed as an anticausative". However, if we consider the meanings 'take pleasure, get amusement' / 'amuse' the verb pair *térpō* 'amuse', 'cause to enjoy' / *térpomai* 'enjoy', 'take pleasure' also occurs, in which it is voice that encodes the alternation, see Luraghi (2020: 256). Besides this isolated occurrence, periphrastic causatives are also attested with the pair 'eat' / 'feed' (see below), but in general they are not a widespread strategy in Homeric Greek.

Three verbs pairs feature suppletion: 'die' / 'kill', 'eat' / 'feed', and 'see' / 'show'. Notably, the first of these verb pairs shows almost exclusively suppletion cross-linguistically (see Haspelmath 1993: 106; Sausa 2016: 220), while the verb pair 'eat' / 'feed' is perhaps not the best choice for instantiating the anticausative alternation. As pointed out by Levin and Rappaport Hovav (2005: 8), with respect to other verbs involved in the anticausative alternation, such as 'break', "the verb eat . . . does not show an intransitive use whose subject is the transitive use's object (*The cookie ate)." Considering the Homeric Greek data, Sausa (2016: 220) remarks that "very often indeed, the causative counterpart of 'eat' is expressed through periphrases" which involve the verb 'give' and a consumption verb ('eat' or 'taste', 'drink' also appears in such periphrases, e.g. *Od.* 9.93; *Od.* 15.373). In any case, if we consider the meanings 'satiate oneself' / 'satiate (someone), feed' we again find a verb pair that features voice alternation, with middle *korénnamai* 'satiate (intr.)'/ active *korénnumi* 'satiate (tr.)' (Luraghi 2020: 257–258). No alternative strategy is available for the pair 'see' / 'show'. Notably, the verb *horáō* 'see' has both active and middle forms, but no detectable semantic difference can be ascribed to voice alternation (see Luraghi 2020: 126–127 with a discussion of the relevant literature on the distribution of voice with this and other sight verbs).

Augmentation is limited: the best instantiation consists in the verb pair *deídō* 'fear' / *deidíssomai* 'frighten', which is quite atypical for the anticausative alternation with experiential verbs even in Homer, as experiential verbs that feature a morphologically encoded alternation do so through voice (Luraghi 2020: 250–265). In Classical Greek, this verb pair was partly replaced by *phobéomai* (middle) 'fear' / *phobéō* (active) 'frighten', which conforms to the pattern of other verbs of emotion, and shows voice alternation (see Section 5.2). The verb pair *édaon* 'learn' /*dédae* 'teach' comes from a defective paradigm, which only features the aorist stem. The reduplicated aorist has a causative meaning, possibly reaching back to PIE, as reduplicated causative aorists also exist in Sanskrit (Burrow 1955: 336–337). Already in Homer, we also find the verb pair *didáskomai* (middle) 'learn' / *didáskō* (active) 'teach' with the valency alternation encoded through voice.

The verb pair 'sit' / 'seat' shows a complex situation. The two plain verbs, *hêmai* and *hízomai* are both middle, but they differ as to lexical aspect: while *hêmai* is stative, and always means 'be seated' in Homeric Greek, *hízomai* indicates a change of state, and means 'sit down'. In addition, the active *hízō* can also be labile. Hence, the proper counterpart of the induced verb is *hízomai* or even *hízō* in its intransitive meaning: with respect to *hêmai* the induced verb does not only introduce a valency change but also adds a dynamic dimension.[4]

Summing up, with animate verbs the only instance of a transitivizing strategy that is not in competition with voice alternation consists in the meaning pair 'fear' / 'frighten', which, however, is replaced by a pair with voice alternation in Classical Greek. Suppletion constitutes a more relevant strategy, with at least two verb pairs that do not also have voice alternation as an alternative. Voice alternation

---

4 This distinction with a stative verb, a plain change-of-state one, and a causative counterpart must possibly be reconstructed for Proto-Indo-European. For example, Nichols (2006) shows that in Old Church Slavic, in the case of stance verbs (i.e. verbs such as 'sit', 'stand', 'lie'), valency changing strategies have been developing interacting with verbal aspect. She remarks that the same pattern exists in Baltic, and indicates as an archaism possibly inherited from PIE a system with a three-fold distinction among static vs. change-of-state (or punctual) vs. transitive, whereby "forms [are] not straightforwardly built on each other", but the fact that the root aorist is punctual (i.e. intransitive) points to the derived nature of transitive forms.

slightly prevails, as it covers four pairs out of nine in Homeric Greek (n. 3, 5, 7 and 9) and in Classical Greek also extends to verb pair n. 8 (see Section 5.1). In addition, for n. 1 and 4 other verb pairs with similar meaning also show voice alternation.

Inanimate verbs encode valency alternations more homogeneously through voice, the only exception being the suppletive pair *píptō* / *hiēmi* 'fall' / 'drop' in which both verbs show active voice. Note that the latter verb does not strictly speaking mean 'drop' but 'throw', 'hurl'. A verb with a meaning closer to 'drop' could perhaps be *ríptō* 'cast'. Sausa (2016) describes the pair *térsomai* 'dry (intr.)' / *tersaínō* 'make dry' as encoding valency alternation via augmentation plus voice: the plain member of the verb pair *térsomai* shows middle voice, while the induced member *tersaínō* is active and features a suffix. Indeed, the causative verb is originally derived from the stem *ters-* plus the addition of a nasal suffix, etymologically connected with causative suffixes in other ancient Indo-European languages (see Luraghi 2012). Importantly, the suffix no longer conveyed causative semantics in Ancient Greek. Finally, Sausa (2016) does not provide a causative counterpart for *zéō* 'boil (intr.)', but one could also consider the verb pair *iaínō* 'warm up'(tr.)' / *iaínomai* 'warm up, relax (intr.)': note however that within this verb pair only active forms preserve their concrete meaning, while middle forms denote a positive emotion of relaxation based on a metonymic shift by which a sensation of warmth denotes wellbeing (Luraghi 2020: 261–262).

Considering now all verbs in Table 3, what strikes one as a regular feature of verb pairs in which the valency alternation is not encoded through voice is the fact that the plain member of the pair is active. With such verbs, suppletion is the most frequent strategy, with augmentation, i.e. overt morphological marking of causativization, possibly reflecting a more ancient Proto-Indo-European state of affairs (Luraghi 2019), clearly marginal. More evidence for the relevance of voice in the encoding of valency alternation is available from other verb pairs, both animate and inanimate, such as those shown in Table 4.

Table 4: Additional verbs with voice alternation encoding valency alternation.

	PLAIN (MIDDLE)	INDUCED (ACTIVE)	STRATEGY
	ANIMATE	VERBS	
i.	*órnumai* 'stand up'	*órnumi* 'lift'	voice alternation
ii.	*mimnḗskomai* 'remember'	*mimnḗskō* 'remind'	voice alternation
iii	*kḗdomai* 'worry'	*kḗdō* 'make worry'	voice alternation
iv	*aiskhúnomai* 'be ashamed'	*aiskhúnō* 'cause shame'	voice alternation
v	*lanthánomai* 'forget'	*lanthánō* 'escape, cause to forget'	voice alternation

Table 4 (continued)

	PLAIN (MIDDLE)	INDUCED (ACTIVE)	STRATEGY
	INANIMATE	VERBS	
vi	tréphomai (middle) 'grow'	tréphō 'let grow'	voice alternation
vii	phaínomai 'appear'	phaínō 'show'	voice alternation
viii	paúomai 'stop (intr.)'	paúō 'stop (tr.)'	voice alternation
ix	barúnomai 'grow heavy'	barúnō 'make heavy'	voice alternation
x	óllumai 'perish'	óllumi 'destroy'	voice alternation

We will return to some of these and more verb pairs featuring voice alternation in Section 5.1.

The verb pairs in Table 3 offer limited evidence for costly processes (in the terminology of Haspelmath 2016) being more readily denoted by verb pairs that encode valency alternation through voice, while only one automatic process corresponds to a verb pair with voice opposition ('catch fire' / 'set on fire'). However, other verb pairs referring to automatic process and featuring voice alternation can easily be found: among those mentioned in Table 4, for example, *tréphomai* 'grow' / *tréphō* 'let grow', *phaínomai* 'appear' / *phaínō* 'show', *barúnomai* 'become heavy' / *barúnō* 'make heavy' refer to automatic processes.

Up to now, we have refrained from specifying the orientation of voice alternation. Indeed, no matter what the nature of the active/middle relation might have been in Proto-Indo-European (see e.g. Willi 2018: 532; Luraghi 2019), in Ancient Greek we can see two different inflections, rather than a relation of morphological derivation of one voice from the other (see Allan 2003; Willi 2018). It is generally assumed that the middle voice is a detransitivizing strategy with respect to the active, however, the distribution of the two voices in Homeric Greek deserves some more discussion. Indeed, in Homeric Greek the percentage of *media tantum* is high, as they account for 38.2% of lemmas in a sample of 355 verbs (data from Romagno 2010). Remarkably, this does not mean that the remaining verbs all feature both voices: much to the contrary, another 14.5 % are either *activa tantum* (i.e. they only feature active morphology), or show a tense based voice distribution, whereby forms of specific tenses, often the future, are middle (our counting in a sample of 200 most frequent verbs in Homer). In other words, verbs that do not feature both voices make up for about half of all verbs in Homeric Greek.

Importantly, among active / middle verb pairs mentioned in this section some were arguably ancient *media tantum*, whose active forms are a recent innovation in Homer, and have apparently been created in order to provide a causative counterpart to the middle. This is the case for example for *mimnḗskō* 'remind' / *mimnḗskomai* 'remember' and *kholóō* 'anger someone' / *kholóomai* 'be(come) angry', see the discussion in Luraghi (2020: 254–256, 263–264) with further references. Strictly speaking, in such cases it is active voice that might be viewed as a transitivizing strategy. Notably, however, whatever one reconstructs as the original function of the middle in PIE, in Homeric Greek it already functioned as passive, though this was not its main function. Hence, the active voice is considered the unmarked member of active/middle opposition (see Willi 2018: 2), and voice alternation, as already noted, is usually considered a detransitivizing strategy.

In fact, the Greek middle was inherited from PIE, and its relation to the active in the proto-language remains discussed. Several scholars hold the view that voice cannot be reconstructed as oppositional in PIE, but that its distribution was largely lexical, a reconstruction which is supported by evidence from the most ancient stages of several Indo-European languages (see Luraghi 2019). What we observe in Homeric Greek is the ongoing implementation of a full-fledged voice system with an oppositional middle, which, at least in Ancient Greek, had also become morphologically heavier than the active and has partly been re-modelled on it, as shown by the present middle ending *-mai* which owes its nasal to analogy with the active (the inherited form should be *-ai*; Cotticelli-Kurras and Rizza 2015).

More in general, middle endings, even though they cannot always be said to be based on the active ones, are usually heavier (see Inglese this volume for similar considerations on Latin). In Table 5 we compare the present indicative active endings of *-mi* verbs with the corresponding middle endings.

Table 5: Present indicative endings in Ancient Greek.

	ACTIVE	MIDDLE
1 SG	mi	mai
2 SG	si	sai
3 SG	ti	tai
1 PL	men	metha
2 PL	te	sthe
3 PL	asi <*nti	ntai

Table 5 shows that middle endings are phonologically heavier than their active counterparts, either because they contain diphthongs in the place of simple vowels, as in the singular and in the third person plural, or because they are bisyllable rather than monosyllable, as in the first person plural. Even the second person plural, which is a monosyllable and contains the same vowel in both voices, contains more phonemes in the middle. Hence, we consider the active morphologically unmarked with respect to the middle, and consider voice alternation as a reduced correspondence.

Still, it must be pointed out that, apart from perhaps the first person singular if we accept the etymology proposed above, there is no relationship of derivation between the active and the middle. For this reason, voice alternation could be viewed as conjugation class change, if it were not for the fact that the two voices belong to the same inflectional paradigm of verbs that feature voice opposition. If one accepts the reconstruction of Proto-Indo-European (possibly Pre-Proto-Indo-European) that views active and middle voice as lexically distributed (see Benveniste 1966; more discussion in Luraghi 2019 with references), then one can view voice alternation as conjugation class change in Proto-Indo-European, i.e. as an undetermined strategy, later becoming a detransitivizing strategy based on a reduced correspondence after the paradigmaticization of voice opposition.

In Homeric Greek, one can also see traces of other, clearly transitivizing strategies such as reduplication and suffixation. Especially the latter is well attested in other ancient Indo-European languages, as argued in Luraghi (2012), and might well have been the basic strategy for valency alternation in Proto-Indo-European. In any case, voice opposition is the most relevant strategy with all types of verb, but with animate verbs suppletion also plays a relevant role, while with inanimate verbs voice opposition is almost the only attested strategy. This points to a distinction between the two groups of verbs, whereby inanimate verbs show a clearer orientation with respect to animate ones.

We will discuss post-Homeric developments in Section 5.

4 Modern Greek

Modern Greek is among the languages in Nichols, Peterson and Barnes' (2004) sample. The authors classify it as predominantly detransitivizing for inanimate verbs and neuter in the case of animate verbs. Our own analysis of the 18 verb pairs shown in Table 6 yielded the following results (the sum is higher than 18 because some verbs pairs show multiple strategies).
- Lability (ambitransitivity): 7
- Suppletion (including partial): 5
- Reduction: 5+2 (middle voice)
- Periphrasis: 1
- Augmentation (+voice): 2

Table 6: Valency alternation in Modern Greek.[5]

PLAIN	INDUCED	PLAIN	INDUCED	STRATEGY
ANIMATE VERBS				
1 laugh	make laugh	ɣeláo[5] (ACT)	káno na ɣelái	PERIPHRASIS
2 die	kill	peθéno (ACT)	skotóno (ACT)	SUPPLETION
3 sit	seat	IMPF NON-PAST: káθome (MID)	IMPF NON-PAST: kaθízo (ACT)	AUGMENTATION (+VOICE)
		PFV NON-PAST: kaθíso (ACT)	PFV NON-PAST: kaθíso (ACT)	LABILE
4 eat	feed	tróo (ACT)	taízo (ACT)	SUPPLETION
5 learn	teach	maθéno (ACT)	ðiðásko (ACT)	SUPPLETION
			maθéno (ACT)	LABILE
6 see	show	vlépo (ACT)	ðíxno (ACT)	SUPPLETION
7 get angry	anger	θimóno (ACT)	θimóno (ACT)	LABILE
8 fear	frighten	fováme (MID)	fovízo (ACT)	AUGMENTATION (+VOICE)
9 hide	conceal	krívome (MID)	krívo (ACT)	VOICE
INANIMATE VERBS				
10 boil	boil	vrázo (ACT)	vrázo (ACT)	LABILE
11 catch fire	set fire	kéɣome (MID)	kéo (ACT)	VOICE
		kéo (ACT)		LABILE
12 break	break	spáo (ACT)	spáo (ACT)	LABILE
13 open	open	aníɣo (ACT)	aníɣo (ACT)	LABILE
14 dry	(make) dry	kserénome (MID)	kseréno (ACT)	VOICE
15 be straight	straighten	isióno (ACT)	isióno (ACT)	LABILE
16 hang	hang (up)	kremιéme / krémome (MID)	kremáo (ACT)	VOICE
17 turn over	turn over	ɣirízo (ACT)	ɣirízo (ACT)	LABILE
18 fall	drop	péfto (ACT)	ríxno (ACT)	SUPPLETION

Let us start by observing some stable features that directly connect the Ancient Greek verb pairs with the Modern Greek ones. In the first place, the pair 'laugh'/ 'make laugh' remains encoded by an intransitive verb and a periphrastic causative. Suppletive pairs of Ancient Greek also correspond to suppletive pairs

---

5 The Medieval and Modern Greek examples are transcribed phonologically in the IPA (with the acute used to mark stress accent).

in Modern Greek, and include: 'die' / 'kill', 'eat' / 'feed', 'see' / 'show' and 'fall' / 'drop'. Notably, four of these verb pairs are animate and only one inanimate.

In fact, the extent of suppletion for animate verbs has become larger in Modern Greek, with the addition of verb pair 5, 'learn' / 'teach'. Valency alternation is described as suppletive in Nichols, Peterson and Barnes (2004).[6] Notably, however, the verb *maθéno* can also exhibit lability, while the active *ðiðásko* 'teach', in turn, also has a middle counterpart *ðiðáskome* 'learn', which is a learned form reintroduced into Modern Greek from Katharévousa (see Section 5.1). The verb can be found in dialectal Medieval and Modern Greek with the form *ðiðáxno*, which is the phonologically regular outcome of the Ancient Greek *didáskō*. Remarkably, transitive *maθéno* and *ðiðásko* are not completely in complementary distribution. This peculiarity has to do with the fact that, as remarked in Section 2, the verb 'learn' is different from other verbs that show the anticausative alternation, as it is transitive in many languages, among which Greek. Its counterpart 'teach', accordingly, is frequently ditransitive. In Greek (both Ancient and Modern), the verb 'teach' can take two objects, one of which is also the object of 'learn' and is typically inanimate, while the second is the argument involved in the alternation, i.e. the subject of the plain verb and the object of the induced one, which is typically animate and has the role of causee. The causee can be omitted: this brings about ambiguity if the labile verb is used. Accordingly, transitive *maθéno* can be used only when the verb is clearly ditransitive, in occurrences such as (7), while in occurrences such as (8) the only possible interpretation would be an intransitive one.

(7) *Ti   sas   émaθe   o   ðáskalos   símera?*
    what   2PL.ACC   learn.PST.3SG ART.NOM   teacher.NOM   today
    'What did the teacher teach you today?'

(8) *Maθénume   angliká*
    learn.PRS.1PL   English
    'We learn/*teach English.'

On the other hand, *ðiðásko* is an unambiguous alternative in any context, both with and without a causee, as shown in (9).

---

6 We thank Johanna Nichols for sharing with us the list of Greek verb pairs used in Nichols, Peterson and Barnes (2004), which does not appear in the article. A list of verb pairs, not coinciding with ours but containing some of those listed in Table 6, is also provided in the Appendix by Haspelmath (1993: 114). For some meanings, Haspelmath selected the same verb pairs as we did, but for some others he selected different verbs. However, choices are not discussed and motivated.

(9) O   kaθiyitís   ðiðáski/   *maθéni
    ART.NOM   professor.NOM   teach.PRS.3SG /   *learn. PRS.3SG
    (tus   fitités)   sto   panepistímio.
    ART.ACC.PL   student.ACC.PL   in_the   university
    'The professor teaches (the students) at the university.'

Variation between lability and voice characterizes verb pair 7. We used the labile verb *θimóno* 'get angry / anger' mainly because it is the same verb pair used by Nichols, Peterson and Barnes (2004); note however that judgments vary among speakers and we might as well have used the more frequent *eknevrízo* as causative counterpart of intransitive *θimóno*.⁷ This would have the effect that lability would play no role among animate verbs (except for perfective forms of *kaθíso* 'sit' / 'seat', on which see below), while the extent of suppletion would grow. Notably, however, lability does not bring about the same degree of ambiguity as in the case of the verb pair 'learn' / 'teach', and lability is also shown by another verb pair *nevriázo* (intr.) / *nevriázo* (tr.) 'be irritated' / 'irritate'. In fact, the pair 'get angry' / 'anger' is different from the pair 'learn' / 'teach' in terms of syntactic transitivity, as the plain verb is a true intransitive, the induced verb is not ditransitive and there is no second object involved. In addition, one also has to reckon with voice alternation, as the plain counterpart of *eknevrízo* 'anger' can also be the middle *eknevrízome* 'be angry, irritated', and the more colloquial pair *tsatízome* 'be irritated'/ *tsatízo* 'irritate' (<Turkish *çat*) also shows that voice alternation can be used in parallel with lability for these meanings.

The pair 'fear'/ 'frighten' *fováme/ fovízo* features augmentation. It constitutes a complex case, as the plain and the induced verb have different stems with the induced verb containing the similative suffix *-iz*, but also show middle vs. active inflection, hence valency alternation is also marked by voice. In Homeric Greek, the corresponding verb pair *deídō / deidíssomai*, though not etymologically related, also shows augmentation, but note that, as we remarked in Section 3, the distribution of voice is not coherent with the role it plays elsewhere, as it is the plain verb (*deídō* 'fear') that is active, while the induced one (*deidíssomai* 'frighten') is middle. Nichols, Peterson and Barnes (2004) regard this an instance of double derivation, but we prefer to view it as augmentation, even though the base for the suffix *-iz* is not the plain verb, but the noun *fóvos* 'fear'. Another possible counterpart of plain *fováme* is *foverízo* 'frighten' formed with

---

7 One reviewer even suggested that "the causative use of *θimóno* is a bit marginal and can be found only in such expressions as *me θimosan ta logia tu* ['your words make me angry']."

the same suffix from the base *foverós* 'frightening' (see further the discussion in Section 5.3.3).

As regards the pair 'sit' / 'seat' *káθome* (mediopassive)/ *kaθízo* (active),[8] even though one might have the impression that the same suffix is involved, this is not the case: in fact, Modern Greek *káθome* derives form Ancient Greek *káthēmai* (*katá* + *hêmai*), while Modern Greek *kaθízo* comes from Ancient Greek *kathízō* (*katá* + *hízō*).[9] As shown in Table 3, the two verbs share the same perfective stem (*kaθis-*) and have a split strategy for the perfective future tense, the perfective past tense and the perfective subjunctive mood.[10] We still considered this as an instance of augmentation, as the induced verb is phonologically heavier than the plain one, but an analysis as double derivation as the one proposed by Nichols, Peterson and Barnes (2004) can also be agued for (or even as suppletion, as in the case of Ancient Greek *hêmai* / *hízō*, see Table 3). Perfective forms of this verb pair are labile. This was the only verb pair that also featured lability in Homeric Greek already, and constitutes a remarkable case of stability over time. As in Ancient Greek, the present imperfective double-marks the alternation through voice.

Some verb pairs may feature more than one strategy. The pair 'burn'/ 'set on fire', which is considered labile by Nichols, Peterson and Barnes (2004), can encode the anticausative alternation through voice, as shown by the plain middle in (11), even though in some contexts the active verb can be labile (cf. Alexiadou and Anagnostopoulou 2004: 124) as in (10).

(10) i   fotiá   kéi/*kéyete
    ART.NOM   fire.NOM   burns.PRS.ACT/*MID.3SG
    'The fire burns.'

(11) to   spíti   kéyete/*kéi
    ART.NOM   house.NOM burns.PRS.MID/*ACT
    'The house is on fire.'

---

[8] The two verbs 'sit' / 'seat' *káθome* (mediopassive)/ *kaθízo* (active) might be cognates historically, even though, strictly speaking, they can hardly be considered derived from each other synchronically: both *hêmai* and *hízō* possibly originate from a common PIE *sed-* root, see further the discussion of the corresponding verb pair in Homeric Greek in Section 3.

[9] The prefixed verbs *káthēmai* and *kathízō* replaced the non-suffixed *hêmai* and *hízō* in 5th century BCE Attic prose already.

[10] 'Sit': imperfective non-past *káθome*/ perfective non-past *kaθíso*; 'seat': imperfective non-past *kaθízo*/ perfective non-past *kaθíso*.

In comparison to our data, Nichols, Peterson and Barnes (2004) have a higher number of inanimate verb pairs in which voice encodes the alternation. These include the pairs 'open', 'straighten' and 'turn over', which deserve some more comments.

The pair 'open' is reported to be *aníyome* (plain) vs. *aníyo* (induced). This is not completely correct, as the verb is normally labile. Interestingly the mediopassive form *aníyome* is only used as an anticausative with animate subjects. Consider examples (12)-(14).

(12) i   pórta   aníyi/*aníyete
     ART.NOM door.NOM   opens.PRS.ACT/*MID.3SG
     'The door opens.'

(13) o   Kóstas   aníyi   tin   pórta
     ART.NOM Kostas.NOM opens.PRS.ACT.3SG ART.ACC   door.ACC
     "Kostas opens the door.'

(14) o   Kóstas   aníyete   éfkola
     ART.NOM door.NOM   opens.PRS.MID.3SG easily
     'Kostas opens up easily.'

The pair 'straighten' is reported as *isiázome* (plain)/ *isiázo* (induced), which is mainly a dialectal form that is nearly obsolete in Standard Modern Greek (cf. Babiniotis 1998) and its voice alternation is attested in Medieval Greek (see Section 5). On the contrary, *isióno* can be used both as a transitive and as an intransitive verb, hence instantiating another case of lability, as shown in (15) and (16).

(15) ta   maliá   mu   ðen   isiónun   éfkola
     ART.NOM.PL   hair.NOM.PL   1SG.GEN   NEG   straighten.PRS.3PL easily
     'My hair does not straighten out easily.'

(16) spánia   isióno   ta   maliá   mu
     rarely   straighten.PRS.1SG ART.ACC.PL   hair.ACC.PL   1SG.GEN
     'I rarely straighten my hair.'

Finally, the pair 'turn over' is incorrectly reported as alternating, with *anapoðoyirízome* being the plain form and *anapoðoyirízo* as the induced one. Regardless of the exact form of the pair (the compound *anapoðoyirízo*[11] or the simple *yirízo*), *(anapoðo)yirízo* is a true labile, as can be seen in (17) and (18).

(17) i   karékla   (anapoðo)yírise/*(anapoðo)yirístike
     ART.NOM   chair.NOM   turn_over.SUBJ.PST.ACT/*MID.3SG
     'The chair turned over.'

(18) o   Kóstas   (anapoðo)yírise   tin   karékla
     the.NOM   Kostas.NOM   turn_over.PST.3SG   ART.ACC   chair.ACC
     'Kostas turned over the chair.'

More verb pairs with similar meanings to those included in Table 6 may feature alternative strategies. So for example for the pair 'dry' besides the pair *kserénome* (plain)/ *kseréno* (induced), which features voice alternation as shown in (19) and (20), another possible instantiation is the labile *steynóno* 'dry'/ *steynóno* 'make dry', which is used in different contexts as shown in (21) and (22).

(19) to   xortári   kseraθike/*kserane
     ART.NOM   grass.NOM   dry.PST.MID.3SG/*dry.PST.ACT.3SG
     'The soil dried up.'

(20) i   zésti   ksérane   to   xortári
     ART.NOM   heat.NOM   dry.PST.ACT.3PL ART.ACC   grass.ACC
     'The heat dried the soil.'

(21) ta   maliá   mu   stéynosan/*steynóθikan
     ART.NOM.PL   hair.NOM.PL   1SG.GEN   dry.PST.ACT.3PL/*dry.PST.MID.3PL
     'My hair got dry.'

(22) o   aeras   stéynose   ta   maliá   mu
     ART.NOM   air.NOM   dry.PST.ACT.3SG ART.ACC.PL   hair.ACC.PL   1SG.GEN
     'The air dried my hair.'

On the other hand, for the meaning 'turn' the pair *stréfome/ stréfo* 'turn/ direct' is also available besides the labile *yirízo*, again used in different contexts (see further Section 5.8), as in (23) and (24).

---

[11] From *anápoðos* "upside-down" (adjective) + *yirízo*.

(23) stréfo   to   vléma   mu   sto   mélon
     turn.PRS.1SG ART.ACC   sight.ACC   1SG.GEN   in_ ART.ACC future.ACC
     'I direct my sight to the future.'

(24) i   néi   stréfonde   stin   texnoloyía
     ART.NOM.PL   young.NOM.PL   turn.PRS.MID.3PL   in_ ART.ACC   technology
     'Young people turn (themselves) to technology.'

It stems from the Ancient Greek verb *stréphomai/ stréphō* 'turn over' and exhibits its ancient counterpart's voice alternation. Its usage is mostly found in higher registers, as it constitutes an influence from Katharévousa.

From the data in Table 6, it turns out that labile verbs (ambitransitive in Nichols, Peterson and Barnes' 2004 terminology) dominate among inanimate verbs, while in the same group voice alternation has become more limited (see Alexiadou and Anagnostopoulou 2004; Alexiadou 2014). On the other hand, animate verbs show a wider variety of strategies, as they already did in Ancient Greek. Labile verbs also are marginal in this group, possibly restricted to the perfective *kaθíso* 'sit down' / 'seat'. Remarkably, this was the only pair that also exhibited lability in Ancient Greek. Both in Ancient and in Modern Greek, the same meanings could also be instantiated by a verb pair that features voice alternation: as already discussed above, in Modern Greek this involves two slightly different verb stems, but note that voice alternation is coherent with other verb pairs that encode valency alternation through voice alone.

The same can be said for the verb pair *fováme* 'fear' / *fovízo* 'frighten' in which two slightly different stems are involved along with voice in the encoding of the alternation. Notably, this was not always the case in Homeric Greek, in which the corresponding verb pair *deídō* (active) 'fear' / *deidíssomai* (middle) 'frighten' does show voice alternation, but is incoherent with the habitual distribution of voice with respect to valency: indeed, in this verb pair the intransitive member *deídō* 'fear' shows active morphology, while the transitive member *deidíssomai* 'frighten' is always inflected in the middle. This verb pair was partly replaced by *phobéomai* (middle) 'fear' / *phobéō* (active) 'frighten' in Classical Greek, with valency encoded by voice alternation, coherently with the distribution of voice in other verb pairs (see Sections 3 and 5).

Possibly labile animate verb pairs are *maθéno* 'learn' / 'teach' (see Section 5.1) and *θimóno* 'be angry' / 'anger' (see Section 5.2). In the first case, however, there is a suppletive alternative for the transitive member of the verb pair, *ðiðásko* 'teach', which is the only possibility in ambiguous contexts. Ambiguity with this verb pair may arise due to syntactic transitivity of the plain verb. In the case of the meanings 'be angry / anger', we saw that several verb pairs exist. Beside the labile verb *θimóno, eknevrízo / eknevrízo* may either encode the alternation through voice, or, with its active forms, provide a suppletive alternative to transitive *θimóno*. Finally, voice encodes valency alternation with another animate verb, *krívome* 'hide' / *krívo* 'conceal'.

In this connection, the verb *aníyo* 'open' is especially interesting. As we showed in examples (12) and (13), the verb is normally labile. In the unusual case that it occurs with an animate subject, the spontaneous event is marked by the middle voice as shown in (14). Remarkably, this is not an isolated case. Alexiadou and Anagnostopoulou (2004: 126) argue that some other verbs may either be labile with inanimate subjects or encode valency alternation through voice with animate subjects, with the middle voice functioning as anticausative. One such verb is *leróno* 'dirty', as in (25)-(27) (adapted from Alexiadou and Anagnostopoulou 2004).

(25) o   yiánis   lérose   to   trapezomándilo
     ART.NOM   John.NOM   dirty.PST.3SG   ART.ACC   tablecloth.ACC
     'John dirtied the tablecloth.'

(26) to   trapezomandilo   lerose/lerothike   apo   mono   tu
     ART.NOM   tablecloth.NOM   dirty.PST.ACT/MID.3SG from   alone   3SG.GEN
     'The tablecloth got dirty by itself.'

(27) o   yiánis   leróθike/*lérose.
     ART.NOM   John.NOM   dirty.PST.MID/*ACT.3SG
     'John got dirty.'

Similarly, the verb *stravóno* 'crook' / 'bend' is labile. It also has the colloquial meaning 'to blind someone' / 'make someone lose their sight temporarily', and in the middle it can occur with animate subjects and means 'become blind':

(28) to   xerúli   strávose
     ART.NOM   handle.NOM   bend.PST.3SG
     'The handle got bent.'

(29) o   yiánis   strávose   to   xerúli
     ART.NOM   John   bend. PST.3SG ART.ACC   handle.ACC
     'John bent the handle.'

(30) ta   fóta   mas   strávosan
     ART.NOM.PL   light.NOM.PL   1PL.ACC   bend.PST.3PL
     'The lights blinded us.'

(31) o   yiánis   stravóθike
    ART.NOM   John   bend.PST.MID.3SG
    'John lost his sight.'

The preference of animate subjects for overt marking of valency reduction through the middle voice seems to be connected with the likelihood for verb pairs in this group to have animate or inanimate subjects when they denote spontaneous events. Indeed, 'open' belongs in the group of inanimate verbs in Nichols, Peterson and Barnes (2004), and 'dirty' and 'bend' can also be ascribed to the same group. Non-overt marking would more likely trigger an agentive reading of the animate subject, hence the need for overt marking. In addition, with some of these verbs a human participant might also act intentionally. In such cases, the plain verb inflected in the middle leaves open the possibility for a reflexive reading. Let us consider the verb *tendóno* 'stretch' in Babiniotis' (1998) dictionary.

(32) min   tendónis   to   skiní, θα   spási
    NEG   stretch.IMPER.2SG   ART   rope   FUT   break
    'Don't stretch the rope, it will break.'
    TRANSITIVE ACTIVE

(33) me   aftes   tis   ambules   to   δérma
    with   DEM.ACC.PL   ART.ACC.PL   ampoule.ACC.PL   ART   skin
    tendóni
    stretch.PRS.3SG
    'The skin stretches with these ampoules.' INTRANSITIVE ACTIVE

(34) tendóθike   yiá   na   δi   ti
    stretch.PST.MID.3SG   for   to   see.SUBJ.PFV.PRS.3SG   what
    yinótan
    happen.PST.MID.3SG
    'He stretched himself so he could see what was happening.' REFLEXIVE MIDDLE (INTENTIONAL)

(35) kíta   pós   tendónete,   ótan   akúi
    look.IMPER.2SG   how   stretch.PRS.MID.3SG   when   hear.PRS.3SG
    kopliménda
    compliment.ACC.PL
    'Look how he stretches (gloats), when he hears compliments.' REFLEXIVE MIDDLE (UNINTENTIONAL)

Notably, verbs that can be labile with inanimate subjects but encode valency alternation through voice with animate ones do not only denote events that typically involve inanimate participants, but also belong to the 'costly' group according to Haspelmath (2016). This means that, on the one hand, animate subjects with active forms are likely to be taken as denoting agents as already pointed out above, while on the other hand the middle voice leaves open the possibility both of a spontaneous and a reflexive interpretation. These options are not available for inanimate subjects, as inanimate participants are typically unable to bring about or control events. As animate participants are more versatile, it comes as no surprise that animate subjects need heavier marking on the verb for disambiguating valency.

It can further be noted that, as signaled by Alexiadou and Anagnostopoulou (2004), deadjectival verbs tend to be labile. These include *aðiázo* 'empty', *asprízo* 'whiten', *kokinízo* 'redden', *mavrízo* 'blacken', *kaθarízo* 'clean', *strongilévo* 'round', *platéno* 'widen', *steynóno* 'dry', *stenévo* 'tighten', *skuréno* 'darken', *kaθisteró* 'delay', *alázo* 'change', *ksepayóno* 'defreeze'. Interestingly, most of these verbs usually take inanimate subjects. On the other hand, among deadjectival verbs that also feature middle morphology, kseréno 'dry up' belongs in the inanimate verbs group, but treléno 'madden' is animate and zesténo 'warm up' is also mostly used with animate subjects, hence again pointing to a bigger need for disambiguation of the verbal valency in cases in which an active form of the verb would allow for an agentive interpretation of the subject.

More in general, it is remarkable that even for verbs that virtually never allow inanimate subjects, such as 'eat' / 'feed', marking is made explicit by suppletion: in this framework, the increase of suppletive pairs in Modern Greek, partly as a recent development that limits lability, offers more evidence for a sharp distinction between inanimate subjects / lability on the one hand and animate subjects / overt marking on the other hand.

5 From Ancient to Modern Greek

In this section we discuss the changes that took place during the time span elapsed from the Homeric Greek stage described in Section 3 to Modern Greek as illustrated in Section 4. We start by outlining the developments emerging from Classical Greek, and argue that the opposition between the middle and the active voice, which already functioned as main strategy for the encoding of the anticausative alternation, became even more extended (Section 5.1). We then show that voice opposition underwent a major change leading to the marginalization of its role in the anticausative alternation, and argue that this development was accompanied by the rise of lability (Section 5.2). As will be shown, the majority of these changes began in late Hellenistic Greek and were consolidated in Medieval Greek.

5.1 Classical Greek

We have argued in Section 3 that the use of voice opposition for the encoding of valency alternation was on the rise in Homeric Greek, and that some verb pairs featured old *media tantum* with active counterparts that constituted an innovation in Homer. This development proceeded further in post-Homeric Greek. Among fear verbs, *atúzomai* 'be terrified' only has middle forms in Homer; in later epics, the active *atúzō* is also attested, with the meaning 'cause terror' (Luraghi 2020: 231). The pair *deídō* 'fear' / *deidíssomai* 'frighten' was still used in post-Homeric Greek, but remained marginal in comparison with the much more frequent pair *phobéomai* 'fear' / *phobéō* 'frighten, threaten'.[12] This verb pair is also attested in Homer, but only with the meaning 'flee' / 'put to flight' (Luraghi 2020: 288–289). The verb pair *édaon* 'learn' *dédae* 'teach', with which valency alternation was indicated by reduplication, hence a transitivizing strategy, disappeared after Homer, and only the pair *didáskomai* 'learn' *didáskō* 'teach' featuring voice opposition remained.

Besides the verbs in Table 1, more verbs that were *media tantum* in Homer developed active forms in Classical and post-Classical Greek, even though some remained sporadic. Examples are *geúomai* 'taste' / *geúō* 'let taste' from Herodotus (5th century BCE), *maínomai* 'be furious' / *maínō* 'make furious' in 5th century Attic tragedy and comedy , *meilaínomai* 'become black' / *melaínō* 'make black' in Aristotle (4th century BCE), *théromai* 'become warm' / *térō* 'warm up' (the active form is attested in Apollonius Rhodius, 3rd century BCE, and Nicander, 2nd century BCE).[13] Thus, the role of voice in the encoding of valency alternation, which was already relevant and still on the rise in Homeric Greek, became even more relevant in Classical Greek, and expanded its relevance in the group of animate verbs. Hence, from the point of view of basic valency Ancient Greek can be considered a detransitivizing language, with voice alternation providing

---

12 See the data in the Perseus database: http://www.perseus.tufts.edu/hopper/wordfreq?lang=greek&lookup=fobe%2Fwhttp://www.perseus.tufts.edu/hopper/wordfreq?lookup=deidi%2Fssomai&lang=greek http://www.perseus.tufts.edu/hopper/wordfreq?lookup=dei%2Fdw&lang=greek
13 See also Lavidas (2010: 67), who also argues that some active intransitive verbs became labile in post-Homeric Greek, and mentions *zéō* 'boil', attested in Apollonius Rhodius (3rd century BCE) in the meaning 'make boil'.

the most frequent strategy whereby the unmarked active voice encodes induced events while the middle voice encodes plain events.

5.2 The middle voice from Classical to Modern Greek

In the Hellenistic and Medieval Greek period, the verb system underwent major changes, which also affected voice. While a complete assessment of the developments that affected the middle voice from Classical Greek up to Modern Greek falls outside the scope of our paper, it needs to be mentioned that some functions of the middle voice, notably the reciprocal and the autobeneficiary were dropped or strongly limited, while the passive function became more relevant. Indeed, passive is often described in reference handbooks as the main function of the Modern Greek middle (Holton, Mackridge and Philippaki-Warburton 1997: 211–216). Contrasting the frequency of middle functions in Ancient and Modern Greek unveils a number of tendencies that we shortly summarize below.

(a) Decrease in the token frequency of *media tantum*: in Homer (8th c. BCE) *media tantum* account for 15.9% total occurrences of the 200 most frequent verbs (see Section 3), while in a corpus of literary Modern Greek from the 1980s they cover 8.5% (Stamatiou 2017, henceforth LitMG). This tendency emerges at an early stage, as the number of oppositional middles is on the rise from Homeric Greek onward as we pointed out above (see further Schwyzer 1959).

(b) Even though the Modern Greek middle largely preserves the semantics of the Ancient Greek middle, token frequency shows a different distribution of the various meanings. Among the 50 most frequent verbs in Homer, out of 15,818 occurrences middle tokens account for 4050, of which 2209 are oppositional middles. Among these occurrences, 861 are from verbs that do not show any semantic differences between voices.

We restricted the observations to verbs with passive, reflexive/reciprocal/autobeneficiary and anticausative middles, and compared them with the verb samples form literary Modern Greek. Comparison yields the results in Table 7 that confirm Holton, Mackridge and Philippaki-Warburton's (1997) description, and show a reversal in the ratio passive / anticausative in the functions of middle forms of verbs in Modern Greek as compared to Homeric Greek.[14]

---

14 The figures in Table 7 point to a sharp decrease of the reflexive, reciprocal and autobeneficiary functions. Concerning the latter, Lavidas (2010: 108) argues that the decline already started in the Hellenistic Koine.

Table 7: Token frequency of middle voice functions in Homeric and Modern Greek.

	PASSIVE	REFL/REC/AUTOB	ANTICAUSATIVE
Homer	19,6%	38,3%/	42,1%/
LitMG	63,9%	12,1%	24%

Indeed, as we have argued in Section 4, the role of voice in the encoding of valency orientation has become more limited as compared to Ancient Greek. Most important in this connection is the rise of lability, which was restricted in Ancient Greek and which we found as extensively used in the encoding of valency alternation in Modern Greek. Karantzola and Lavidas (2014) identify the following patterns in the diachrony in post-Classical Greek:

i. Intransitive verb with active morphology → labile verb, e.g. Ancient Greek *eksamartánō* 'fail' (intr.) → Hellenistic Koine *eksamartánō* 'fail' (intr.)/ 'do wrong to someone' (tr.)

ii. Intransitive verb with active/middle morphology → alternating verb (active causative, active/nonactive anticausative), e.g. Classical Greek *leukaínō* (ACT)=*leukaínomai* (MID) 'become white' → Hellenistic Koine *leukaínō* (ACT intr.)=*leukaínomai* (MID) 'become white'/ *leukaínō* (ACT tr.) 'whiten'

iii. Intransitive verb with middle morphology → alternating verb (causative type with active morphology and anticausative type with middle morphology), e.g. Classical Greek *hḗdomai* 'enjoy' (MID intr.) → Hellenistic Koine *hḗdomai* 'enjoy' (MID intr.)/ *hḗdō* 'enjoy' (ACT tr.)

With regard to the exact origin of labilization, it should be noted that none of the pairs under examination involved the labile strategy in Ancient Greek apart from *hízō* 'sit' / 'seat', for which the mediopassive *hízomai* was also available for the plain meaning.[15] Another verb that could occasionally encode valency alternation through lability is *auksánō* (ACT tr.) 'increase'/ *auksánomai* (MID intr.) 'increase'

---

[15] Lavidas (2010: 68) discusses some cases of verbs that he considers labile in Ancient Greek. Notably, however, he does not distinguish between P- (or Patient-preserving) lability and A- (or Agent-preserving) lability (see Dixon 1994; Letuchiy 2009). Only the former is relevant for the anticausative alternation, which involves events in which a patient undergoes a change of state either spontaneously (plain) or because it is brought about by another participant (induced). On the other hand, A-lability refers to transitive verbs used without a direct object, preserving the Agent in subject position. In traditional Indo-European linguistics this is called 'absolute' use of transitive verbs, and in Ancient Indo-European languages it does not require any special marking, as in e.g. *siōpáō* 'stay silent (intr.)' / 'keep secret (tr.)' mentioned by Lavidas (2010: 68).

→ *hē selḗnē auksánei* (ACT intr.) 'the moon increases (in size)' Aristotle, *Analytica priora et posteriora* 78b (4th c. BCE). This influence on other verbs must have been especially successful when the anticausative meaning of a verb could be expressed by both its active and a non-active form, cf. *leukaínō* (ACT)=*leukaínomai* (MID) 'become white'.

5.3 Developments within verb pairs

In the following sub-sections the pairs of Table 6 with diachronic changes in their strategies will be discussed as part of the verb-specific approach of our paper. More specifically, we will focus on the following pairs: 'learn' / 'teach' (Section 5.3.1), 'be angry' / 'anger' (Section 5.3.2), 'fear' / 'frighten' (Section 5.3.3), 'catch fire' / 'set fire' (Section 5.3.4), 'break' / 'break' (Section 5.3.5), 'open' / 'open' (Section 5.3.6), 'dry' / 'make dry' (Section 5.3.7), 'be straight' / 'straighten' (Section 5.3.8), and 'turn over' / 'turn over' (Section 5.3.9).

5.3.1 'Learn' / 'teach'

As was mentioned in Section 4, the presence of *ðiðáskome/ ðiðásko* 'learn' / 'teach' in Modern Greek is due to influence of Katharévousa, which was the official language of Greece for nearly 150 years (1830–1976), which replaced *ðiðáxnome/ ðiðáxno*, the direct descendant of the ancient verb that occurs in some Medieval Greek and Modern Greek varieties. In Modern Greek, the active form *ðiðásko* 'teach' provides an induced counterpart to plain *maθéno* 'learn', which is the only possible choice in cases in which lability would bring about ambiguity, as argued at length in Section 4.

The labile *maθéno* stems from the Classical Greek *manthánō* 'learn' and was formed on the basis of the aorist stem *math-* and the derivational suffix *-ain-*. The Ancient Greek *manthánō* had a mediopassive future (*mathḗsomai*), but true passive uses of the verb were rare, as only seven occurrences can be found in Classical Greek and all them are attested in Plato, as shown in (36).

(36) *mathḗmata   mēdamê̂   toutôn   iatikà*
      lesson.NOM.PL not   this.GEN.PL healing.NOM.PL
      ek   néōn   manthánētai
      out_of   young.GEN.PL   learn.SUBJ.PRS.MID.3SG
      'No healing lessons at all are learnt from a young age.' Plato, *Timaeus* 87b (4th c.BCE)

Given the fact that the ditransitive use of the verb with the semantic extension to 'teach' does not seem to be attested until the vernacular late Medieval Greek texts, the change most likely took place at some point in the early Medieval period of the language (5th-10th c. CE) and not earlier. An example is (37).

(37) *máθe   to   tsangárin   to   peðín   su*
     learn.IMPER.2SG ART.ACC shoemaker.ACC ART.ACC child.ACC 2SG.GEN
     'Teach your child to be a shoemaker.' *Ptochoprodromica* 3.112 (12th c. CE)

As regards the course of this change, it is uncertain whether the mediopassive morphology of the future tense of the verb could have played a role in the reanalysis of the active future forms that started to appear in late Hellenistic Koine.[16] Among our verb pairs, this is the only case in which the plain member of the pair is transitive and the induced member can be ditransitive. From the point of view of the rise of lability, we witness an extension to the ditransitive construction of a transitive verb. Morphology remains active throughout this development.

5.3.2 'Be angry' / 'anger'

The Modern Greek labile *θimóno* stems from the Ancient Greek media tantum *thumóomai* 'be angry', whose active intransitive forms first appear in Hellenistic Koine: *ethýmōsen Ephraím* 'Ephrem got angry' *Septuagint, Hosea* 12.15. The labilization of the verb must have been completed relatively recently, as in Medieval Greek (Karantzola and Lavidas 2014: 1036) the intransitive meaning was still expressed by the middle form of the verb. The causative *thumóō* in the Hellenistic Koine was modeled after other pairs with voice alternation and similar meaning, cf. Classical Greek *kholóomai/ kholóō* 'be angry' / 'get angry', *eksorgízomai/ eksorgízō* 'be enraged' / 'enrage'.

When compared with *maθéno*, which also developed lability, *θimóno* shows a different morphological development, as the plain verb, as we highlighted, originated from a *medium tantum*, i.e. a verb that only featured middle morphology. Only later an active causative counterpart was created. In Modern Greek, only active forms survive, covering the semantics of both the ancient active and the ancient middle.

---

16 *Mathḗsete* (ACT) 'you will learn' in Galen, *De compositione medicamentorum per genera libri vii* 13.450 (2nd c. CE); see the discussion of example (41) in Section 5.3.6.

5.3.3 'Fear' / 'frighten'

This verb pair constitutes an interesting case of preservation of an otherwise marginal, if not absent, pattern, that is, augmentation. In Homer, the verb pair *deídō / deidíssomai* features augmentation, as a suffix *-iss* is added to the base. Note, however, that this is a peculiar formation, as the suffix is normally used as denominal, and derives factive verbs from adjectives or nouns (Schwyzer 1953: 733). In this case, *deidíssomai* is certainly based on the non-derived verb as it also contains reduplication, while the noun *déos* 'fear' does not (see Chantraine 1977: 255–256). The two members of the verb pair show different voice, but, as remarked in Section 3, they do so incoherently with the valency reducing function of the middle voice in other verb pairs: indeed, the plain verb is an *activum tantum*, while the induced verb is a *medium tantum*. In Classical Greek, this verb was increasingly replaced by *phobéomai* 'fear' / *phobéō* 'frighten', which encodes valency alternation through voice as many other verb pairs. This provides evidence for the fact that valency encoding through voice was still on the rise in Homer (see Section 5.1). By the time of the New Testament, the pair *deídō / deidíssomai* had disappeared, and only the adverb *deinós* 'terrible, awful' occurs twice.

In the meantime, the verb *phobízō* 'frighten' had made its appearance in inscriptions from the first century BCE, and *phoberízō* 'frighten' is attested even earlier, in the Greek translation of the Bible (*Septuagint*), which was accomplished from the 3rd century BCE onward. These verbs are both denominal: the former is based on the noun *phóbos* 'fear', and the latter on the adjective *phoberós* 'frightening', plus the addition of the similative suffix *-iz-*. These two verbs eventually replaced *phobéō* and, as we have argued in Section 4, their Modern Greek outcomes *fovízo* and *foverízo* express the meaning 'frighten' and represent the induced counterpart of *fováme* 'fear', which in its turn derives form the Classical Greek middle *phobéomai* 'fear'. As derivation with the suffix *-iz* remains productive in Modern Greek, the two verbs are still analyzable as denominal (see Section 4).

5.3.4 'Burn (intr.)' / 'burn (tr.)'

As mentioned in Section 4, Modern Greek *kéo* presents a split strategy, as the active and mediopassive intransitive forms have different meanings and are in complementary distribution, whereas Ancient Greek *kaíō* had voice alternation and its active form could not be used intransitively. The intransitive use of the active form is attested in Medieval Greek. According to Lavidas (2010: 146) it likely originated in transitive structures with object omission.

(38) eán   káfsi   me   to   pir
     if   burn.ACT.3SG   1SG.ACC   ART.NOM   fire.NOM
     'If the fire burns me' John Malalas, *Chronographia* 18.16 (5th-6th c. CE)

(39) to   pir   kéi
     ART.NOM   fire.NOM   burn.ACT.3SG
     'The fire burns.'

5.3.5 'Break' (intr.) / 'break' (tr.)

While Ancient Greek *rhḗgnumai/ rhḗgnumi* involved voice alternation, Modern Greek *spáo* is used for both meanings, as does its synonym *rayízo*, which actually stems from the ancient verb. In fact, the diachrony of *rayízo* is worth examining, as it may have facilitated the labilization of *spáo*. More specifically, it was formed from the aorist stem *rhag-* of the ancient verb: Classical Greek *er-rhág-ēn* (MID)→ late Hellenistic Koine/ early Medieval Greek *e-ráy-in* (MID*)* → **e-ráy-is-a* (ACT)→ present tense *ray-íz-o* (ACT).

Spáo, with its variant *spázo*, comes from the Ancient Greek *spáō* 'draw'. This verb was mostly used in the middle in Homeric Greek. The meaning later expanded to 'tear' and, in Classical Greek, the middle voice was increasingly limited to the passive function. It eventually acquired the meaning 'break'. The role of animacy should be mentioned at this point, as the middle form *spázome* is used in Modern Greek with an animate subject with the meaning 'I am annoyed/ enraged', as already in Medieval Greek, example (40).

(40) Axiléfs   espázeto   ði'   ekínin
     Achilles.NOM   break.PST.MID.3SG   for   DEM.ACC
     'Achilles was hurting about her' *Achilleid* (e cod. Brit. Mus. addit. 8241) 567 (14th c. CE).

5.3.6 'Open' (intr.) / 'open' (tr.)

Modern Greek *aníyo* stems from the ancient *anoígnumi* (<*aná* + *oígnumi*) and the first attestations of its active intransitive use can be found in the Hellenistic Koine, as Lavidas has shown (2010: 113), citing an occurrence from the New Testament, in which however the middle voice is still routinely used. According to Lavidas (2010: 113–114), an intransitive interpretation of some forms with active morphology may have been facilitated by phonological developments of Koine

Greek, as the third person singular middle *anoígetai* had become phonologically identical to the second person plural active *anoígete*, as shown by orthographic errors, as in (41), in which the form *anúgete* should be emendated in *anoígetai*.[17]

(41) kroúei   thúran   kaì   anúgete   (anoígetai)[17]
     push.PRS.3SG door.ACC and open.PRS.2PL open.PRS.MID.3SG
     'He pushes the door and it opens.' (Wilcken 1927, 79.7 p. 365).

Note that a passive interpretation is also possible, as the following context makes clear that another person is involved, met by the agent of *kroúei* 'push' after the opening of the door. The whole passage goes as follows: "I saw Ptolemaios walking in the street with a knife in his hand, he knocks on a door, it opens / it is opened and there is a scuffle as he wants to harass him (i.e. the person who opened the door)."

5.3.7 'Dry' / 'make dry'

As shown in Section 4, the pair 'dry' / 'make dry' is not only expressed by *kserénome/ kseréno*, whose voice alternation is identical to its Ancient Greek ancestor *kseraínomai/ kseraínō* 'dry' / 'make dry', but also by the labile *steynóno*, which is used in different contexts.

Steynóno stems from the Ancient Greek *stegnóomai/ stegnóō*, which could be a Hellenistic Koine formation, as it is attested only in Hippocrates' *Epidemics I*[18] (5th c. BCE) in Classical Greek and its initial meaning was 'make something watertight' with voice alternation. The intransitive use of the active verb is attested in Medieval Greek and it must have developed similarly to the previous pairs in discussion. An examples is (42).

(42) ta   ommátia   tu   uk   estéynosan
     ART.NOM.PL eye.NOM.PL 3SG.GEN NEG dry.PFV.PST.3PL
     'His eyes didn't dry up.' *Achilleid* l. 1754 (14th c. CE)

---

[17] The emendation comes from the edition by Wilcken (1927: 365–366), who also provides the translation; see further Shushan (2006: 133).
[18] This is perhaps an indication of the spuriousness of the text.

5.3.8 'Be straight' / 'straighten'

Both the Modern Greek *isióno* and the obsolete *isiázo* stem from the ancient verbs *isóō* and *isázō*,[19] whose meaning was 'make equal' and whose strategy was voice alternation. The first attestations of the lability of these verbs come from Medieval Greek/ Early Modern Greek (Kriaras 2006), e.g.

(43) sti ziɣarán esáza
 in_ ART scale.ACC be_equal.PST.3PL
 'They matched on the scale' *Erotocritus* A37.

As argued in Section 4, animacy plays an important role again, as *isiázome* (MID) is used with animate subjects with various meanings, e.g. 'make amends', 'stretch oneself out'. This was already the case in Medieval Greek, as shown in (44).

(44) isiásti o prínɡipas metá ton vasiléa
 be_equal.PST.MID.3SG ART.NOM prince.NOM with ART.ACC king.ACC
 'The prince made amends with the king' *Chronicle of Morea* H 2624 (14th c. CE).

5.3.9 'Turn over (intr.)' / 'turn over (tr.)'

The Modern Greek *ɣirízo* is related to the Hellenistic Koine *gyróō* 'make round' (<*gûros* 'ring, circle'). Quite interestingly, the intransitive use of the active verb is attested already in late Hellenistic Koine: *gyrṓsas* 'as he coiled himself up' Oppian, *Cynegetica* 3.440 (2nd-3rd c. CE). The labile use of *ɣirízo* is further attested in the vernacular Medieval Greek texts, in which the intransitive mediopassive is also used, but only with animate subjects with various meanings, e.g. 'turn (myself) around', 'change my mind' etc. (Kriaras 2006).

As regards the fate of the Ancient Greek *stréphomai/ stréphō*, it underwent a phonological change, as it became *strívo* in Medieval Greek,[20] and also a semantic one, as its meaning shifted from 'turn' to 'twist' / 'rotate'. In Modern Greek *strívo*, always with active morphology, is also labile, as shown by the two occurrences in (45).

---

[19] The -*i*- is due to the reshaping of the adjective *ísos* 'equal' with the suffix -*ios* in Medieval Greek: *ísios* 'straight'.
[20] Perhaps by analogy to *trívo* 'rub' (<Ancient Greek *tríbō*).

(45) *Prospáθisa   na   strípso   to   xerúli,*
      try.IMPF.PST.1SG COM   rotate.PFV.PRS.1SG   ART.ACC   handle.ACC
      alá ðen éstríve
      but   NEG rotate.IMPF.PST.3SG
      'I tried to turn the handle, but it wasn't turning.'

As noted in Section 4, *stréfome / stréfo* does exist in Modern Greek with its ancient meaning, but it is a reintroduction from Katharévousa restricted to higher registers.

6 Discussion

The diachrony of the Greek language shows both similarities and differences between the earliest and the latest language stages. Comparing Ancient with Modern Greek, it is noticeable that, at both temporal stages, inanimate verbs show a much more uniform pattern of valency alternation than animate verbs. The latter feature a variety of strategies in Homeric Greek, but a clearer prevalence of voice in Classical Greek, with a sizable percentage of suppletive pairs. Modern Greek in turn shows a preference for suppletion, with voice still playing a relevant role, and a limited degree of lability. On the other hand, inanimate verbs consistently encode valency alternation through voice in Homeric Greek and through lability in Modern Greek.

As we have argued in Section 5, the active/middle opposition was still on the rise in Homer, and an increasing number of verb pairs adopted this strategy to indicate valency alternation in Classical Greek. At the dawn of the Hellenistic age, in the Koine, one can detect a tendency for different types of verb, mostly active but also some *media tantum*, to develop lability, hence being used both transitively and intransitively. As we argued in detail in Sections 4 and 5.3, this tendency involved by the most part inanimate verbs, but also some animate ones. Among the latter, *θimóno* 'get angry' / 'anger' shows that the direction of labilization is not necessarily from active to labile, as this labile verb originated from an Ancient Greek medium tantum *thumóomai* 'be angry'.

Interestingly, labile verbs that normally take inanimate subjects such as *isióno* 'become straight' / 'straighten' or *aníyo* 'open (intr./tr.)' can be used only as transitive with animate subjects. If they are occasionally used as intransitive with animate subjects, they show middle inflection, pointing to a tendency for animate subjects to need overt marking in connection with valency change. We remarked in Section 4 that this is connected with common expectations for animate subjects to be agents with such verbs, and with possible reflexive reading of the middle voice, which, in such cases, leaves open an interpretation of the event as intentional or non-intentional (compare for example (34) and (35)).

In general, however, overt marking is preferred even by verb pairs that denote events almost only restricted to human subjects. In some cases, there may be a syntactic motivation for this, as in the case of *maθéno* / *ðiðásko* 'learn' / 'teach': while the plain verb can also be labile when it occurs in a ditransitive construction (see example (7)), possible ambiguity prevents it to occur with the meaning 'teach' elsewhere, as argued at length in Section 4 (see examples (8) and (9)).
For the pair 'get angry' / 'anger', we found that several verbs are available, featuring both lability, as *θimóno* (intr.) / *θimóno* (tr.) and *nevriázo* (intr.)/ *nevriázo* (tr.), and voice, as *eknevrízome* / *eknevrízo* or *tsatízome* / *tsatízo*.

In this framework, it is interesting to note that the pair 'sit' / 'seat' features lability in the perfective stem (*kaθíso* (intr.) / *kaθíso* (tr.)), and that lability for this verb already originated in Homeric Greek (*hízō* (intr.) / *hízō* (tr.)) thus constituting a stabile feature of the verb pair. Similarly, in the imperfective stem the verb pair shows two different stems at both stages, *káθome* / *kaθízo* in Modern Greek and *hêmai* / *hízō* in Homeric Greek. We considered the latter an instance of suppletion and the former an instance of augmentation, even though both members of the verb pairs are etymologically related. In whatever way one considers the morphological relation between members of the two verb pair, this constitutes a remarkable instance of preservation of the same patterns.

A similar development concerns the pair 'fear' / 'frighten', discussed in Sections 4 and 5.3.3, in which augmentation (*deídō* / *deidíssomai*) was attested in Homeric Greek. It was then replaced by voice in Classical Greek (*phobéomai* / *phobéō*), but eventually augmentation was restored, as shown in Modern Greek (*fováme* / *fovízo*).

Letuchiy (2010) matched lability against Haspelmath's (2016) spontaneity scale, to see whether verbs denoting spontaneous events tend to be labile with more frequency than verbs that denote events that rank lower on the scale. He found that this is only true for detransitivizing languages: in his sample, these are French, German, Romanian, Udmurt and Greek. Let us now consider Table 8, in which we show how inanimate verb pairs included in our sample rank on the spontaneity scale as represented in Table 2.

The first observation is that our verbs are evenly distributed over the whole scale, ranging from first to 28th position. Hence, our data do not seem to support the claim that events that rank lower on the scale tend to be encoded more easily by labile verbs as opposed to events that rank higher. The same even distribution characterized voice alternation in Ancient Greek, thus offering evidence for the replacement of the latter strategy with lability in Modern Greek, at least as long as inanimate verbs are concerned.

Table 8: Verb pairs on the spontaneity scale.

	RANKING ON THE SPONTANEITY SCALE	MEANING	ANCIENT GREEK	MODERN GREEK
1	1	boil	(voice)	labile
2	3	dry	voice	voice (labile)
3	10	turn	voice	labile
4	12	burn	voice	voice/labile
5	27	open	voice	labile
6	28	break	voice	labile

As we described voice alternation as a detransitivizing strategy already at the Homeric Greek stage, we can observe a shift in basic valency from detransitivizing orientation to unoriented for what concerns inanimate verbs. In addition, leaving aside the other languages mentioned by Letuchiy (2010), one can note that Modern Greek can be considered to be detransitivizing only inasmuch as it relies on voice opposition for a minority of verb pairs, since prevailing strategies, i.e. lability and suppletion, are both undetermined.

7 Conclusion

In this paper, we discussed changes in the encoding of basic valency in Greek over a time span of three millennia. From the data surveyed in the paper, it turns out that, in spite of preferred strategies that can be singled out at every language stage, a stabile feature of the Greek language is a split between animate and inanimate verbs, whereby animate verbs show a much wider range of variation in the choice of strategies at all language stages, while inanimate verbs are much more uniform.

The strategy adopted by most inanimate verbs in Homeric and in Classical Greek was voice alternation, whereby the middle morphology occurred on plain verbs and active morphology on induced ones. We argued that voice opposition represented a reduced strategy at the Homeric Greek stage, and characterized Ancient Greek as an intransitivizing language (Section 3). At the Classical Greek stage, the extent to which voice was involved in the encoding of valency alternations also increased for animate verbs, as shown in Section 5.1.

A shift toward lability started in the Hellenistic Koine and continued during the Middle Ages: at this stage, the role of voice in the encoding of valency alternations was strongly reduced, and several verbs, especially in the inanimate group, became labile. In Section 5.2, we argued that this shift was accompanied by a reduction of several other functions of the middle voice, which became increasingly connected with the passive function. As discussed in Sections 5.3.1–5.3.9, the verb pairs that we surveyed in our analysis show various developments, whereby labilization often affected the active voice, but might also take ancient *media tantum* as its starting point, as in the case of *thimóno* 'get angry' (Section 5.3.2).

In Table 9 we summarize the distribution of different strategies for the encoding of basic valency from Homer to the present.[21] While voice plays the most important role as a means for the encoding of valency changes in Ancient Greek, its relevance is more limited in Modern Greek, though still covering a number of verb pairs. The extent to which suppletion is used remains virtually unchanged at all language stages, while the most important change consists in the rise of lability, which features prominently especially among inanimate verbs. Interestingly, the only verb pair that shows lability in Homeric Greek, 'sit' / 'seat', is animate.

Table 9: The encoding of valency alternations from Ancient to Modern Greek.

	ANCIENT GREEK			MODERN GREEK	
	ANIMATE		INANIMATE	ANIMATE	INANIMATE
	HOM.	CL.			
PERIPHRASIS	1	1	-	1	-
SUPPLETION	4	3	1	4	1
AUGMENTATION	2	1	1	2	-
VOICE	4	6	8	3	3
LABILITY	1	1	-	3	6

Changes in orientation are summarized in Table 10. Tentatively, we also add the indication of the prevalent strategy reconstructed for PIE, that is augmentation, and, even more tentatively, we introduce an intermediate stage at which voice alternation should better be described as conjugation class change, rather than as a reduction strategy. In the slot of animate verbs in Ancient Greek, the arrow indicates the extended role of voice in Classical Greek as compared to Homeric Greek. In the corresponding Modern Greek slot, we show that, though suppletion is the most frequent strategy, we still think that the variety of strategies does not allow for one to be considered prevalent, as even suppletion only accounts for less than half of the verb pairs.

---

21 The sum is higher than the number of verb pairs because some of them rely on multiple strategies.

Table 10: Valency orientation from Proto-Indo-European to Modern Greek.

	***PIE**	**??**	**ANCIENT GREEK**		**MODERN GREEK**
ORIENTATION	Transitivizing	(Undetermined)	Detransitivizing		Undetermined
STRATEGY	Augmentation	(Conj. class change)	**ANIMATE**	No prevalent strategy ↓ Voice	No prevalent strategy / Suppletion
			INANIMATE	Voice	Lability

Abbreviations

1	1st person
2	2nd person
3	3rd person
ACC	accusative
ACT	active
ART	article
ASSOC	associative
c.	century
COM	complementizer
FUT	future
G.ACT	generalized active
G.APPL	generalized applicative
GEN	genitive
IMPER	imperative
IMPF	imperfective
intr.	intransitive
MID	middle
NEG	negation
NOM	nominative
O	direct object
PFV	perfective
PL	plural
PRS	present, non-past
PST	past
REFL	reflexive

S   subject
SG   singular
SUBJ   subjunctive

References

Alexiadou, Artemis & Elena Anagnostopoulou. 2004. Voice morphology in the causative-inchoative alternation: Evidence for a non unified structural analysis of unaccusatives. In Artemis Alexiadou, Elena Anagnostopoulou & Martin Everaert (eds.). *The unaccusativity puzzle*, 114–116. Oxford: Oxford University Press.

Alexiadou, Artemis. 2014. Active, middle, and passive: The morpho-syntax of Voice. *Catalan Journal of Linguistics* 13. 19–40.

Allan, Rutger. 2003. *The middle voice in Ancient Greek: A study of polysemy*. Leiden: Brill.

Babiniotis, Georgios. 1998. *Lexiko tis neas ellinikis glossas* [Dictionary of the Modern Greek language]. Athens: Centre for Lexicology.

Benveniste, Emile 1966. *Problèmes de linguistique générale*, vol. 1. Paris: Gallimard.

Burrow, Thomas. 1955. *The Sanskrit language*. London: Faber & Faber.

Chantraine, Pierre. 1977. *Dictionnaire etymologique grec*. Paris: Klinksiek.

Cotticelli-Kurras, Paola & Alfredo Rizza. 2015. Zur Entstehung der Medialendungen: Überlegungen zu einigen Bildungsstrategien. In Thomas Krisch & Stefan Niederreiter (eds.), *Diachronie und Sprachvergleich*, 45–55. Innsbruck: IBS.

Dixon, R. M. W. 1994. *Ergativity*. Cambridge: Cambridge University Press.

Gelderen, Elly van. 2011. Valency changes in the history of English. *Journal of Historical Linguistics* 1 (1). 106–143.

Grünthal, Riho & Johanna Nichols. 2016. Transitivizing-detransitivizing typology and language family history. *Lingua Posnaniensis* 58 (2). 11–31.

Haspelmath, Martin. 1987. *Transitivity alternations of the anticausative type*. Köln: Universität zu Köln Arbeitspapiere N.F. 5.

Haspelmath, Martin. 1993. Change-of-state/causative verb alternations. In Bernard Comrie & Maria Polinsky (eds.) *Causatives and transitivity*, 87–120. Amsterdam & Philadelphia: John Benjamins.

Haspelmath, Martin. 2016. Universals of causative and anticausative verb formation and the spontaneity scale. *Lingua Posnaniensis* 58 (2): 33–63.

Holton, David, Peter Mackridge & Irene Philippaki-Warburton. 1997. *Greek. A comprehensive grammar of the modern language*. London: Routledge.

Karantzola, Eleni & Nikolaos Lavidas. 2014. On the relation between labilizations and neuter gender: Evidence from the Greek diachrony. *Linguistics* 52 (4): 1025–1059.

Kriaras, Emmanouil. 2006. *Epitomi tou lexikou tis meseonikis ellinikis dimodoys grammatias* [Abridged version of the Dictionary of the Medieval Greek vernacular literature] *1100–1669 (A-K)*. Athens: Center for the Greek Language.

Lavidas, Nikolaos. 2010. *Transitivity alternations in diachrony: Changes in argument structure and voice morphology*. Newcastle: Cambridge Scholars Publishing.

Letuchiy, Alexander. 2009. Towards a typology of labile verbs: Lability vs. derivation. In Patience Epps & Alexandre Arkhipov (eds.), *New challenges in typology: Transcending the borders and refining the distinctions*, 223–244. Berlin & New York: Mouton de Gruyter.

Letuchiy, Alexander. 2010. Lability and spontaneity. In Patrick Brandt & Marco García García (eds.), Transitivity, 237–256. Amsterdam & Philadelphia: John Benjamins.

Levin, Beth & Malka Rappaport Hovav. 2005. *Argument realization*. Cambridge: Cambridge University Press.

Luraghi, Silvia, Guglielmo Inglese & Daniel Kölligan. 2021. The passive in Indo-European. *Folia Linguistica Historica* 42.

Luraghi, Silvia. 2012. Basic valency orientation and the middle voice in Hittite. *Studies in Language* 36 (1). 1–32.

Luraghi, Silvia. 2019. Basic valency orientation, the anticausative alternation, and voice in PIE. In Melanie Malzahn (ed.), *Akten der 16th Fachtagung der Indogermanischen Gesellschaft*, 259–274. Wiesbaden: Reichert.

Luraghi, Silvia. 2020. *Experiential verbs in Homeric Greek. A constructional approach*. Leiden: Brill.

Malchukov, Andrej & Bernard Comrie (eds.). 2015. *Valency classes in the world's languages*. Berlin & New York: Mouton De Gruyter.

Nedjalkov, Vladimir P. & Georgij Sil'nitsky. 1973. The Typology of Morphological and lexical causatives. In Ferenc Kiefer (ed.), *Trends in Soviet theoretical linguistics*, 1–32. Dordrecht: Springer.

Nedjalkov, Vladimir P. 1969. Nekotorye verojatnostnye universalii v glagol'nom slovoobrazovanii [Some statistical universals in verbal derivation]. In I. F Vardul' (ed.), *Jazykovye universalii i lingvističeskaja tipologija* [Language universals and linguistic typology], 106–114. Moskva: Nauka.

Nichols, Johanna. 2006. Stance verbs and the linguistic Europeanization of the Slavs. Paper presented at the 1st Meeting of the Slavic Linguistics Society, Indiana University, Bloomington, Indiana, 7–10 September.

Nichols, Johanna, David Peterson & Jonathan Barnes. 2004. Transitivising and detransitivising languages. *Linguistic Typology* 8 (2). 149–211.

Nichols, Johanna. 2007. Lexical Valence Typology project: Instructions for elicitation of causative-noncausative verb pairs. https://www.eva.mpg.de/lingua/tools-at-lingboard/pdf/Nichols_TransDetransQues.pdf (accessed on 24 April 2021)

Plank, Frans & Aditi Lahiri. 2015. Microscopic and macroscopic typology: Basic valence orientation, more pertinacious than meets the naked eye. *Linguistic Typology* 19 (1). 1–54.

Romagno, Domenica. 2010. Anticausativi, passivi, riflessivi: Considerazioni sul medio oppositivo. In Ignazio Putzu, Giulio Paulis, Gianfranco Nieddu & Pierluigi Cuzzolin (eds.), *La morfologia del greco tra tipologia e diacronia*, 430–441. Milano: FrancoAngeli.

Sausa, Eleonora. 2016. Basic valency orientation in Homeric Greek. *Folia Linguistica Historica* 37. 205–23.

Schwyzer, Eduard. 1953. *Griechische Grammatik*. Vol. 1. Munchen: C. H. Beck.

Schwyzer, Eduard. 1959. *Griechische Grammatik*. Vol. 2: *Syntax und Syntaktische Stilistik*, vervollständigt von Albert Debrunner. Munchen: C. H. Beck.

Shushan, Gregory. 2006. Greek and Egyptian dreams in two Ptolemaic archives: Individual and cultural layers of meaning. *Dreaming* 16 (2). 129–142.

Stamatiou, Irini. 2017. *Meleti tis mesopathitikis fonis sto stoma kimenon tou IEL* [A study of the mediopassive voice in the corpus of IEL]. Athens: National and Kapodistrian University of Athens Unpublished BA Thesis.

Wilcken, Ulrich. 1927. *Urkunden der Ptolemäerzeit I: Papyri aus Unterägypten*. Berlin & New York: Mouton De Gruyter.

Willi, Andreas. 2018. *Origins of the Greek verb*. Cambridge: Cambridge University Press.

Zúñiga, Fernando & Seppo Kittilä. 2019. *Grammatical voice*. Cambridge: Cambridge University Press.

Riho Grünthal, Heini Arjava, Jyri Lehtinen and Johanna Nichols
Basic causative verb patterns in Uralic: Retention and renewal in grammar and lexicon

Abstract: This paper presents the formation of causative verbs and different causativization strategies in the Uralic languages as evidenced by six verb sets in 22 languages. The sample is a selection of basic verbs from a larger database including altogether 21 non-causal and causal verb pairs based on a slightly revised version of Nichols, Peterson and Barnes (2004). Our sample illustrates the big picture of causativization in Uralic in the light of three animate verb pairs 'eat' / 'feed', 'see' / 'show', 'fear, be afraid' / 'frighten, scare' and three inanimate non-causal / causal pairs, namely 'burn (intr.); catch fire' / 'burn (tr.); set afire', 'dry (intr.); get dry' / 'dry (tr.), dry out' and 'be straight; straighten out' / 'straighten; make straight'. The sample shows some variation in the causativization strategies across the language family and different lexical types. However, the dominating characteristic of almost all investigated cases is that the Uralic languages prefer valency changing affixal morphology whereas other strategies are more random and result from verb-specific and language-specific historical development. A qualitative analysis of the diachronic development shows that, actually, most deviating patterns originate from former valency changing affixal morphology patterns as well.

Keywords: causative verbs, causativization, morphology, derivation, Uralic languages, language change

1 Introduction

This paper aims to shed light on the most typical features of causal verbs and their non-causal pairs in the Uralic languages from a diachronic perspective. We discuss verb pairs like the following, which we use here to present our terminology:

Riho Grünthal, University of Helsinki, e-mail: Riho.Grunthal@helsinki.fi
Heini Arjava, University of Helsinki, e-mail: heini.arjava@helsinki.fi
Jyri Lehtinen, University of Helsinki, e-mail: jyri.lehtinen@helsinki.fi
Johanna Nichols, University of Berkeley and University of Helsinki, e-mail: johanna@berkeley.edu

∂ Open Access. © 2021 Riho Grünthal, et. al, published by De Gruyter. This work is licensed under the Creative Commons Attribution-NonCommercial-NoDerivatives 4.0 International License.
https://doi.org/10.1515/9783110755657-007

Table 1: Morphological causativization strategies of six verb sets in the Uralic languages: Non-causal and causal verb pairs in Finnish.

	Non-causal	Causal
Finnish	nukk-u-a 'sleep'	nuk-u-tta-a 'put to sleep'
	sleep-REFL/PASS-INF	sleep-REFL/PASS-CAUS-INF
	syö-dä	syö-ttä-ä
	eat-INF	eat-CAUS-INF
	kätke-yty-ä 'hide'	kätke-ä 'hide (s.th.)'
	hide-DECAUS-INF	hide-INF

In all three of these pairs the verb semantics is the same: the non-causal describes a state or activity and the causal describes causation of the state or activity. But the morphology differs: in the first two pairs the causal member has a causative suffix -*tta*, while in the third pair the causal has no suffix and the non-causal has a decausative, or reflexive, suffix -*yty*. The essence of causativization is derivation of a causal verb from a non-causal one by some overt morphological means, and causative is the usual term for a verb affix that does this, or for the whole derived verb. Decausative is morphology that derives a non-causal from a causal; reflexive is a common term for such morphology in various grammatical traditions.[1]

The pair 'sleep' : 'put to sleep' has a suffix -*u*-, glossed REFL/PASS above, which originated as a decausative or more generally intransitive marker, but by now has lost its function and is just a part of the verb stem. Henceforth we ignore such suffixes.

Fairly standard terms for the valency and argument structure are given in Table 2.

However, since there remain open theoretical questions in the syntactic and semantic description, and none of this is at issue in this paper, we maintain that argument structure, valency, and semantic roles just describe the syntactic roles as subject for intransitives, subject and object for transitives, and agent, causee, and object for causativized transitives.

Studies on causatives have shed light on their typological properties from a cross-linguistic viewpoint and shown differences in causativization and decausativization strategies across the world's languages. The scale of causativizing strategies alternates between synthetic and analytic verb constructions. Lexically and morphologically totally independent suppletive pairs form the most transparent con-

---

[1] We note that the term anticausative also exists in the literature, but it mostly describes the syntax of a construction with a decausative verb. We use decausative only for morphology that derives a non-causal verb from a derived causal verb.

Table 2: Functional properties of non-causal/causal verb pairs.[2]

	nukkua 'sleep'		*nukuttaa* 'put to sleep'		
Arguments	S		A		O
Valency	NOM		NOM		GEN/PART
Semantics	Theme		Agent		Patient
	syödä	'eat'	*syöttää*	'feed'	
Arguments	A	O	A	R/A	O
Valency	NOM	GEN/PART	NOM	ALL	GEN/PART
Semantics	Agent	Patient	Agent	Causee	Patient

trast between causal and non-causal verbs, while ambiguous (labile, ambitransitive) verbs have both functions: they do not distinguish formally between the non-causal and causal verb but make a distinction in the argument structure (such verbs are frequent cross-linguistically). In general, valency classes and changes in valency, such as causativization, have a direct influence on clausal argument structure, alignment and transitivity prominence (Haspelmath 1993; Shibatani and Pardeshi 2002; Nichols, Peterson and Barnes 2004; Malchukov and Comrie 2015a, 2015b).

Since a wordlist-based typology of basic valency orientation was proposed in 2004 (Nichols, Peterson and Barnes 2004) there has been work on individual languages, some historical comparison using the typological idea (Kulikov 2009; Luraghi 2012; Arkadiev and Pakerys 2015; Holvoet 2015; Nau 2015; Lavidas and Kulikov 2018), but no exhaustive survey of a language family, and virtually no work of this type on Uralic. This paper remedies these gaps with a survey of causativization strategies in this particular North Eurasian language family, using an expanded version of the wordlist of Nichols, Peterson and Barnes (2004), and proposing some major typological and historical trends in Uralic.

Most Uralic languages heavily rely on affixal valency-changing morphology, i.e. deriving a causal verb from a non-causal one, which is the most frequent way to form causative verbs. The basic pattern involves derivation from an underived verb stem as in North Saami *borrat* 'eat' → *borahit* 'feed' (1–2) (cf. Nickel and Sammallahti 2011: 580–591).

North Saami
(1) *Dat mearkkaša ahte dat borrá eará elli-id*
    it   mean.3SG   that it eat.3SG other animal-PL.GEN(-ACC)
    'It means that it eats other animals.'

---

[2] Abbreviations of the arguments: A = agent, O = object, R = recipient, S = subject.

(2) Ma-id   sii   galge-t   **bora-hi-t**
    what-PL.GEN(-ACC)   they   must-3PL   eat-CAUS-INF
    mána-i-de?
    child-PL-ILL
    'What should they give the children to eat?'

The Saamic verb *borra-t* eat-INF 'eat' belongs to the inherited Uralic vocabulary, and both the root etymology and the grammatical pattern of causativization, with underived noncausal, come from the protolanguage. As a rule, causativization as illustrated in (1–2) involves valency change and increases the number of arguments. The syntactic arguments agent, object, and causee are obligatory in the causal sentence (2), whereas the non-causal verb in (1) has no causee because its subject corresponds to the causee of the causative example. For verbs like 'eat' the object is not always obligatory but always possible. Thus, verbs like Saami *borrat* 'eat' may function as both intransitive and transitive, whereas the causal counterpart is derived and always transitive.

Theoretically, both causativizing and decausativizing are possible. Decausative verbs can be derived from causative ones in many Uralic languages. North Mansi (cf. Dolovai 2001), for instance, mainly follows the pattern manifested in North Saami, above (1)–(2). A default causative verb such as North Mansi *kotarenkwe* burn-INF 'burn (something)', from which the non-causal pair *kotartaxtuŋkwe* 'get burned' is derived, is very rare (3)–(4).

North Mansi
(3) n'ēlmu-m   tērpi-n   ta   **kotara-we**
    tongue-1SG.PX medicine-LAT   it   burn-3SG
    'My tongue burns because of the medicine.'

(4) manr-iɣ   naskass-iɣ   **kotər-ta-xt-uŋkwe?**
    what-TRA   in.vain   burn-CAUS-REFL-INF
    'Why would you burn yourself in vain?'

More generally speaking, causative derivations can be easily decausativized by applying the same strategy as in (4). A closer look at individual languages and selected verb sets shows exceptions to our hypothesis that in Uralic causal verbs are based on affixal causatives (alternatively augmentation, the cover term for causativization and other kinds of affixally marked derivation of causals). Ambitransitive (labile) verbs, for instance, are far less frequent in Uralic than in many other languages (Creissels 2015), and in fact they are almost non-existent in Uralic.

In Uralic causatives are formed from both intransitive and transitive verbs as well as nouns and adjectives. As a rule, the character of the non-causal member in terms of parts of speech does not influence the way causatives are used. Denominal and deadjectival causative verbs behave syntactically like those derived from intransitive verbs and have the same kind of argument structure. In Finnish *syö-dä* eat-INF 'eat' → *syö-ttä-ä* eat-CAUS-INF 'make (one) eat' and *kuiva* 'dry' (adjective) → *kuiva-tta-a* dry-CAUS-INF 'make (one) dry', for instance, the non-causal roots differ in part of speech but syntactically both agent and object are obligatory dependents of the causative (5)–(6).

Finnish
(5) *Itse-kin* **syö-tä-n** *koira-lle-ni* *myös*
oneself-FOC eat-CAUS-1SG dog-ALL-1SG.PX also
kana-n *luu-t.*
chicken-GEN bone-PL
'I myself feed my dog with chicken bones, too.'

(6) *Tuuli* **kuiva-ttaa** *kasve-ja.*
wind dry-CAUS.3SG plant-PL.PART
'The wind dries the plants up.'

The relative proportion of denominal causatives is, however, small and they are considerably less frequent than deverbal causatives. Diachronically, distinguishing deverbal from denominal causatives is important for describing the origins of individual pairs but not for typologizing languages or the whole family.

We may assume that aside from language-specific varying causativization strategies there are verb-specific reasons that explain the use of deviating strategies from the assumed main pattern based on derivation (specifically, augmentation). Syntactically, the most salient characteristic of causativized transitive verbs is the optional ditransitive argument structure (see (5)) involving a similar valency change and increase of arguments as causativized intransitive verbs have. Furthermore, decausativization is also typical of Uralic causative verbs and may allow even secondary causativization of decausativized verbs (as in Finnish *kasta-a* dip-INF 'dip' → *kast-u-a* dip-REFL-INF 'get wet' → *kast-u-ttaa* dip-REFL-CAUS 'make wet'). The strong tendency to causativize any non-causal verbs, either underived or derived, correlates with the universal proposing that if a language allows synthetic causatives of transitive verbs used in three-argument clauses, it also allows synthetic causatives of intransitive verbs (Nedjalkov 1966; Haspelmath 2016: 40–42). This, however, remains outside of the scope of this article.

We next introduce the data and verb sample used here (Section 2). This will be followed by a typological overview on the main morphological differences of causativized verbs in Uralic in the light of the selected six verbs (Section 3). Finally, diachronic tendencies that affect the verb/noun/adjective + CAUS relationship either by preserving the inherited pattern or deviating from it will be discussed in the light of the verbs 'straighten' and 'dry' in individual languages (Section 4).

2 Language sample and data

The data used in this paper mainly come from the database of the project *The causative alternation in Uralic* (UrCaus) (University of Helsinki). The database contains information from 22 Uralic languages ranging from the easternmost Samoyedic languages in Siberia to the westernmost Saamic languages in Northern Scandinavia and consists of 21 verb sets with morphological analysis, type of derivation, synonyms, valency, and glossed examples; additional examples from other sources are used here. The sampling of data is based on the verb list in Nichols, Peterson and Barnes (2004), which has been slightly revised. The identification of causal verbs takes place by determining causal pairs on functional and morphological grounds involving valency change. The database contains altogether roughly 2300 causal verb entries. Besides the basic pair consisting of a non-causal and causal verb, synonyms and near-synonyms displaying either the same or different verb root were included. Given that derivational morphology is widely used in Uralic, different aspectual features such as boundedness and continuity increase the number of adjacent verbs.

The current article investigates a more limited set of six verb sets and the causativizing pairs in more detail. The verb pairs under observation are (numbers refer to the numbering of Nichols, Peterson and Barnes (2004)) 4. 'eat' / 'feed; give food', 6. 'see' / 'show', 8. 'fear, be afraid' / 'frighten, scare', 11. 'burn; catch fire' / 'burn, set afire', 14. 'dry; get dry' / 'dry (out)' and 15. 'be straight; straighten (out)' / 'straighten; make straight'. The first three pairs typically have animate S/O and the last three have inanimate S/O. The selected verbs include both inherited verbs ('eat', 'see', 'fear', 'burn') and predicates that are usually adjectives in Uralic languages ('dry', 'straight').

The formation of causal pairs of these six verb sets in 22 selected Uralic languages could maximally give 132 hits based on the selection of primary correspondence between a word and meaning. The total found is 129 as information was not available in some individual cases. Six parameters were chosen to distinguish between alternating causativization strategies on morphological grounds. Table 3 summarizes the distribution of the six strategies in the sample. Causativizing affixal morphology assigns segmental derivation (augmentation). Other changes in affixal morphology such as derivation of the non-causal pair from an unmarked causative verb are very rare in Uralic. Synchronically unproductive valency changing opaque morphology partly overlaps with changes in the verb root, which may contain a consonant originating from an affix that is non-transparent from the perspective of synchronic morphology. Radical indicates change in the verb root. Suppletion shows asymmetric pairs that display different verb roots, while analytic forms are light verb pairs or other phrases consisting of free words. Functionally ambiguous (labile) verbs that can be described as both causal and non-causal do not occur in the selected sample and are not mentioned in the table.

Table 3: Morphological causativization strategies of six verb sets in the Uralic languages.[3]

Language	eat / feed	see / show	fear / scare	burn	dry	straight
Kamas	S	S	S	R	C	C
Selkup	C	C	C	S	C	
Tundra Nenets	C	C	C	C	C	C
Nganasan	C	C		C	C	
East Khanty	C	S	C	C	C	A
North Khanty	C	S	C	A	A	A
(North) Mansi	C	C	C	S	C	A
Hungarian	C	S	S	C	C	C
Udmurt	S	C	C	C	C	C
Komi	S	S	C	R	R	C
Mari	S	S	C	C	R	C
Erzya	S	C	S	O	R	O
Livonian	C	C	S	S	O	A
South Estonian	C	C	S	C	R	C
Estonian	C	C	S	C	C	C
Votic	C	C	S	C	C	C
Veps	C	S	S	C	C	N
Finnish	C	C	C	C	C	C
Kildin Saami	C	S	C	C	R	O

---

3 Abbreviations: A = analytic, C = affixal causative, N = affixal non-causal, O = opaque, R = radical morphology, S = suppletion.

Table 3 (continued)

Language	eat / feed	see / show	fear / scare	burn	dry	straight		
Inari Saami	C	S	C	C	R	R		
North Saami	C	S	C	C	C	C		
South Saami	C	N	C	C	R	C		
Morphology							Total	
Analytic				1	1	4	= 6	(4.65%)
Affixal causative	17	11	13	15	13	12	= 81	(62.79%)
Affixal non-causal		1				1	= 2	(1.55%)
Opaque				1	1	2	= 4	(3.10%)
Radical morphology				2	7	1	= 10	(7.75%)
Suppletion	5	10	8	3			= 26	(20.16%)
Total							= 129	(100%)

The sample shows the dominating role of derivational morphology and causativizing affixes in contemporary Uralic languages in all selected verb sets. The number of diverging patterns varies, whereas deviations from the main type are, as a rule, relevant only for the analysis of individual verbs in the narrow sample. If individual languages deviate from this pattern, it is probably caused by secondary development in most cases. Yet, individual verbs such as 4. 'see' / 'show' demonstrate that suppletion can be a lexically relevant strategy as well. A large cross-linguistic sample may show relevant tendencies concerning the historical development of the language family. However, this topic will be discussed on another occasion.

3 Regularities and irregularities in causativization strategies

This section will include examples of the six verb sets to illustrate the typological and cross-linguistic divergence of causal verbs in Uralic. Conservative morphological and morphosyntactic patterns illustrate inherent long-term characteristics of this particular language family. Language and branch-specific deviations from the dominating pattern are hypothetically either areally or verb-specifically limited innovations highlighting the areas in which inherent features are prone to change or depend on lexical typology. Differences in the behavior of animate and inanimate verbs will also be pointed out.

3.1 Affixal morphology

Affixal causativization is most frequent in all six verbs selected for this paper, although in individual cases such as 'see' / 'show' other morphological strategies may be almost as frequent. As a rule, the derivational suffixes descend from the assumed Proto-Uralic *-pt- (*-kt-), which has preserved its productivity as a segmental affix in most investigated verbs in most languages. South Estonian verb 'eat' / 'feed' shows the maintenance of the inherited causative affix, although morphological erosion has, in general, strongly affected South Estonian (7)–(8). This is a more fundamental characteristic of the Uralic languages and their inherent typological characteristics, because they typically display a larger set of derivative affixes adding specific semantic and syntactic features to individual verbs. The main rule is that, although a given affix such as the causative suffix may be very frequent, there are always exceptions which distinguish derivational affixes from considerably more regular inflectional categories.

South Estonian
(7) mi **süü-miq** kolm kõrd päävä-n
we eat-1PL three time day-LOC
'We eat three times a day.'

(8) ta **süü-t** tsiko
(s)he eat-CAUS.3SG pig.PL.PART
'(s)he is feeding pigs'

As Table 3 shows, there is a good deal of divergence between verb sets in individual languages, although rather similar patterning between the Finnic languages on the one hand, and Saamic languages, on the other hand, suggests that the degree of genealogical affinity has some importance as well. Affixal causativization in North Khanty, for instance, is not dominant as shown by other verb pairs as well, whereas the low frequency of affixal morphology in Erzya is caused by more random options in Table 3. North Khanty diverges from all other languages in the sample, and alternative strategies are frequently used. Individual verb pairs may use segmentable affixes, and have a parallel possibility for more productive analytic patterns. The verb łeti 'eat' is etymologically different from semantically corresponding words in other Uralic languages and illustrates alternating causativization strategies in North Khanty as both an affixal causative and an analytic construction are possible: łe-ti eat-INF 'eat' ~ jŏχi łe-ti ASP eat-INF 'eat (momentanous)' / ła-pət-ti eat-CAUS-INF 'feed' ~ nŏχ ła-pət-ti ASP eat-CAUS-INF 'feed (continuous)'. The basic pattern based on affixal valency change (9–10) and the use of the affix *-pt- can be considered as the inherited one, which has mostly been replaced by secondary means in the causativization of other verbs.

North Khanty
(9) *Maša jŏχi lŏŋ-m-aləm ma łat **łe-s-əm***
Masha home enter-PTCP.PST-3SG I soup eat-PST-1SG
'When Masha entered home, I was eating soup.'

(10) *ant-em ńawrem-əł **ła-pət-əł***
mother-1SG child-3SG eat-CAUS-3SG
'My mother is feeding her child.'

Considering Table 3, above, it is striking that all Uralic languages spoken in Central Russia, namely Udmurt, Komi, Mari and Erzya covering three distinct branches, display a suppletive pattern for 'eat' + CAUS. Mostly 'eat' in these languages descends from old inherited vocabulary, although semantic changes have taken place between them and etymologically corresponding lexemes. The causal pairs, in turn, either manifest semantic changes in comparison with their etymological cognates, cf. Erzya *andoms*, Moksha (Mordvinic) *andəms* 'feed' ~ Finnish *antaa* 'give' and Hungarian *ad-* 'give', or they do not have cognates in other Uralic languages as Udmurt *śudyny* 'feed', Mari *pukšaš* 'feed'.

3.2 Other affixal changes

Given the dominating role of affixal morphology, any other affixal changes are very rare in the data (cf. Table 3). In Veps the causal *oigeta* 'straighten' is an exception to the rule as the non-causal pair *oigetas* 'straighten (oneself); make one's way' displays valency-decreasing morphology (11a-b) and not the causativizing type (12a-b). Unlike the derivational morphology that is characteristic of causativization, the non-causal verb is morphologically more complex in comparison with the causal. Historically, both verbs are based on the adjective *oiged* 'straight; even; right'. The non-causal member is a reflexive verb, which inflects for a specific conjugation type. Both verbs display secondary meanings and, actually, the most typical meaning of *oigeta* is 'send; direct', *oigetas* 'take one's way (further)' in contemporary Veps.

Veps

(11) a. *rungu-n*   *kibišta-b,*   **oige-tas**   *emboi*
back-GEN(-ACC)   hurt-3SG   straight-REFL.INF   NEG.1SG.can
'My back is hurting, I cannot straighten myself.' (SVJa 377)

(11) b. *Me-ide-n*   *kanz*   *most*   **oige-ti-he**   *ede-mba.*
we-PL-GEN   family   again   straight-PST-REFL.3PL   further-CMP
'Our family made one's way further, again.'

(12) a. **oige-ta**   *naglo-i-d*   *pal'l'aiže-l*
straight-INF   nail-PL-PART   hammer-ADE
'straighten nails with a hammer'

(12) b. *Muga*   *hän*   *tahto-i*   **oige-ta**   *naiž-ide-n*
so   (s)he   want-PST.3SG   straight-INF   woman-PL-GEN
energia-d   *da*   *väge-d*   *voina-ha.*
energy-PART   and   power-PART   war-ILL
'So she wanted to direct women's energy and power to the war.'

A distinct reflexive conjugation is not very widespread in the Uralic languages, although non-causal derivative verbs that display an affix labeled reflexive(-passive) occur very widely. In Finnic, a reflexive conjugation is attested in the contact zone of Russian involving South Estonian, Votic, Ingrian, Karelian and Veps (Koivisto 1995). In Veps, this is a fairly productive feature which, in the given case, enables a parallel use of another parameter, the contrast between reflexive and non-reflexive verbs (Grünthal 2015: 120–149). In the context of this article, this feature is secondary and both language- and verb-specific.

3.3 Causativizing change in verb root

Introductions to the Uralic languages often emphasize the role of suffixal morphology, whereas flexion, stem alternations and analytic constructions, for instance, exist as well but are less characteristic (Majtinskaja 1979, 1993: 24–29; Comrie 1988: 455, 459–469; Hajdú 1993: 12–19; Abondolo 1998: 30–31). This, however, admits many exceptions as some kind of stem alternation occurs across the language family. In our sample, the verb 'dry', for instance, illustrates the minority pattern, in which causativization is based on changes limited to the verb root. In Inari Saami, a language that displays both affixal morphology and vowel metaphony, the verb set *kuškâ-ď* dry.up-INF 'dry (up)' (intr.), *kuški-ď* dry.up-INF 'dry (up)' (tr.) and a secondary affixal causal *kuškâ-di-ď* dry.up-CAUS-INF 'dry (up) (something)' are all related to the adjective *koškes* 'dry'.

Inari Saami

(13) *Juuva-h* **koške-h** *pakkâ já arvettis*
river-PL dry-3PL hot and rainless
keesi ääigi.
summer(NOM-GEN-ACC) time.GEN-ACC
'Rivers dry up during a hot and rainless summer.'

(14) *Piäiváš já pieggâ* **kuški-v** *jotelávt*
sun and wind dry-3DU fast
Myerji pihtâs-ijd.
Myerji.GEN cloth-PL.ACC
'The sun and wind dried Mary's clothes fast.'

Examples (13)–(14) illustrate the overlapping of lexically ruled morphology with category-based morphology, which has regular affixal inflection. In the given case, the inflectional categories are segmentable, whereas valency change is merely radical. Synchronically, this is a language-specific deviation from more frequent causativization strategies in Inari Saami. This unexpected feature has parallels in several other Uralic languages (see Table 3, above), which suggests that the reasons can be found in the historical development of these particular forms. We return to this issue in Section 4.4, below.

3.4 Suppletion

After affixal causativization suppletion is the second most frequent way of forming non-causal / causal contrasts in Uralic, which emphasizes the importance of lexical properties for valency change. There are some other individual cases in which the basic verb and its causal counterpart both lack a productive causal or non-causal marker, which is functionally unnecessary, if the semantic difference between the verb pair is lexically encoded. In this respect suppletion shares some of the characteristics of changes in the verb root, which were discussed in Section 3.3. In example (15)–(16) the causativizing strategy of a basic animate verb 'eat' / 'feed' in Udmurt, a language with regular affixal morphology, is based on suppletion and diverges from the more frequent derivational pattern X + CAUS (see (1), (2), (5)–(9) above).

Udmurt
(15) *čapak* **si-s'ky-sa** *puki-s'ko-my val*
just eat-REFL-CVB sit-PRES-1PL be.PST
'We were just sitting and eating.'

(16) *so pinal-z-e* **s'ude**
(s)he child-3SG-ACC feed.PRES.3SG
'(S)he is feeding her/his child.'

Cross-linguistically, a wide-spread exception is the verb pair 'die' and 'kill', which typically form a suppletive pair in global typological data (Botne 2003; WATP). This is valid in the Uralic languages as well. In our sample of six verb sets, the verb pair that has most suppletive pairs is 'see' / 'show'. This kind of pattern is attested in three different macro-areas, namely Siberia (Khanty (17)–(18), Kamas), languages of Central Russia (Komi and Mari), as well as Saamic (19)–(20) in Scandinavia, and Hungarian as the geographical outsider. Hence, the tendency to use suppletion for this particular verb is probably more due to lexical typology than language-specific or areal factors. Khanty, unlike other Uralic languages, displays a different alignment pattern and manifests an ergative structure with a non-nominative agent. In Inari Saami (20), the causal verb *čäitti-d* show-INF additionally has a causative suffix -t-, which, given the lack of an underived counterpart from the same root, cannot be distinguished from the verb stem. The evidence for the assumed underived word stem is found in the South Saami cognate *tjaajie-h* show-INF, cf. *vuojne-dh* see-INF 'see' → *vuesie-hti-dh* show-CAUS-INF 'show' (for reconstruction of the Inari Saami word descending from '(to) head', see Sammallahti 1998: 234).

North Khanty
(17) *Mašaj-a jăm-a* **ni-ɬ-a**
Maša-LAT good-LAT see-PASS-3SG
'Masha sees well.'

(18) *ant-em ńawrem-a χŏr-ət* **aɬ-əɬ**
mother-1SG child-LAT picture-PL show-3SG
'The mother shows pictures to the child.'

Inari Saami
(19) *Tarja* **ooin-ij** *Raansu aauto.*
Tarja see-PST.3SG Ransu.GEN auto.NOM-GEN-ACC
'Tarja saw Ransu's car.'

(20) Ransu **čaait-ij** aauto-s Taarja-n.
    Ransu show-PST.3SG car-3SG.PX Tarja-ILL
    'Ransu showed Tarja his car.'

The number of lexically dissimilar expressions of 'see' / 'show' is almost as high as that of pairs with affixal morphology, which reflects the fact that almost all Finnic languages display it, and they are more numerously represented in the sample than other Uralic branches (cf. Table 3, above). In Finnic, suppletion is typically used for verbs expressing 'fear' / 'frighten', as in South Estonian (21)–(22), which like Inari Saami in (20) displays a causative suffix in the causal member. In this case the causal member is a derivative of another non-causal verb *(h)irmu-daq* get.scared-INF 'get scared' but the basic meaning 'fear' is expressed by another inherited verb, which etymologically belongs to the older Proto-Uralic layer.

South Estonian
(21) latś **pelä-ś** ütsindä kodo min-näq.
    child be.afraid-PST.3SG alone home.ILL go-INF
    'The child was afraid of going home alone.'

(22) susi piśt akna-st saba si-sse,
    wolf put.PST.3SG window-ELA tail.GEN-ACC in.ILL
    irmu-t lamb-i-t.
    frighten-CAUS.PST.3SG sheep-PL-PART
    'A wolf put its tail in from the window and frightened the sheep.'

Compared to affixal morphology, suppletion lacks predictability and is less systematic in the way it assigns valency change and causativization both in individual languages and verb sets. Hence the way valency change is assigned depends primarily on verbal semantics in individual languages and verb sets. The result is that affixal causatives partly resemble inflectional units and tend to be category-based, while suppletion is lexically based. The shaded areas in Table 4 show those slots which display absolute or optional suppletion for the pairs 'eat' / 'feed' and 'fear' / 'frighten, scare' in our sample. Absolute suppletion indicates that there is no synonymic alternation that would allow the selection of the same root for both the causal and non-causal verb. Optional suppletion makes a distinction between the primary non-causal verb and its causal counterpart but the verb set involves a synonym which is a lexical cognate of one or the other verb.

Udmurt and Erzya display absolute suppletion in the causal member of 'eat' / 'feed', whereas Hungarian is the only language that displays absolute suppletion of 'fear' / 'frighten'. The number of possible suppletion pairs is higher, if one con-

Table 4: The causal pair of 'eat' / 'feed' and 'fear' / 'frighten, scare' based on suppletion (shaded areas).

	'eat'	'feed; give food'	'fear'	'frighten, scare'
Selkup	am-	apsətə-	lęri- / lęrimpi-	lęrəpčə-
North Khanty	łeti	łapətti	păłti	păłtaptəti
Mansi	teenkwe	titunkwe	pilunkwe	piluptankwe
Hungarian	eszik	etet	fél	ijeszt
Udmurt	s´iyny	s´udyny	kurdany	kurda-ty-ny
Mari	kočkaš	pukšaš	lüdaš	lüdyktaš
Erzya	jarsams	andoms	pel´ems ~ tandadoms	tandavtoms
Estonian	sööma	söötma	kartma ~ hirmuma	hirmutama ~ hirmu tegema
Finnish	syödä	syöttää	pelätä	pelästyttää ~ pelottaa
North Saami	borrat	borahit	ballat ~ suorganit	suorgahit

siders the difference between the primary verb denoting 'fear' and its causal pair. In this case, Erzya, Estonian and North Saami causal pairs could be considered as suppletive. However, in Erzya *tanda-vto-ms* get.scared-CAUS-INF 'frighten' has a non-causal counterpart *tanda-do-ms* get.scared-MOM-INF 'get scared', whereas the old inherited Uralic verb *pel'e-ms* fear-INF is the primary verb denoting 'fear'. Likewise, North Saami *balla-t* fear-INF 'fear' belongs to the inherited Uralic lexicon, while causal *suorga-hi-t* get.scared-CAUS-INF 'frighten' is a counterpart of *suorga-ni-t* get.scared-TRA-INF 'get scared'.

3.5 Analytic verb pairs

Assuming that language contacts may affect the distribution of various causativization patterns, one would expect that analytic constructions are gaining more space in western Uralic languages such as Livonian and Estonian that have been heavily influenced by the neighboring Baltic and Germanic languages. And in fact, the spread of analytic constructions has taken place in some other verb phrase types and several Estonian verbs (23–24) display alternative causativization strategies (Erelt 2017: 231–235).

Estonian
(23) a. Mees **käivi-ta-s** auto.
man walk-CAUS-PST.3SG car.GEN-ACC
'The man started the car.'
(23) b. Mees **pan-i** auto **käi-ma.**
man put-PST.3SG car.GEN-ACC walk-INF
'The man started the car.' (Erelt 2017: 231)

(24) a. Kee-gi **rõõmus-ta-b** mind.
who-FOC happy-CAUS-3SG I.ACC
'Someone is making me happy.'
(24) b. Kee-gi **tee-b** mind **rõõmsa-ks.**
who-FOC do-3SG I.ACC happy-TRA
'Someone is making me happy.' (Erelt 2017: 235)

For (23b) our claim is not that the verb *panema* 'put' calques any particular Germanic or Baltic causal construction, but that the whole structure of auxiliary or light verb plus lexical verb is presumably influenced by Germanic and/or Baltic patterns.

In the sample of basic verbs analyzed in this paper, a general tendency of shifting towards more analytic constructions is not seen. The language that diverges most in this limited sample is North Khanty, spoken in Northwestern Siberia. There the expression 'burn' is a phrasal predicate based on the construction 'fire' + 'eat' (25), and a similar construction occurs in some other Uralic languages in Siberia, such as Mansi and Eastern Khanty. The causativization of 'burn' is the same as for the independent verb to 'eat' / 'feed' (26).

North Khanty
(25) tŭt łe-ł
fire eat-3SG
'burn'

(26) imi tut ła-pt-əs
woman fire eat-CAUS-3SG
'A woman makes a fire.'

The Khanty verb phrase displays more analytic constructions than most other Uralic languages. While analytic constructions are secondary in southern Finnic languages, such as Livonian, South Estonian and Estonian, the age of analytic constructions in the Ugric languages is a more ambiguous question (Honti 1999,

2013: 303–317; Honti and Kiefer 2003). It must also be noted that certain North Khanty verbs, such as *łeti* 'eat' / *łapətti* 'feed', which is included in the column of affixal morphology in Table 3, above, actually have phrasal verb synonyms *jŏχi łeti* 'eat (momentaneous)' / *nŏχ łapətti* 'feed (continuous)' showing the increase of analytic constructions.

These few examples show the structural and lexical diversity which characterizes the Uralic causatives. We will next proceed with an overview of main diachronic trends in their development.

4 Diachronic tendencies

Given that the default causal verb in Uralic is based on augmentation and a derivative verb, the diachronic analysis of most verb sets has to account for the maintenance and renewal of morphological units. The diachronic development of individual verbs in individual languages is hypothetically open for three alternatives either maintaining or compensating the earlier pattern. The alternatives for preserving the inherited pattern are gradual erosion and lexicalization of one member of a verb pair or replacement of a synthetic causal verb by analytic constructions. Gradual reduction of a formerly segmentable causative structure eventually creates a non-segmentable lexeme with causative semantics. Thus, considering affixally marked causatives, we may assume three basic mechanisms affecting their diachronic development:
(i) The inherited augmentation pattern X + CAUS is preserved, although the affix may undergo some phonological changes.
(ii) The inherited pattern X + CAUS has eroded and gradually led to the fusion of the two morphemes.
(iii) The inherited pattern X + CAUS is no longer productive, and secondary analytic light verb constructions have emerged instead.

All three alternatives suggest that the causativized verb undergoes the diachronic development of alternating causal patterns, whereas changes in the argument structure are sensitive to the semantic properties of the verb regardless of the morphological structure.

The wide-spread similarity between causative affixes in contemporary Uralic languages displaying affixal -*t*- presumably originates from a shared proto-language stage. The high degree of stability of the proto-language affix *-kt- or *-pt- and its maintenance in every branch shows the importance of inherited derivative affixes for causative verbs and, more generally speaking, the word formation typology of the Uralic languages. Nevertheless, in certain cases, the inherited causativization strategy is blurred by the parallel influence of language contacts. For instance, the heavy Turkic influence on Mari is manifested in causal verbs, too, with the result that the number of different causative suffixes has increased under language contact.

This section will be limited on two diachronic aspects, which are (a) the evolution of the inherited Uralic causative affix, (b) the gradual erosion of segmentable affixes and the lexicalization of affixal causatives. Other diachronically relevant processes such as the decausativization and secondary causativization of individual verbs, the emergence of analytic causatives, and affixal borrowing in a language contact situation will not be discussed here. The following sections are organized so that they correspond to the horizontal parameters in Table 3 and Section 3, above.

4.1 Evolution of the inherited causative affix

As examples in Table 4 show, the transparent feature in the causative affixes of Uralic languages is the derivational segment -*t*-, which typically follows a two-syllable word stem, although in individual cases, such as Hungarian *e-tet-ni* eat-CAUS-INF 'feed' the stem may be shorter. The historical development of the Proto-Uralic involves two alternatives. The Samoyedic and Ob-Ugric languages suggest that the Proto-Uralic affix used to be *-pt- as evidenced in Selkup *lẹri-* 'fear' / *lẹrǝ-pčǝ-* fear-CAUS 'frighten, scare', North Khanty *păł-ti* fear-INF 'fear' / *păłta-ptǝ-ti* fear-CAUS-INF and (North) Mansi *pilu-nkwe* fear-INF 'fear' / *pilu-pta-nkwe* fear-CAUS-INF 'frighten'. The more western languages, Mari and Erzya, in which -vt- descends from *-kt-, provide evidence for the variant *-kt as in Mari *lüda-š* fear-INF 'fear' / *lüdy-kt-aš* fear-CAUS-INF 'frighten'. In standard North Saami the causative affix is reflected as -*h*- as in *suorga-hi-t* fear-CAUS-INF 'frighten' but, historically, it originates from a plosive as well, as the Inari Saami variant *polâ-tti-đ* fear-CAUS-INF 'frighten' indicates.

The main point here is that the affixal status of the inherited causative derivational affix *-pt- ~ *-kt- has been preserved consistently in all Uralic branches and the vast majority of individual languages. The degree to which descendants of the inherited affix are the dominating means of causativization varies.

4.2 Erosion and fusion of the causative affix in the lexical stem

In Table 3 Erzya and Kildin Saami show greater diversity of causativization strategies than other Uralic languages. This is somewhat surprising, because both Mordvinic languages, Erzya and Moksha, have a rich derivative morphology, which is especially characteristic of verbs, and there is a productive causative affix.

The ultimate result of the erosion of morphological affixes is fusion to the stem. The erosion of affixes characteristically leads to the increase of dissimilarity between related languages either through morphological restructuration or complete loss. However, in our sample there are very few cases in which the verb presumably displays a historical affix, which synchronically is a part of the stem, manifesting a complete loss of the affix. The verb pair 'be straight; straighten (out)' / 'straighten; make straight' in Erzya is an example of this process (27)–(28).

Erzya
(27) *nuvara   ser'e-m   mon* **vit'-an**
     depressed length-1SG.PX   I   straighten-1SG
     'I will straighten my downcast posture.' (MdWb 2657)

(28) *ves'i* **vit'e-v-s'**   *mon'   mel'-n'e-m*
     all   straighten-REFL-PST.3SG   I.GEN mind-DEM-1SG.PX
     'My mind has been fully brightened up.' (MdWb 2658)

Morphologically, the non-causal pair *vit'e-ve-ms* straighten[CAUS]-REFL-INF is derived from the causative basic stem *vit'e-ms* straighten[CAUS]-INF as reflexive(-passive) derivations are often used as non-causativizing affixes in Mordvinic. Nevertheless, the stem *vit'e-* historically originates from the adjective *vijed'e ~ vid'e* 'straight' and there are numerous nominal and verbal derivations from this particular word (MdWb 2652–2658). Most of them are based on *vid'e*, which is secondary and shortened from *vijed'e* (cf. UEW 824–825). The intervocalic voiceless plosive -*t'*- of the verb *vit'e-ms* straighten.CAUS-INF 'straighten' diverges from the voiced -*d'*- of the adjective *vid'e* because the historical causative affix *-kt-, Proto-Mordvinic -vt-, has merged in the stem. This explains the phonological contrast between -*d'*- in *vid'e* 'straight' and -*t'*- in *vit'e-ms* straighten.CAUS-INF. The merger is partly caused by the fact that second-syllable mid vowels *e* and *o* drop in front of an affix.

This example is language- and verb-specific to a very large extent. The next section deals with another example that reflects the diachronic properties of the word in Uralic in a more general way.

4.3 Verb root alternation

Change in the verb root is, as a rule, secondary if it occurs in strongly suffixal languages such as Uralic. In our sample, 'dry' shows considerably more frequent change in the verb root than the rest of the six verb sets (cf. Table 3, above). Change in the verb root is not attested in Samoyedic and Ugric, whereas at least one language in every Uralic branch on the European side manifests it. In this case, the point of the diachronic development is the historical development of non-verbal predication and verbal nouns, which inflect both as nouns and verbs.

The vast majority of Uralic verbs denoting 'dry' in the non-causal (intransitive) and causative (transitive) meaning are derived from the adjective 'dry'. Synchronically, the stem alternation is seen either in vowel alternation as in Inari Saami *kuškâ-ď* dry-INF 'dry (non-causal)' / *kuškiď* dry.CAUS-INF 'dry (causal)', or consonant alternation as in Mari *košk-aš* dry-INF 'dry (non-causal)' / *košt-aš* dry.CAUS-INF 'dry (causal)' (29)–(30). A similar relationship occurs between Erzya *kos'ke-ms* dry-INF 'dry (non-causal)' and *kos't'a-ms* dry.CAUS-INF 'dry (causal)' (31)–(32). The relating adjectives are Mari *kukšo* 'dry (adj.)', which does not correspond phonologically to the verbs, whereas Erzya *kos'ke* 'dry (adj.)' is simply the same stem without verbal markers.

Mari
(29) *pušeŋge* **košk-en**
  tree   dry-PST2.3SG
  'the tree withered'

(30) *šinčal-an kočkyš logary-m   košt-a*
  salt-ADJR food   throat-ACC dry-3SG
  'Salty food makes you thirsty.'

Erzya
(31) *kos'ke čevn'e-ks   mon kos'k-i-n'*
  dry   kindling-TRA I   dry-PST-1SG
  'I dried out like a dry kindling.' (MdWb 873)

(32) *lis'-n'e-s'   či-ze,   n'ej kos't'-i-nz'e*
  exit-CONT-PST.3SG sun-3SG.PX now dry.CAUS-PST-3SG>3SG
  'The sun rose, now it has dried it/her/him.' (MdWb 874)

Synchronically, the distinction between Mari non-causal and causal verb is based merely on the alternation of the plosive (k ~ t). The causal stem suggests that, historically, the use of -*t*- in the causal pair could originate from a causative affix. The Erzya parallel sheds more light on the diachronic development. Since the stem *kos'ke* inflects both for nominal and verbal categories, the non-causal variant *kos'ke-ms* must be considered as primary, whereas the causal pair *kos't'a-ms* historically reflects the loss of the word stem mid vowel -*e*- and, probably, the simplification of a consonant cluster *kos'k(e)-(k)ta-ms.

Similarly, the Inari Saami verb pair *kuškâ-đ* dry-INF 'dry (non-causal)' / *kuškiđ* dry.CAUS-INF 'dry (causal)' reflects the ambiguous character of Proto-Uralic *kośka 'dry' in terms of parts of speech in that it displays two distinct verb stems, an intransitive and transitive one, both of them verbs, while in most of the languages the intransitive is an adjective. Inari Saami also displays a secondary causative derivation *kuškâ-di-đ* dry-CAUS-INF 'dry (caus.)', which is based on the prevailing affix-changing morphology and compensates for the higher morphological burden caused by lexically encoded and stem-based valency change. In North Saami this is the only alternate (33)–(34) that causes a slight difference between valency changing patterns in comparison with Inari Saami, a neighboring language.

North Saami
(33) *Muđui   muorra **guoiká**,   go   mátta*
     otherwise   tree   dry.3SG   when   butt
     gáhčči-luvvá   hui   jođanit.
     resin-CONT.PASS.3SG   very   fast
     'Otherwise the timber will dry out, when the butt rapidly becomes resinous.'

(34) *Ma-s   don   dál   galgga-t   **goika-di-t**   biktas-iid?*
     where-LOC you   now   must-2SG   dry-CAUS-INF   cloth-PL.GEN(-ACC)
     'Where will you dry your clothes now?'

The tendency to prefer affixal valency changing is more stable across the Uralic family than the other ways of forming causative pairs. Both verb root alternation and non-segmental affixal changes are secondary and characteristically random, whereas affixal derivation is diachronically stable in most verb sets. There is not much evidence that secondary analytic light verb constructions would have emerged instead and led to a large-scale typological compensation of eroded constructions. In our sample, exceptions to the rule show some traces of earlier affix changing morphology.

5 Conclusion

The empirical sample of this paper represents a larger database showing variation in causativizing strategies of selected Uralic verb pairs. The limited pilot consisting of six verb pairs shows that synchronically, there is considerable divergence. While affixal morphology is the most frequent and regular way of forming causal verbs across the language family, other strategies such as suppletion and changes in verb root are less regular. The fact that more than sixty percent of the verb sets display causativizing affixes suggests that this is an inherited typological characteristic of the Uralic languages, which, more generally speaking, typically display rich affixal morphology of both nominal and verbal categories.

The number of deviations from the main pattern is not irrelevant, either. Those verb sets that show more than random exceptions to the rule have significance for the analysis of verb-specific and areal development. Verbs like 'see' / 'show' for instance are clearly prone to replace valency changing pattern with suppletion.

A brief diachronic analysis shows that, historically, the picture of causativizing individual verbs is probably more uniform than the synchronic divergence shows. The erosion of affixal morphology explains the emergence of irregular direction in valency change between the non-causal and causal verbs. Likewise, the emergence of root alternation, a secondary feature in the morphology of several Uralic languages, originates from the loss of morpheme boundaries and merger of morphemes, usually including a causative morpheme.

Abbreviations

ACC	accusative
ADE	adessive
ADJR	adjectivizer
ALL	allative
ASP	aspectual
CAUS	causative
CMP	comparative
CONT	continuous
CVB	converb
DECAUS	decausative
DEM	deminutive
DU	dual
ELA	elative
FOC	focus
FRE	frequentative(continuous)

GEN	genitive
ILL	illative
INF	infinitive
LAT	lative
LOC	locative
MOM	momentanous
NEG	negative
NOM	nominative
PART	partitive
PASS	passive
PL	plural
PRES	present
PST	past tense
PTCP	participle
PX	possessive suffix
REFL	reflexive
SG	singular
TRA	translative

Appendix – Uralic languages of the sample

(Languages and subgroups are primarily organized from East to West with respect to the whole language family and the division of subbranches, and secondarily from South to North, if the assumed spread of the subbranch had this direction.)

Samoyedic
KAM = Kamas
SEL = Selkup
NENT = Tundra Nenets
NGA = Nganasan

Ugric
KHAE = East Khanty
KHAN = North Khanty
MAN = (North) Mansi
HUN = Hungarian

Permic
UDM = Udmurt
KOM = Komi

Mari
MAR = (Meadow) Mari

Mordvinic
ERZ = Erzya

Finnic
LIV = Livonian
ESTS = South Estonian
EST = (Standard) Estonian
VOT = Votic
FIN = Finnish
VEP = Veps

Saamic
SAAKld = Kildin Saami
SAAIn = Inari Saami
SAAN = North Saami
SAAS = South Saami

References

Abondolo, Daniel. 1998. Introduction. In Daniel Abondolo (ed.), *The Uralic languages*, 1–42. London: Routledge.

Arkadiev, Peter & Jurgis Pakerys. 2015. Lithuanian morphological causatives: A corpus-based study. In Axel Holvoet & Nicole Nau (eds.), *Voice and argument structure in Baltic*, 39–97. Amsterdam & Philadelphia: John Benjamins.

Botne, Robert. 2003. To die across languages: Toward a typology of achievement verbs. *Linguistic Typology* 7. 233–278.

Comrie, Bernard. 1988. General features of the Uralic languages. In Denis Sinor (ed.), *The Uralic languages: Description, history and foreign influences*, 451–477. Leiden: Brill.

Comrie, Bernard, Iren Hartmann, Martin Haspelmath, Andrej Malchukov & Søren Wichmann. 2015. Introduction. In Andrej L. Malchukov & Bernard Comrie (eds.), *Valency classes in the world's languages*, 3–26. Berlin & New York: Mouton de Gruyter.

Creissels, Denis. 2015. Valency properties of Mandinka verbs. In Andrej Malchukov & Bernard Comrie (eds.), *Valency classes in the world's languages*, 221–260. Berlin & New York: Mouton de Gruyter.

Dolovai, Dorottya. 2001. A többszörös műveltés az obi-ugor nyelvekben [Multiple causativization in the Ob-Ugric languages]. *Néprajz és nyelvtudomány* 41. 77–93.

Erelt, Mati. 2017. Öeldis [Verb]. In Mati Erelt & Helle Metslang (eds.), *Eesti keele süntaks* [The syntax of the Estonian language], 93–239. Tartu: Tartu Ülikooli Kirjastus.

Grünthal, Riho. 2015. *Vepsän kielioppi* [Veps grammar]. Helsinki: Finno-Ugrian Society.

Hajdú, Péter 1993 = П. Хайду: Уральские языки [Uralic languages]. In В. Н. Ярцева (ed.), *Языки мира: Уральские языки* [World's languages: Uralic languages], 7–19. Moscow: Linguistic Institute of the Russian Academy of Sciences.
Haspelmath, Martin. 1993. More on the typology of inchoative/causative verb alternations. In Bernard Comrie & Maria Polinsky (eds.), *Causatives and transitivity*, 87–120. Amsterdam & Philadelphia: John Benjamins.
Haspelmath, Martin. 2016. Universals of causative and anticausative verb formation and the spontaneity scale. *Lingua Posnaniensis* 58 (2). 33–63.
Holvoet, Axel. 2015. Extended uses of morphological causatives in Latvian. In Axel Holvoet & Nicole Nau (eds.), *Voice and Argument Structure in Baltic*, 147–177. Amsterdam & Philadelphia: John Benjamins.
Honti, László. 1999. Das Alter und die Entstehungsweise der "Verbalpräfixe" in uralischen Sprachen. *Linguistica Uralica* 35. 81–97, 161–176.
Honti, László. 2013. *Magyar nyelvtörténeti tanulmányok* [Studies on Hungarian language history]. Budapest: L'Harmattan.
Honti, László & Ferenc Kiefer. 2003. Verbal "prefixation" in the Uralic languages. *Acta Linguistica Hungarica* 50. 137–153.
Koivisto, Vesa. 1995. *Itämerensuomen refleksiiviverbit* [Reflexive verbs in Finnic]. Helsinki: Finnish Literature Society.
Kulikov, Leonid. 2009. Valence-changing categories in Indo-Aryan and Indo-European: A diachronic typological portrait of Vedic Sanskrit. In Anju Saxena & Åke Viberg (eds.), *Multilingualism. Proceedings of the 23rd Scandinavian Conference of Linguistics*, 75–92. Uppsala: Uppsala University.
Lavidas, Nikolaos & Leonid Kulikov. 2018. Voice and valence orientation in Indo-European: A diachronic typological perspective. Paper presented at the 51st Annual Meeting of the Societas Linguistica Europaea (SLE 2018) 29 August – 1st September 2018. University of Tallinn, Estonia.
Luraghi, Silvia. 2012. Basic valence orientation and the middle voice in Hittite. *Studies in Language* 36. 11–32.
Majtinskaja, K. E. 1979 = К. Е. Майтийская: *Историко-сопоставительная морфология финно-угорских языков* [Historical-comparative morphology of the Finno-Ugric languages]. Moscow: Nauka.
Majtinskaja, K. E. 1993 = К. Е. Майтийская: Финно-угорские языки [Finno-Ugric languages]. In В. Н. Ярцева (ed.), *Языки мира: Уральские языки* [World's languages: Uralic languages], 20–31. Linguistic Institute of the Russian Academy of Sciences.
Malchukov, Andrej & Bernard Comrie (eds). 2015a. *Valency classes in the world's languages, Vol 1: Introducing the framework, and case studies from Africa and Eurasia*. Berlin & New York: Mouton de Gruyter.
Malchukov, Andrej & Bernard Comrie (eds). 2015b. *Valency Classes in the World's Languages, Vol. 2: Case studies from Austronesia, the Pacific, the Americas, and theoretical outlook*. Berlin & New York: Mouton de Gruyter.
MdWb = *H. Paasonens Mordwinisches Wörterbuch* I–VI. Zusammengestellt von Kaino Heikkilä. Bearbeitet und herausgegeben von Martti Kahla. Lexica Societatis Fenno-Ugricae XXIII. Helsinki: Finno-Ugrian Society 1990–1999.
Nau, Nicole. 2015. Morphological causatives in contemporary Latvian. In Axel Holvoet & Nicole Nau (eds.), *Voice and argument structure in Baltic*, 99–145. Amsterdam & Philadelphia: John Benjamins.

Nedjalkov, V. P. 1966 = В. П. Недялков: Об ареальных универсалиях (на материале каузативных глаголов). *Конференция по проблемам изучения универсальных и ареальных свойств языка. Тезисы* [On areal universals (on the basis of causative verbs). Conference on the problems in the research of universal and areal characteristics in language. Theses.], 55–58. Moscow: Nauka.

Nichols, Johanna, David A. Peterson & Jonathan Barnes. 2004. Transitivizing and detransitivizing languages. *Linguistic Typology* 8 (2). 149–211.

Nickel, Karl & Pekka Sammallahti. 2011. *Nordsamisk grammatikk* [North Saami grammar]. Karasjok: Davvi Girji.

Sammallahti, Pekka. 1998. *The Saami Languages. An Introduction*. Karasjok: Davvi Girji.

Shibatani, Masayoshi & Prashant Pardeshi. 2002. The causative continuum. Masayoshi Shibatani (ed.), *The Grammar of Causation and Interpersonal Manipulation*, 85–126. Amsterdam & Philadelphia: John Benjamins.

SVJa = М. И. Зайцева и М. И. Муллонен. 1972. *Словарь вепсского языка* [Dictionary of Veps language]. Leningrad: Nauka.

UEW = Károly Rédei. 1988. *Uralisches etymologisches Wörterbuch* I–II. Akadémiai Kiadó, Budapest.

WATP = *The World Atlas of Transitivity Pairs*. Tokyo: National Institute for Japanese Language and Linguistics. https://watp.ninjal.ac.jp/en (accessed 30 April 2021)

Sonja Riesberg, Kurt Malcher and Nikolaus P. Himmelmann
The many ways of transitivization in Totoli

Abstract: This paper investigates the basic valency orientation and different ways of transitivization in Totoli, a western Austronesian symmetrical-voice language of Indonesia. Totoli can be considered a transitivizing language that makes use of four major valency-increasing strategies: causativization proper, transitive-intransitive alternation within the stative paradigm, alternation between the stative and the dynamic paradigms, and the use of applicative morphology. Taking a closer look at the unique relationship between the symmetrical-voice and applicative systems in Totoli we claim that the language occupies an intermediary position between Philippine-type and non-Philippine-type symmetrical-voice languages, and that the development of applicatives as a system independent from voice may have arisen with the emergence of transitivity as a distinction relevant in the grammar of western Austronesian languages of the non-Philippine-type.

Keywords: symmetrical voice, basic valency orientation, transitivization, applicativization, (non-)Philippine type

1 Introduction

This paper investigates the basic valence orientation and different ways of transitivization in Totoli, a western Austronesian symmetrical-voice language.[1] In western

---

[1] The research for this article was carried out within the Collaborative Research Centre SFB1252 Prominence in Language (Project-ID 281511265) funded by the Deutsche Forschungsgemeinschaft (DFG, German Research Foundation) at the University of Cologne – support we very gratefully acknowledge. Sonja Riesberg also gratefully acknowledges funding and support from the Australian Research Council as a postdoc in the Centre of Excellence for the Dynamics of Language. Nikolaus Himmelmann and Sonja Riesberg are especially thankful to the Volkswagen Foundation for long-term support and funding of their research and fieldwork in Tolitoli. A very special thanks to all Totoli speakers who helped us understand the 'mysteries' of Totoli voice and applicative morphology. Thank you also to Sophia Little for proof reading this chapter. For a brief characterization of Austronesian symmetrical voice systems see Himmelmann (2005: 167–170).

Sonja Riesberg, Universität zu Köln, Australian National University and CNRS-LACITO, e-mail: sonja.riesberg@cnrs.fr
Kurt Malcher, Universität zu Köln, e-mail: kmalcher@smail.uni-koeln.de
Nikolaus P. Himmelmann, Universität zu Köln, e-mail: sprachwissenschaft@uni-koeln.de

∂ Open Access. © 2021 Sonja Riesberg et al., published by De Gruyter. [CC BY-NC-ND] This work is licensed under the Creative Commons Attribution-NonCommercial-NoDerivatives 4.0 International License.
https://doi.org/10.1515/9783110755657-008

Austronesian symmetrical-voice languages, voice alternations do not decrease transitivity, i.e. unlike the active-passive alternation, a symmetrical-voice alternation does not involve the suppression or demotion of a core argument to oblique status. Rather, it can be described as a means to rearrange the linking of arguments and select different arguments as syntactic pivots. In some symmetrical-voice languages of Indonesia,[2] formatives which are historically associated with the Austronesian voice system are used as applicatives. That is, they signal the promotion of a peripheral participant to core status.

Totoli is interestingly different from many other Indonesian symmetrical-voice languages in two ways: first, it exploits the same formatives for both voice and applicative functions and thus exhibits a rather puzzling polysemy in the voice-changing and valency-increasing paradigms. Second, the extent to which Totoli makes use of different transitivization operations seem to be exceptionally high.

In the first part of the paper, we will be concerned with the different valence increasing strategies in Totoli. These include 'proper' causativization – i.e. the addition of an AGENT by means of a designated causative prefix, and 'proper' applicativization – i.e. the application of a GOAL by means of an applicative suffix. Due to the symmetrical nature of the voice system, and unlike in asymmetrical languages, neither causativization nor applicativization in Totoli install the applied argument to a predetermined syntactic function (i.e. new agent to subject for causatives and new undergoer to object for applicatives, as would be the case in asymmetrical languages). Rather, they install the new argument in core function, which, depending on the voice, can either be the subject or a non-subject direct core argument (Zúñiga and Kittilä 2019: 14 call this process 'nucleativization'). Furthermore, Totoli exhibits the applicative-causative syncretism found in many western Austronesian languages (cf. Hemmings 2013 for references and discussion). That is, depending on the basic valency of the verb, the same set of affixes is used to either promote different undergoer participants to core arguments or to add a (new) AGENT/CAUSER. With transitive bases, the suffix *-an* applies a BENEFACTIVE or an INSTRUMENT. With intransitive bases, a new AGENT/CAUSER is added to the verb's argument structure. Making use of Nichols, Peterson and Barnes' (2004) method to determine the BASIC VALENCE ORIENTATION of

---

Riesberg (2014) provides the most detailed discussion available to date. A comparison between western Austronesian symmetrical voice systems and similar phenomena in languages of the Americas is found in Zúñiga and Kittilä (2019: 120–150).

2 The symmetrical-voice languages of Indonesia are found west of Lombok and in the northern half of Sulawesi.

a language, we show that Totoli is a strongly transitivizing language, and we will see that transitivization is an important aspect of Totoli grammar.

In the second part of the paper, we will place the Totoli system into the wider western Austronesian context and demonstrate that Totoli is exceptional in the way it employs the same set of formatives for different voice-changing and valency-increasing alternations. Based on the Totoli system, we also provide some comments on a possible historical development of western Austronesian voice and applicative marking systems.

In Section 2, we will provide some grammatical background information on Totoli. In particular, we will describe the voice system, the applicative paradigm, and the distinction between dynamic and stative predications. In Section 3 we turn to the issue of transitivity and basic valence orientation. In addition to the above-mentioned strategies of 'proper' causativization (Section 3.1), and transitivization with applicative morphology (Section 3.4), we will discuss causativization within the stative paradigm (Section 3.2), and causativization by conjugation class change (Section 3.3). Section 4 introduces the Philippine-type voice system and the non-Philippine-type voice/applicative system and argues that the Totoli system is somewhere in between the two.

2 Grammatical background – voice and applicative marking in Totoli

Totoli is a Western Malayo-Polynesian language spoken by up to 5000 speakers in the northern part of Central Sulawesi (see Himmelmann 2001, 2010 for further details on the social and linguistic setting). Most examples used in this paper are from the DoBeS Totoli corpus (Leto et al. 2005–2010) and can be cross-checked there. A few examples are from the corpus by Bracks et al. (2017–2020), which will be available online in the near future. Examples from spontaneous discourse are referenced for name of the session and line number. Elicited examples are not further indexed. To further highlight the difference between natural and elicited data, we represent the two data types differently: Elicited examples all adhere to capitalization conventions and include punctuation, while examples from natural spontaneous speech do not.

2.1 Voice in Totoli

Totoli is a western Austronesian language of the non-Philippine type (see Section 4 for further details). It has two basic transitive constructions, the actor voice and the undergoer voice. If the NP in subject function[3] is an actor, the verb will be marked by actor-voice morphology. If the subject is an undergoer, undergoer-voice morphology will be used. The undergoer voice comes in two different paradigms, here simply called UNDERGOER VOICE 1 (UV1) and UNDERGOER VOICE 2 (UV2). The choice between paradigm 1 and 2 is lexically determined. That is, some verbal bases mark undergoer voice with UV1 and others with UV2 without there being a functional difference between the two undergoer voices. Note that this differs crucially from Philippine-type languages like Tagalog (cf. Section 4, example (18)), where the different undergoer voices are functionally distinct, each voice selecting a participant with a different semantic role as a subject. Both the actor voice and the undergoer voice in Totoli are fully transitive, that is, in both voices the non-subject argument has core argument status. There is also a locative voice, in which the subject is a stative locative argument (i.e. a place where something happens). Unlike in Tagalog (cf. example (18d)), however, the locative voice in Totoli is less basic than the actor and the undergoer voices, as it is syntactically more restricted (cf. Himmelmann and Riesberg 2013: 412). The following examples illustrate actor- and undergoer-voice uses of the verb *taip* 'peel' (a verb which takes paradigm 1 for undergoer-voice marking), and a locative-voice form of the verb *kaan* 'eat'.

(1) a. *I Rinto manaip taipang.*
i Rinto **moN-**taip taipang
HON PN **AV-**peel taipang
'Rinto is peeling a mango'

b. *Taipang kodoong taip i Rinto.*
taipang ko-doong taip i Rinto
mango POT-want peel.**UV1** HON PN
'The mango will be peeled by Rinto.'
'The house is where they eat.'

c. *Bale ia pangaani ssia.*
bale ia **poN-**kaan-**i** sisia
house PRX **SF-**eat-**LV** 3PL
'The house is where they eat.'

---

[3] The position of the subject NP is flexible. It can occur either before or after the verb + non-subject complex. In the examples used in this paper the subject occurs consistently in sentence-initial position (in the actor voice SVO order is more frequent, in the undergoer voice OVS order is preferred (cf. Riesberg, Malcher and Himmelmann 2019: 537)). Note that we use the term 'subject' here as equivalent to what is termed 'privileged syntactic argument' (PSA) in Van Valin (2005) and elsewhere. A PSA is defined as the syntactic element that controls coding properties such as agreement and that is the pivotal element in complex constructions such as relativization, NP deletion, control, etc.

All examples shown above are in non-realis mood, which is not indicated in the glosses. Table 1 summarizes the full set of voice affixation, including the respective realis forms.[4] Riesberg (2014) provides an in-depth discussion of symmetrical-voice alternations, including more data from Totoli.

Table 1: Totoli voice formatives (dynamic paradigm).

	NON-REALIS	**REALIS**
ACTOR VOICE	mo-/moN-/mog-	no-/noN-/nog-
UNDERGOER VOICE 1	∅	ni-
UNDERGOER VOICE 2	-i	ni- + -an
LOCATIVE VOICE	po-/poN-/pog- + -i	ni- + po-/poN-/pog- + -an

As can be seen in Table 1, UV1 is unmarked in non-realis mood, the form simply consisting of the bare stem. In realis mood, UV1 is only marked by the undergoer-voice realis prefix *ni-*, which occurs in all realis forms except actor voice. The choice of the different prefixes in the actor and locative voices is partially phonologically, partially lexically conditioned.

2.2 Applicativization in Totoli

There are two applicative paradigms in Totoli (shown in Table 2 below) which increase the valency of a predicate by one place. One of these, marked by *-an* in non-realis mood, introduces an argument whose semantic role depends on the valency of the stem. If the stem is monovalent, it adds a (new) causer argument, if it is bivalent, the added argument can either be a BENEFICIARY/ RECIPIENT or an INSTRUMENT. We call this APPLICATIVE 1, even though it partly has a causative function. The other one, which uses the suffix *-i* in non-realis mood, typically adds a GOAL argument. We call this APPLICATIVE 2.

Both applicative markers occur in all voices and in both realis and non-realis mood. Table 2 summarizes the rather intricate system of applicative formatives in Totoli. As can be seen, there is significant syncretism between plain voice forms (cf. Table 1) and applicative (voice) marking. The suffixes *-an* and *-i* are part of

---

[4] Realis mood denotes past events or situations that already exist and are still ongoing. Non-realis mood is used in reference to situations that do not (yet) obtain at the time of speaking, inter alia. Its distribution is in fact considerably wider than realis mood. It is both morphologically and distributionally the unmarked member of the pair.

the applicative paradigm, but they also occur in 'plain', non-applicative voice forms (UV2). Likewise, bare (i.e. non-suffixed) verb forms can be found in both functions, non-applicative realis undergoer voice (UV1) and APPLICATIVE 1 realis undergoer voice. For a detailed argument supporting the analysis summarized in the two tables, see Himmelmann and Riesberg (2013). As illustrated in Table 2, it is especially in realis undergoer voice forms that applicative marking is less transparent and partially homophonous with non-applicative undergoer voice marking.

Table 2: Totoli applicative formatives (dynamic paradigm).

	NON-REALIS	REALIS
APPLICATIVE 1 AV	mo-/moN-/mog- + -an	no-/noN-/nog- + -an
APPLICATIVE 1 UV	-an	ni- + -Ø
(SUBJ = THEME) APPLICATIVE 1 UV	po-/poN-/pog- + -an	ni- + po-/poN-/pog- + -Ø
(SUBJ= BEN/INSTR) APPLICATIVE 2 AV	mo-/moN-/mog- + -i	no-/noN-/nog- + -i
APPLICATIVE 2 UV	-i	ni- + -an

Example (2) illustrates the basic, i.e. non-applicative form of the monovalent verb *sake* 'ascend'. Example (3) shows the use of APPLICATIVE 1 (with non-realis applicative suffix *-an*), where the promoted argument (*tau ana* 'those people') is an external CAUSER, which becomes the subject in the actor voice (example a), and a (not overtly expressed, but unambiguously implied) non-subject core argument in the undergoer voice (example b). The GOAL argument *kapa'* 'ship' remains oblique, marked by the locative preposition *dei* or its proclitic form *i=*. In (4) we see the use of APPLICATIVE 2 (with non-realis applicative suffix *-i*) occurring with the same verb, and it is the GOAL argument, i.e. the ship, that is promoted to become a non-subject core argument in the actor voice, and the subject in the undergoer voice. In these examples, the THEME is marked as oblique.

(2)   *sumake*   *pesawat heli*
       -um-sake   pesawat heli
       -AUTO.MOT-ascend airplane helicopter
       'the helicopter ascended' [lelegesan_a.020]

(3) a. *Tau*   *ana*   *meseo*   *manakean*   *balaan dei kapa'.*[5]
      tau   ana   mo-seo   **moN**-sake-**an**   balaan dei kapa'
      person MED ST-busy AV-ascend-APPL1 goods LOC ship
      'Those people are busy loading goods on the ship.'

b. *Balaan isake ikapa'.*
   balaan **ni**-sake i=kapa'
   goods **RLS.UV**-ascend:**APPL1** LOC=ship
   'The goods were loaded onto the ship.'

(4) a. *Douamo no ondo sisia manakei kapa' (takin balaan).*
   doua=mo no ondo sisia **moN**-sake-**i** kapa' (takin balaan)
   two=CPL LK day 3PL **AV**-ascend-**APPL2** ship with goods
   'For two days already they are loading the ship (with goods).'
   b. *Kapa' ana lalau sakei sisia (takin balaan).*
   kapa' ana lalau sake-**i** sisia (takin balaan)
   ship MED presently ascend-**APPL2.UV** 3PL with goods
   'They are loading the ship (with goods).'

The two examples in (5) illustrate how the use of APPLICATIVE 1 with a bivalent base can either add a BENEFICIARY argument (5a), or an INSTRUMENT (5b).

(5) a. *Aku notookamo nipanaipna taipang.*
   aku no-tooka=mo **ni-poN**-taip=na taipang
   1SG ST.RLS-finished=CPL **RLS.UV-SF**-peel.**APPL1**=3SG.GEN mango
   'He peeled a mango for me.'
   b. *Kode gopas nanasi nipadaamkuko*
   kode gopas nanasi **ni-po**-daam=ku=ko
   only yarn pineapple **RLS.UV-SF**-sew.**APPL1**=1SG.GEN=AND
   ulos ana.
   ulos ana
   sarong MED
   'I only use the yarn from the pineapple leaf to sew that sarong.'

2.3 Stative predicates in Totoli

The paradigms illustrated in Table 1 and Table 2 above pertain to dynamic events. But besides the obligatory mood-distinction that holds for all verbs, Totoli also morphologically distinguishes between dynamic and non-dynamic eventualities.

---

5 The base form for 'ship' is kapal, but word-final laterals after vowels are regularly replaced by vowel lengthening in Totoli (i.e. kapal is [kapa:]). Elided laterals are indicated by an apostrophe <'> in the practical orthography used here. See Himmelmann (1991) and Bracks (forthc.) for more on Totoli phonology.

The latter denote non-dynamic state of affairs, including bodily states, qualities, and emotional and cognitive states. Like dynamic predicates, stative predicates participate in the actor- vs. undergoer-voice alternation. Note, however, that in the stative paradigm, there is only one (transitive) undergoer voice form, but there is an additional set of formatives (*mo-* in the non-realis, *no-* in the realis) that is designated for intransitive uses, and which also takes an undergoer subject (cf. Table 3).

Table 3: Totoli voice formatives (stative paradigm).

	Non-Realis	**Realis**
Stative AV	*mo-* + *ko-*	*no-* + *ko-*
Stative Intr	*mo-*	*no-*
Stative UV	*ko-* + *-i*	*ni-* + *ko-* + *-an*

In this paper, we will mainly be concerned with intransitive stative predicates. But in Section 3.2 we will also see that the alternation between intransitive and transitive stative forms shown in Table 3 involves a sense of causativization. The examples in (6) illustrate some common uses of intransitive stative predicates in Totoli.

(6) a. *mo-linggo deuk dei saa*
     ST-afraid dog LOC snake
     'the dog is afraid of the snake' [maptask_1 0560]
  b. *ai anu mpido ssaakan*
     ai anu mo-pido sasaakan
     and REL ST-good all
     'and all of them are good' [monkey_turtle 069]
  c. *ana waktuu mo-lotok sasik*
     if time ST-calm sea
     'in times when the sea was calm' [tau_bentee 014]

Here the stative predicates take non-agentive subjects. It is this construction type that frequently constitutes the morphologically basic member in a causative – non-causative pair, as we will further discuss in Section 3.

3 Basic valence orientation in Totoli

Nichols, Peterson and Barnes (2004) argue that languages can be classified according to their BASIC VALENCE ORIENTATION, which is determined by how they treat intransitive-transitive verb pairs such as 'learn' and 'teach' or 'die' and 'kill'. They propose four types: TRANSITIVIZING, DE-TRANSITIVIZING, NEUTRAL, and INDETERMINATE. See Table 4 for the respective morphological patterns and their descriptions.

Table 4: Types of basic valence orientation (adapted from Nichols, Peterson and Barnes 2004: 159).

TYPE	CORRESPONDENCE	DESCRIPTION
transitivizing	augmented	induced verb is derived
detransitivizing	reduced	plain verb is derived
neutral	double derivation	both verbs are derived
	auxiliary change	different auxiliaries
	ablaut	consonant/vowel change with same morphology
indeterminate	suppletion	different verb roots
	ambitransitive	same verb, same morphology
	conjugation class change	different conjugation class, otherwise underived

In their study, Nichols, Peterson and Barnes (2004) investigate 18 verb pairs in 80 languages, each pair consisting of a plain (i.e. intransitive and semantically non-causative) and an induced (i.e. transitive and semantically causative) member. The list of verb pairs is shown in Table 5.

Table 5: Plain-induced verb pairs studied in Nichols, Peterson and Barnes (2004: 186).

PLAIN	INDUCED	PLAIN	INDUCED
1. laugh	make laugh	10. (come to) boil	(bring to) boil
2. die	kill	11. burn, catch fire	burn, set fire
3. sit	seat	12. break	break
4. eat	feed	13. open	open
5. learn, know	teach	14. dry	dry
6. see	show	15. be/become straight	straighten
7. be/become angry	make angry	16. hang	hang (up)
8. fear, be afraid	frighten, scare	17. turn over	turn over
9. hide, go into hiding	hide, put into hiding	18. fall	drop, let fall

In Totoli, 14 of these 18 pairs are transitivizing, i.e. the induced member of the pair is morphologically derived – either by applicativization and by causativization – from its plain counterpart. Table 6 shows the 18 verb pairs and the evidence for their basic valence orientation in Totoli.

Table 6: Plain and induced verb pairs in Totoli.

Plain	Induced	Morphological marking	Correspondence
1. *kekek* 'laugh'	*po-kekek* 'make laugh'	causative	augmented
2. *mate* 'die'	*pate* 'kill'	---	suppletion
3. *sugo* 'sit'	*po-sugo-an* 'seat'	causative + applicative	augmented
4. *kaan* 'eat'	*po-kaan* 'feed'	causative	augmented
5. *koto* 'learn, know'	*po-koto-i* 'teach'	causative + applicative	augmented
6. *ita* 'see'	*po-ita* 'show'	causative	augmented
7. *ngasa* 'be/become angry'	*moko-ngasa* 'make angry'	transitive stative	augmented
8. *linggo* 'fear, be afraid'	*moko-linggo* 'frighten, scare'	transitive stative	augmented
9. *buni* 'hide, go into hiding'	*buni-an* 'hide, put into hiding'	applicative	augmented
10. *lolok* '(come to) boil'	*lolok-an* '(bring to) boil'	applicative	augmented
11. *mo-tutung* 'burn, catch fire'	*moN-tutung* 'burn, set fire'	stative vs. dynamic paradigm	conjugation-class change
12. *kolog* 'break'	*kudut* 'break'	---	suppletion
13. *mo-buka* 'open'	*moN-buka* 'open'	stative vs. dynamic paradigm	conjugation-class change
14. *tuu* 'dry'	*moko-tuu, po-tuu* 'dry'	transitive stative, causative	augmented
15. *nonto'* 'be/become straight'	*nonto'-an* 'straighten'	applicative	augmented
16. *toeng* 'hang'	*toeng-an* 'hang (up)'	applicative	augmented

Table 6 (continued)

Plain	Induced	Morphological marking	Correspondence
17. *balli* 'turn over'	*balli-an* 'turn over'	applicative	augmented
18. *dabu* 'fall'	*moko-dabu, dabu-i* 'drop, let fall'	transitive stative, applicative	augmented

As can be seen in Table 6, two of the pairs (numbers 11 and 13) exhibit conjugation-class change, with the plain member occurring in the stative and the induced member in the dynamic paradigm. Pairs 2[6] and 12 involve suppletion. These two strategies can be considered instances of indeterminate valency alternation. For pair number 17, no induced form is attested in our corpus. Note that there is no detransitivization process in Totoli. We will discuss the first three strategies in the following subsections.

3.1 Transitivization by causativization – the causative prefix po-

Totoli has a designated causative marker *po-* that adds a new CAUSER argument to the argument structure of a verb. Causativized forms can occur in both actor and undergoer voice. In the dynamic paradigm, the causative marker follows the voice prefix (if present). Consider the following two example pairs that illustrate the causative alternation for the dynamic verbs *kaan* 'eat' (in the actor voice, (7)) and *ita* 'see' (in the undergoer voice, (8)).

(7) a. *sia   geiga kode   mangaanmo   kukis*
       isia   geiga kode   mog-kaan=mo   kukis
       3SG   NEG   only   AV-eat=CPL   cake
       'she doesn't only eat cake' [conv_cl 671]
    b. *aa   mpakaan   bou   ana*
       aa   mo-**po**-kaan   bou   ana
       INTJ   AV-**CAU**-eat   turtle   MED
       'ah, he feeds that turtle' [Mansur's_work 0865]

---

[6] Note that in pair number 2, the Totoli induced form *pate* 'kill' is historically most likely a causative formation /po-ate/ of the plain form *ate* 'die'. Synchronically, however, these are clearly two different roots.

(8) a. niitaanna   sellengget   tadinmoko
       ni-ita-an=na   se-RDP1-lengget   tadin=mo=ko
       RLS.UV-see-APPL1=3SG   one-RDP1-basket   lost=CPL=AND
       'he saw (that) one basket was already missing' [pearstory_2 310]
    b. bali kau nippoitanamo
       bali kau ni-po-ita-na=mo
       SO   2SG RLS.UV-SF-**CAU**-see.UV1=3SG.GEN=CPL
       'so he already showed it to you' [Abdullah's_dream 002]

The causative prefix *po-* can also occur with semantically stative predicates, again, both in the actor voice, here illustrated with the verb *linggo* '(be) afraid' in (9a), and in the undergoer voice, as exemplified with *itom* '(be) black' in (9b).

(9) a. Aku   mo-**po**-linggo   tau   moane   ia.
       1SG   AV-**CAU**-be.afraid   person   man   PRX
       'I scared this man.'
    b. Mangana   ana   nipoitom   ai   buling.
       mangana   ana   ni-**po**-itom   ai   buling
       child   MED   RLS.UV-**CAU**-black.UV1   with   charcoal
       'The child was made (i.e. painted) black with charcoal.'

Note that there is no additional stative marking on the predicates in either of the two examples in (9). It is conceivable that in these two instances, the focus is on the (causative) event that is initiated and conducted by the newly added, volitionally acting causer. Compare this to the examples in (10), where in addition to voice morphology and the causative prefix, we find the stative marker *ko-*.

(10) a. Aku   mo-**po-ko**-linggo   tau   moane   ia.
        1SG   AV-**CAU-ST**-be.afraid   person   man   PRX
        'I made this man (really) scared.'
     b. Dinding   ia   nipokoitamku.
        dinding   ia   ni-**po-ko**-itam=ku
        wall   PRX   RLS.UV-**CAU-ST**-black.UV1=1SG.GEN
        'I painted this wall (really) black.'

Compared to the examples in (9), it seems to be the case that in (10) the result state is more important than the activity. This is in line with the judgement expressed by some speakers that the latter examples include an increased intensity, as also indicated in the translations (i.e. '*really* scared' and '*really* black'). Yet, the differences between 'plain' causativized statives and causativized statives with stative marking are subtle and require more research.

3.2 Valency alternation within the stative paradigm – intransitive vs. transitive statives

As illustrated in Table 3, the Totoli stative paradigm includes one set of intransitive formatives, and two sets of transitive ones – one for the actor voice and one for the undergoer voice. The availability of regular transitive forms for all stative predicates might seem typologically unusual, and indeed these forms never convey a purely stative meaning in Totoli.[7] Rather, they always involve the entailment of causation, and like in the causative alternation discussed in the previous section, transitive stative forms add a causer argument to the semantically more basic intransitive counterpart. In the following two example pairs, example (a) illustrates the intransitive, non-causative form of the pair. Example (b) shows the transitive, causative version (in (11b) in the actor voice, in (12b) in the undergoer voice). As also seen in these examples, transitive forms of stative predicates preferably involve inanimate causers.

(11) a. *tapi* **mo**-*ongot* *tian* *sisia*
but **ST**-painful stomach 3PL
'but their stomach is aching' [maptask_1 1138]
b. *i* *dulian* **mo-ko**-*ongot* *tian*
HON durian **AV-ST**-painful stomach
'durian causes stomach ache' [lelegesan_a 057]

(12) a. *tau-i* *asin* *saddek* *injan* **mo**-*lutu*
put-APPL2 salt a.little after **ST**-cook
'put in a bit of salt after it is done (cooked)' [making_ambaa_siote 0797–0799]

---

7 The actor voice formations for stative predicates are not fully productive, but the undergoer voice formations appear to be so.

b. *ikolutu*   *tuak*   *nolumolok*   *nabali*
   i-ko-lutu   tuak   no-um-lolok   no-bali
   RLS.UV-ST-cook.UV1   palm.wine   AV.RLS-AUTO.MOT-boil   ST.RLS-become
   manisan
   manisan
   Manisan
   'the palm wine is being cooked, it boils and turns into Manisan (a kind of drink)' [explanation-making-red-sugar_IS.572] (Bracks et al. 2017–2020)

Note that the verb *lutu* in (12) basically means 'ripe, done' and is typically used for fruit and vegetables that are ready to eat. The verb *lolok*, which occurs in (12b), translates as 'boil', but unlike English *boil*, *lolok* actually denotes a process and cannot be used transitively without further derivation.

3.3 Valency alternation by conjugation class change – stative vs. dynamic

Some verbal bases may occur both with stative and dynamic formatives without requiring any further derivation. As seen in example (13a), the stative form is intransitive and typically denotes a result state, while the dynamic forms are transitive and allow for both actor and undergoer voice, as seen in (13b) and (13c).

(13) a. *mottung*   *tooka*   *itu*   *laengna*   *itu*
        mo-tutung   tooka   itu   laeng=na   itu
        ST-burn   already   DIST   leaf=3SG.GEN   DIST
        'its leafs are already burnt' [making_ambaa_siote.1027]
     b. *ha*   *rayat*   *montung*   *danna*   *iatur*   *baik*
        ha   rayat   **moN**-tutung   danna   i-atur   baik
        INTJ   people   AV-burn   then   RLS.UV-organize.UV1   good
        'the people burned (it) down, and then organized (it) properly' [bajugan 169f]
     c. *kututungmo*   *kau*   *tiana*
        ku-tutung=mo   kau   tingana
        1SG.ACT-burn.UV1=CPL   2SG   QUOT
        'I will burn you, she says' [story-monkey-turtle_RSM.050] (Bracks et al. 2017–2020)

For reasons discussed in the following section, to date it is not clear how productive this pattern really is. We suspect that this class is fairly small. Another verbal base that patterns in the same way is, for example, the verb *botak* 'split', which denotes the result state (e.g. a coconut being split open) with stative morphology (*mbotak*), but with dynamic voice morphology can denote a transitive event (e.g. s/he split a coconut) without additional marking (*momotak* in AV, *botak* in UV).

3.4 Transitivization by applicativization

Section 2.2 has introduced the Totoli applicative paradigms, and illustrated use of applicativization with the dynamic monovalent base *sake* 'ascend'. In examples (3) and (4) above, we have seen how the one set of applicative formatives (APPLICATIVE 1) adds a causer argument to the monovalent bases and a benefactive or an instrument to bivalent bases, while the other set of applicative markers (APPLICATIVE 2) promotes goals or locatives to direct core arguments. Example (14) illustrates the same process with the verb *seok* 'enter'.

(14) a. *Isia   mosumeok   dei   lalom   bale.*
       isia   mo-um-seok   dei   lalom   bale
       3SG   AV-AUTO.MOT-enter   LOC   inside   house
       'She enters into the house'
   b. *Deinako   carana   meneokan   bau   ana?*
       deinako   cara=na   moN-seok-**an** bau   ana
       how   manner=3SG.GEN   AV-enter-**APPL1** fish   MED
       'How did you put in the fish?'
   c. *Isia   neneokiko   bale.*
       isia   noN-seok-**i**=ko   bale
       3SG   AV.RLS-enter-**APPL2**=AND   house
       'She entered the house.'

The verb *seok* 'enter', like *sake* 'ascend' in Section 2.2, can be considered to be UNERGATIVE, i.e. an intransitive base that takes an agentive theme in S function, which usually is volitionally acting, as in (14a), or at least has some control over the activity denoted by the verb (like the helicopter in (2)). With unergative bases, APPLICATIVE 1 adds a new, external causer (see (14b)). The former S argument becomes the no longer agentive theme of the derived transitive predicate. In (14c) the goal argument is promoted to core-argument status. But applicative suffixes also occur on monovalent stative bases, which we can call UNACCUSATIVE, because they take a non-agentive argument as their subject. In this case as well, an external causer is added, but there is no change in the semantic role of the former S argument.

(15) a. *kuitai*   *maaling*   *konising*
       ku-ita-i   **mo**-aling   konising
       1SG.ACT-see-UV2   **ST**-disappear fingernail
       'I see that the fingernails are gone' [siote_2 151f]
   b. *magalingan*   *strees* *itu*   *ee*
      mog-aling-**an**   stress   itu   ee
      AV-disappear-**APPL1**   stress   DIST   EMPH
      '(fishing) makes the stress go away' [fishing_2 430]

This kind of multifunctionality of applicative and causative morphology is typical for cognate morphological markers throughout Indonesian symmetrical-voice languages (Himmelmann 2005; Hemmings 2013). The extent to which this transitivization strategy is found varies across the languages of the area. It seems to be particularly productive in Totoli. That is, many verbs that seem to express transitive events at first sight, turn out to be intransitive verbs transitivized by applicativization. The overlap between the plain voice paradigm and the applicative paradigm (compare again Table 1 and Table 2) often poses an analytical challenge. We explicate this challenge in the following with the two verbs *tutung* 'burn' and *pio'* 'twist'.

The dataset in (16) shows these two verbs marked by the (undergoer voice) realis prefix *ni-* only: *nitutung* in (16a), and *nipio'* in (16b).

(16) a. *lemba   itu   i-teleb=na   injan*
       valley   DIST   RLS.UV-clear.UV1=3SG.GEN   after
       *tooka=mo   i-teleb   **ni-tutung**=mo*
       finish=CPL   RLS.UV-Clear.UV1   **RLS.UV-burn.UV1**-CPL
       'he cleared the valley (of the bushes), after clearing (it), (he) burned it' [podok_langgat 076ff]
   b. *Lima=ku   **ni-pio'**   i   inang=ku.*
      hand=1SG.GEN   **RLS.UV-twist.APPL1**   HON   mother=1SG.GEN
      'My mother twisted my hand.'

We have already seen in example (13) that *tutung* 'burn' is a transitive base that can be used in transitive contexts without any applicative marking (cf. (13b) and (13c)). The base *pio'* 'twist', on the other hand – though in undergoer voice and realis mood formally identically marked as *tutung* – is monovalent, and the form *nipio'*, unlike *nitutung*, is an APPLICATIVE UNDERGOER VOICE 1 form and not a plain undergoer voice 1 form. This difference, obviously, cannot be spotted when only looking at the two examples above. Rather, for each verb, we need to know either the respective actor voice form, or the non-realis undergoer voice form. Only these slots in the paradigm are unambiguously marked as either plain voice or applicative voice forms. For *tutung* 'burn', example (13) shows that the transitive actor voice form is *moN-tutung*, and the respective non-realis undergoer voice form is *tutung*. Example (17a) shows that the base *pio'*, like *tutung*, can be used as an intransitive stative verb. But examples (17b) and (17c) reveal that *pio'* needs to be applicativized in order to be used transitively; the (realis) actor voice form is thus *noN-pio'-an* and the non-realis undergoer voice form is *pio'-an*.

(17) a. *Dopi   ana   noppiomo.*
        dopi   ana   **no-RDP1-pio'**=mo
        cardboard MED   **ST-RDP1-twist**=CPL
        'The cardboard twisted.'
   b. *I   Tuti   nomiolan   lima   i   Iskander.*
        i   Tuti   **noN-pio'-an**   lima   i   Iskander
        HON   PN   **AV.RLS-twist-APPL1** hand   HON   PN
        'Tuti twisted Iskander's hand.'
   c. *Usatku   molinggo   piolan   singgayanna.*
        usat=ku   mo-linggo   **pio'-an**   singgayan=na
        sibling=1SG.GEN ST-afraid   **twist-APPL1.UV** friend=3SG.GEN
        'My sibling is afraid to be twisted (pinched) by his friend.'

Table 7 summarizes the differences in the transitive use of the two verbal bases discussed here. It shows the partial overlap (marked in grey) of plain and applied voice forms for verbs that take the UNDERGOER VOICE 1. Remember that the overlap is even more severe in the paradigm of UNDERGOER VOICE 2, where plain undergoer voice and applicative marking is identical in both non-realis and realis mood (cf. Table 1 and Table 2).

When we look at the actual distribution of voice marked verbal forms in Totoli, we can see that the undergoer voice – i.e. the voice in which the syncretism between plain and applicative form occurs – is by far the more frequent one; Totoli displays a ratio of 73% undergoer voice and 28% actor voice (cf. Riesberg et al., in print). Of all the undergoer voice forms in our Totoli corpus of spontaneous speech, more than half (i.e. 53%) are ambiguous.[8]

---

[8] These numbers pertain to an annotated subset of our documentation corpus. This sub-corpus amounts to 02h 50 minutes of spoken texts recorded during various field trips to the Tolitoli Regency, Sulawesi, between 2006 and 2018, with the exception of one recording which dates from 1989. It consists of 27 texts involving a total of 53 different speakers, 26 female and 27 male, mainly adults (with the exception of one text), and all of whom live in bilingual Totoli/Indonesian-speaking households (as is the case for virtually all of the Totoli-speaking population). The texts amount to 16.272 words and consist of 6.745 intonation units, as defined in Himmelmann et al. (2018).

Table 7: Transitive uses of the bases tutung 'burn' and pio' 'twist'.

	NON-REALIS	REALIS
ACTOR VOICE	*moN-tutung* AV-burn	*noN-tutung* AV.RLS-burn
	moN-pio'-an AV-twist-APPL1	*noN-pio'-an* AV.RLS-twist-APPL1
UNDERGOER VOICE	*tutung* burn.UV1	*ni-tutung* RLS.UV-burn.UV1
	pio'-an twist-APPL1.UV	*ni-pio'* RLS.UV-twist.APPL1

4 Totoli in the context of western Austronesian symmetrical-voice languages

Western Austronesian symmetrical-voice languages can be roughly divided into two major types: Philippine-type and non-Philippine-type languages. The latter include a somewhat heterogeneous set of languages sometimes referred to as 'Indonesian-type' languages. In using 'non-Philippine type' to refer to these languages, we emphasize the fact that their main commonality pertains to the fact that they do not show all the defining features of Philippine-type languages (see Himmelmann 2005: 112–114). Among the defining features of Philippine-type languages is the presence of phrase-marking clitics and a rich voice system, i.e. more than two transitive constructions, including those which allow semantically peripheral arguments to be selected as subjects (further illustrated below). Importantly, Philippine-type languages lack applicative marking altogether.

Non-Philippine-type western Austronesian symmetrical-voice languages, on the other hand, have a much more reduced voice system, usually only exhibiting one actor and one undergoer voice (sometimes in addition also a proper, agent-demoting passive). Furthermore, and unlike Philippine-type languages, they often display a set of applicative markers that increase the valency and introduce new core arguments to the verb's argument structure. These applicative markers typically differ formally from the voice marking morphology in the same language.

The purpose of this section is to show that Totoli, which belongs to the non-Philippine-type languages, occupies an intermediary position between typical Philippine-type and typical non-Philippine-type languages and may thus provide a glimpse into the historical development of western Austronesian voice and applicative marking systems. For reasons given below, however, all remarks regarding historical developments must remain fairly speculative for the time being. The following examples illustrate the basic four voice alternations in the Philippine-type language Tagalog:

(18) TAGALOG
    a. *Bumabasa*   *ng*   *diyaryo*   *ang*   *titser.*
        <um>RDP-basa   ng   diyaryo   ang   titser
        <AV>RDP-read   GEN   newspaper   NOM   teacher
        'The teacher is reading a newspaper.' (Schachter and Otanes 1972: 69)
    b. *Kinain*   *ng*   *pusa*   *ang*   *daga.*
        <in>kain-ø   ng   pusa   ang   daga
        <RLS>eat-PV   GEN   cat   NOM   rat
        'The cat ate the rat.' (Kaufman 2017: 603)
    c. *iniabot*   *ng*   *manggagamot*   *sa*   *sundalo*   *ang*   *itlog*
        <in>i-abot   ng   manggagamot   sa   sundalo   ang   itlog
        <RLS>CV-reach   GEN   doctor   DAT   soldier   NOM   egg
        'The physician handed the egg to the soldier.' (Himmelmann 2008: 265)
    d. *Kinainan*   *ng*   *pusa*   *ng*   *daga*   *ang*   *pinggan.*
        <in>kain-an   ng   pusa   ng   daga   ang   pinggan
        <RLS>eat-LV   GEN   cat   GEN   rat   NOM   plate
        'The cat ate the rat on/from the plate.' (Kaufman 2017: 603)

The Tagalog sentences above illustrate the actor voice (18a) and three undergoer voices – patient voice (18b), conveyance (displaced theme/instrumental) voice (18c), and locative voice (18d). The important points for the current investigation are as follows: All four voices basically have the same structure. Verbs are initial and are followed by one or more non-subject arguments, marked by the phrase-marking particles *ng* or *sa*. The term referring to the subject – i.e. the actor, the patient, the theme, and the locative respectively – occurs in final position and is introduced by the phrase marker *ang*. All constructions are equally transitive. The voice marker on the verb marks only the semantic role of the subject argument, the other roles can be deduced by implicature. All voices make use of an overt marker in at least one of the two moods, as seen in Table 8. All undergoer voices have in common that the realis mood is marked by <*in*> or its phonologically conditioned allomorph *ni-*.

Table 8: Voice paradigm in Tagalog.

	NON-REALIS	REALIS
ACTOR VOICE	‹um›/mag-/maN-	‹um›/nag-/naN-
PATIENT VOICE	-in	‹in›/ni-
LOCATIVE VOICE	-an	‹in›/ni- + -an
CONVEYANCE VOICE	i-	i- + ‹in›

Comparing Table 8 with the Totoli voice marking formatives shown in Table 3, repeated here for convenience as Table 9, it is clear that, with one exception, the Totoli formatives constitute a proper subset of the Tagalog ones.

Table 9: Totoli voice formatives (dynamic paradigm).

	NON-REALIS	REALIS
ACTOR VOICE	mo-/mog-/moN-	no-/nog-/noN-
UNDERGOER VOICE 1	∅	ni-
UNDERGOER VOICE 2	-i	ni- + -an
LOCATIVE VOICE	po-/poN-/pog- + -i	ni- + po-/poN-/pog- + -an

The one exception is the UV2 suffix -*i* in non-realis mood. However, the lack of a suffix of this shape is a somewhat idiosyncratic property of Tagalog. Most other closely related Meso-Philippine languages such as Cebuano, Bikol, Waray-Waray, etc. include such a suffix in their voice paradigms, usually in the so-called subjunctive mood, which has been lost in Tagalog. Table 10 illustrates this with Cebuano data.

Table 10: Cebuano voice-mood paradigm for dynamic verbs (cf. Wolff 1972: xvi, 2001:123; quoted from Himmelmann 2005:168).

	NON-REALIS	REALIS	SUBJUNCTIVE
ACTOR VOICE	mu-	mi-/ni-	mu-
PATIENT VOICE	-un	gi-	-a
LOCATIVE VOICE	-an	gi- + -an	-i
CONVEYANCE VOICE	i-	gi-	i-

The most conspicuous difference between the Philippine and the Totoli paradigms is the lack of a conveyance voice, which is marked by a prefix while the other undergoer voices are marked by suffixes. There is also no voice formative in the Totoli paradigm that specifically signals patient voice, corresponding to Tagalog -*in* and Cebuano -*un*.

Before further discussing similarities and differences between Philippine-type languages and Totoli, it will be useful to take a brief look at a more typical non-Philippine-type symmetrical-voice language, using Madurese as our example. In Madurese, there is a simple actor voice vs. undergoer voice distinction, both marked by prefixes, as seen in example (19).

(19) MADURESE
    a. *Ale' noro' Ebu.*
        yngr.sibling AV.follow mother
        'Little Brother followed Mother.'
    b. *Ebu e-toro' Ale'.*
        mother UV-follow yngr.sibling
        'Little Brother followed Mother. /Mother was followed by Little Brother.'
        (Davies 2010: 249)

There are no multiple undergoer voices in Madurese which would alternate in accordance with the semantic role of the undergoer subject as in the case of Tagalog shown above. But Madurese also allows for superficially very similar constructions to the ones illustrating the Tagalog locative and conveyance voices. The crucial difference pertains to the fact that these constructions are clearly applicative constructions in that they usually alternate with a non-applicative construction. Furthermore, all applicatives come in both actor and undergoer voice.

(20) MADURESE
    a. *Ennyor rowa gaggar ka motor-ra Ahmad.*
        coconut that fall to car-DEF PN
        'That coconut fell on Ahmad's car.'
    b. *Motor-ra Ahmad e-gaggar-i ennyor rowa.*
        car-DEF PN UV-fall-APPL coconut that
        'That coconut fell on Ahmad's car.'
    c. *Ennyor rowa ngaggar-i motor-ra Ahmad.*
        coconut that AV.fall-APPL car-DEF PN
        'That coconut fell on Ahmad's car.' (Davies 2010: 295)

(21) MADURESE
    a. *Ale' nambu' burus bi' bato.*
        yngr.sibling AV.hit dog with rock
        'Little Brother hit the dog with rocks.'

b. *Ale'   nambu'-agi   bato dha' burus.*
   yngr.sibling AV.hit-APPL rock to   dog
   'Little brother hit the dog with rocks.'
c. *Bato e-tambu'-agi (dha') burus bi' ale'.*
   rock UV-hit-APPL   to   dog   by   yngr.sibling
   'Little Brother hit the dog with rocks.' (Davies 2010: 309)

Here the applicative suffixes -*e* (and its allomorph -*i*) and -*agi* can be used with verbs marked for actor voice or undergoer voice. Example (20a) differs from (20b) and (20c) in that, in the latter (featuring the applicative suffix -*e/i*), the locative expression is a direct argument, whereas in (20a) it is an oblique, introduced by the preposition *ka*. Similarly, in (21a), an instrument is treated as an oblique. In (21b) and (21c), which are marked with the applicative suffix -*agi*, the erstwhile oblique instrument is promoted to core argument status. In the actor voice (21b), it is assigned direct object status, in the undergoer voice (21c), it is selected as subject.

There is of course an interaction between the systems in that the subject function is determined by the voice. In the actor voice the applied argument is the object and in the undergoer voice it is assigned the subject function. Nevertheless, the systems can be clearly distinguished formally and functionally. The Madurese voice and applicative paradigms are shown in Table 11.

Table 11: Madurese voice and applicative formatives (Davies 2010).

Actor Voice	N- (ng-/m-/n-/ny-) /a-
Undergoer Voice	e-
Applicative (Locative/Goal)	-e/-i
Applicative (Benefactive/Instrumental)	-agi

Comparing the Madurese system with the Totoli and the Philippine-type systems, there are major differences. In Madurese, voice marking is exclusively done by prefixes, applicative marking by suffixes. In Totoli, voice marking is mixed, as it is in the Philippine-type languages. But Totoli applicatives are exclusively suffixes, as in Madurese. Madurese, like many other non-Philippine-type symmetrical-voice systems in Indonesia (but unlike Totoli), does not distinguish realis from non-realis forms. Totoli and Madurese are similar in that functionally there is a simple actor voice – undergoer voice alternation, though Totoli still has two formally distinct undergoer voices. And, of course, both languages have applicative marking, which is completely absent in the Philippine-type languages.[9]

Furthermore, voice marking and applicative formatives in Totoli and Madurese constitute subsets of the forms attested in the Philippine languages, with the exception of the Madurese applicative suffix *-agi*. The latter is an innovation, as argued by Adelaar (2011). The Madurese undergoer voice prefix *e-* is cognate with the widely attested (realis) undergoer voice prefix *i-*, which is a reduced form of the prefix *ni-* attested in Totoli and some Philippine languages. Madurese N in actor voice, which assimilates to and sometimes replaces the base-initial consonant, is cognate with the N in the widely attested actor voice prefix *maN-*.

The above comparisons should make it clear that Totoli is exceptional in formally intertwining two otherwise formally and functionally different systems: voice and applicative marking. Philippine-type languages only mark voice. Most non-Philippine-type languages mark voice and applicatives, but by two clearly distinct set of formatives (prefixes and suffixes). In Totoli, however, the same formatives may sometimes mark an applicative, and sometimes a voice.

The above comparisons also make it clear that in all three languages – Totoli, Tagalog and Madurese – we are basically dealing with the same formatives, except for Madurese *-agi*. It is thus tempting to speculate about which kind of changes may have lead from one system to the other.

Before doing so however, a caveat is in order. Following the pioneering work of Wolff (1973), it has been widely assumed that Proto-Austronesian clause structure and verb morphology looked very much like they do in current Meso-Philippine languages (see Ross 2009 for some recent modifications). That is, all of the formatives illustrated for Tagalog in Table 8 and Cebuano in Table 10 have been reconstructed to the proto-level, also with essentially the same meanings and functions. It is very likely that this picture is considerably oversimplified. To date there is no comprehensive account for the attested historical developments for a single one of these formatives, let alone the many changes found in each individual system. As further detailed in Himmelmann (2020: 1045–6, 1057–8), it is not uncommon that even something so basic as the directionality of a given change is unclear. In the case at hand, for example, it is not established beyond all doubt that Totoli represents the innovation and Tagalog/Cebuano the inherited system.

---

[9] There are, however, approaches to Philippine-type voice systems which claim that locative and conveyance voices are to be analyzed as applicatives. See Chen and McDonnell (2019: 180–184) for references and counterarguments.

The following remarks are largely framed within the widely shared hypothesis that the general direction of historical developments affecting Austronesian voice and applicative affixes is from close to Philippine-type to non-Philippine-type. However, it should be kept in mind that the reverse direction has also been proposed and that it is, in fact, not straightforward to decide between competing views at our current stage of knowledge.

If it is assumed that the ambiguous Totoli voice/applicative suffixes *-i* and *-an* were originally patient and/or locative voice suffixes in a Philippine-type system of voice alternations (compare again the Tagalog examples in (18)), then the main question pertaining to the transition from the Philippine-type system to the Totoli system is how the new applicative uses came about. Note that, strictly speaking, the introduction of a new argument into the case frame of a verb is not an innovation. Tagalog locative voice, for example, also allows for assigning subject status to the place where something happens (compare 'The cat ate the rat on/from the plate' in (18d) above). Consequently, the major change in the transition to Totoli consists in the fact that the suffixes *-i* and *-an*, which continue to be used as regular undergoer voice suffixes, may co-occur with the actor voice prefixes, thus making for a proper applicative where the 'applied' argument functions as a non-subject core argument. See the examples (3a) and (4a), repeated here in (22).

(22) a. *Tau   ana   meseo   manakean   balaan dei   kapa'.*
     tau   ana   mo-seo   **moN**-sake-**an**   balaan dei   kapa'
     person   MED   ST-busy   AV-ascend-APPL1   goods   LOC   ship
     'Those people are busy loading goods on the ship.'
   b. *Douamo   no   ondo   sisia   manakei   kapa'   (takin balaan).*
      doua=mo   no   ondo   sisia   **moN**-sake-**i** kapa'   (takin balaan)
      two=CPL   LK   day   3PL   AV-ascend-APPL2   ship   with   goods
      'For two days already they are loading the ship (with goods).'

Another apparent innovation in Totoli, not discussed in the preceding sections, is the occurrence of verbal forms with pronominal prefixes such as *ku-ita-i* 'I see it/them' exemplified in (15a) above. Such forms do not occur in Philippine-type languages. They may have provided a major stepping stone for forms with an actor voice prefix and the former undergoer voice suffixes *-i* and *-an* such as *manakei* and *manakean* in (22) above. The development of the forms with pronominal prefixes themselves, however, is complex and cannot be further expounded here (Wolff 1996 and Himmelmann 1996, 2020 provide further details and discussion).

In the current context, the role played by transitivity and the basic valency profile in the development of the Totoli system is of particular interest. Transitivity distinctions do not play a major role in the grammar of Philippine-type voice alternations and there are reasons to assume that the lexical bases of verbal items are essentially intransitive (see Kaufman 2009 on the so-called nominalist hypothesis for Tagalog and other Philippine languages). In Totoli, on the other hand, there are clear differences in the transitivity of the different verbal formations. Furthermore, while a large number of verbal bases, also ones which denote semantically transitive eventualities, are intransitive (see Section 3.4 above), there are also some bases which are clearly transitive. Consequently, it would appear that the innovation of proper applicative forms is correlated with a beginning change in the basic valency profile of the language: from a stage where essentially all base forms are (syntactically) intransitive to one where transitivity distinctions become not only more relevant in the verbal grammar of the language overall, but also manifest themselves on the level of lexical base forms.

Further developments then would lead to a stage where transitive and intransitive verbal bases are clearly distinguished on the lexical level, as is the case in Madurese and other Indonesian symmetrical-voice languages. The emergence of a new valency profile in these languages would further correlate with a change in function of the former undergoer voice suffixes -*i* and -*an* (for the latter, such a change is in fact rarely attested). These fully lose their function as markers of different types of undergoer voices and only occur in their applicative function. To emphasize the point made above once again: while this scenario may have some plausibility, it is highly speculative and very sketchy. There are very many details that need to be worked out in much more detail. Among many other points, we would need proper basic valency profiles for all the languages mentioned here (including Tagalog and Madurese) as well as for a few additional representatives of the two basic types, i.e. Philippine vs. non-Philippine type.

5 Summary

In this paper, we investigated the basic valency orientation and different ways of transitivization in Totoli. Following the approach in Nichols, Peterson and Barnes (2004) to determine basic valency orientation, Totoli can be considered a transitivizing language. Comparing verb pairs whose meaning differs in the presence or absence of an entailment of external causation ('induction' in the terms of Nichols, Peterson and Barnes (2004)), the 'plain' (i.e. 'non-induced') member can be considered as non-derived or basic in the majority of cases. Alternations in which both 'plain' and 'induced' meanings are coded in a way that may be considered equally basic (or derived) are also attested but detransitivization proper seems to be absent in the language. Leaving aside suppletion, four valency-increasing strategies were identified in Totoli: causativization proper, transitive-intransitive alternation within the stative paradigm, alternation between the stative and the dynamic paradigms, and the use of applicative morphology. Applicative marking in Totoli is sensitive to the argument structure of the verbal base, resulting in causative-applicative syncretism. With transitive bases, applicative morphology signals the promotion of a participant to core-argument status, while with intransitive bases the entailment of external causation is added.

The unique relationship between the symmetrical-voice and applicative systems in Totoli is of particular interest, as the language seems to occupy an intermediary position between Philippine-type and non-Philippine-type symmetrical-voice languages. The situation is as follows: Philippine-type languages have a rich symmetrical-voice system but lack applicatives. Typical non-Philippine-type languages have applicative markers, which are – with the exception of some innovations – cognate with voice formatives in Philippine-type languages. But in non-Philippine-type languages the voice and applicative systems are clearly distinct. Voice and applicative morphology in Totoli, in contrast, exhibits substantial formal overlap. This suggests that the development of applicatives as a system independent from symmetrical-voice alternations may have arisen with the emergence of transitivity and valency as distinctions relevant in the grammar of western Austronesian languages of the non-Philippine-type.

Abbreviations

1	first person
2	second person
3	third person
ACT	undergoer voice agent
AND	andative
APPL	applicative
APPL1	applicative1
APPL2	applicative2
AV	actor voice
AUTO.MOT	autonomous motion
CAU	causative
CPL	completive
CV	conveyance voice
DAT	dative
DEF	definite
DIST	distal
EMPH	emphatic
GEN	genitive

HON	honorific
INTJ	interjection
LK	linker
LOC	locative
LV	locative voice
MED	medial
NEG	negation
NOM	nominative
NP	noun phrase
ONE	one
PL	plural
PN	proper or personal name
POT	potentive
PRX	proximal
PV	patient voice
QUOT	quotative
RDP	reduplication
RDP1	reduplication1
REL	relative
RLS	realis
SG	singular
SF	stem formant
ST	stative
UV	undergoer voice
UV1	undergoer voice 1
UV2	undergoer voice 2

References

Adelaar, Alexander. 2011. Javanese *-aké* and *-akən*: A short history. *Oceanic Linguistics* 50 (2). 338–350.

Bracks, Christoph A. forthcoming. *The syntax-prosody interface in Totoli*. Cologne: University of Cologne PhD thesis.

Bracks, Christoph A., Datra Hasan, Maria Bardají i Farré, Sumitro Pogi & Nikolaus P. Himmelmann. 2017–2020. *Totoli documentation corpus 2*. LAC – Language Archive Cologne. https://lac2.uni-koeln.de/de/ (accessed May 15th, 2020).

Chen, Victoria & Bradley McDonnell. 2019. Western Austronesian voice. *Annual Review of Linguistics* 5 (1). 173–195. https://doi.org/10.1146/annurev-linguistics-011718-011731.

Davies, William D. 2010. *A grammar of Madurese*. Berlin & New York: Mouton de Gruyter.

Hemmings, Charlotte. 2013. Causatives and applicatives: The case for polysemy in Javanese. *SOAS Working Papers in Linguistics* 16. 167–194.

Himmelmann, Nikolaus P. 1991. Tomini-Tolitoli sound structures. *NUSA* 33. 49–70.

Himmelmann, Nikolaus P. 1996. Person marking and grammatical relations in Sulawesi. In Hein Steinhauer (ed.), *Papers in Austronesian Linguistics* No. 3, 115-136. Canberra: Pacific Linguistics.

Himmelmann, Nikolaus P. 2001. *Sourcebook on Tomini-Tolitoli languages. General information and word lists*. Canberra: Pacific Linguistics.

Himmelmann, Nikolaus P. 2005. The Austronesian languages of Asia and Madagascar: Typological characteristics. In Alexander Adelaar & Nikolaus P. Himmelmann (eds.), *The Austronesian languages of Asia and Madagascar*, 110–181. London & New York: Routledge.

Himmelmann, Nikolaus P. 2008. Lexical categories and voice in Tagalog. In Peter K. Austin & Simon Musgrave (eds.), *Voice and grammatical relations in Austronesian languages*, 247–293. Stanford, CA: CSLI Publications.

Himmelmann, Nikolaus P. 2010. Language endangerment scenarios: A case study from northern Central Sulawesi. In Margaret Florey (ed.), *Endangered languages of Austronesia*, 45–72. Oxford: Oxford University Press.

Himmelmann, Nikolaus P. 2020. Grammaticisation processes and reanalyses in Sulawesi languages. In Andrej Malchukov & Walter Bisang (eds.), *Grammaticalization scenarios. Areal patterns and cross-linguistic variation*, 1043–1075. Berlin & New York: Mouton de Gruyter.

Himmelmann, Nikolaus P., Meytal Sandler, Jan Strunk & Volker Unterladstetter. 2018. On the universality of intonational phrases in spontaneous speech – a cross-linguistic interrater study. *Phonology* 35 (2). 207–245.

Himmelmann, Nikolaus P. & Sonja Riesberg. 2013. Symmetrical voice and applicative alternations: Evidence from Totoli. *Oceanic Linguistics* 52 (2). 396–422. https://doi.org/10.1353/ol.2013.0021.

Kaufman, Daniel. 2009. Austronesian nominalism and its consequences: A Tagalog case study. *Theoretical Linguistics* 35 (1). 1–49.

Kaufman, Daniel. 2017. Lexical category and alignment in Austronesian. In Jessica Coon, Diane Massam & Lisa D. Travis (eds.), *The Oxford Handbook of Ergativity*, 589–630. Oxford: Oxford University Press.

Leto, Claudia, Winarno S. Alamudi, Nikolaus P. Himmelmann, Jani Kuhnt-Saptodewo, Sonja Riesberg & Hasan Basri. 2005–2010. *DoBeS Totoli documentation*. https://hdl.handle.net/1839/da11addf-bef3-4742-9c00-d85a446f2cdb (accessed May 15th, 2020).

Nichols, Johanna, David A. Peterson & Jonathan Barnes. 2004. Transitivizing and detransitivizing languages. *Linguistic Typology* 8 (2). 149–211. https://doi.org/10.1515/lity.2004.005.

Riesberg, Sonja. 2014. *Symmetrical voice and linking in western Austronesian languages*. Berlin & New York: Mouton de Gruyter.

Riesberg, Sonja, Maria Bardají i Farré, Kurt Malcher & Nikolaus P. Himmelmann. In print. Predicting voice choice in symmetrical-voice languages. All the things that do not work in Totoli. *Studies in Language*.

Riesberg, Sonja, Kurt Malcher & Nikolaus P. Himmelmann. 2019. How universal is agent-first? Evidence from symmetrical voice languages. *Language* 95 (3). 523–561.

Ross, Malcolm D. 2009. Proto Austronesian verbal morphology: A reappraisal. In Alexander Adelaar & Andrew Pawley (eds.), *Austronesian historical linguistics and culture history: A festschrift for Robert Blust*, 295–326. Canberra: Pacific Linguistics.

Schachter, Paul, & Fe T. Otanes. 1972. *Tagalog reference grammar*. Berkeley: University of California Press.

Van Valin, Robert D. 2005. *Exploring the syntax semantics interface*. Cambridge: Cambridge University Press.
Wolff, John U. 1972. *A dictionary of Cebuano Visayan*, 2 vols. Ithaca: Cornell University Southeast Asia Program.
Wolff, John U. 1973. Verbal inflection in Proto-Austronesian. In Andrew B. Gonzales (ed.), *Parangal kay Cecilio Lopez*, 71–91. Quezon City: Linguistic Society of the Philippines.
Wolff, John U. 1996. The development of the passive verb with pronominal prefix in western Austronesian languages. In Bernd Nothofer (ed.), *Reconstruction, classification, description – festschrift in honor of Isidore Dyen*, 15–40. Hamburg: Abera-Verlag.
Wolff, John U. 2001. Cebuano. In Jane Garry & Carl Rubino (eds.), *Facts about the world's languages*, 121–126, New York: New England Publishing Associates.
Zúñiga, Fernando & Seppo Kittilä. 2019. *Grammatical voice*. Cambridge: Cambridge University Press.

Michela Cennamo
Anticausatives and lability in Italian and French: a diachronic-synchronic comparative study

Abstract: This article explores the interplay of the event structure template of verbs with the verb's inherent meaning (the 'root') and the nature of the subject (e.g., animacy and control) in shaping the distribution of the different strategies available to mark anticausativization – the active intransitive (i.e. lability) and the reflexive (SE) – in Italian and French, both diachronically and synchronically, in light of their Latin antecedents, the -*r* form, the reflexive and the active intransitive. It is shown that both in Italian and French SE comes to be gradually associated with verbs lexicalizing telic change, interacting with the voice domain, starting from the alternation between the reflexive and the active intransitive in Old Italian, and from the active intransitive as the sole/main anticausative strategy in Old French. The aspectual specification of verbs also affects the synchronic distribution of the anticausative strategies, with the reflexive being not only a marker of thematic reduction, but also signalling in some of its uses the presence of a final goal/result or target state in the lexical meaning of a verb, occurring with verbs lexically encoding a scalar change, either in all their uses or in some of them.

Keywords: anticausative, reflexive, lability, aspect, scalar change

1 Introduction

This article investigates diachronic and synchronic aspects of the morphosyntax of anticausatives in two Romance languages, Italian and French, in light of their Latin antecedents, in relation to the distribution of the different strategies available to mark anticausativization: the active intransitive (i.e. lability) and the reflexive in Italian and French, the (mediopassive) -*r* form, the reflexive pattern and the active intransitive in Latin. The analysis focuses on the persistence of the parameters determining variability in the encoding of anticausatives in Latin – (i) *aspectual* (reflecting the event structure template of the verbs allowing this type of intransitive alternation), (ii) *thematic* (relating to the nature of the subject, i.e. its affectedness/animacy/control), (iii) *lexical*, resulting from the nature of the

---

Michela Cennamo, University of Naples Federico II, e-mail: micennam@unina.it

∂ Open Access. © 2021 Michela Cennamo, published by De Gruyter. This work is licensed under the Creative Commons Attribution-NonCommercial-NoDerivatives 4.0 International License.
https://doi.org/10.1515/9783110755657-009

verb's inherent meaning, the lexical root (e.g., the type of change encoded) –, and on the function of the reflexive morpheme in this type of intransitive alternation. The latter is viewed as a marker of Actor suppression and/or telicity, according to the language and the diachronic stage of the change.

The discussion is organized as follows. Section 2 provides the theoretical background on the notion of anticausativization. Section 3 illustrates diachronic aspects of the anticausative alternation in Latin and two of its Romance continuants, Italian and French. Section 4 describes the synchronic distribution of the anticausative strategies in Italian and French. Section 5 shows the relevance of a scale-based classification of verbs for a better understanding of the diachrony of anticausativization in the languages investigated, as well as of the synchronic distribution of the labile and reflexive strategies. Finally, section 6 draws the conclusions.[1]

2 The anticausative alternation: its encoding and semantic constraints

In the anticausative alternation the original inanimate object (i.e. the Undergoer)[2] of a transitive pattern occurs as subject and the eventuality described by

---

[1] Earlier versions of the present work were presented at the *Cambridge Workshop on Voice*, Cambridge, 22 - 24 May 2017, at the *50th Annual Meeting of the Societas Linguistica Europaea*, Zurich, 10-13 September 2017, at the *Institut National des Langues et Civilisations Orientales*, Paris, 18 May 2018 and at the Workshop *The Shaping of Transitivity and Argument Structure: Theoretical and Empirical Perspectives*, Pavia, 25-27 October 2018. I wish to thank the audiences, in particular Delia Bentley, Francesco Ciconte, Carmen Dobrovie-Sorin, Rita Manzini and Alexandru Mardale for their insightful questions. Thanks are also due to Steffen Heidinger and two anonymous reviewers for most helpful comments on an earlier draft of this article. They all contributed to refine my arguments and to improve my analysis. All shortcomings and misinterpretations are, of course, mine.

The following abbreviations are used (partly in accordance with the Leipzig rules): ABL = ablative; ACC = accusative; F = feminine; FUT = future; IMPF = imperfect; IND = indicative; INF = infinitive; M = masculine; MPASS = mediopassive; N = neuter; NOM = nominative; PL = plural; PP =past participle; PRF = perfect; PRS = present; PTCP = participle; PST = past tense; RFL = reflexive; SBJV = subjunctive; SG = singular.

[2] Actor and Undergoer are syntactico-semantic categories, acting as the interface between thematic and syntactic relations, subsuming the different thematic relations of a verb's argument. More specifically, Actor is the generalized Agent-type argument (e.g. Agent, Effector, Instrument, Experiencer) and Undergoer is the generalized Patient-like argument (e.g. Patient, Theme, Experiencer) (Van Valin and La Polla 1997: 141; Van Valin 2005: 60–67).

the verb is presented as occurring spontaneously (Haspelmath 1993, 2016). The spontaneous manifestation of an eventuality and its related feature, "unspecific change of state" (Haspelmath 1987: 15), are the main semantic properties characterizing the anticausative pattern (see also Haspelmath 2016 for a formalization of this notion within the "spontaneity scale"). Only transitive, lexically causative verbs denoting events which may come about spontaneously, without a wilful animate causer, thus most typically lexicalizing a final goal/result state may occur in the anticausative alternation (Haspelmath 1987: 15; Levin and Rappaport Hovav 1995: 102). Therefore, verbs including a manner component in their root, denoting for instance "specific instruments or methods" (Haspelmath 1993: 93) (e.g. *bite, cut, dig, paint* . . .) (Haspelmath 1987: 15, 1993: 94), are excluded from this type of construction (Rappaport Hovav and Levin 2010). An additional semantic characteristic is the *thematic underspecification of the causer*: verbs with a thematically specified subject (i.e. an agent), such as the English *assassinate*, do not allow anticausativization, unlike *break, open*, whose subject has a lower degree of thematic specification, since it may also be instantiated by an instrument and a natural force, and which, by contrast, undergo the anticausative alternation (see Koontz-Garboden 2009: 80–90, also for a discussion of counterexamples to this generalization; Beavers and Koontz-Garboden 2012; Levin 2017, among others).

Depending on the perspective taken, the (unexpressed) Actor is viewed either as both syntactically and semantically suppressed (Haspelmath 1987: 7), or as lacking only at the level of argument structure (i.e. the lexical syntactic representation), while retained in the lexical semantic representation (Levin and Rappaport Hovav 1995: 84; Bentley 2006: 126–131; Schäfer 2008, 2009; Koontz-Garboden 2009; Alexiadou 2010; Heidinger 2015, 2019; Alexiadou, Anagnostopoulou and Schäfer 2015; Haspelmath 2016 and further references therein).

As for the encoding of this alternation, as well-known and thoroughly investigated in the literature, the anticausative pattern may be either morphologically unmarked, so-called 'lability', as in (1a), or both morphologically unmarked and marked, as in (1b-c) for German and in (1d-e) for French, signalled, in the marked form, by a dedicated morpheme, e.g., the reflexive marker in (1c) and (1e). The distribution of the two strategies varies across languages, often reflecting the diachronic stage(s) investigated (Lazzeroni 2009; Heidinger 2010, 2014 for French; Cennamo 2012 for Italian; Cennamo, Ciconte and Andriani 2020 for some early Italo-Romance varieties, among others):

(1) a. *The window shattered* (< *John/the stone shattered the window*) (unmarked)
   b. *Das Segel **zerriss***
      the sail tear.PST.3SG
      'The sail tore.'
      (Schäfer 2008: 11)
   c. *Die Tür **öffnete** sich* (marked)
      the door open.PST.3SG RFL
      'The door opened.'
   d. *Le ciment a durci* (unmarked)
      the cement have.PRS.3SG harden.PTCP
      'The cement hardened.'
   e. *Le vase (se) casse* (optionally marked)
      the vase RFL break.PRS.IND.3SG
      'The vase breaks.'

In several languages the core of the category is instantiated by verbs lexicalizing a final goal/result state (i.e. achievements/accomplishments) (Levin and Rappaport Hovav 1995: 93, among others),[3] as illustrated in (1a) for English, (1b) for German and (2a) for Italian. This pattern, however, may occur also with atelic eventualities, as with (continuation of) activity verbs and states in Italian and French, exemplified in (2b) for Italian and (2c) for both Italian and French (cf. also Cennamo 1995: 92–99; Cennamo and Jezek 2011):

(2) a. *Lo specchio si è frantumato*
      the mirror RFL be.PRS.IND.3SG smash.PST.PTCP.M.SG
      'The mirror smashed.'
   b. *Il brutto tempo è continuato*
      The bad weather be.PRS.IND continue.PST.PTCP.M.SG
      per tutta la settimana
      for whole the week
      'The bad weather has continued for the whole week.'

---

[3] I follow the Vendler (1967)/Dowty (1979) classification of verbs/predicates according to their temporal characteristics. *Accomplishments* are durative dynamic predicates with an inherent endpoint (i.e. telic); *achievements* are dynamic, non-durative predicates denoting an instantaneous (i.e. punctual) event with an inherent endpoint; *activities* are dynamic, durative predicates lacking an inherent endpoint; *states* are non-dynamic predicates involving no change (cf. Levin and Rappaport Hovav 2005: 88–105, among others, and references therein).

c. *Una   comunità   omogenea   **si   basa***
   *une   communauté   homogéne   **se   fonde/se base***
   a   community   homogeneous   RFL   base.PRS.IND.3SG
   anche   su   una   mediocrità   di   fondo
   aussi   sur   une   médiocrité   de   base
   also   on   a   mediocrity   of   background
   'A homogeneous community is based also on some sort of underlying mediocrity.'

3 Diachronic paths in anticausativization

3.1 Latin antecedents of Romance anticausatives: synchronic and diachronic aspects

In Latin, three strategies were available for the encoding of this type of intransitive alternation: (i) the mediopassive *-r* form,[4] (ii) the reflexive pattern, *se* + verb in the active voice, (iii), the active intransitive (i.e. lability) (Feltenius 1977; Cennamo 1998, 2019; Adams 2013: 686–711; Gianollo 2014; Cennamo, Eythórsson and Barðdal 2015).

The mediopassive *-r* form is attested throughout the history of Latin, with all verb classes allowing the anticausative alternation: achievements (3a), accomplishments (3b), gradual completion verbs (i.e. verbs denoting the gradual approximation to a terminal point along a scale, which may not be attained; Bertinetto and Squartini 1995:12–13), also referred to in the literature as degree achievements (Hay, Kennedy and Levin 1999), e.g. *minuere* 'to decrease' (3c) and activities (3d). The possible ambiguity between an anticausative and a passive reading was resolved only by the context, as shown in (3d):

(3) a. ***frangitur***   *aestus*
      breaks.MPASS.PRS.IND.3SG   tide.NOM
      'The rolling tide breaks.'
      (Lucr. *De Rer. Nat.* 6, 121)

---

[4] Although it gets used as such in Latin, the mediopassive character of the Indo-European *–r* ending is by no means certain. For instance, in Vedic it appears not only in the mediopassive, but also in the form *–ur*, as an active ending. It also turns up as such in Sanskrit (cf. Kuryłowicz 1964: 60-61, 65). In Latin the *-r* ending is employed for different types of intransitive patterns, including middles, anticausatives, passives, and impersonals (cf. Cennamo 1998: 79, 2020: 210-212 and related literature).

b. (humanae   res)   quae   fluxae   et
    human.NOM.PL affair.NOM.PL which.NOM.PL unstable.NOM.PL and
    mobiles   semper in advorsa   **mutantur**
    mobile.NOM.PL always in opposite.N.PL change.MPASS.PRS.IND.3PL
    '(Human affairs), which, unstable and fluctuating, are always changing to opposite extremes.'
    (Sall. *Iug.* 104, 2)
c. *Memoria*   **minuitur**
    memory.NOM   decrease.MPASS.PRS.IND.3SG
    'Memory is impaired.'
    (Cic. *Sen.* 7, 21)
d. *animi* ... *circum*   *terram*   **volutantur**
    soul(M).PL   around   earth.ACC   roll.MPASS.PRS.IND.3PL
    'Souls ... whirl/are whirled around this world.'
    (Cic. *Rep.* 6, 28)

As for the reflexive pattern, in Early and Classical Latin this construction occurs as an anticausativization strategy with achievements and accomplishments, i.e. with inherently telic verbs, lexically encoding a final goal/result or target state[5] (e.g. a reversible change) (Parsons 1990: 234–235), as shown in (4a-c):

(4) a. *lutamenta*   **scindunt**   *se*
        plaster(N).PL crack.PRS.IND.3PL RFL
        'Plaster cracks.'
        (Cat. *Agr.* 128)
    b. *brassica* ... **commutat**=*que*   *sese*   *semper* *cum*   *calore*
        cabbage.NOM   change.PRS.IND.3SG=and RFL   always   with   heat.ABL
        'Cabbage constantly changes its nature with heat.'
        (Cat. *Agr.* 157, 1)
    c. *valvae*   *se*   *ipsae*   **aperuerunt**
        door.NOM.PL   RFL   themselves.NOM.PL open.PRF.IND.3PL
        'The doors suddenly opened of their own accord.'
        (Cic. *Div.* 1, 34, 74)

The reflexive also seems to be preferred (to the mediopassive -*r* form) when the subject, although inanimate, is personified, showing some degree of control,

---

[5] Unlike result states, that "hold for ever after the culmination of the event", target states "may or may not last for a long time" (Parsons 1990: 235).

as in (4c). The latter can be contrasted with (4a-b), where no personification is involved, and *se* simply marks the intransitive (anticausative) variant (Ronconi 1968: 21; Cennamo 1998; Adams 2013: 690–691).

Se+active verb is not attested in anticausative function with verbs of variable/reduced telicity, e.g. gradual completion verbs (**irae se leniunt* anger.PL RFL heal.PRS.IND.3PL 'anger abates') and with activities (**saxa se volutant* stones RFL roll.PRS.IND.3PL 'stones roll'), for which only the *-r* form (3d) and the non-reflexive, labile pattern occur (5c-d) (Cennamo 1998, 2001). By contrast, the active intransitive in Early and Classical Latin is mainly found with gradual completion verbs (e.g. *lenire* 'to soothe', *ampliare* 'to enlarge', *minuere* 'to decrease', *sedare* 'to calm down') (5a–b), and, marginally, activities (e.g. *quassare* 'to shake', *volutare* 'to roll') (5c-d):

(5) a. *irae* **leniunt**
    anger.NOM.PL soothe.PRS.IND.3PL
    'Anger abates.'
    (Plaut. *Mil.* 583)
  b. *tempestas* **sedavit**
    storm.NOM calm-down.PRF.IND.3SG
    'The storm went down/calmed down.'
    (Gell. *NA* 18, 12,6)
  c. *capitibus* **quassantibus**
    head(N).ABL shake.PRS.PTCP.ABL
    'While their heads shook.' (lit. 'their heads shaking')
    (Plaut. *Bacch.* 304)
  d. *confusaque* *verba* **volutant**
    confused.PP.N.PL=and word(N).PL roll.PRS.IND.3PL
    'And confused reports flit about.'
    (Ov. *Met.* 12,54/55)

Lability is not found in anticausative function with verbs lexically encoding a final goal/result state, i.e. achievements (e.g. *rumpere* 'to break', *scindere* 'to crack') (6a-c), the core of the category in Latin and in other languages that show this type of transitive/intransitive alternation. An exception to this tendency is instantiated by accomplishments such as *aperire* 'to open' in Early Latin, e.g. Plautus (6d). This verb, however, denotes a reversible change of state, i.e. a target state, unlike *scindere* 'to crack' and *rumpere* 'to break', which denote a non-reversible change, i.e. a result state, and which therefore lexicalize a higher degree of telicity:

(6) a. *foris   **rumpit**[6]
       door.NOM   break.PRS.IND.3SG
       'The door breaks.'
    b. *lutamenta **scindunt**
       plaster(N).PL crack.PRS.IND.3PL
       'Plaster cracks.'
    c. ***corrumpit***   iam   cena
       spoil.PRS.IND.3SG   already   dinner.NOM
       'Dinner is spoiling already.'
    d. foris   **aperit**
       door.NOM   open.PRS.IND.3SG
       'The door opens.'
       (Plaut. *Persa*. 300)

3.1.1 Interim summary

Summing up the main characteristics of the distribution of anticausativizaton strategies in Early and Classical Latin, it can be noted that the alternation among the different voice forms marking anticausativization is aspectually streamlined, reflecting the interplay of the event structure template of verbs with the meaning components lexicalized in their root, e.g. the type of change, reversible/target ~ non-reversible/result state (Parsons 1990) (cf. also Cennamo, Eythórsson and Barðdal 2015). More specifically, (i) the -*r* form is found with all verbs which allow anticausativization, (ii) the reflexive pattern occurs with telic verbs [±punctual] (e.g. *scindere* 'to crack', *movere* 'to move', *aperire* 'to open', *frangere* 'to crack', *rumpere* 'to break'), (iii) the active intransitive is found with verbs which do not lexicalize the attainment of a final state, i.e. the endpoint of the process, as with gradual completion verbs (e.g. *lenire* 'to soothe', *minuere* 'to decrease', *sedare* 'to calm down'), albeit also attested with accomplishments denoting a target state (e.g., *aperire* 'to open') (Cennamo 1998, 2001) and with activities (e.g. *quassare* 'to shake', *volutare* 'to roll'). These factors interact, in the course of time, with changes in the voice system and the encoding of argument structure (Cennamo 1998, 2009; Cennamo, Eythórsson and Barðdal 2015: 693-704).

---

[6] The asterisk (*) for the Latin examples indicates that a pattern is not attested with a particular verb in the data investigated, consisting of literary and non-literary texts from III BC to IX A.D., collected from Pirson (1906), Svennung (1935), Wistrand (1942), Feltenius (1977), and the P(ackard) H(umanities) I(institute)-5 CD-ROM (see also Cennamo, Eythórsson and Barðdal 2015: 683-93, note 1).

3.1.2 Anticausatives and Transitivity in Late Latin

In Late Latin the semantics of predicates and the inherent and relational properties of the subject no longer play a role in the morphological realization of anticausatives. Thus, the reflexive and the active intransitive also mark anticausativization with aspectual classes with which they are not found in Early and Classical Latin. The reflexive is also attested with *gradual completion* verbs (e.g. *minuere* 'to decrease') (7a), and *other types of accomplishments*, such as *coquere* 'to cook', and de-nominal verbs such as *cicatricare* 'to heal' (< noun *cicatrix* 'scar') (7c), at times alternating with the *r*- form in one and the same text, as shown in (7c-d) (Pirson 1906; Feltenius 1977):

(7) a. **minuente** se morbo
 decreasing.PRS.PTCP.ABL RFL disease.ABL
 'When the disease is on the decline.'
 (Plin. *Nat.* 23, 50)
 b. *memoria* **minuitur**
 memory.NOM decrease.MPASS.PRS.IND.3SG
 'Memory is impaired/diminishes.'
 (Cic. *Sen.* 7, 21) (Classical Latin)
 c. *vulnera* *cum* **se** **cicatricaverint**
 wound(N).PL when RFL heal.FUT.PRF.3PL
 'When the wounds will have healed.'
 (Orib. *Syn.* 7, 10 Aa)
 d. *vulnera* **cicatricantur**
 wound(N).PL heal.MPASS.PRS.IND.3PL
 'The wounds heal.'
 (Orib. *Syn.* 7, 3)

Conversely, *se* + active also occurs with activities (e.g. *vexare* 'to oppress', *servare* 'to keep', *excusare* 'to justify, excuse') (Cennamo 1998, 2001: 238), at times with ambiguity between an anticausative and a passive interpretation, i.e. between a spontaneous vs. an induced process reading, as in (8) (Cennamo 1998, 2001, 2006):

(8) *mala...* *toto* *anno* **servare** *se* **possunt**
 apple(N).PL whole.ABL year.ABL keep.INF RFL can.PRS.IND.3PL
 'Apples . . . can keep/be kept for the whole year.'
 (Pall. *De agr.* 3, 25, 18; Ronconi 1968: 24)

In Late Latin the use of the active intransitive in anticausative function increases, and is well attested in 4th century technical works (e.g. veterinary texts such as the *Mulomedicina Chironis*) (Pirson 1906). This pattern also occurs with achievements (9a) and accomplishments (9b), alternating with the reflexive (9c) (Feltenius 1977: 82; Cennamo 2006: 317):

(9) a. *postea* **rumpunt** *dentes*
     afterwards break.PRS.IND.3PL tooth(F).NOM.PL
     'Afterwards teeth break'
     (*Mul. Chir.* 775, 14)
   b. *ut* **confirmet** (sc. *vulnus*)
     in_order_to heal.SBJV.PRS.3SG (wound)
     'So as it (sc. the wound) heals.'
     (*Mul. Chir.* 670)
   c. *donec cicatrix oculo* **se confirmet**
     till scar.NOM eye.DAT RFL heal.SBJV.PRS.3SG
     'Until the scar in its eye heals.' (*Mul. Chir.* 76)

The three strategies appear to be fully interchangeable at this stage, occurring with all verb classes (cf. Pirson 1906; Feltenius 1977; Cennamo 1998, 2020; Cennamo, Eythórsson and Barðdal 2015, among others). Thus, in Late Latin, with clear examples from the 4th century A.D., the reflexive strategy is found not only with inherently telic verbs, i.e., achievements and accomplishments (e.g. *scindere* 'to crack', *frangere* 'to break', *mutare* 'to change'), but also with non-inherently telic and atelic ones (e.g. *citare, provocare* 'to cause', *minuere* 'to decrease', *servare* 'to keep', i.e., accomplishments of variable/reduced telicity as well as activities; Cennamo 2001). With these aspectual classes in Early and Classical Latin either only the mediopassive *-r* form (in passive function) occurred (cf. (10a) vs (10b), (10d)), or the active intransitive/the *-r* form, in anticausative function (10c-d). If the pattern clearly marked an induced process (passive interpretation) only the *-r* form occurred, as illustrated in (10a) and (10d) (Cennamo 1998, 2006, 2020):

(10) a. *stercora* **provocantur**
      excrement.PL cause.PRS.IND.MPASS.3PL
      'Excrement is induced.'
    b. *stercora **se provocant**
      excrement.PL RFL cause.PRS.IND.3SG
      '*Excrement causes itself.'
    c. *memoria* **minuitur** /**minuit**
      memory.NOM decrease.MPASS.PRS.IND.3SG /PRS.IND.3SG
      'Memory is impaired (lit. memory decreases).'

d. *mala* **servantur**
   apple(N).PL keep.MPASS.PRS.IND.3PL
   'Apples are kept.'

In some Late Latin texts (e.g. Oribasius, 6th century A.D.), the reflexive pronoun and the -*r* form in anticausative function may co-occur, at times in one and the same sentence, with possible ambiguity between an anticausative and a passive reading, depending on the verb and on the syntactic context, as shown in (11):

(11) *si autem* **minutetur** *se medicamen*
     if then pulverize.MPASS.PRS.SBJV.3SG RFL drug
     'If then the drug pulverizes/gets pulverized.'
     (Orib. *Eup.* 4, 63; Svennung 1935: 463, n. 2) (VI A.D.)

The co-occurrence of the -*r* form and the reflexive pronoun in (11) witnesses the functional equivalence of the two anticausativization strategies.[7] This phenomenon is part and parcel of a wider change, the restructuring of the voice system taking place in Late Latin, resulting in the gradual demise of the mediopassive -*r* form from the spoken language and its replacement by other syntactic tools in the Romance languages, the reflexive coming to cover over time the functional domains of the –*r* suffix (passive, anticausative, middle) (cf. Cennamo 1998, 2009; Cennamo, Eythórsson and Barðdal 2015; Gianollo 2014: 990–993; Cennamo 2019 for a detailed analysis), alongside the active intransitive, as illustrated in (9a-b).

One of the outcomes of the functional equivalence among voice forms in Late Latin is the so-called deponentization, the use of the passive morphology in active function, affecting the whole verbal paradigm (Flobert 1975; Feltenius 1977), as shown in (12) for the analytic passive pattern, BE+PP, in active function in the perfect, replacing the reflexive pattern (12a) and the active intransitive (12b) (Norberg 1943: 151–174):

---

[7] The co-occurrence of *se* and the –*r* form in one and the same pattern is already found for the reflexive/middle function of these strategies in Early Latin (although its incidence needs to be investigated) as in (i), hinting at an early weakening of the –*r* form, collocating with *se* to strengthen its reflexive/middle values, anticipating later examples (e.g. *se iungi* RFL join.MPASS. INF 'to join oneself') (Norberg 1943: 167; Cennamo 1998: 80):

(i) *nemo se excalceatur*
    nobody.NOM RFL take-off-the-shoes.MPASS.PRS.IND.3SG
    'Nobody takes off his shoes.'
    (Varro. *Men.* 439)

(12) a. *qui* (sc. *Alciocus*) *in marca Vinedorum* **salvatus**
 who Alzeco in marsh Wends.GEN save.PST.PTCP.M.SG
 est (= ***se salvavit***)
 be.PRS.IND.3SG RFL save.PRF.3SG
 'Who (sc. Alzeco) found safety in the Wendish marsh.'
 (Fredeg. *Chron.* 4, 72; Norberg 1943: 158)
 b *Eo anno luna oscurata*
 that.ABL year.ABL moon.NOM darken.PST.PTCP.F.SG
 est (= *o(b)scuravit/ se o(b)scuravit*)
 be.PRS.IND.3SG darken.PST.3SG/ RFL darken.PST.3SG/RFL
 'That year the moon darkened.'
 (Fredeg. *Chron.* 4, 11.5)
 c *foris aperta est* = *foris aperuit* (/ *se aperuit*)
 door.NOM open.PST.PTCP.F.SG be.PRS.IND.3SG door.NOM open.PRF.IND.3SG
 'The door opened.'

Therefore, at some point in time in Late Latin, the sequence BE+PP, formed from a telic predicate such as *aperire* 'to open', in a pattern such as *foris aperta est* (12c), could be ambiguous between a dynamic passive ('the door was opened'), a resultative stative passive ('the door has been opened'), a stative/adjectival ('the door is open') and an anticausative reading ('the door opened'), with the analytic 'deponential'/passive perfect form (*aperta est*) used instead of the active perfect (*aperuit*), alongside the reflexive, as shown in (12c) (cf. also Cennamo 2005: 180–181, 2012: 406, note 14).

In the next sections we explore some Romance developments in the encoding of this type of intransitive alternation, starting from the functional ambiguity among voice forms illustrated above, leading to the construction exemplified in (12).

3.2 Anticausatives in Old Italian

The following (intertwined) paths emerge in the diachrony of anticausativization in the two Romance languages investigated, varying according to the language and the diachronic stage(s) considered: (i) the gradual emergence of aspectual notions such as telicity in determining the occurrence of/preference for the reflexive strategy with highly telic verbs (e.g. achievements and accomplishments lexicalizing a final goal/result state), (ii) the retrenching / loss ~ subsequent remodulation of lability, witnessed by Italian and French, respectively. In both changes the aspectual properties of verbs and the meaning components lexicalized in their root (e.g. the type of change encoded) appear to play a key-role, interacting with the voice domain.

3.2.1 The anticausative alternation in Old Italian (Old Florentine)

In Old Florentine – the Old Tuscan vernacular (based on the 14th century language of the so-called three crowns, the great Tuscan writers Dante, Petrarca and Boccaccio), which became codified as the national standard language at the beginning of the 16th century (Maiden 1995: 5, 10; Lepschy and Lepschy 2006: 546 among others), already in the early texts (13th century) –, two strategies alternate in the marking of anticausativization in simplex tenses, the reflexive and the active intransitive, i.e. the labile form.[8] They occur with the verb classes allowing this type of intransitive alternation, instantiated by achievements and accomplishments. With activity verbs, instead, the presence of the reflexive morpheme gives the pattern a passive interpretation (cf. Cennamo 2012: 405 and discussion further below). In compound tenses, the non-reflexive strategy, i.e. lability, is the form generally found, and the presence/absence of the reflexive morpheme reflects the gradual reconstitution of the tense-aspectual and voice systems consequent to the loss of the grammatical dimension of voice in the passage to Romance, described in section 3.1.2 for Late Latin in relation to the encoding of anticausativization.

The analysis reveals a higher frequency of the reflexive with verbs which lexicalize a final/result state, e.g. achievements such as *spezzare* 'to crack', for which the non-reflexive form is hardly attested in Old Florentine, as shown in (13b), where the only attested example of the labile form with this verb in the corpus investigated is ambiguous between an anticausative ('the spears broke') and a transitive reading ('they broke the spears'), with an unexpressed subject and *le lance* 'the spears' as direct object (Cennamo 2012: 406). *Si* generally functions as a marker of thematic reduction, but its presence also seems to be aspectually

---

[8] The texts investigated, both literary and non-literary, taken from OVI (*Opera del Vocabolario Italiano*) (available at http://ovi.cnr.it), cover a time span dating from the 13th to the 15th century. They include prose, poetry, letters, volgarizzamenti (i.e. adaptations from Latin), testimonies of minute-books, deeds, contracts, transactions and court trials, in the wake of the approach by Vincent, Parry and Hastings 2004 (see also Cennamo 2012). The approach taken in the present study is qualitative, rather than quantitative, and the generalizations put forward, based on the figures obtained from the electronic search, are meant to suggest tendencies, to be tested on a wider range of lexical verbs in subsequent research.

streamlined, since it tends to occur more prominently with verbs which lexicalize a terminal point, alternating with the active intransitive, i.e. with the labile form. Thus, fluctuation between the two strategies is found with achievements (e.g. *frangere* 'to smash', *rompere* 'to break') (13)-(15), and different types of accomplishments (e.g. *aprire* 'to open', *mutare* 'to change', *cuocere* 'to burn'/'cook', *allagare* 'to flood'), including gradual completion verbs (*scurare* 'to darken', *seccare* 'to dry', *ampliare* 'to enlarge', *aumentare* 'to increase') (16) – (17). The alternation also involves aspectual verbs (e.g. *cominciare* 'to begin', *cessare* 'to stop', *continue* 'to continue', denoting the beginning, termination and continuation of an activity, respectively), illustrated in (17) for *continuare*:

(13) a. la   spada   sì   **si**   **spezza**   presso   alla
       the   sword   thus   RFL   break.PRS.IND.3SG   near   to-the
       punta   (achievement)
       tip
       'The sword breaks near the tip'
       (*Tavola ritonda*, [cap. 18 | page 71.19–20])
   b. si   feriscono   per   tale   vigoria, che
      RFL   wound.PRS.IND.3PL   for   such   strength that
      le   lance   **spezzarono**   in   many   pezzi
      the   spears   break.PST.3PL   in   più   pieces
      'They wound each other fiercely, so that the spears break (lit. broke) into several pieces/so as to break the spears in several pieces'
      (*Tavola ritonda*, [cap. 18 | page 70.28])

(14) a. Come   **si**   **frange**   il   sonno
       how   RFL   break.PRS.IND.3SG   the   sleep
       'As sleep gets interrupted'
       [p. B284] (Dante. *Commedia*, [Purg. 17 | page B283, 40])
   b. e'l   mar   che   **frange**
      and-the sea   that   break.PRS.IND.3SG
      'And the sea that breaks'
      (Petrarca. *Canzoniere*, 277, 7)

(15) a. (lo stato di Roma)   quasi   ogne   die   di
       (the state of Rome)   almost   every   day   of
       diverse   maniere   **si**   **muta**   (accomplishment)
       different   ways   RFL   change.PRS.IND.3SG
       'The State of Rome changes almost every day'
       (Bono Giamboni. *Orosio*, [L. 6, cap. 12 | page 384]a)

b. *(lo giorno) poi ver' mezzo giorno ... **muta***
   the day then towards noon... change.PRS.IND.3SG
   'Then the day changes towards noon'
   (Percivalle Doria (ed. Contini) 1264 (Old Tuscan) [Parte non numerata 1 | page 162])

(16) a. *per la qual cosa la fama*
       owing_to the which thing the fame
       *sua **s'amplió** molto* (gradual completion verb)
       his RFL-increase.PST.3SG a_lot
       'Owing to this his fame increased'
       (Boccaccio. *Esposizioni,* [par. 22 | page 692])
   b. *poi **amplió** la fama di Santa Maria in Pruneta*
       then increase.PST.3SG the fame of Saint Mary in Pruneto
       'Then the fame of Saint Mary in Pruneto increased'
       (Sacch. L, 9,29; Brambilla Ageno 1964: 64)

(17) a. *dalle altre due parti, onde **si***
       from-the other two parts where RFL
       ***continua** la terra* (aspectuals-continuation of activity)
       continue.PRS.IND.3SG the earth
       'From the other two areas, where the earth continues'
       (Bono Giamboni. *Orosio,* [L. 1, cap. 2 | page 19])
   b. *In questa prima parte (il capitulo) **continua***
       in this first section the chapter continue.PRS.IND.3SG
       'In the first section the chapter continues ... '
       (Chiose falso Boccaccio. *Inf.,* 1375 *(fior.)*)

With activity/process verbs such as *bollire* 'to boil', only the non-reflexive form is found (18a). The reflexive pattern, in fact, has a passive interpretation, as expected, since it is an activity verb. Thus, *l'acqua si bolle* in (18b) does not mean 'water boils' but 'water is boiled', with *si* signalling external causation (see also Cennamo 2012: 409):

(18) a. *perocché il mosto ancora **bolliva***
       since the grape-must still boil.IMPF.IND.3SG
       'Since the grape must was still boiling'
       (Marchionne di Coppo, *Cronaca fiorentina,* [Rubr. 876 | page 382])

b.	la	cui	acqua	**si**	**bolle**		in	caldare
	the	whose	water	RFL	boil.PRS.IND.3SG		in	containers
	di	piombo	e	*fasse=ne*				sale
	of	lead	and	make.PRS.IND.3SG.RFL=of_it			salt

'Whose water is boiled in three lead containers and salt is made with it.'
(Metaura d'Aristotile volgarizzata, App. B, 2, 29, page 327. 2–3)

The two strategies alternate with the verb *cuocere* 'to cook, burn' under its processual interpretation, 'to burn' (19a-b). By contrast, when the verb lexicalizes a result, i.e. under the meaning 'to cook', the reflexive form occurs, as shown in (19c) (cf. also Cennamo 2012: 408; Cennamo, Ciconte and Andriani 2020: 165):

(19) a. quanto il fuoco è più ristretto, più **cuoce** (= arde)
        when the fire is more strong more cook.PRS.IND.3SG (=burns)
        'When the fire is stronger, it burns more'
        (Boccaccio, *Esposizioni*, [c. X, par. 7 | page 514])
   b. per che 'l ciel, come pare ancor, **si cosse**
      since that the sky as seems yet RFL cook.PST.3SG
      'As a result of which, as it still seems, the sky burnt'
      (Dante. *Commedia*, [Inf. 17| page a290]109)
   c. metti=vi uno bicchiere d'acqua che
      put=there a glass of-water that
      si cuoca con essa a conpimento
      RFL cook.PRS.SBJV.3SG with it thoroughly
      'Add a glass of water, so that it cooks thoroughly'
      (*Ricette di cucina*, XIV m. LVII)

The different encoding at times also reveals the existence of regional variation: for instance, whereas in Old Florentine the achievement verb *accendere* 'to ignite' occurs mainly in the reflexive form (20a), in Old Pisan (20b-c) both strategies are well-attested, as shown in (20b-c):

(20) a. nel tempio de' Dei **s' accese** il fuoco
        in-the temple of-the gods RFL ignite.PST.3SG the fire
        'Fire ignited in the gods' temple'
        (Giamboni, Bono. *Delle Storie contra i Pagani di*..., [L. 4, cap. 12| page 230])
   b. come carbon, che'n fuoco **accende**
      like charcoal that-in fire ignite.PRS.IND.3SG
      'Like charcoal that ignites'
      (Fazio degli Uberti. *Dittamondo*, [L. 5, cap. 25 | page 409])

c. (*il fuoco*) *che* **s' accese** *in quell'anno*
   the fire   that RFL ignite.PST.3SG in that-year
   'The fire that ignited that year'
   (Fazio degli Uberti. *Dittamondo*, [L. 1, cap. 24 | page 69])

In compound tenses the reflexive mainly occurs with telic verbs (i.e. achievements and different types of accomplishments), such as *accendere* 'to ignite' in (21a) and *mutare* 'to change' in (21b). There are also rare examples with gradual completion verbs, e.g. *ampliare* 'to enlarge' (21c) (Cennamo 2012):

(21) a. *credeano   di   spontanea   volontà*
       thought.3PL   of   spontaneous   will
       acceso   *si   fosse*   (sc. *il tumulto*)
       ignite.PP.F.SG RFL be.IMPF.SBJV.3SG (sc. the turmoil)
       'They thought that [the tumult] had arisen spontaneously (lit. ignited)'
       (Deca terza di Tito Livio [L 10, cap. 6, page 454])
    b. *se in tenebre   si   fosse   mutato   sì fatto*
       if in darkness RFL be.IMPF.SBJV.3SG   change.PP.M.SG such
       giorno!
       day
       'If the day had turned to night'
       (Boccaccio. *Fiammetta*, [cap. 1, par. 8 | 25])
    c. *verso   l'Occidente   miserabilmente   s'*
       towards   the-West   wretchedly   RFL
       era   ampliata   (sc. *pestilenza*)
       be.IMPF.IND.3SG   spread.PP.F.SG   (sc. plague)
       'The plague had spread towards West'
       (Boccaccio. *Decameron*, [Introduzione | 9])

However, most typically the non-reflexive, labile form is found in compound tenses, as shown in (22a-b) for the verbs *gelare* 'to ice' and *cuocere* 'to cook' (see also Cennamo 2012: 407–410):

(22) a. *del   sangue... della   sua   madre   che   è*
       of-the blood... of-the his   mother that be.PRS.IND.3SG
       gelato (**si è gelato*)
       freeze.PP.M.SG
       'Of his mother's blood ... that froze'
       (*Libro di Sidrach*, [cap. 294 | page 323])

b. *e   quando   è   cotto   a*
   and   when   be.PRS.IND.3SG cook.PP.M.SG at
   compimento (*si è cotto)
   completion
   'And when it has cooked completely'
   (*Ricette di cucina* XIV, 11, page 10)

In compound tenses the occurrence of the reflexive morpheme resolves the ambiguity of the pattern BE + PP in the perfect/pluperfect, which allows for three possible readings: active (anticausative), (resultative stative) passive and adjectival (i.e. result state) with telic predicates, as in (23a), continuing the Late Latin ambiguity of the sequence BE + PP discussed in section 3.1.2 (see Brambilla Ageno 1964: 186–199; Cennamo 2003; Cennamo 2012; Cennamo, Ciconte and Andriani 2020 for other early Italo-Romance varieties):

(23) a. *Ora   mi   fate   venire una lancia, perciò*
        now   to.me make   come   a   spear   since
        che   la   mia   è   rotta
        that the   mine   be.PRS.IND.3SG break.PSTP.PTCPF.SG
        'Now let me have a spear, since mine broke (anticausative)/has been broken (passive)/is broken (result state)'
        (*Tristano Ricc. App.*, page 376)
   b. *la   cordellina   del   pesce di   legno s'   era*
        the little_cord   of-the   fish   of   wood   RFL be.IMPF.IND.3SG
        rotta
        break.PP.F.SG
        'The wooden fish's string had broken.'
        (Sacchetti. *Trecentonovelle*, 216, page 561. 24)

By contrast, when SE occurs, only the active (anticausative) interpretation of the construction is possible, as illustrated in (23b).

3.2.2 Constraints on the distribution of the anticausative strategies in Old Italian

The analysis of some 13th-14th century Florentine texts shows the relevance of the aspectual template of verbs and the meaning components lexicalized in the verbal root (e.g. the type of change) in determining the distribution of the anticausativization strategies.

More specifically, in simplex tenses the reflexive, albeit occurring in apparently free variation with the active intransitive (i.e. lability), tends to be the only/main anticausative strategy with some achievements, and is excluded with activity verbs, with which its occurrence gives the pattern a passive interpretation. Conversely, the non-reflexive, labile pattern shows a wider range of uses, since it is found also with telic/punctual predicates, e.g. with achievements and accomplishments, including also gradual completion verbs. The alternation between the reflexive and the labile strategies also involves aspectuals.

In compound tenses the pattern without the reflexive is more frequent. The rare examples with *si* are confined to achievements and accomplishments, i.e. verbs which lexicalize a final goal/result state.

Thus, the data reveal the tendency for the reflexive morpheme to occur with inherently telic, punctual verbs in both simplex and compound tenses, as well as the use of the labile strategy with gradual completion verbs and generally with verbs which do not lexicalize a final goal/result state in compound tenses, as schematized in Table 1.

Table 1: Anticausative strategies and their distribution in Old Florentine

Strategy	Verb class	Simplex tenses	Compound tenses
+SI (only/mainly)	(some) **achievements** (*spezzare* 'to crack')	+	+ (rare)
±SI (free alternation in simplex tenses)	(some) **achievements** (*frangere* 'to smash', *rompere* 'to break')	+	– SI (rarely +SI)
	(different types of) **accomplishments** (*aprire* 'to open', *mutare* 'to change', *cuocere* 'to burn', *allagare* 'to flood')	+	– SI (rarely +SI)
	gradual completion verbs (*scurare* 'to darken', *seccare* 'to dry', *ampliare* 'to enlarge', *aumentare* 'to increase')	+	– SI
	aspectuals (beginning, termination, continuation of an eventuality) (*cominciare* 'to begin', *cessare* 'to stop', *continuare* 'to continue')	+	
–SI (lability)	(some) **accomplishments** (*cuocere* 'to cook')	+	+
	(some) **activities** (*bollire* 'to boil')		

Summing up, the analysis of early Florentine texts shows the gradual establishing of the reflexive as the main/only anticausative strategy with some aspectual classes of verbs, namely those which lexically encode a final goal/result state, both in simplex and compound tenses, where *si* is gradually penetrating into the anticausative domain starting from telic verbs. *Si*, however, has not become a marker of telicity yet, i.e. of a final goal/result or target state, as in contemporary Italian (Cennamo and Jezek 2011; Cennamo 2012), as revealed by the free alternation between the reflexive/non reflexive forms with verbs which allow both an activity/processual reading and a result interpretation (e.g. *cuocere* 'to cook, burn', *gelare* 'to freeze', *ardere* 'to burn'). Interestingly, in compound tenses with these verbs the only auxiliary used with the non-reflexive strategy is BE, unlike in contemporary Italian, where both HAVE and BE occur (see section 4).

3.3 Diachrony of anticausatives in French

The Old French texts reveal the existence of only one anticausativization strategy at the end of the 12th century, the active intransitive, i.e. the labile pattern, as shown in (24a-d), with apparently only one example with the reflexive form attested in the early 12th century *Chanson de Roland* (25a) (and one in the *Bestiaire*) (Hatcher 1942: 126, note 72).[9] In Old French (12th – 13th century) anticausativization, most typically encoded through the formally unmarked, labile pattern, occurs with change of state verbs, the core of the category: achievements (24a-f), accomplishments (24g), aspectuals denoting the beginning and termination of an eventuality such as *begin* and *end/complete*, as shown in (24h) for the verb *commenser* 'to begin' (examples and discussion from Heidinger 2010: 33, 94, 2014: 1013–1014):

---

[9] The corpus employed for the analysis consists of the texts investigated by Heidinger (2010), covering all stages of the history of the language, from Old French to contemporary French, including the *Chanson de Roland* (Rol.) (1100), *Le Voyage de Saint Brendan* (Bre.) (1112), the *Roman de Thèbes* (Thè.) (1160), *Lancelot* (Lanc.) (1171) and *Guillaume d'Angleterre* (Gui.) (1175) as well as the *Altfranzösischen Wörterbuch* for Old French, the electronic text corpus *Dictionnaire de Moyen Français* (DMF) for Middle French (14th-15th century), the *Frantext* for Pre-Classical and Classical French (16th-18th century), the *Trésor de la Langue Française informatisé* (*TFLi*) for Modern French (19th century onwards) (see discussion in Heidinger 2010: 25-32, 68, note 1 and references therein).

(24) a. *L'espee* **cruist,** *ne* **fruisset** *ne*
the-sword creak.PRS.IND.3SG not burst.PRS.IND.3SG neither
ne **brise**
not break.PRS.IND.3SG
'The sword creaks, but does not burst nor break'
(Rol.; Heidinger 2010: 31) (1100)

b. *Que sa lance a estros* **peçoie**
that his lance suddenly break.PRS.IND.3SG
'That his lance breaks into pieces'
(Lanc., verse 859) (1171)

c. *Vos plaies* ... **escrevastes**
your wounds break_open.PRS.IND.3SPL
'Your wounds
burst open'
(Lanc., verse 4899f.) (1171)

d. *La voile* **ront** *et li maz* **froisse**
the canvas break.PRS.IND.3SG and the mast crush.PRS.IND.3SG
'The canvas breaks and the mast breaks into pieces'
(Gui., verse 239) (1175)

e. **Tranche** *li fuz et* **ront** *li fers*
splinter.PRS.IND.3SG the wood and break_up.PRS.IND.3SG the iron
'The wood splinters and the iron breaks'
(Lanc., verse 2702)

f. *Tuz lur escuz* **i fruissent** *et* **esquassent**
all their shields burst.PST.3PL and shatter.PST.3PL
'Their shields burst and shattered'
(Rol., verse 3879) (1100)

g. *Idunc* **agreget** *le doel et la pitet*
then aggregate/join.PRS.IND.3SG the pain and the grief
'then pain and grief increase'
(Rol., verse 2206)

h. *Des or* **comance** *sa raison*
thus now begin.PRS.IND.3SG his story
'Thus now his story begins'
(Lanc., verse 30)

The first rare examples of the reflexive strategy to mark anticausativization are attested by the 12th century, and comprise different types of change of state verbs: accomplishments (e.g. *guerir* 'to heal', *tordre* 'to bend', *changer* 'to change', *descouvrir* 'to manifest', *ouvrir* 'to open', *monter* 'to go up, rise', *deviser* 'to divide, intersect', *lever* 'to rise') (25a-d), also with variable telicity (e.g. gradual completion verbs such as *refroidir* 'to cool', *accoître* 'to increase', *décroîte* 'to decrease'), aspectuals (e.g. *commenser* 'to begin') (25e), alternating with the labile form (Heidinger 2014: 1009) (see also Table 2). Some aspectuals (e.g. *parfaire* 'to finish/complete', only appear with SE in an anticausative pattern, already in 12th century Old French (cf. Table 2). From the 15th century onwards (i.e. from late Middle French) and even more so in Modern French, the use of SE as a marker of anticausativization increases, spreading to a wider number of telic predicates (both achievements and accomplishments) (Heidinger 2010: 29; 73), alternating with the active intransitive, albeit an increasing number of verbs only displays SE in the anticausative pattern (Table 2).

(25) a. ***se levet   la   puldre***
        RFL rise.PRS.IND.3SG the dust
        'The dust rises'
        (Rol., verse 3633; Hatcher 1943: 126, note 72)
   b. *quant li   segrei de mon cour   s   **ouvre***
      when   the secret of my   heart RFL open.PRS.IND.3SG
      *et   mis corage   **se**   **descovre***
      and my   courage RFL manifest.PRS.IND.3SG
      'When the secret of my heart opens and my courage reveals itself'
      (*Le livre des manieres de Etienne de Fougeres*, 1776; NCA; mod. StH)
   c. *la   vie   terrienne **se**   **change**   sovant*
      the path earthly   RFL change.3SG often
      'The earthly life often changes'
      (*L'Historie de Barlaam et Josaphat*, 1250; NCA; Heidinger 2010: 86)
   d. *Ils   (sc. les cœurs) **se**   **fondent** aux rayons du   soleil*
      they   the hearts   REFL melt.3PL   at   rays   of.the sun
      'They (sc. the hearts) melt in the rays of the sun'
      (Camus, 1615; Frantext; Heidinger 2010: 80)
   e. *e   **se**   **commensse** le   seruise*
      and RFL begin.3SG   the service
      'And the service begins'
      (*La vie du pape Saint Gregoire*, 1175; NCA; Heidinger 2010: 86)
   f. *Car   justice divine **se**   **manifeste** en extermination des*
      because justice divine RFL manifest. 3SG in estermination of.the
      reprouvés
      reprobates
      'Because divine justice manifests itself in the extermination of the reprobates'
      (Chartier, 1429; DMF1; Heidinger 2010: 80)

g. ou   la   plume   en   l   air   **se**   **souslieve**
   where the   feather in   the air   RFL   raise.3SG
   'Where the feather rises in the air'
   (*Le Bestiaire d'amour rimé*, 1250; NCA; Heidinger 2010: 80)
h. *L'* eue   en   la   terre   **s**   **abaisse**
   the   water into the earth   RFL   go_down.PRS.IND.3SG
   'The water sinks into the earth'
   (*Chronicle des ducs de Normandie par Benoit*, 1175; NCA; Heidinger 2010: 30)

Already from its early (12th-13th century) attestations, anticausative SE is found in compound tenses, with the auxiliary BE, as illustrated in (26a-b) for the gradual completion verbs *refreidier* 'to cool (down)' and *monter* 'to go up, to rise'. The non-reflexive pattern, however, is the strategy most typically found, also in Middle French, as shown in (26c-d), from the 14th century (Heidinger 2010: 191):

(26) a. *quant   la   paie   **s**   **est**   **refreidie**
        when   the wound RFL   be.PRS.IND.3SG   cool.PST.PTCP.F.SG
        'When the wound cooled'
        (*Miracle de Notre Dame de Chartres de Jean le Marchant*, 1262; NCA; Heidinger 2010: 30)
    b. **S'**   **est**   antre eus   la   tançons **montee**
       RFL   be.PRS.IND.3SG   among them the tensions rise.PST.PTCP.F.PL
       'The tensions between them increased'
       (*Guillaume d'Angleterre*, 1061 (1175); Heidinger 2010: 34)
    c. *par ou   il   **est**   **rompu**
       where   it   be.PRS.IND.3SG   break.PST.PTCP.M.SG
       'Where it broke'
       (*Miracles de Nostre Dame*; Förster 1908: 93)
    d. *Més   ma   vie   **est**   **tournée**   en   desespoir
       but   my   life be.PRS.IND.3SG turn.PST.PTCP.F.SG   into   despair
       'But my life turned into despair'
       (Froissart I, 129, 1471; Förster 1908: 83)

With some achievement verbs such as *briser* 'to break', the labile pattern is the only attested form in early Old French (e.g. the *Chanson de Roland*), alternating with the reflexive strategy at a later stage (e.g. in Classical French), which remains the only allowed strategy in Modern and contemporary French. By contrast, accomplishments of variable telicity, gradual completion verbs such as *abaisser* 'to make/become less', *adoucir* 'to make/become softer', indefinite change verbs such as *changer* 'to change', and other accomplishments such as *ouvrir* 'open', denoting a target state, alternate the two strategies already in Old French. Aspectuals denoting the termination of an eventuality such as *parfaire* 'to complete', on the other hand, occur in the *se* form only, from their early attestations, as shown in Table 2. Other gradual completion verbs (e.g. *augmenter* 'to increase', *grossir* 'to grow, gain weight', *empirer* 'to worsen'), alternating the reflexive and labile patterns in Pre-Classical and Classical French (i.e. the 16th-17th centuries) (Heidinger 2010: 157–171), subsequently show an increase in the labile form, which ousts the reflexive in contemporary French (Heidinger 2014: 1013–1018). According to Heidinger (2010, 2014), no differences are detectable among the verb classes with which the reflexive strategy is gradually introduced as a marker of the anticausative alternation, apart from the occurrence of a high number of change of state verbs.

However, the diachronic data from French also appear to show the gradual association of SE with verbs lexicalizing change, becoming fixed, i.e. obligatory with some *achievements and accomplishments*, i.e. highly telic verbs, already in their first attestations (cf. Old French *parfaire* 'to complete', Middle French *remplir* 'to fill', 18th century *briser* 'to break', etc.), subsequently also with some verbs of variable telicity, including some gradual completion verbs (e.g. *accroître* 'to increase', *amplifier* 'to increase, intensify', *vider* 'to become empty').

3.3.1 Constraints on the distribution of anticausative strategies in the diachrony of French

Also for the diachrony of French, therefore, the data appear to witness the gradual emergence of aspectual notions, interacting with the idiosyncratic aspects of the verb meaning, such as the type of change lexicalized in its root (e.g., target/result state, attainment/non-attainment of a final state), in determining the (optional/obligatory) occurrence of SE. The diachronic data point to the gradual spread of SE as an anticausativization strategy, starting from the core of the category, (+ telic, ± punctual) verbs of change. The extension of SE strongly increases after the Middle French period, especially from the 17th century onwards, and nowadays the reflexive morpheme is very widespread as an anticausative strategy, either optional or obligatory, depending on the verb, a change that is still ongoing (Heidinger 2010: 107-109 and Table 2).

Two different hypotheses have been put forward in the literature for the gradual penetration of the reflexive morpheme in a domain where lability was the only strategy available, in both simplex and compound tenses. The first hypothesis (i), concerns the ambiguity of interpretation of a pattern consisting of an inanimate argument and a verb in active morphology, between the O vs

S_O[10] function of the verbal argument, owing to the relatively free word order and to the optionality of the subject (Heidinger 2010: 36). This is shown in (27a), where, out of context, the theme argument, *sa lance* 'his lance', could be interpreted either as the object (O) of a transitive clause 'He broke his lance into pieces', or as the subject (S_O) of an anticausative pattern 'his lance broke into pieces'. The second hypothesis (ii), involves the ambiguity of meaning of the sequence BE + past participle, between an eventive (anticausative) and a (dynamic/ resultative stative) passive reading of the construction, depending on the aspectual characteristics of the verb and on the context. The former type of ambiguity is viewed as accounting for the spread of SE in simplex tenses, the latter is regarded as interacting with the gradual replacement of the auxiliary BE with HAVE for unmarked anticausatives in compound tenses in Modern French (cf. 27c), that is part and parcel of a wider change involving the demise of BE as a perfective auxiliary with intransitive verbs (Förster 1908; Heidinger 2010: 187–193 with reference to anticausative patterns). The decrease of BE as a perfective auxiliary with non-reflexive (i.e. labile) anticausative structures (27b), would have favored the high increase of SE in compound tenses attested at this stage, with the reflexive coming to mark the eventive (i.e. anticausative) function of the construction and focus on the final goal/result state, as in (27d). This value was originally conveyed by BE, whereby the BE+past participle sequence comes to have a passive reading only (dynamic/resultative passive) (Heidinger 2010: 192–193):

(27) a. *sa lance* **peçoie**
  his lance break.PRS.IND.3SG
  'He breaks his lance; his lance breaks'
 b. *il* **est** *rompu*
  it be.PRS.IND.3SG break.PST.PTCP.M.SG
  'It broke/it is broken/it has been broken'
 c. *Des pieces de bois... n'* **ont** *pas* **rompu**
  some pieces of wood not have.PRS.IND.3PL not break.PST.PTCP
  'Some pieces of wood have not broken'
  (Littré, 18th c.; Förster 1908: 94)

---

[10] S, A, O are syntactico-semantic categories, referring to the sole participant of an intransitive eventuality and to the Agent-like/Patient-like participants of a transitive eventuality, respectively (Mithun and Chafe 1999; Haspelmath 2011, among others).

d. (= 26b) **S'**   **est**   antre   eus   la   tançons
          RFL   be.PRS.IND.3SG   among   them   the   tensions
          montee
          rise.PST.PTCP.F.PL
          'The tensions between them increased'

This hypothesis, however, does not account for the presence of reflexive anticausatives in compound tenses (with the auxiliary BE) already in Old French (albeit rarely), illustrated in (27d), **s' est antre eus la tançons montee** 'the tension increased'), at a time when BE was the only perfective auxiliary for intransitive verbs/patterns.

By contrast, the presence of SE in compound tenses can be interpreted as disambiguating the eventive (i.e. anticausative) from the passive/resultative stative reading of the pattern BE+past participle and can be more clearly understood as a part of the more general phenomenon involving the reconstitution of grammatical voice in the transition from Latin to Romance (Old French in the examples illustrated above).

Summing up, the path of development emerging in the diachrony of anticausatives in French reveals that the two anticausative strategies, SE and the active intransitive, gradually come to distribute according to the aspectual properties of verbs, with SE becoming associated with verbs lexically encoding a final goal/result state already in the first occurrences of this strategy in the early Old French texts, the active intransitive being preferred for gradual completion verbs, starting from lability as the sole/main anticausative strategy. Over time, however, SE also becomes the only strategy for a number of gradual completion verbs (e.g. *accroître* 'to grow, increase', *amplifier* 'to increase, intensify', *réduire* 'to reduce') and other accomplishments (e.g. *remplir* 'to fill', *transformer* 'to change'), as shown in Table 2 for Modern French. This was part of the general trend of expansion of the reflexive as a marker of anticausativization to all verb classes, as witnessed by the contemporary distribution, illustrated in section 4.

Table 2: Anticausative strategies from Old to Modern French (adapted from Heidinger 2010: 94).

Period	Strategy	Verb class	Simplex tenses	Compound tenses
Old French	+SE (*–SE) ±SE	some **aspectuals** (*parfaire* 'to complete, end')	+	
		achievements (*tordre* 'to bend')	+	

Table 2: (continued)

Period	Strategy	Verb class	Simplex tenses	Compound tenses
		accomplishments (*changer* 'to change', *guérir* 'to heal', *muer* 'to change', *ouvrir* 'to open', *tourner* 'to turn', *lever* 'to rise')	+	+
		gradual completion verbs (*abaisser* 'to lower', *refroidir* 'to cool')	+	+
	− SE (*+SE)	**achievements** (*briser* 'to break')	+	+
Middle French	+SE (*−SE)	**accomplishments** (*démontrer* 'to show, demonstrate', *manifester* 'to show', *prouver* ' to prove', *remplir* 'to fill') **aspectuals** (*parfaire* 'to complete, end')	+	
	±SE	**achievements** (*briser* 'to break')	+	
		accomplishments (*convertir* 'to convert, change', *redoubler* 'to double', *ouvrir* 'to open') **aspectuals** (*terminer* 'to end')	+	
		gradual completion verbs (*accoître* ' to increase', *amollir* 'to soften', *décroîte* 'to decrease', *renforcer* ' to strengthen')	+	+
	−SE (*+SE)		−	−
1610–1615	+se (*−se)	**accomplishments** (*agiter* 'to shake', *dessécher* 'to dry out', *transformer* 'to change', *perfectionner* 'to complete', *éteindre* 'to turn off, estinguish')	+	
		aspectuals (*parfaire* 'to complete, end)	+	
		gradual completion verbs (*putréfier* 'to rot', *vider* 'to empty', *fortifier* 'to strengthen')	+	
	±SE (= free alternation in simplex tenses)	**achievements** (*éclater* 'to burst')	+	
		accomplishments (*ouvrir* 'to open', *changer* 'to change', *brûler* 'to burn')	+	+
		gradual completion verbs (*augmenter* 'to increase', *enlaidir* 'to make ugly', *fondre* 'to melt')	+	+
	−SE (*−SE)		−	−

Table 2: (continued)

Period	Strategy	Verb class	Simplex tenses	Compound tenses
1745	+SE (*–SE)	**achievements** (*blesser* 'to hurt')	+	
		accomplishments (*effacer* 'to erase', *enflammer* 'to inflame', *irriter* 'to irritate', *convertir* 'to convert, change into')	+	
		aspectuals (*terminer* 'to end')	+	
		gradual completion verbs (*accroître* 'to increase', *affaiblir* 'to weaken', *dessécher* 'to dry out', *fortifier* 'to strengthen')		+
	±SE	**achievements** (*romper, briser* 'to break') (rare)	+	
		accomplishments (*fermer* 'to close', *ouvrir* 'to open', *multiplier* 'to multiply', *changer* 'to change')	+	
		gradual completion verbs (*augmenter* 'to increase', *embellir* 'to embellish', *enfler* 'to swell', *fondre* 'to melt')	+	
	–SE (*+SE)		–	–
1990	+SE (*–SE)	**achievements** (*briser* 'to break') **accomplishments** (*éteindre* 'to turn off, estinguish', *remplir* 'to fill', *transformer* 'to change')	+	+
		gradual completion verbs (*accroître* 'to increase', *amplifier* 'to increase, intensify', *aplatir* 'to flatten', *arrondir* 'to round', *réduire* 'to decrease', *vider* 'to empty')	+	+
	±SE	**achievements** (*plier* 'to bend', *romper, casser* 'to break')	+	+
		accomplishments (*fermer* 'to close', *muer* 'to change', *ouvrir* 'to open', *arrêter* 'to stop')	+	+
		gradual completion verbs (*allonger* 'to lengthen', *multiplier* 'to multiply')	+	+
Contemporary French	–SE (*+SE)	**achievements** (*crever* 'to burst')	+	+
		gradual completion verbs (*augmenter* 'to increase', *grossir* 'to grow/gain weight', *empirer* 'to worsen')	+	+

4 Anticausatives in contemporary Italian and French

In contemporary Italian and French, three subclasses are usually identified in the literature, on the basis of the presence, absence, optionality of the reflexive and of auxiliary selection (HAVE, BE or both). As illustrated in (28)-(30), the three subclasses are not aspectually homogenous, neither in Italian or French.

Class 1, characterized by verbs always taking SE in the anticausative construction, with selection of the auxiliary BE, comprises achievements (Fr. *se briser* 'to break'; It. *spezzarsi* 'to crack'), different types of accomplishments (Fr. *se calcifier* 'to become chalky', *s'agrandir* 'to get larger'; It. *chiudersi* 'to close', *gonfiarsi* 'to swell'), as well as activities (Fr. *s'exprimer*/It. *esprimersi* 'to express') and states (Fr. *se fonder*/It. *fondarsi* 'to be based') (Labelle 1992; Legendre and Smolensky 2009: 231; Martin and Schäfer 2014 on French; Folli 2002; Bentley 2006; Cennamo and Jezek 2011; Cennamo 2012 for Italian; Manente 2008; Schäfer 2008, among others), as shown in (28) (French examples from Legendre and Smolensky 2009: 231):

(28) Class 1 [+SE] (aux BE)
Achievements: Fr. *se briser* 'to break'; It. *spezzarsi* 'to crack', *rompersi* 'to break', *spegnersi* 'to turn out'.
Accomplishments: Fr. *s'ameliorer* 'to get better', *se calcifier* 'to become chalky', *se deteériorer* 'to get worse', *se gâter* 'to go bad', *s'alléger* 'to get lighter', *s'assécher* 'to dry out', *s'agrandir* 'to get larger', *s'amaigrir* 'to get thinner', *s'alourdir* 'to get heavier'; It. *svuotarsi* 'to empty', *gonfiarsi* 'to swell', *aprirsi* 'to open', *chiudersi* 'to close', *dividersi* 'to divide'.
Activities: Fr. *s'exprimer*/It. *esprimersi* 'to express'.
States: Fr. *se fonder, se baser*/It. *fondarsi, basarsi* 'to be based'.

Class 2 [-SE] (selecting the auxiliary BE in Italian, HAVE in French in compound tenses), includes mostly accomplishments with variable telicity, such as gradual completion verbs (Fr. *durcir* 'to harden', *sécher* 'to dry'; It. *aumentare* 'to increase', *migliorare* 'to improve'), as well as some achievements (e.g. *crever* 'to burst', *claquer* 'to slam') and accomplishments lexicalizing a final point, such as French *moisir* 'to grow moldy', *fletrir* 'to wither' and Italian *affondare* 'to sink', *guarire* 'to heal':

(29) Class 2 [–SE] (aux HAVE (Fr.); aux BE (It.))
Achievements: Fr. *crever* 'to burst', *claquer* 'to slam'.
Accomplishments: Fr. *moisir* 'to grow moldly', *fletrir* 'to wither', *durcir* 'to harden', *sécher* 'to dry'; It. *aumentare* 'to increase', *diminuire* 'to decrease', *migliorare* 'to improve', *cambiare* 'to change', *affondare* 'to sink', *guarire* 'to heal'.
Activities: Fr. *bouiller*/It. *bollire* 'to boil'.

Class 3 ([±SE]), exemplified in (30), comprises different types of accomplishments, including also gradual completion verbs such as *(se) ramollir* 'to soften', *(s')augmenter* 'to increase', as well as achievements in French (e.g. *(se) rompre* 'to break up'). In Italian verbs with optional SE in the anticausative pattern are accomplishments consisting of a change process and an optional *telos* (e.g. *cuocer(si)* 'to cook', *bruciar(si)* 'to burn') (Folli 2002; Cennamo and Jezek 2011, Cennamo 2012: 401-403, among others). In both languages the non-reflexive pattern focuses on the transition itself, on the process, whilst in the reflexive form the focus is on the endpoint of the process, the attainment of a result state (see Labelle 1992; Manente 2008; Legendre and Smolensky 2009; Heidinger 2010, 2015, 2019 and references therein for French; Martin and Schäfer 2014; Heidinger 2019 for a different interpretation of the optionality of the reflexive). In French in compound tenses the auxiliary selected is always HAVE in the non-reflexive pattern; in Italian in the [–SE] pattern both HAVE and BE may occur, conveying an aspectual difference. The construction with BE tends to have a telic interpretation, signalling either a result state (31a) or an event (31b), whereas the structure with HAVE tends to trigger an atelic reading (31c). However, with some verbs (e.g. *bruciare* 'to burn', *stingere* 'to fade') BE is acceptable also in an atelic context and HAVE may occur in a telic one, as shown in (31d) (Cennamo 2012: 402; Cennamo and Jezek 2011: 817–818):

(30) Class 3 [±SE] (+SE: aux BE; -SE: HAVE/BE (It); HAVE (Fr.))
Achievements: *(se) casser* 'to break', *(se) rompre* 'to break up'.
Accomplishments: Fr. *(se) cristalliser* 'to crystallize', *(se) gonfier* 'to swell up', *(se) tarir* 'to dry up', *(se) rétrécir* 'to shrink', *(se) noircir* 'to blacken', *(se) refroidit* 'to cool down', *(se) ramollir* 'to soften', *(se) couler* 'to sink', *(s')augmenter* 'to increase', *(s')enfler* 'to swell'; It. *seccar(si)* 'to dry (out)', *bruciar(si)* 'to burn', *cuocer(si)* 'to cook', *gelar(si)* 'to ice', *fonder(si)* 'to melt'.

(31) a. Il   bosco è   bruciato   (result state)
        the   wood   be.PRS.3SG burn.PST.PTCP.M.SG
        'The wood is burnt down'

b. *Il   bosco   è   bruciato   in*
   the   wood   be.PRS.3SG   burn.PST.PTCP.M.SG   in
   pochi   minuti (telic event)
   few   minutes
   'The wood burnt in a few minutes'
c. *Il   bosco   ha   bruciato   per*
   the   wood   have.PRS.3SG   burn.PST.PTCP.M.SG   for
   giorni (atelic event)
   days
   'The wood burnt for days'
d. *La   carne   ha   bruciato/*
   the   meat   have.PRS.3SG   burn.PST.PTCP.F.SG
   è   bruciata   per   alcuni
   be.PRS.3SG   burn.PST.PTCP.F.SG   for   some
   minuti/   in   pochi   minuti
   minutes/   in   few   minutes
   'The meat burnt for some minutes/in a few minutes'

5 Aspectually relevant lexical properties of verbs and the distribution of anticausative strategies

The data investigated fall within a more general diachronic tendency, clearly attested in Late Latin for its final stage, whereby anticausative SE spreads to all verbs classes, regardless of their aspectual characteristics, a change that is also clearly perceivable in the diachrony of French and still ongoing in the language (Heidinger 2010: 107), interacting with the voice domain in the languages analysed. The synchronic and diachronic distribution of the anticausativization strategies discussed can be insightfully accounted for by means of a scale-based classification of the temporal structure of verbs (Beavers 2008; Rappaport Hovav 2008), which takes into account the role played by the properties encoded in the lexical meaning of the verb, the root, in determining the aspectual schemas and morphosyntactic realization of predicates (Levin and Rappaport Hovav 2005; Rappaport Hovav 2008, and recent discussion of the internal structure of roots and their including both templatic and idiosyncratic aspects in Beavers and Koontz-Garboden 2020). This model allows us to describe the aspectual variability and the different morphosyntactic behavior of verbs entering the anticausative alternation in the languages investigated, both synchronically and diachronically (sections 5.1- 5.2).

5.1 A scale-based classification of verbs

Following a recent proposal concerning the classification of verbs on the basis of their aspectually relevant lexical properties (Beavers 2008; Rappaport Hovav 2008), dynamic verbs which can be viewed as involving the notion of change (Dowty 1979; Rappaport Hovav 2008: 16) can be classified accordingly, in relation to the type of change, as scalar/non-scalar change verbs. The change lexicalized by change of state verbs (i.e. a property scale) is scalar, involving a set of ordered values for a particular attribute, as with English *widen* and *open*. By contrast, the change lexicalized by activities such as *jog, run, waltz* is nonscalar (i.e. it involves a complex, unordered change and it is not associated with a scale) (Rappaport Hovav 2008: 17-20). Verbs that lexically specify a scalar change, may be further distinguished, in relation to the nature of the scale, as associated with a binary, two-point scale, or a polar, multi-point scale (Beavers 2008; see also binary and polar opposition in Pustejovsky 2001).

In light of these assumptions, Rappaport Hovav (2008: 38–39) puts forward the classification in (32):

(32)   *Nonscalar changes*: activities (*play, jog*) [+change]
   Scalar change verbs:
   – Two-point scalar change verbs (presence/absence of a property): achievements (e.g. *die, break, crack*)
   – *Multi-point scalar change verbs* (existence of many values for the particular attribute lexicalized in the scale): different types of accomplishments (e.g. *widen, increase, open, swell*)
   States: [-change] (e.g., *resemble, have, know*)

The different morphosyntactic behavior of a verb may reflect the different meaning component(s) which it lexicalizes (Levin and Rappaport Hovav 2005; Rappaport Hovav 2008). States encode no change; achievements encode a two-point scalar change, accomplishments encode a multi-point scalar change. The lexical encoding of a scalar change is responsible for the varying aspectual interpretation of gradual completion verb, their 'hybrid' nature (i.e. their showing properties of activities, achievements and accomplishments) (Rappaport Hovav 2008: 22–28, 2014: 263–266, 274–281).

5.2 Relevance of a scale-based verb classification for Latin, Italian and French anticausatives

The notion of scalar change, in particular the distinction between a two-point and a multi-point scalar change, together with the idea that the different morphosyntactic behavior of a verb may reflect the different meaning components lexicalized in its various uses, seems to offer an interesting generalization for capturing the occurrence of the reflexive morpheme SE with anticausatives in Latin, Italian and French, both diachronically and synchronically.

More specifically, the reflexive morpheme SE in some of its anticausative uses may be regarded as a marker of the presence of a final goal/result/target state in the lexical meaning of a verb, occurring with verbs lexically encoding a scalar change, either in all their uses or in some of them. Achievements (i.e. two-point scalar change verbs), such as Classical Latin *rumpere se*/Italian *rompersi*/French *se briser*, 'to break', and de-adjectival verbs whose root denotes the maximal/minimal value of a closed/open scale, such as Italian *(s)vuotarsi* /French *se vider* 'to empty' and Italian *gonfiarsi* 'to swell, inflate', always entail the presence of a final goal/result/target state and appear with the reflexive marker in the anticausative pattern. Accomplishment verbs denoting a change process with an optional telos, such as Italian *bruciar(si)* 'to burn', *cuocer(si)* 'to cook', *gelar(si)* 'to freeze', *fonder(si)* 'to melt', French *(se) ramollir* 'to soften', *(se) refroidir* 'to cool down', entail the presence of a final goal/result/target state only in some of their uses, this being signalled by the presence of SE. These verbs appear instead in the intransitive form without SE under their processual/transitional reading, i.e. when they do not lexicalize a final goal/result/target state (see also Sorace 2000: 872).

The lack of SE with verbs which lexicalize a final state such as Italian *affondare* 'to sink', *guarire* 'to heal', *cambiare* 'to change'[11] and with achievements such as French *crever* 'to burst', and punctual activities (i.e. semelfactives) such as *claquer* 'to slam', can be accounted for if the synchronic distribution is viewed as a part of a long-term diachronic change, involving the extension of the reflexive to all verb classes, a change that is aspectually streamlined, and takes place at different 'paces' in the languages analysed. In Latin, SE initially occurs only with two-point scalar change verbs (i.e. achievements) and multipoint scalar change

---

11 These verbs, however, always take SE in southern regional varieties of Italian and dialects, e.g. Neapolitan/Molisan *il tempo s'è cambiato* the weather RFL-be.PRS.3SG change.PST.PTCP.M.SG 'the weather changed', thereby confirming the generalization put forward, concerning the presence of the reflexive marker in the anticausative pattern with verbs lexically encoding a scalar change (cf. also Cennamo and Jezek 2011: 814; Cennamo 2012: 400–401).

verbs lexically encoding a result/target state). Only at subsequent stages is SE found with multi-point scalar change verbs of variable telicity such as gradual completion verbs, and with non-scalar change verbs (i.e. activities). In French the reflexive penetrates into the original labile system from scalar change verbs (two-point and multi-point), i.e. some achievements and accomplishments, gradually spreading to other verbs with the same aspectual characteristics, becoming obligatory initially with two-point scalar change verbs, i.e. achievements and multipoint-scalar change verbs lexicalizing a result state (e.g. accomplishments such as *remplir* 'to fill'), gradually extending to nonscalar change verbs (e.g. activities such as *exprimer* 'to express') and even states (e.g. *baser* 'to base'). Italian shows a similar path of development, though taking off from a different starting point, the alternation between the reflexive and labile strategy with all aspectual classes allowing anticausativization (except activities). A deeper investigation of the factors determining the behavior of verbs which escape the generalization proposed needs to be carried out, however, in order to confirm the diachronic tendencies described and the hypothesis put forward.

6 Conclusions

Two paths of change emerge in the diachrony of anticausatives in the Romance languages investigated and their Latin antecedents:

- the gradual association of SE with verbs lexicalizing telic change in Italian and French, starting from the alternation between the reflexive and the active intransitive in Old Italian, and lability as the sole/main anticausative strategy in Old French, with aspectual notions such as telicity gaining ground in determining the obligatory occurrence/preference for SE over the active intransitive in Old Florentine and Old/Middle French;
- the demise of the interplay of thematic and aspectual notions in the encoding of anticausatives in Latin, leading to the equivalence and ensuing alternation among the anticausativization strategies, with SE no longer occurring only with telic and/or punctual verbs.

More specifically, the reflexive morpheme SE can be interpreted as a marker of Actor suppression at argument structure, and of the presence of a final goal/result/target state in the lexical meaning of a verb, occurring with verbs lexically encoding a scalar change, either in all their uses, or in some of them. Thus, the data investigated appear to offer an interesting contribution to the current debate on the role played by the idiosyncratic and templatic aspects of verb meaning, and their interaction and integration in determining argument realization. In point of fact, they show the relevance of these notions also for the diachrony of anticausativization, a syntactic domain which lies at the heart of the issue of the non-homogeneous internal temporal properties of accomplishments and of how particular components of lexicalized meaning may determine the aspectual properties of predicates and argument realization.

References

Adams, James N. 2013. *Social variation and the Latin language*. Cambridge: Cambridge University Press.
Alexiadou, Artemis. 2010. On the morpho-syntax of anticausative verbs. In Malka Rappaport Hovav, Edith Doron & Ivy Sichel (eds.), *Syntax, lexical semantics and event structure*, 177–203. Oxford: Oxford University Press.
Alexiadou, Artemis. 2014. The problem with internally caused change-of-state verbs. *Linguistics* 52. 879–910.
Alexiadou, Artemis, Elena Anagnostopoulou & Florian Schäfer. 2015. *External arguments in transitivity alternations: A layering approach*. Oxford: Oxford University Press.
Beavers, John. 2008. Scalar complexity and the structure of events. In Johannes Dölling, Tatjana Heyde-Zybatow & Martin Schäfer (eds.), *Event structures in linguistic form and interpretation*, 245–265. Berlin & New York: Mouton de Gruyter.
Beavers, John & Andrew Koontz-Garboden. 2012. Manner and result in the roots of verbal meaning. *Linguistic Inquiry* 43 (3). 331–369.
Beavers, John & Andrew Koontz-Garboden. 2020. *The roots of verbal meaning*. Oxford: Oxford University Press.
Bentley, Delia. 2006. *Split intransitivity in Italian*. Berlin & New York: Mouton de Gruyter.
Bertinetto, Pier Marco & Mario Squartini 1995. An attempt at defining the class of 'gradual completion verbs'. In Pier Marco Bertinetto, Valentina Bianchi, James Higginbotham & Mario Squartini (eds.), *Temporal reference, aspect and actionality*. Vol. 1: *Semantic and syntactic perspectives*, 11–26. Torino: Rosenberg & Sellier.
Brambilla Ageno, Franca. 1964. *Il verbo nell'italiano antico*. Milano & Napoli: Ricciardi.
Cennamo, Michela. 1995. Transitivity and VS order in Italian reflexives. *Sprachtypologie und Universalienforschung* 48 (1/2). 84–105.
Cennamo, Michela. 1998. The loss of the voice dimension between Late Latin and early Romance. In Monika Schmid, Jennifer R. Austin & Dieter Stein (eds.), *Historical Linguistics 1997*, 81–100. Amsterdam & Philadelphia: John Benjamins.
Cennamo, Michela. 2001. Classi verbali e cambiamento sintattico: La reinterpretazione passiva del costrutto riflessivo. In Zsuzanna Fàbiàn & Giampaolo Salvi (eds.), *Semantica e lessicologia storiche. Atti del XXXII Congresso Internazionale della Società di Linguistica Italiana*, 225–242. Roma: Bulzoni.

Cennamo, Michela. 2003. Perifrasi passive in testi non toscani delle origini. In Nicoletta Maraschio & Teresa Poggi Salani (eds.), *Italia linguistica anno Mille. Italia linguistica anno Duemila*, 105–127. Roma: Bulzoni.
Cennamo, Michela. 2005. Passive auxiliaries in Late Latin. In Sándor Kiss, Luca Mondin & Giampaolo Salvi (eds), *Latin et langues romanes. Études de linguistique offertes à József Herman à l'occasion de son 80ème anniversaire*, 177–194. Tübingen: Niemeyer.
Cennamo, Michela. 2006. The rise and grammaticalization paths of Latin *fieri* and *facere* as passive auxiliaries. In Werner Abraham & Larisa Leisö (eds.), *Passivization and typology*, 311–336. Amsterdam & Philadelphia: John Benjamins.
Cennamo, Michela. 2009. Argument structure and alignment variations and changes in Late Latin. In Johanna Barðdal & Shobana L. Chelliah (eds.), *The role of semantic, pragmatic and discourse factors in the development of case*, 307–346. Amsterdam & Philadelphia: John Benjamins.
Cennamo, Michela. 2012. Aspectual constraints on the (anti)causative alternation in Old Italian. In Johanna Barðdal, Michela Cennamo & Elly van Gelderen (eds.), *Argument realization and change. Transactions of the Philological Society* 110 (3). 394–421. Special issue.
Cennamo, Michela. 2016. Voice. In Adam Ledgeway & Martin Maiden (eds.), *The Oxford guide to the Romance languages*, 967–980. Oxford: Oxford University Press.
Cennamo, Michela, Francesco Ciconte & Luigi Andriani. 2020. The syntax and semantics of anticausatives in Early Italo-Romance. *L'Italia Dialettale* 81: 1–28
Cennamo, Michela, Thórhallur Eythórsson & Johanna Barðdal. 2015. Semantic and (morpho) syntactic constraints on anticausativization: evidence from Latin and Old Norse-Icelandic. *Linguistics* 53.4: 677–729.
Cennamo, Michela & Elisabetta Jezek. 2011. The anticausative alternation in Italian. In Giovanna Massariello & Serena Dal Masi (eds.), *Le interfacce*, 809–823. Roma: Bulzoni.
Dowty, David R. 1979. *Word meaning and Montague Grammar*. Dordrecht: Reidel.
Feltenius, Leif. 1977. *Intransitivizations in Latin*. Uppsala: Almkvist & Wiksell.
Flobert, Pierre. 1975. *Les verbes déponents Latins des origines à Charlemagne*. Paris: Les Belles Lettres.
Gianollo, Chiara. 2014. Labile verbs in Late Latin. In Leonid Kulikov & Nikolaos Lavidas (eds.), *Typology of labile verbs: Focus on diachrony. Linguistics* 52 (4). 945–1002. Special Issue.
Haspelmath, Martin. 1987. Transitivity alternations of the anticausative type. In *Arbeitspapier nr. 5*, Institut für Sprachwissenschaft, Universität zu Köln, 1–51.
Haspelmath, Martin. 1993. More on the typology of inchoative/causative verb alternations. In Bernard Comrie and Maria Polinsky (eds.), *Causatives and transitivity*, 87–120. Amsterdam & Philadelphia: John Benjamins.
Haspelmath, Martin. 2011. On S, A, P, T and R as comparative concepts for alignment typology. *Linguistic Typology* 15. 535–567.
Haspelmath, Martin. 2016. Universals of causative and anticausative verb formation and the spontaneity scale. *Lingua Posnaniensis* LVIII (2). 33–63.
Hay, Jen, Christopher Kennedy & Beth Levin. 1999. Scalar structure underlies telicity in degree achievements. In *Proceedings of SALT IX*, 127–144.
Heidinger, Steffen. 2010. *French anticausatives. A diachronic perspective*. Berlin & New York: Mouton de Gruyter.

Heidinger, Steffen. 2014. The persistence of labile verbs in the French causative-anticausative alternation. In Leonid Kulikov & Nikolaos Lavidas (eds.), *Typology of labile verbs: focus on diachrony*. *Linguistics* 52 (4): 945–1002. Special Issue.

Heidinger, Steffen 2015. Causalness and the encoding of the causative-anticausative alternation in French and Spanish. *Journal of Linguistics* 51 (3). 562–594.

Heidinger, Steffen. 2019. Reflexive and unmarked anticausatives in French and Spanish: Frequency of transitive use and undergoer overlap. *Langages* 216. 53–69.

Koontz-Garboden, Andrew. 2009. Anticausativization. *Natural Language and Linguistic Theory* 27. 77–138.

Kuryłowicz, Jerzy. 1964. *The inflectional categories of Indo-European*. Heidelberg: Carl Winter.

Labelle, Marie. 1992. Change of state and valency. *Journal of Linguistics* 28. 375–164.

Lazzeroni, Romano. 2009. Causativi e transitivi indoeuropei: Fra comparazione e tipologia. *Studi e Saggi Linguistici* 47. 7–23.

Legendre, Geraldine & Paul Smolensky. 2009. French inchoatives and the Unaccusative Hypothesis. In Donna Gerdts & Maria Polinsky (eds.), *Hypothesis A/Hypothesis B*, 229–246. Cambridge: MIT Press.

Lepschy, Anna Laura & Giulio Lepschy. 2006. Italian. In Keith Brown (ed.), *Encyclopedia of language and linguistics*, 2nd edn. Vol 6, 545–549. Oxford: Elsevier.

Levin, Beth & Malka Rappaport Hovav. 1995. *Unaccusativity*. Cambridge: MIT Press.

Levin, Beth & Malka Rappaport Hovav. 2005. *Argument realization*. Cambridge: Cambridge University Press.

Levin, Beth. 2017. The elasticity of verb meaning revisited. *Proceedings of SALT* 27. 571–599.

Maiden, Maiden. 1995. *A linguistic history of Italian*. London: Longman.

Manente, Mara. 2008. *L'aspect, les auxiliaires 'être' et 'avoir' et l'hypothèse inaccusative dans une perspective comparative Français/Italien*. Venice: University of Venice PhD thesis.

Martin, Fabienne & Florian Schäfer. 2014. Anticausatives compete but do not differ in meaning: A French case study. In *Actes du Congrès Mondial de Linguistique Française 2014*, 2485–2500. Berlin: FU.

Mithun, Marianne & Wallace Chafe. 1999. What are S, A and O?. *Studies in Language* 23. 569–596.

Norberg, Dag. 1943. *Syntaktische Forschungen auf dem Gebiete des Spätlateins und des frühen Mittellateins*. Uppsala: Almkvist & Wiksell.

Parsons, Terence. 1990. *Events in the semantics of English*. Cambridge, MA: MIT Press.

Pirson, Jules. 1906. Mulomedicina Chironis: La syntaxe du verbe. In *Festschrift zum Allgemeinen Deutchen Neuphilologentage*, 390–431. Erlangen.

Pustejovsky, James. 2001. Type construction and the logic of concepts. In Pierre Bouillon & Federica Busa (eds.), *The syntax of word meaning*. Cambridge: Cambridge University Press.

Rappaport Hovav, Malka. 2008. Lexicalized meaning and the internal temporal structure of events. In Susan Rothstein (ed.), *Crosslinguistic and Theoretical Approaches to the Semantics of Aspect*, 13–42. Amsterdam & Philadelphia: John Benjamins.

Rappaport Hovav, Malka. 2014. Building scalar changes. In Artemis Alexiadou, Hagit Borer & Florian Schäfer (eds.), *The syntax of roots and the roots of syntax*, 261–281. Oxford: Oxford University Press.

Rappaport Hovav, Malka & Beth Levin. 2010. Reflections on Manner/Result complementarity. In Edith Doron, Malka Rappaport Hovav & Ivy Sichel (eds), *Syntax, lexical semantics and event structure*, 21–38. Oxford: Oxford University Press.

Ronconi, Alessandro. 1968. *Il verbo latino. Problemi di sintassi storica*. Firenze: Le Monnier.

Schäfer, Florian. 2008. *The syntax of (Anti-)Causatives. External arguments in change-of-state contexts*. Amsterdam & Philadelphia: John Benjamins.
Schäfer, Florian. 2009. The causative alternation. *Language and Linguistics Compass* 3 (2). 641–681.
Sorace, Antonella. 2000. Gradients in auxiliary selection with intransitive verbs, *Language* 76. 859–890.
Svennung, Josef. 1935. *Untersuchungen zu Palladius and zur lateinischen Fach und Folkssprache*. Uppsala: Almkvist & Wiksell.
Van Valin, Robert D. Jr. 2005. *Exploring the syntax-semantics interface*. Cambridge: Cambridge University Press.
Van Valin, Robert D. Jr. & Randy La Polla. 1997. *Syntax: structure, meaning and function*. Cambridge: Cambridge University Press.
Vendler, Zeno. 1967. *Linguistics in phylosophy*. Ithaca, NY: Cornell University Press.
Vincent, Nigel, Mair Parry & Robert Hastings. 2004. Il progetto SAVI: presentazione, procedure e problemi. In Maurizio Dardano & Luca Frenguelli (eds.), *La sintassi dell'italiano antico: Atti del Convegno Internazionale di Studi,* Roma TRE, 18–21 September 2002, 501–528. Roma: Aracne.
Wistrand, Eric. 1942. *Über das Passivum*. Gothenburg: Wettergren.

Textual sources

Latin

PHI-5 CD-ROM (*The Packard Humanities Institute's Collection of Digital Latin Texts*).
Cat. *Agr.* = Mazzarino, Antonio. 1982. (ed.), *M. Porci Catonis de Agri Cultura*. Leipzig: Teubner.
Cic. *Div.*; *Rep.* = Müller, Carl Friedrich W. 1890. (ed.), *M. Tulli Ciceronis Scripta quae manserunt omnia*. Part 4, Vol. 2. Leipzig: Teubner.
Cic. *Sen.* = Simbeck, Karl. 1917. (ed.), *M. Tulli Ciceronis Scripta Quae Manserunt Omnia*. Fasc. 47. Leipzig: Teubner.
Fredeg. Chron. = Krusch, Bruno. 1888. (ed.), *Fredegarii et aliorum Chronica. Vitae sanctorum. MGH Scriptores rerum Merovingicarum 2.* Hanover.
Gell. *NA* = Marshall, Peter K. 1968. (ed.), *A. Gelli Noctes Atticae*. Vols. 1–2. Oxford: Clarendon Press.
Lucr. *RN* = Martin, Joseph. 1969. (ed.), *De Rerum Natura Libri Sex*. Leipzig: Teubner.
Mul. *Chir.* = Oder, Eugenius. 1901. (ed.), *Claudii Mermerii Mulomedicina Chironis*. Leipzig: Teubner.
Orib. = Mørland, Henning. 1940. (ed.), *Oribasius Latinus. Synops*is, I–II. Oslo: Brøgger.
Ovid. *Met.* = Miller, Frank J. & George P. Goold. 1977–1984. (eds.), *Ovid: Metamorphoses in Two Volumes*. Cambridge MA & London: Harvard University Press & William Heinemann.
Pall. = J.C. Schmitt. 1898. (ed.), *Palladius Rutilius Taurus Aemilianus. Opus Agriculturae*. Leipzig: Teubner.
Plaut. *Bacch.* = Leo, Friedrich. 1895. (ed.), *Plauti Comoediae*. Vol. 1. Berlin: Weidmann.
Plaut. *Mil.*; *Persa* = Leo, Friedrich. 1896. (ed.), *Plauti Comoediae*. Vol. 2. Berlin: Weidmann.

Plin. *Nat.* = Mayhoff, Karl. 1892–1909. (ed.), *C. Plini Secundi Naturalis Historiae libri XXXVII*. Vols. 1–5. Leipzig: Teubner.

Sall. *Iug.* = Kurfess, Alfons. 1951–1957. (ed.), *C. Sallusti Crispi Catilina. Iugurtha. Fragmenta Ampliora*. Leipzig: Teubner.

Varr. *Men.* = Astbury, Raymond. 1985. (ed.), *M. Terentii Varronis Saturarum Menippearum Fragmenta*. Leipzig: Teubner.

Old Florentine

Boccaccio, *Decameron* = Branca, Vittore, (ed.), 1976. *Decameron*, Florence: Accademia della Crusca.

Boccaccio, *Esposizioni* = Padoan, Giorgio, (ed.), 1965. Boccaccio, Giovanni. *Esposizio sopra la Comedia di Dante*, in Id., *Tutte le opere di Giovanni Boccaccio*. Vol. VI. Milan: Mondadori.

Boccaccio, *Fiammetta* = Ageno, Franca, (ed.), 1954. Boccaccio, Giovanni. *L'Elegia di Madonna Fiammetta*. Paris: Tallone.

Bono Giamboni, *Orosio* = Tassi, Francesco, (ed.), 1849. Giamboni, Bono. *Delle Storie contra i Pagani di Paolo Orosio libri VII*. Florence: Baracchi.

Chiose falso Boccaccio, *Inf.* = Vernon, William Warren, (ed.), 1846. *Chiose Dette del Falso Boccaccio (Inferno)*. Florence: Piatti.

Dante, *Commedia* = Petrocchi, Giorgio, (ed.), 1966–67. *Dante Alighieri, La Commedia secondo l'antica vulgata, vol. II Inferno, vol. III Purgatorio, vol. IV Paradiso*. Milan: Mondadori.

Deca terza di Tito Livio = *Gli ultimi sei libri della terza Deca di Tito Livio volgarizzata*, in Pizzorno, Francesco, (ed.), 1845. *Le Deche di T. Livio*. Vol. IV. Savona: Sambolino.

Fazio degli Uberti, *Dittamondo* = Corsi, Giuseppe, (ed.), 1952. Fazio degli Uberti. *Il Dittamondo e le Rime*. Bari: Laterza.

Libro di Sidrach = Bartoli, Adolfo, (ed.), 1868. *Il Libro di Sidrach. Testo inedito del secolo XIV. Parte prima (testo)*. Bologna: Romagnoli.

Marchionne di Coppo, *Cronaca fiorentina* = Rodolico, Niccolò, (ed.), 1903. *Cronaca Fiorentina di Marchionne di Coppo Stefani*. Rerum Italicarum Scriptores, vol. XXX. Città di Castello: Lapi.

Metaura d'Aristotile volgarizzata = Librandi, Rita, (ed.), 1995. *La Metaura D'Aristotile. Volgarizzamento Fiorentino Anonimo del XIV secolo*. Vols 1–2. (Text: vol. 1, 157–328). Naples: Liguori.

OVI (*Opera del Vocabolario Italiano*). http:www.ovi.cnr.it (accessed 30 April 2021)

Percivalle Doria = *Come lo giorno quand'è dal maitino/canzone*. In Contini, Gianfranco, (ed.), 1962. *Poeti del Duecento*, 161–163. Naples: Ricciardi.

Petrarca, *Canzoniere* = Contini, Gianfranco, (ed.), 1964. Petrarca, Francesco. *Canzoniere*. Turin: Einaudi.

Ricette d'un libro di cucina = Morpurgo, Salomone, (ed.), 1890. *LVII Ricette d'un libro di cucina del buon secolo della lingua*. Bologna: Zanichelli.

Sacchetti, *Rime* = Chiari Alberto, (ed.), 1936. Sacchetti, Franco. *Il Libro delle Rime*. Bari: Laterza.

Tavola ritonda o l'Istoria di . . . = Polidori, Luigi, 1864. *La Tavola Ritonda o l'Istoria di Tristano*. Bologna: Romagnoli.

Tristano Ricc. = Heijkant, Marie J. (ed.), 1991. *Tristano Riccardiano*. Rome: Carocci.

Old French

Altfranzösischen Wörterbuch = Bluhmenthal, Peter & Achim Stein. 2002. *Tobler-Lommatzsch*: *Altfranzösisches Wörterbuch*. Stuttgart: Steiner.
Bre. = *Le Voyage de Saint Brendan*. Ruhe, Ernstpeter (ed.), 1977. *Le Voyage de Saint Brendan*. Munich: Fink.
DMF = ATILF (CNRS, Université Nancy 2). *Dictionnaire de Moyen Français 2009*. Nancy. http://www.atilf.fr (accessed 30 April 2021).
DMF1 = ATILF (CNRS, Université Nancy 2). *Base de Lexique de Moyen Français* (DMF1). Nancy. http://www.atilf.fr (accessed 30 April 2021).
Frantext = ATILF (CNRS, Université Nancy 2). *Base Textuelle de Frantext*. Nancy. http://www.frantext.fr (accessed 30 April 2021).
Gui. = *Guillaume d'Angleterre*. Klüppelholz, Heinz. 1987. *Guillaume d'Angleterre*. Munich: Fink.
Lanc. = Lancelot. Jauss-Meyer, Helga (ed.), 1974. *Lancelot*. Munich: Fink.
NCA = Stein, Achim, Pierre Kunstmann & Martin-D. Gleßgen. *Nouveau Corpus d'Amsterdam. Corpus Informatique de Textes Littéraires d'Ancien Français* (cs. 1150–1350), établi par Anthonij Dees (Amsterdam 1987), remanié par Achim Stein, Pierre Kunstmann et Martin-D. Gleßgen. Stuttgart: Institut für Linguistik & Romanistik.
Rol. = *Chanson de Roland*. Steinsieck, Wolf (ed.), 1999. *Das Altfranzösische Rolandslied*. Stuttgart: Reclam.
Thè. = *Roman de Thèbe*. Olef-Krafft, Felicitas. 2002. *Roman de Thèbes*. Munich: Fink.
TLFi = ATILF (CNRS, Université Nancy 2). *Trésor de la Langue Française Informatisé*. Nancy. http://www.atilf.fr (accessed 30 April 2021).

Denis Creissels
Phonologically conditioned lability in Soninke (West-Mande) and its historical explanation

Abstract: In Soninke (West Mande), all non-monosyllabic transitive verbs ending with a front vowel are P-labile, whereas P-lability is almost inexistent among the transitive verbs that end with a non-front vowel. In this article, I show that this unusual distribution of lability results from the evolution of a detransitivizing suffix *-i* that fused with the ending of non-monosyllabic verb stems, with the final outcome that intransitive verb stems originally formed from a transitive verb stem ending with a front vowel via the addition of *-i* became homonymous with the transitive stem from which they derived.

Keywords: Mande, Soninke, transitivity, lability, mediopassive.

1 Introduction

This paper analyzes the historical origin of the phonological conditioning of P-lability that characterizes the transitivity system of Soninke (*sòonìnkànqánnè*), a Mande language spoken mainly in Mali, Mauritania, Senegal, and The Gambia.

Soninke belongs to the Soninke-Bozo sub-branch of the western branch of the Mande language family. It is only distantly related to the Manding languages (Bambara, Maninka, Mandinka, etc.), which are the best-documented group of Mande languages. The only relatively well-documented Soninke variety is that spoken in Kaedi (Mauritania), for which two comprehensive grammars are available (O.M. Diagana 1984, 1995; Y. Diagana. 1990,1994), as well as a dictionary (O.M. Diagana 2011). The only other publications directly relevant to the topic of this article are Creissels (1992) on Kaedi Soninke and Creissels and Diagne (2013) on Bakel Soninke. Dialectal variation in Soninke is relatively weak, and I am aware of no dialectal variation that could have an incidence on the analysis of valency-changing derivations and lability. The data presented here are from the Kaedi and Kingi varieties (two geographically distant, but linguistically very close Soninke varieties).

Denis Creissels, University of Lyon, e-mail: denis.creissels@univ-lyon2.fr

 Open Access. © 2021 Denis Creissels, published by De Gruyter. This work is licensed under the Creative Commons Attribution-NonCommercial-NoDerivatives 4.0 International License.
https://doi.org/10.1515/9783110755657-010

P-lability is a widespread phenomenon across the Mande language family, and several Mande languages are known for having not only morphologically unmarked causal-noncausal alternation (i.e. the type of P-lability illustrated by English *break*), but also morphologically unmarked active-passive alternation. Among Mande languages, as rightly observed by Cobbinah and Lüpke (2009), active-passive lability is particularly productive in Bambara and other Manding varieties. In Bambara, whatever the semantic nature of the object, all verbs that can be used in a transitive construction can also be used without any specific marking, and without any change in the argument structure they express, in an intransitive construction in which their subject is assigned the same semantic role as the object in the transitive construction, as in (1). Apart from the total lack of passive morphology, this construction has all the properties of a canonical passive, including the possibility of expressing the agent as an oblique phrase. Moreover, in Bambara, as illustrated by example (2), with some transitive verbs (but not all), the intransitive construction is ambiguous between a passive reading and a noncausal (anticausative) reading.[1]

(1) a Wùlû   má   sògô   dún.   (Bambara)
       dog.D   CPL.NEG   meat.D   eat
       S   pm   O   V
       'The dog didn't eat the meat.'

(1) b Sògô   má   dún   (wùlú   fɛ̀).   (Bambara)
       meat.D   CPL.NEG   eat   dog.D   by
       S   pm   V   X
       'The meat was not eaten (by the dog).'

(2) a Ń   má   dàgá   cì.   (Bambara)
       1SG   CPL.NEG   pot.D   break
       S   pm   O   V
       'I didn't break the pot.'

(2) b Dàgâ   má   cì.   (Bambara)
       pot.D   CPL.NEG   break
       S   pm   V
       'The pot didn't break.' OR 'The pot was not broken.'

---

[1] The third line of the examples gives indications about the structure of the clause, using the following abbreviations: S = subject, pm = predicative marker (see section 2), O = object, V = verb, X = oblique.

The same phenomenon is found in Soninke, but with a phonological conditioning. In Soninke, P-lability is exceptional among the verbs whose stem ends with non-front vowels (*a, o, u*), whereas all non-monosyllabic transitive verbs whose stem ends with a front vowel (*i* or *e*) are P-labile. This unusual distribution of lability calls for a historical explanation, since it cannot have a functional (or semantic) explanation, and accounting for it in terms of lexical properties of individual verbs would miss an obvious (although surprising) generalization.

The paper is organized as follows. Section 2 briefly presents the most basic aspects of Mande clause structure. Section 3 provides a typological profile of the transitivity system of Soninke. Section 4 discusses the historical scenario responsible for the phonological conditioning of P-lability found in Soninke. Section 5 summarizes the conclusions.

2 The basics of Mande clause structure

From the point of view of morphosyntactic typology, Mande languages are remarkably homogeneous, and sharply contrast in several respects with the other language families with which they are in contact. The most striking characteristic of Mande clause structure is the rigid (and typologically unusual) S (O) V (X) linear ordering of the constituents in verbal predication, found in all Mande languages without exception.[2] As a rule, multiple-object constructions are not allowed in Mande languages.[3] In general, Mande languages have very reduced verbal inflection, and express most grammaticalized TAM distinctions, as well as polarity, by means of so-called *predicative markers* (pm). The predicative markers are grammatical words or clitics placed immediately after the subject NP (and consequently, separated from the verb by the object NP in the transitive construction).[4] In addition to TAM and polarity, they may express subject indexation and/ or provide information about the information structure of the clause, depending on the individual languages.

Example (3) illustrates this type of organization of verbal predication in Soninke, with the two predicative markers *má* 'completive, negative', and *wá*,

---

2 S = subject, O = object, V = verb, X = oblique.
3 The only exception to this rule I am aware of concerns the construction of derived causative verbs in Beng (South Mande).
4 The predicative markers are sometimes called 'auxiliaries', but most linguists working on Mande languages avoid using this term because it may suggest that the grammatical words in question have a verbal origin, and for the vast majority of the Mande predicative markers, there is no evidence supporting the hypothesis of a verbal origin.

locational copula fulfilling the function of incompletive auxiliary. In Soninke, the form of the verb is determined by the predicative marker according to a very simple rule: with the locational copula used as an incompletive auxiliary, the verb is in a suffixed form called gerundive, otherwise it occurs in its bare lexical form. Moreover, some predicative markers trigger the replacement of the lexical tones of the verb by a grammatical tone pattern entirely low (indicated in the gloss by superscript L, as in (3a-b)).[5]

(3) a Ké   yúgó má   xàrà.
       DEM   man   CPL.NEG   study^L
       S   pm   V
       'This man did not study.'

(3) b Lémínè-n   m(á)   í   hàabá   tù.
       child-D   CPL.NEG   3REFL   father^{LH} recognize^L
       S   pm   O   V
       'The child did not recognize his father.'

(3) c Hàatú   wá   táaxú-nú   dàagó-n   kànmá.
       Fatou   ICPL   sit-GER   mat-D   on
       S   pm   V   X
       'Fatou will sit on the mat.'

(3) d Múusá   wá   dòròkê-n   qóbó-nó   í   yàqqé-n   dà.
       Moussa   ICPL   dress-D   buy-GER   3REFL   wife-D^{LH} for
       S   pm   O   V   X
       'Moussa will buy a dress for his wife.'

In some Mande languages, the predicative markers include an obligatory subject index, but Soninke, like most West Mande languages, has no core argument indexation at all. As a rule, Mande languages do not have core argument flagging, but Soninke is an exception. However, core argument flagging in Soninke is limited to the use of an enclitic -n with interrogative pronouns and NPs including the focus marker `yá in subject function (see 3.4).

---

5 In (3d), superscript LH indicates the grammatical low-high tone pattern whose substitution to the lexical tones of nouns marks the construct form of Soninke nouns. On tonal processes in Soninke, see Creissels (2016).

3 The transitivity system of Soninke

3.1 Alignment

Soninke has no core argument indexation, but shows nominative-accusative alignment in flagging (since the mechanism of differential flagging described in 3.4 is shared by the agent of prototypical transitive verbs and the sole argument of semantically monovalent verbs) and in the linear ordering of constituents (since the agent of prototypical transitive verbs and the sole argument of semantically monovalent verbs equally occur before the predicative markers, whereas the patient of prototypical transitive verbs occurs between the predicative markers and the verb).

3.2 The formal distinction between transitive and intransitive predication

A striking feature of Soninke is the particularly clear-cut distinction between transitive and intransitive predications. This follows not only from the rigid S (O) V (X) pattern, which excludes ambiguity between the syntactic roles of object and oblique, but also from the fact that three of the morphemes occurring in the predicative marker slot immediately after the subject are sensitive to the *transitive* vs. *intransitive* distinction:

- in the completive positive, a morpheme *dà* is obligatorily found in transitive constructions, but does not occur in the corresponding intransitive constructions – example (4), and the same morpheme *dà* also occurs with the same distribution in the imperative plural – example (5);
- the subjunctive positive is marked by *nà* in transitive constructions and *nàn* in intransitive constructions – example (6);[6]
- in clauses including a focalized term, the locational copula *wá* used as an incompletive marker has two variants depending on the transitivity of the construction: Ø in intransitive constructions, and *nà* (homonymous with the subjunctive positive marker) in transitive constructions – example (7).

---

[6] The predicative marker labeled 'subjunctive' combines with noun phrases in subject function in uses broadly similar to those fulfilled by forms traditionally labeled 'subjunctives' in grammars of European languages, but it is also found without an overt subject in uses broadly similar to those of European infinitives. In particular, it is spontaneously used by speakers as the quotation form of verbs.

(4) a Hànŋé   ké   Ø   káawá   hàné   yírígí.
       river   DEM   CPL.INTR   dry_up   early   this_year
       S   pm   V   X   X
       'The river dried up early this year.'

(4) b Yàxàré-n   dà   tíyè-n   qóbó   sáxà-n   ŋá.
       woman-D   CPL.TR   meat-D   buy   market-D   at
       S   pm   O   V   X
       'The woman bought meat at the market.'

(5) a Qà   Ø   táaxú   yíttè-n   ŋùré!
       2PL^L IMPER.INTR   sit   tree-D   under
       S   pm   V   X
       'Sit under the tree!'

(5) b Qà   dà   lémínè-n   qírí!
       2PL^L IMPER.TR   child-D   call
       S   pm   O   V
       'Call the child!'

(6) a Lémúnù   kú   nàn   táaxú   yíttè-n   ŋùré.
       child.PL   DEM   SUBJ.INTR   sit   tree-D   under
       S   pm   V   X
       'These children should sit under the tree.'

(6) b Lémúnù   kú   nà   tíyè-n   ñigá.
       child.PL   DEM   SUBJ.TR   meat-D   eat
       S   pm   O   V
       'These children should eat meat.'

(7) a À   wá   sállì-ní.
       3SG   ICPL   pray-GER
       S   pm   V
       'He is praying.'

(7) b À   Ø   sállì-ní   yà.
       3SG   ICPL.FOC.INTR   pray-GER   FOC
       S   pm   V
       'He is PRAYING.'

(7) c À   wá   hàrê-n   gáagà-ná.
       3SG   ICPL   donkey-D   sell-GER
       S   pm   O   V
       'He is selling the donkey.'

(7) d À   nà   hàrê-n   gáagà-ná yà.
      3SG ICPL.FOC.TR donkey-D sell-GER FOC
      s   pm   o   v
      'He is SELLING the donkey.'

3.3 Ban on null subjects or objects

Like most Mande languages, Soninke has a total ban on null core arguments, either with a non-specific or anaphoric reading. With the exception of the imperative singular (in which the 2nd person singular subject is not overtly expressed), the subject NP slot must obligatorily be filled in independent clauses, and the object NP slot must obligatorily be filled in the clauses that include a predicative marker marking the clause as transitive.

3.4 Differential subject flagging

In Soninke, interrogative words and focalized NPs in subject function (in transitive as well as intransitive clauses) are obligatorily flagged by a special enclitic -*n* (glossed SBJF for 'subject flag'). This enclitic never occurs with subjects other than interrogative words or focalized NPs, and it cannot attach to interrogative words or focalized NPs in functions other than subject either. This is consequently a quite clear instance of differential subject flagging, whose conditioning fully confirms the typological regularities observed by Fauconnier and Verstraete (2014).

As illustrated in (8), the introduction of the focus particle `yá requires the addition of -*n* if the focalized NP fulfills the subject function (8a-b), but not if it fulfills the object or oblique function (8c-d).

(8) a Ó   yà-n   Ø   gòllì   dáàrú.
       1PL FOC-SBJF CPL.INTR work^L yesterday
       s   pm   v   x
       'WE worked yesterday.'

(8) b Ó   yà-n   dà   Múusá   qìrì.
       1PL FOC-SBJF CPL.TR Moussa call^L
       s   pm   o   v
       'WE called Moussa.'

(8) c Ó   dà   Múusá   yà   qìrì.
       1PL   CPL.TR   Moussa   FOC   call^L
       S   pm   O   V
       'We called MOUSSA.'

(8) d Ó   dà   Múusá   qírí   Démbà   yá   dànŋá.
       1PL   CPL.TR   Moussa   call   Demba   FOC   for
       S   pm   O   V   X
       'We called Moussa FOR DEMBA.'

(9) illustrates the use of the subject flag -*n* with interrogative words.

(9) a Kó-n   Ø   gòllì   dáàrú?
       who-SBJF   CPL.INTR   work^L yesterday
       S   pm   V   X
       'Who worked yesterday?'

(9) b Kó-n   dà   Múusá   qìrì?
       who-SBJF   CPL.TR   Moussa   call^L
       S   pm   O   V
       'Who called Moussa?'

(9) c Qá   dà   kó   qìrì?
       2PL   CPL.TR   who   call^L
       S   pm   O   V
       'Who did you call?'

(9) d Qá   dà   Múusá   qírí   kó   dànŋá?
       2SG   CPL.TR   Moussa   call   who   for
       S   pm   O   V   X
       'For whom did you call Moussa?'

3.5 Transitivity prominence

A general characteristic of Mande languages is their moderate degree of transitive prominence, similar to that found in the languages of Western Europe. In Mande languages, the basic transitive construction extends to many bivalent verbs that are not, semantically speaking, prototypical transitive verbs. For example, in the construction of Soninke *ŋàrí* 'see' (10b), the perceiver and the stimulus are encoded exactly like the agent and the patient of a typical transitive verb such as *kárá* 'break' (10a). However, as illustrated in (10c), a sizeable minority of bivalent verbs have an 'extended intransitive' construction in which one of the arguments is encoded as an oblique (i.e. is represented by an adpositional phrase whose postverbal position (X) contrasts with the immediate preverbal position (O) typical for objects).

(10) a *Léminè-n   dà   qóllèn   kárá.*
         child-D   CPL.TR   calabash-D   break
         S   pm   O   V
         'The child broke the calabash.'

(10) b *Léminè-n   dà   sámáqqè-n   ŋàrí.*
         child-D   CPL.TR   snake-D   see
         S   pm   O   V
         'The child saw the snake.'

(10) c *Ń   Ø   mùngú   dò   ké   léminé   tòxó-n   ŋà.*
         1SG   CPL.INTR   forget   with   DEM   child   name-D^{LH} POSTP
         S   pm   V   X
         'I have forgotten the name of this child.'

3.6 Valency-changing derivations

Soninke has two morphological devices encoding detransitivization or valency-decrease, and one encoding transitivization or valency-increase.

3.6.1 The detransitivizing suffix -*i*

3.6.1.1 Formal properties of the detransitivizing suffix -*i*

Most verbs that have a transitive stem ending with *a*, *o*, or *u* also have an intransitive stem that can be analyzed as derived from the transitive stem by the addition of a detransitivizing suffix whose underlying form is -*i*. However, this detransitivizing suffix surfaces as a distinct segment (-*yí* or -*nŋí*) with monosyllabic stems only:

kǎ 'insult' → *kà-yí*   'be insulted'
tǔ 'know'   → *tù-yí*   'be known'
ñá 'do'   → *ñá-nŋí* 'be done'

With non-monosyllabic stems, the presence of detransitivizing -*i* is manifested by a change in the last vowel of the stem that can be explained as the result of the amalgamation of an underlying *i* according to the following rules:[7]

a + *i* → *e* (sometimes *í*) as in *kúppè* 'capsize (intr.)' < *kúppà* 'capsize (tr.)'
o + *i* → *e* as in *sòxé* 'be cultivated' < *sòxó* 'cultivate'
u + *i* → *i* as in *fúutí* 'stretch (intr.)' < *fúutú* 'stretch (tr.)'

The lack of distinct detransitivized forms for non-monosyllabic verbs ending with *e* or *i* will play a crucial role in the analysis of phonologically conditioned lability that will be put forward in section 4.

The detransitivizing suffix -*i* is tonally neutral: stems including this suffix invariably show the same tone pattern as the transitive stems from which they derive.

3.6.1.2 Syntactic and semantic properties of the detransitivizing suffix -*i*

Depending on the individual verbs with which it combines, -*i* may express various detransitivizing operations, but it is not equally productive in all its possible uses.

Agent demotion is by far the most productive use of the detransitivizing suffix -*i*. Two semantic subtypes can be recognized, anticausative (in which the agent is deleted from argument structure), as in (11b), and passive (in which the agent is maintained in argument structure, although syntactically demoted), as in (12b).

(11) a *Yúgò-n   dà   wùllì-tùurìntê-n   ñóolà.*
        man-D   CPL.TR   dog-rabid-D   drown
        S   pm   O   V
        'The man drowned the rabid dog.'

(11) b *Lémìnè-n   Ø   ñóolè   hànŋé-n   ŋà.*
        child-D   CPL.INTR   drown.DETR   river-D   at
        S   pm   V   X
        'The child drowned in the river.'

(12) a *Yàxàré-n   dà   yìllé-n   gòró.*
        woman-D   CPL.TR   millet-D   pound
        S   pm   O   V
        'The woman pounded the millet.'

---

[7] In Soninke, coda consonants are allowed in stem-internal position, but all nominal, verbal or adjectival stems invariably end with a vowel.

(12) b *Yìllé-n* Ø   *gòré.*
        millet-D CPL.INTR   pound.DETR
        S   pm   V
        'The millet was pounded.'

With a few verbs among those that have the ability to combine with the detransitivizing suffix *-i* in anticausative or passive function, the same form also has a reflexive or autocausative use:[8]

bóorà 'undress (tr.)'   → *bóorè* 'undress oneself' – example (13)
kàhú 'gather (tr.)'   → *kàhí* 'gather (intr.)'
húutú 'stretch (tr.)'   → *húutí* 'stretch (intr.)'

(13) a *Yúgò-n* *d(à)*   *í*   *rèmmê-n*   *bóorà.*
        man-D   CPL.TR   3REFL   son/daughter-D^LH undress
        S   pm   O   V
        'The man undressed his son/daughter.'
(13) b *Yúgò-n* Ø   *bóorè.*
        man-D   CPL.INTR undress.DETR
        S   pm   V
        'The man undressed.'

With a very small set of verbs (ten or so), the detransitivizing suffix *-i* may also have an antipassive function. As illustrated in (14) by *yígé*, intransitive form of *yígá* 'eat', with some transitive verbs, the same detransitivized form can be found in passive and antipassive function.

(14) a *Lémúnù*   *kú*   *dà*   *tíyè-n*   *ñígá.*[9]
        child.PL   DEM.PL   CPL.TR   meat-D   eat
        S   pm   O   V
        'The children ate the meat.'

---

[8] Soninke has two pronouns used productively to express reflexivity: *í* is used in logophoric contexts, and as a reflexive possessive (as in (3b) and (3d) above), whereas *dú* is used for object or oblique reflexivization (cf. 3.7.1). The term 'autocausative' is taken from Geniušienė (1987). For the discussion of a possible historical relationship between the detransitivizing suffix *-i* and the reflexive pronoun *í*, see Creissels (2020).
[9] In Soninke, *y* in contact with a nasal consonant is automatically converted into *ñ*, hence the *ñígá* variant of the verb *yígá* 'eat', and the *ñígé* variant of its intransitive derivate *yígé*.

(14) b Lémúnù   kú   Ø   yígé.
        child.PL DEM.PL   CPL.INTR eat.DETR
        S   pm   V
        'The children ate.'

(14) c Tíyè-n   Ø   ñígé.¹⁰
        meat-D   CPL.INTR eat.DETR
        S   pm   V
        'The meat was eaten.'

3.6.2 The antipassive suffix -ndì ~ -ndí

3.6.2.1 Formal properties of the antipassive suffix -ndì ~ -ndí

The antipassive suffix has disyllabic allomorphs with monosyllabic stems:

kǎ 'insult' → (antip.) kà-yìndí
sí 'shave' → (antip.) sí-yíndì

With non-monosyllabic stems, the antipassive suffix is invariably realized as -ndì or -ndí (depending on the tonal contour of the stem), and triggers no segmental modification of the stem to which it attaches.

Tonally, the antipassive suffix interacts with the stem as indicated in the following chart, where H* and L* must be understood as abbreviations for 'one or more successive H-toned syllables' and 'one or more successive L-toned syllables', respectively:[11]

tonal types of non-derived verbs	tonal contour of derived antipassives
(H*)HH	(H*)HH-L
(H*)HL	(H*)HH-L
(L*)LH	(L*)LL-H
(L*)LHL	(L*)LHL-H
H(L*)LH	H(L*)LL-H

---

[10] See footnote 9.

[11] Of the four Soninke varieties for which I have tonal data, Kaedi Soninke, Jaahunu Soninke and Kingi Soninke have very similar tone systems, whereas Bakel Soninke shows a marked tendency toward losing tonal contrasts. The tonal data presented in this paper are identical in the three varieties (Kaedi, Jaahunu, and Kingi) for which I have data and in which the existence of a tone system is unquestionable.

3.6.2.2 Syntactic and semantic properties of the antipassive suffix -ndì ~ -ndí

The antipassive function is the only possible function of this suffix – example (15).

(15) a Sámáqqè-n dà lémìnè-n qíñí.
 snake-D CPL.TR child-D bite
 S pm O V
 'The snake bit the child.'

(15) b Sámáqqè-n Ø qíñí-ndì.
 snake-D CPL.INTR bite-ANTIP
 S pm V
 'The snake bit (someone).'

The antipassive suffix -ndì ~ -ndí is very productive. In Soninke, the transitive verbs that can be used intransitively in their underived form with a subject representing the agent (A-labile verbs), are quite marginal, the transitive verbs with which the detransitivizing suffix -i can be used in antipassive function are not very numerous either, and all transitive verbs that do not belong to one of these two subsets are compatible with the antipassive marker -ndì ~ -ndí. In Soninke discourse, the use of the antipassive marker -ndì ~ -ndí is quite obviously the standard strategy to avoid specifying the identity of the participant that would be encoded as the object in the transitive construction. I have no explanation to put forward for the existence of a limited number of transitive verbs with which another strategy is used (either A-lability, or detransitivization by means of -i).

3.6.3 The causative suffix -ndí

3.6.3.1 Formal properties of the causative suffix -ndí

With very few exceptions, the causative suffix has the form -ndí and triggers no segmental modification of the stem to which it attaches. The irregular causative forms include:

tǔ	'know'	→ (caus.) tù-yìndí
wú	'cry'	→ (caus.) wú-ndì
qàrá	'learn'	→ (caus.) qàrá-nŋùndí
bángé	'appear'	→ (caus.) bángá-ndí
dìré	'make noise'	→ (caus.) dìrà-ndí

Tonally, as indicated by the following chart, the only interaction between the causative suffix and the stem to which it attaches is the conversion of LH-H sequences into LL-H:

tonal types of non-derived verbs	tonal contour of derived causatives
(H*)HH	(H*)HH-H
(H*)HL	(H*)HL-H
(L*)LH	(L*)LL-H
(L*)LHL	(L*)LHL-H
H(L*)LH	H(L*)LL-H

As can be seen by comparing this chart with that given above for antipassive derivates, the distinction between causative and antipassive forms is ensured by tone for stems whose inherent tone pattern includes no LH sequence, but it is not apparent in the case of stems whose inherent tone pattern includes a LH sequence. The risk of confusion is however virtually inexistent, since the antipassive suffix combines exclusively with transitive stems, and the causative suffix has only limited possibilities of combination with transitive stems.

3.6.3.2 Syntactic and semantic properties of the causative suffix -ndí

As illustrated by example (16), causativization by means of the causative suffix -ndí is fully productive with verbs used intransitively in their non-derived form.

(16) a Lémínè-n   Ø   cáxú.
        child-D   CPL.TR   lie_down
        S   pm   V
        'The child went to bed.'

(16) b Yàxàré-n   dà   léminè-n   cáxú-ndí.
        woman-D   CPL.TR   child-D   lie_down-CAUS
        S   pm   O   V
        'The woman put the child to bed.'

Morphological causativization is less productive with a transitive input. There are transitive verbs for which morphological causativization is usual (for example yígá 'eat' > (caus.) yígá-ndí), or at least accepted by consultants in elicitation, but with most transitive verbs, analytical causatives are clearly preferred.

As illustrated by example (17), the object of causative verbs derived from transitive verbs may correspond semantically either to the subject or the object of the transitive verb from which they derive, but if both are expressed, as in (17c), the object of the initial construction is maintained as the object of the causative verb.

(17) a *Lémìnè-n dà tíyè-n ñìgá.*
child-D CPL.TR meat-D eat
S pm O V
'The child ate meat.'

(17) b *Fàatú dà lémìnè-n ñìgá-ndí.*
Fatou CPL.TR child-D eat-CAUS
S pm O V
'Fatou made the child eat.'

(17) c *Fàatú dà tíyè-n ñìgá-ndí lémìnè-n ŋá.*
Fatou CPL.TR meat-D eat-CAUS child-D by
S pm O V X
'Fatou made the child eat meat.'

3.7 Reflexivity and reciprocity

3.7.1 Reflexivity

Apart from a very limited set of transitive verbs whose detransitivized form may express object reflexivization, object and oblique reflexivization is expressed in Soninke by means of the dedicated reflexive pronoun *dú* 'self' marking coreference with the subject, either alone or combined with a possessive, without any change in the construction. (18) illustrates object reflexivization. The tonal change undergone by *dú* in (18c) is a general property of the adnominal possession construction.

(18) a *Yàxàré-n dà lémìnè-n tàngá.*
woman-D CPL.TR child-D protect
S pm O V
'The woman protected the child.'

(18) b *Yàxàré-n dà dú tàngá.*
woman-D CPL.TR self protect
S pm O V
'The woman protected herself.'

(18) c *Yàxàré-n d(à) í dù tàngá.*
woman-D CPL.TR 3REFL self^L protect
S pm O V
same meaning as (18b)

3.7.2 Reciprocity

Reciprocalization is expressed in Soninke by *mé* 'each other' (cognate with the noun *mê*, plural *mèenû* 'the like of'). *Mé* can be found in any syntactic role other than subject, depending on the syntactic roles involved in the reciprocal relation. (19) illustrates object reciprocalization.

(19) a *Múusá   dà   Démbà   dèemá.*
       Moussa   CPL.TR   Demba   helped
       S   pm   O   V
       'Moussa helped Demba.'

(19) b *Múusá   dò   Démbà   dà   mé   dèemá.*
       Moussa   and   Demba   CPL.TR   each other   helped
       S   pm   O   V
       'Moussa and Demba helped each other.'

3.8 Object incorporation

Soninke has a productive mechanism of object incorporation yielding morphological compounds in which the noun, interpreted as non-specific, occurs in a form distinct from the form it takes as an autonomous word. Interestingly, as illustrated in (20), with verbs ending with a non-front vowel, compound N+V verbs are marked as intransitive by the detransitivization marker -*i*.[12]

(20) a *Yàxàrú-n   dà   kónpè-n   céllà.*
       woman.PL-D   CPL.TR   room-D   sweep
       S   pm   O   V
       'The women swept the room.'

(20) b *Yàxàrû-n   Ø   kónpó-séllè.*
       woman.PL-D   CPL.INTR   room-sweep.DETR
       S   pm   V
       'The women did room sweeping.'

For a detailed analysis of incorporation in Soninke and its implications for transitivity, see Creissels and Dramé (2018).

---

[12] In Soninke, *s* in contact with a nasal consonant is automatically converted into *c*, hence the *céllà* variant of the verb *séllà* 'sweep'.

3.9 Valency classes of verbs

3.9.1 Strictly transitive and strictly intransitive verbs

Soninke has strictly intransitive verbs (for example *bíré* 'live' or *bònó* 'become spoilt') and strictly transitive verbs (for example *yígá* 'eat' or *séllà* 'sweep'). Strictly intransitive verbs form cannot be used transitively in their underived form with a participant encoded as the object,[13] and strictly transitive verbs in their underived form can only be used transitively with an overtly expressed object. As illustrated by example (21), strictly transitive verbs must undergo morphological derivation before being used in intransitive constructions, whatever the semantic nature of the intransitive construction.[14]

(21) a *Hàatú dà kónpè-n céllà.*
Fatou CPL.TR room-D sweep
S pm O V
'Fatou swept the room.'

(21) b *Hàatú Ø séllá-ndì.*
Fatou CPL.INTR sweep-ANTIP
S pm V
'Fatou did the sweeping.'

(21) c *Kónpè-n Ø céllè.*
room-D CPL.INTR sweep.DETR
S pm V
'The room was swept.'

3.9.2 A-labile verbs

Among potentially transitive verbs, A-labile verbs can be used intransitively with a subject representing the same agent-like participant as the subject of the transitive construction, but must undergo a detransitivizing derivation in order to be used intransitively with a subject representing the same patient-like participant as the object of the transitive construction. This behavior, illustrated in example (22) by *sòxó* 'cultivate',[15] is extremely rare among Soninke verbs.

---

[13] However, some intransitive verbs can be found in a formally transitive construction with 'atypical objects' expressing the temporal or spatial delimitation of the event, cf. Creissels (2017).
[14] On the alternation affecting the initial *s* of *séllà* 'sweep', see footnote 12.
[15] On the alternation between *sòxó* and *còxó*, see footnote 12.

(22) a Yúgò-n dà té-n còxó.
man-D CPL.TR field-D cultivate
S pm O V
'The man has cultivated the field.'

(22) b Yúgò-n Ø còxó.
man-D CPL.INTR cultivate
S pm V
'The man has cultivated.'

(22) c Té-n Ø còxé.
field-D CPL.INTR cultivate.DETR
S pm V
'The field has been cultivated.'

3.9.3 P-labile verbs

Among potentially transitive verbs, P-labile verbs can be used intransitively with a subject representing the same patient-like participant as the object of the same verb used transitively, but must undergo antipassive derivation in order to be used intransitively with a subject corresponding to the subject of the transitive construction. This behavior is illustrated in (23) by *ŋàrí* 'see'.

(23) a Dénbà dà Hàatú ŋàrí sáxà-n ŋá.
Demba CPLTR Fatou see market-D at
S pm O V X
'Demba saw Fatou at the market.'

(23) b Hàatú Ø ŋàrí sáxà-n ŋá.
Fatou CPL.INTR see market-D at
S pm V X
'Fatou was seen at the market.'

(23) c Hìnkàntê-n ntá ŋàrì-ndì-nì.
blind-D ICPL.NEG see-ANTIP-GER[L]
S pm V
'The blind do not see.'

In their intransitive use, P-labile verbs may have a noncausal or passive reading, depending on their lexical meaning.

P-lability is restricted to a subset of the verbs that can be used transitively. Moreover, it is striking that the vast majority of P-labile verbs end with *i* or *e*, and conversely, all the verbs that end with *i* or *e* and can be used transitively are

P-labile, which raises the question whether this is really P-lability, or perhaps rather vacuous detransitivization, since Soninke has a detransitivizing suffix -*i* that fuses with the last vowel of non-monosyllabic stems. The historical explanation of this particularity of Soninke will be discussed in section 4.

3.9.4 Reflexive lability

Yánqí 'wash' is to the best of my knowledge the only Soninke verb that can be used intransitively in its underived form, not only with a passive or anticausative reading, but also with a reflexive reading.

3.9.5 A/P-labile verbs

A/P-labile verbs have three possible types of uses in their underived form: they can be used transitively with a participant encoded as the object, intransitively with a subject corresponding semantically to the subject of the transitive construction, and intransitively with a subject corresponding to the object. This behavior, illustrated in (24) by *mìní* 'drink', is extremely rare among Soninke verbs.

(24) a *Léminè-n   dà   qátì-n   mìní   bà?*
         child-D   CPL.TR   milk-D   drink   Q
         S   pm   O   V
         'Did the child drink the milk?'

(24) b *Léminè-n   Ø   mìní   bà?*
         child-D   CPL.INTR   drink   Q
         S   pm   V
         'Did the child drink?'

(24) c *Qátì-n   Ø   mìní   bà?*
         milk-D   CPL.INTR   drink   Q
         S   pm   V
         'Was the milk drunk?'

4 The phonological conditioning of P-lability in historical perspective

As already mentioned above, in Soninke, all the non-monosyllabic verbs ending with *i* or *e* that can be used transitively are P-labile, whereas for monosyllabic verbs and for non-monosyllabic verbs ending with *a*, *o* or *u* that can be used transitively, the general rule is that an intransitive use with a noncausal or passive meaning requires overt detransitivization by means of the detransitivizing suffix -*i*.

Crucially, the detransitivizing suffix has morphophonological properties that explain this distribution of lability and overt detransitivizing derivation in the expression of the noncausal-causal alternation. The point is that the detransitivizing suffix surfaces as a distinct segment with monosyllabic stems only, whereas with non-monosyllabic ones, it obligatorily fuses with the last vowel of the stem in a way that can be described as the addition of a palatal feature:

$a + i > e$
$o + i > e$
$u + i > i$

Since *i* and *e* already include a palatal feature, they cannot be modified by fusion with *i*. Synchronically, the (quasi-)complementarity between P-lability and overt detransitivizing derivation can therefore be analyzed as a consequence of the fact that detransitivizing derivation would apply vacuously to non-monosyllabic stems ending with *i* or *e*.

Historically, non-concatenative morphology often results from phonological processes that blur the boundary between formatives that originally constituted successive segments. Consequently, one may assume that, initially, the ancestor of the suffix -*i* did not fuse with the stems to which it attached, and its use was not constrained by the phonological structure of the stem.

One may therefore assume that, originally, P-lability was inexistent (or at least exceptional) in Soninke, as it still is for verbs whose stem ends with nonfront vowels. When the detransitivizing suffix -*i* fused with the stem of non-monosyllabic verbs, the fusion operated according to the following rule:

$i + i > i$
$e + i > e$
$a + i > e$
$o + i > e$
$u + i > i$

And, consequently, the non-monosyllabic transitive verbs ending with *i* or *e* became homonymous with their mediopassive derivate.

Interestingly, the observation of vowel length provides some additional support for this hypothesis. In present-day Soninke, vowel length is distinctive in non-final syllables of non-monosyllabic words, but in monosyllabic words and in the final syllables of non-monosyllabic words, no length contrast is possible. Phonetically, vowels in word-final position are invariably short. This also applies to monosyllabic words, which are invariably pronounced with a short vowel. The fact that there are some morphological alternations with short vowels in word-final position alternating with long vowels in word-internal position suggests that, originally, vowel length was distinctive in all positions, and long vowels in word-final position lost their length at some point in the history of Soninke.

Turning to the historical scenario sketched above about the detransitivizing suffix -*i*, it is interesting to observe that, when the gerundive suffix attaches to intransitive verb stems derived by means of -*i*, at least with some verbs, the ending of the stem (i.e. the vowel resulting from the fusion of the stem-final vowel and the suffix -*i*) sporadically occurs as a long vowel. For example, the final *a* of *yígá* 'eat' is invariably short, and the gerundive of this verb is also invariably *yígá-ná*, whereas the gerundive of the intransitive derivate *yígé* may optionally be *yígé-né* or *yígée-né*.

In a language in which vowel length is distinctive, the fusion of two adjacent vowels can be expected to create long vowels. Consequently, it is reasonable to assume that, originally, the fusion of the detransitivizing suffix -*i* with the last vowel of non-monosyllabic stems created long vowels, which ensured the distinction between transitive stems and their intransitive derivates even in the case of stems ending with *i* or *e*:

i + *i* > *ii*
e + *i* > *ee*
a + *i* > *ee*
o + *i* > *ee*
u + *i* > *ii*

Subsequently, long vowels in word-final position lost their length, so that the last vowel of the intransitive verb stems derived by means of -*i* automatically lost its length when no other suffix followed the detransitivizing suffix. The sporadic occurrence of forms such as *yígée-né* (variant of *yígé-né*, gerundive of the intransitive derivate of *yígá* 'eat') suggests that, in the initial stage, the length of the vowel resulting from the fusion of the detransitivizing suffix -*i* with the last vowel of the verb stem was maintained in word-internal position.

Finally, the variant ending with a short vowel generalized to all contexts, although the variant ending with a long vowel is still sporadically found in contact with the gerundive suffix.

5 Conclusion

In general, the transitivity system of Soninke shows the features typical for Mande transitivity systems. However, Soninke also has some interesting specificities: a formal distinction between transitive and intransitive predication more marked than in the other Mande languages, a system of differential subject flagging, productive detransitivizing derivations (with both mediopassive and antipassive functions), a productive mechanism of object incorporation, and phonologically conditioned P-lability.

On this latter point, I have shown that this unusual situation is the result of a sequence of typologically unremarkable morphophonological changes:
- fusion of a suffix with the ending of the stems to which it attaches,
- loss of vowel length in word-final position,
- replacement of the form taken by a stem in combination with suffixes by the form it shows in the absence of any suffix.

As a by-product of this sequence of changes, which by themselves have nothing to do with the transitivity system, the distinction between transitive stems ending with front vowels and the corresponding intransitive stems derived by means of the detransitivizing suffix -*i* was blurred, giving rise to P-lability for a subset of transitive verbs characterized by the phonological nature of their final vowel.

Abbreviations

ANTIP	antipassive
CAUS	causative
CPL	completive
D	default determiner[16]

---

[16] A default determiner is a grammatical element that has the syntactic distribution of a determiner, but whose presence has implications for the interpretation of noun phrases in limited contexts only, and can otherwise be analyzed as resulting from a mere syntactic constraint.

DEM	demonstrative
DETR	detransitivization marker
FOC	focalization
GER	gerundive
H (superscript)	high morphotoneme
ICPL	incompletive
IMPER	imperative
INTR	intransitive
L (superscript)	low morphotoneme
LH (superscript)	low-high morphotoneme
NEG	negative
O	object
PL	plural
pm	predicative marker
REFL	reflexive
S	subject
SBJF	subject flag
SG	singular
SUBJ	subjunctive
TR	transitive
V	verb
X	oblique

References

Cobbinah, Alexander & Friederike Lüpke. 2009. Not cut to fit – zero coded passives in African languages. In Matthias Brenzinger & Anne-Maria Fehn (eds.), *Proceedings of the 6th World Congress of African Linguistics*, 153–165. Cologne: Köppe.

Creissels, Denis. 1992. La voix en soninké. *Mandenkan* 23. 1–24.

Creissels, Denis. 2016. Phonologie segmentale et tonale du soninké (parler du Kingi). *Mandenkan* 55. 3–174.

Creissels, Denis. 2017. Atypical objects in Soninke (West Mande). *Italian Journal of Linguistics* 29 (1). 25–52.

Creissels, Denis. 2020. The detransitivizing suffix *-i* and the reconstruction of Pre-Proto-Mande constituent order. *Language in Africa* 1(4). 85–97.

Creissels, Denis & Anna Marie Diagne. 2013. Transitivity in Bakel Soninke. *Mandenkan* 50. 5–37.

Creissels, Denis & Djibril Dramé. 2018. Transitivity and incorporation in Soninke. *Frankfurter Afrikanistische Blätter* 26. 37–54.

Diagana, Ousmane Moussa. 1984. *Le parler soninké de Kaedi, syntaxe et sens*. Habilitation thesis. Paris: Paris Descartes University.

Diagana, Ousmane Moussa. 1995. *La langue soninkée: morphosyntaxe et sens*. Paris: L'Harmattan.

Diagana, Ousmane Moussa. 2011. *Dictionnaire soninké-français (Mauritanie)*. Paris: Karthala.
Diagana, Yacouba. 1990. *Éléments de grammaire du soninké*. Paris: INALCO PhD thesis.
Diagana, Yacouba. 1994. *Éléments de grammaire du soninké*. Paris: Association Linguistique Africaine.
Fauconnier, Stefanie & Jean-Christophe Verstraete. 2014. A and O as each other's mirror image? Problems with markedness reversal. *Linguistic Typology* 18 (1). 3–49.
Geniušienė, Emma. 1987. *The typology of reflexives*. Berlin & New York: Mouton de Gruyter.

Index of Authors

Abondolo, Daniel 219
Adams, James N. 269, 217
Adelaar, Alexander 257
Aissen, Judith. 14
Aldai, Gontzal 2, 4, 7, 14, 127
Alexiadou, Artemis 135–136, 185, 188–189, 191, 267
Allan, Rutger 179
Anagnostopoulou, Elena 135–136, 185, 188–189, 191
Andriani, Luigi 267, 280, 282
Annerholm, Hjalmar 31
Antonov, Anton 15, 22
Arkadiev, Peter 20, 211
Arkhangelskij, Timofey 22–23

Babiniotis, Georgios 186, 190
Balles, Irene 153
Bammesberger, Alfred 31
Barðdal, Jóhanna 32, 41–42, 60, 134–136, 140, 145, 147–148, 158, 269, 272, 274–275
Barnes, Jonathan 2, 5–8, 17, 31, 42, 133–135, 137–141, 143–144, 146, 156–157, 159, 161, 169, 172–175, 181, 183–186, 188, 190, 209, 211, 214, 236, 253, 259
Barshi, Immanuel 57
Bauer, Bernhard 91, 97
Baumann, Luisa 59
Beavers, John 267, 295–296
Bentley, Delia 267, 293
Benveniste, Émile 181
Bernhardt, Ernst 47
Berrettoni, Pierangiolo 151
Bertinetto, Pier Marco 269
Bhaskararao, Peri 5
Bickel, Balthasar 14–16, 21, 24
Bisagni, Jacopo 101
Bisang, Walter 122
Bjarnadóttir, Valgerður 44
Bökenkrüger, Wilhelm 31
Borer, Hagit 135
Bortolussi, Bernard 140
Botne, Robert 221

Bozzone, Chiara 150, 153
Bracks, Christoph A. 237, 241, 248
Brambilla Ageno, Franca 279, 282
Brousseau, Anne-Marie 20
Brucale, Luisa 141–142, 153
Brugmann, Karl 147
Budassi, Marco 149, 151
Burridge, Kathryn 20
Burrow, Thomas 177
Bybee, Joan L. 142

Cennamo, Michela 10, 32, 35–36, 41–42, 49, 60, 65, 134–136, 140, 145, 147–148, 158–159, 267–269, 271–277, 279–282, 284, 293–294, 297
Cerbasi, Donato 141, 159
Chafe, Wallace 289
Chantraine, Pierre 197
Chappell, Hilary 20
Chen, Victoria 257
Chomsky, Noam A. 3
Ciconte, Francesco 267, 280, 282
Clackson, James 146, 157
Cobbinah, Alexander 306
Comrie, Bernard 1–2, 9, 19, 32, 34, 36, 49–51, 89–90, 117, 133, 137, 140, 159–161, 211, 219
Conti, Luz 52
Cotticelli-Kurras, Paola 180
Covini, Andrea Lorenzo 140, 156, 158
Creissels, Denis 10, 154, 212, 305, 308, 315, 320–321
Cristofaro, Sonia 15, 25
Croft, William 1, 45, 146
Curme, George O. 33
Cysouw, Michael 137

D'Agostino, Giulia 61, 66
Dahl, Östen 117
Dalrymple, Mary 14
DeLancey, Scott 14
Delatte, Louis 141, 146
Delbrück, Berthold 147
Dell'Oro, Francesca 150

Diagana, Ousmane Moussa 305
Diagana, Yacouba 305
Diagne, Anna Marie 305
Dixon, R. M. W. 14, 34, 194
Dolovai, Dorottya 212
Doornebal, Marius Albert 21
Downing, Laura J. 14
Dowty, David R. 268
Drinka, Bridget 41, 160
Dryer, Matthew S. 15
Dunkel, George E. 147

Ebert, Karen 21
Egge, Albert E. 31
Epps, Patience 20
Erelt, Mati 223–224
Evans, Nicholas 69
Eythórsson, Thórhallur 32, 41–42, 60, 134–136, 140, 145, 147–148, 158, 269, 272

Fabrizio, Claudia 35–36
Falluomini, Carla 33
Fauconnier, Stefanie 311
Fedriani, Chiara 44
Feltenius, Leif 145, 269, 272–275
Ferraresi, Gisella 41–42, 48–50
Flobert, Pierre 145, 275
Fortson, Benjamin W. 157
Fraurud, Kari 117
Friedrichsen, George W. S. 33
Fruyt, Michèle 149–153, 155, 158

García Castillero, Carlos 91, 93, 118
García García, Luisa 31, 43, 51, 134, 139, 160
van Gelderen, Elly 7, 43, 139, 141, 159–160
Geniušienė, Emma 315
Gianollo, Chiara 137, 140, 145, 147–148, 154, 159, 269, 275
Givón, Talmy 13
Glare, Peter W. G. 141
Goldberg, Adele E. 3
Graver, Jenny 93
Grebe, Paul 3
Greenberg, Joseph H. 21
Griffith, Aaron 91–92, 97, 101, 105, 113, 120
Grossman, Eitan 6–8, 15, 19, 23–24, 160
Grünthal, Riho 7, 9, 169, 219

Hahn, Adelaide E. 149, 151–153
Haig, Geoffrey 19
Hajdú, Péter 219
Hay, Jen 269
Harbert, Wayne 62
Harðarson, Jón A. 41, 44
Harris, Alice 15
Hartmann, Iren 3–4, 32, 89–90, 93, 100, 109, 111, 127
Haspelmath, Martin 3–5, 8, 13, 16–17, 32, 42, 49–51, 59, 89–93, 95, 100, 107, 109, 111, 126–127, 129, 135–137, 144–145, 159, 172–176, 179, 183, 191, 202, 211, 213, 267, 289
Hastings, Robert 277
Haverling, Gerd 151, 156
Heidinger, Steffen 267, 284–290, 294, 295
Heine, Bernd 20
Hellan, Lars 32
Hemmings, Charlotte 236, 250
Herbst, Thomas 3
Hermodsson, Lars 31
Hettrich, Heinrich 47
Hewson, John 40, 53
Himmelmann, Nikolaus P. 9, 235, 237, 239, 241, 250–251, 253–254, 257–258, 260
Hock, Hans H. 51
Hoffmann, Roland 140, 144, 155
Holton, David 191
Holvoet, Axel 32, 44, 211
Honti, László 224–225
Hopper, Paul J. 4, 13, 45, 54
Horrocks, Geoffrey 58, 146, 157
Huumo, Tuomas 52

Iemmolo, Giorgio 14
Inglese, Guglielmo 8, 36, 56, 147, 151–152, 154, 156, 172, 180

Jacques, Guillaume 15, 22–23
Janda, Richard D. 34
Jasanoff, Jay H. 150–151, 153
Ježek, Elisabetta 268, 284, 293–294, 297
Joseph, Brian D. 31, 34, 62

Karantzola, Eleni 194, 196
Karsten, Torsten E. 31

Katz, R. Moses Jr. 41, 61
Kaufman, Daniel 253, 259
Kavanagh, Séamus 97, 125
Keidan, Artemij 33
Kemmer, Susanne 147
Kennedy, Christopher 269
Keydana, Götz 56
Kibrik, Andrej A. 92
Kiparsky, Paul 46, 51
Kittilä, Seppo 135, 170, 236
Kleyner, Svetlana 34, 60–61, 65–66
Koivisto, Vesa 219
Kölligan, Daniel 147, 172
Koontz-Garboden, Andrew 136, 267, 295
Kotin, Michail L. 61
Krämer, Peter 31
Kriaras, Emmanouil 200
Kulikov, Leonid 32, 134–135, 139, 154, 211
Kuryłowicz, Jerzy 40, 269
Kuteva, Tania 20

La Polla, Randy 266
Labelle, Marie 293–294
Lahiri, Aditi 7, 32, 134, 137, 139–140, 169
Lash, Elliott 94, 107, 113, 120
Lavidas, Nikolaos 154, 192–194, 196–198, 211
Lavine, James E. 44
Lazzeroni, Romano 42, 139, 267
Le Mair, Esther 99, 102
Lecaudé, Peggy 140
Lefevre, Claire 20
Legendre, Geraldine 293–294
Lehmann, Christian 34, 64, 96, 100, 116–117, 120, 125, 128, 140–141, 145
Leiss, Elisabeth 51
Lepschy, Anna Laura 277
Lepschy, Giulio 277
Leto, Claudia 237
Letuchiy, Alexander 154, 174, 194, 202–203
Levin, Beth 2, 34, 48, 56, 136, 176, 267–268, 269, 295–296
Lewis, Charlton T. 141
Litta, Eleonora 149, 151
Lüpke, Friederike 306
Luraghi, Silvia 5, 7, 9, 32, 46–48, 51–53, 56–57, 60, 134, 137, 139–141, 146–148, 153–154, 157–158, 172, 176–181, 192, 211

Mackridge, Peter 193
Maiden, Martin 277
Majtinskaja, K. E. 219
Malcher, Kurt 9, 238
Malchukov, Andrej 1.2, 4–5, 8, 14, 17, 19, 32, 34, 36, 44, 49–51, 89, 90, 95, 97, 109, 126–127, 129
Malicka-Kleparska, Anna 160
Malzahn, Melanie 150
Manente, Mara 293–294
Martin, Fabienne 293
Maslova, Elena 15
Matras, Yaron 19, 21
Mattiola, Simone 151
McDonnell, Bradley 257
McGregor, William 14
Mel'čuk, Igor' Aleksandrovič 3
Melis, Chantal 14
Mendoza, Julia 147
Metlen, Michael 33
Michaelis, Susanne Maria 19
Mignot, Xavier 150
Miller, Gary D. 33, 41–44, 46–54, 57–58, 61–62, 67–69
Mithun, Marianne 289
Mocciaro, Egle 141, 152–153
Montaut, Annie 14

Næss, Åshild 4, 136
Napoli, Maria 52
Nau, Nicole 7, 32, 44, 211
Nedjalkov, Vladimir P. 5, 69, 135, 137, 213
Nichols, Johanna 2, 5–9, 17, 25, 31, 42, 133–135, 137–141, 146, 156–157, 159, 161, 169, 172–175, 177, 181, 183–186, 188, 190, 209, 211, 214, 236, 243, 259
Nickel, Karl 211
Nikolaeva, Irina 14
Norberg, Dag 275–276
Norman, Jerry 20
Nussbaum, Alan 150

Ó Gealbháin, Séamas 121
Oettinger, Norbert 151
Olsen, Birgit Anette 150

Otanes, Fe T. 253
Ottósson, Kjartan 7–8, 31–32, 41–42, 71, 134, 139, 160

Pagliarulo, Giuseppe 61
Pakerys, Jurgis 7, 211
Pardeshi, Prashant 211
Parry, Mair 277
Parsons, Terence 270, 272
Payne, Doris L. 57
Peterson, David A. 2, 5–8, 17, 31, 42, 59, 133–135, 137–141, 143–144, 146, 156–157, 159, 161, 169, 172–175, 181, 183–185, 188, 190, 209, 211, 214, 236, 243, 259
Petit, Daniel 147
Pflugmacher, Miriam 56
Philippaki-Warburton, Irene 193
Pinkster, Harm 134, 140, 145–146
Piras, Antonio 33
Pirson, Jules 272–274
Plank, Frans 7, 32, 134, 137, 139–140, 169
Polis, Stephane 15
Puddu, Nicoletta 147
Pustejovsky, James 296

Quirk, Randolph 3

Rappaport Hovav, Malka 2, 34, 56, 135–136, 176, 267–268, 295–296
Ratkus, Artūras 33–34, 60–61, 65–66
Rau, Jeremy 150
Reinöhl, Uta 158
Rice, Allan L. 33
Riecke, Jörg 31
Riesberg, Sonja 9, 236, 238–240, 251
Ringe, Don 42
Rizza, Alfredo 180
Rizzo, Giuseppe 56
Roma, Elisa 8, 36, 91–92, 100, 111, 118, 121
Romagno, Domenica 156, 179
Ronconi, Alessandro 271, 273
Ross, Malcolm D. 257
Rousseau, André 41, 43, 49
Ruijgh, Cornelius J. 153

Sakel, Jeanette 19, 21
Sammallahti, Pekka 211, 221

Sanchez, Liliana 21
Sanfelici, Emanuela 95
Sansò, Andrea 112
Sausa, Eleonora 7, 32, 53, 56, 134, 139, 141, 144, 146, 175–176, 178
Say, Sergey 18, 24
Schachter, Paul 253
Schäfer, Florian 135–136, 267–268, 293–294
Schindler, Jochem 150, 153
Schwerdt, Judith 41–42
Schwyzer, Eduard 193, 197
Seržant, Ilja A. 14, 19, 52
Shibatani, Masayoshi 211
Short, Charles 141
Shushan, Gregory 199
Siewierska, Anna 44
Sil'nitsky, Georgij 5, 135, 172
Simone, Raffaele 141, 159
Smolensky, Paul 293–294
Sorace, Antonella 297
Squartini, Mario 269
Stamatiou, Irini 193
Stavrou, Melita 58
Stefanowitsch, Anatol 3
Stein, Achim 24
Stifter, David 92
Stokes, Whitley 91, 97, 113, 125
Strachan, John 91, 97, 113, 125
Streitberg, Wilhelm 33
Stüber, Karin 95, 98, 105, 107, 109, 125–126
Subbarao, Karumuri 5
Sundén, Karl F. 31
Suzuki, Seiichi 31, 41–42
Svennung, Josef 272, 275

Taylor, Bradley 32, 89–90
Tenser, Anton 19
Tesnière, Lucien 1–2
Thomason, Olga 40–41, 55
Thompson, Sandra A. 4, 13, 45, 54, 136
Thurneysen, Rudolf 91, 94, 98, 107, 112, 115, 121, 125–126
Trips, Carola 24
Tsunoda, Tasaku 4, 8, 13–14, 17, 127, 129

Usacheva, Maria 22–23

de Vaan, Michiel 143, 158
Van Valin, Robert D. 238, 266
Vendler, Zeno 268
Verhoeven, Elisabeth 5
Verstraete, Jean-Christophe 311
Vincent, Nigel 277
Viti, Carlotta 44, 147

Watkins, Calvert 150–151, 155
Weiss, Michael 143, 147, 150, 155, 157
West, Jonathan 41–42
Wichmann, Søren 2, 4, 7, 14, 21–24, 127, 159
Wiemer, Björn 44
Wilcken, Ulrich 199

Willi, Andreas 179–180
Witzlack-Makarevich, Alena 6–7, 14, 16, 19, 21, 24
Wohlgemuth, Jan 21–24
Wolfe, Brendan N. 58
Wolff, John U. 254, 257–258
Wright, Joseph 46, 51, 68–69

Yoshioka, Jiro 33

Zakharko, Taras 15–16, 21, 24
Zanchi, Chiara 8, 34, 46, 48, 51, 53, 60, 139, 141
Zúñiga, Fernando 20, 135, 170, 236

Index of Subjects

Ablaut 6, 41, 63, 64,65, 84, 138, 172, 183
Accomplishment, accomplishments
    268–274, 276–277, 281, 283–288,
    290–294, 296–299
Achievement, achievements 140, 268–271,
    274, 276–278, 280–281, 283–284,
    286–288, 290–294, 296–298
Active perfect 276
Activity, activities 45, 56, 59, 77, 81–82, 210,
    246, 249, 268–269, 271–274, 277–279,
    283–284, 293–294, 296–298
Adpositional arguments 99, 108
Affixal morphology 9, 209, 215, 217–220,
    222, 225, 230
Ambivalent (labile) 6, 172
Animacy 10, 14, 16, 22, 47, 54, 79, 105,
    116–117, 119, 128, 156, 198, 200, 265
Anticausative alternation 5, 32, 116, 134–137,
    161, 174, 176–177, 183, 185, 191–192,
    194, 266–267, 269, 277, 288, 295
Antipassive 112, 315–318, 322, 326
Applicative 9–10, 31, 37, 47–48, 59–60, 70,
    82, 172, 235–237, 239–241, 244–245,
    249–253, 255–260
Aspectual verbs 278
Aspectuals 279, 283–284, 286, 288,
    290–292
Autocausative 317
Auxiliary change 6, 138, 172, 243
Auxiliary selection 284, 289, 293–294

Basic valency orientation 8, 31–32, 42,
    13–134, 137, 139–140, 211, 235, 259, 265
BE+past participle 289–290
Bound arguments 91

Caland System 150, 158
Case-marking 13, 15, 17, 19, 21, 40–41,
    90–91, 99, 107, 109
Case alternations 5, 51–55, 80–82, 92, 114
Causal verb 15, 61, 209–214, 216, 218,
    221–222, 225–226, 229–230
Causal-noncausal alternation 8, 40, 42,
    63–68, 306

Causative verbs 45, 68, 150, 155, 178, 209,
    211–213, 215, 225, 267, 307, 318–319
Causativization strategies 9, 158–159,
    209–211, 213, 215–217, 220, 223, 226–227
Coding alternations 92
Cognate/kindred object 31, 58, 70, 82, 118
Compound tenses 277, 281–284, 287–294
Conjugation class change 6, 138, 140, 143,
    146, 151, 172, 181, 201, 237, 243, 248
Control 10, 62, 105–106, 148, 191, 238, 249,
    265, 270
Correspondences
 – augmented 172
 – reduced 6, 172, 180–181
 – undetermined 6, 172
Criteria for argumenthood 3, 100

Decausativization 210, 213, 226
Deponentization 275
Derivational morphology 51, 139, 157, 214,
    216, 218
Detransitivizing 6, 9–10, 19, 22, 169,
    172–173, 179–181, 192, 202–203, 205,
    243, 305, 313–315, 317, 321, 323–326
Differential argument marking 14, 16
Differential subject flagging 311, 326
Double derivation 6, 138, 148, 150, 156, 172,
    176, 184–185, 243

Event Structure Template 265, 272
Experiential verb 4–5, 46, 47, 55, 77–80, 82,
    84, 126, 127, 177
External Causation 259–260, 279
External possessor 31, 57–58, 69–70, 82

Final goal/result/state 265, 268, 270–271,
    276, 283–284, 289–290, 297–298

Gradual Completion Verbs 269, 271–273,
    278, 281, 283, 286–288, 290–294, 298

Impersonal verb 43, 46
Impersonal construction 35, 44, 55, 63, 93,
    108

Incorporation 23–24, 320, 326
Intransitivization 9, 133–134, 146–147, 155, 159–161, 306, 313, 321

Lability 9–11, 43, 133, 138–139, 143, 154, 156, 159, 161, 169, 172, 181, 183–186, 188, 191–192, 194–196, 200–205, 265, 267, 269, 271, 276–277, 283, 288, 290, 298, 305–307, 309, 323–324
– A-lability 317, 321
– P-lability 9, 10, 154, 305, 307, 322–324, 326
Language contact 7, 8, 11, 13, 15–20, 24–25, 160, 223, 226
Lexical restrictions 12, 117–120

Matter replication 13, 21, 24–25
Multi-point scalar change 296–298
Multi-point scale 296

Neutral correspondence 6, 172
Non-causal verb 210–213, 218, 222
Non-Philippine-type 10, 235, 237, 252–253, 255–257, 260
Null objects 31, 52–53, 56, 69–70, 81, 311
Null subjects 311

One-place verb 45, 77, 82–83

Passivization and passive alternation 43, 60–62, 99, 108, 122, 236, 306 (see also Voice)
Passive perfect 276
Pattern replication 13, 19, 25
Perfective auxiliary 289–290
Philippine-type 10, 235, 237–238, 252–253, 256–258, 260
Possessives 109, 119–121

Reciprocal 31, 68–70, 85, 193, 320
Reflexive
– conjugation 219
– pattern 148, 265, 269–270, 272, 275, 279, 287, 294
– pronoun 9, 58, 66–69, 71, 133, 145–147, 160–161, 275, 315, 319

– strategy 10, 274, 276–277, 284–285, 287–288
Relative clause 47, 92, 112, 117–118, 124
Resultative stative passive 276
r-form/ inflection 146–148, 158

Scalar change 10, 265, 296–298
Simplex tenses 277, 283, 289–292
Spontaneity scale 174, 202–203, 267
States 242, 268, 270, 293, 296–298
Stative predicate 241–242, 246–247
Suppletion 6, 9, 133, 139, 141–145, 155–156, 158–159, 161, 169, 172, 174, 175–176, 177–178, 181–185, 191, 201–205, 215–216, 220–223, 230, 243–245, 259
Symmetrical-voice language 235–236, 250, 252, 255, 259–260

Telicity 149, 266, 271, 274, 276, 284, 286–288, 293, 298
Thematic reduction 265, 277
Thematic underspecification of the causer 267
Three-place verb 43, 49, 56, 70, 79, 81–84, 116
Transfer verb 43, 49, 50–51, 79–80
Transitivity
– index 8, 89–90, 116, 122–124, 126–129
– prominence 16–18, 127, 211, 312
Transitivizing 6, 9, 113, 134, 138–139, 145, 153, 155, 157, 159–161, 172–173, 177, 180–181, 192, 205, 235, 243–244, 259
Two-place verb 45, 48, 53, 78, 81–85, 127
Two-point scalar change / Two-point scale 296–298

Unspecific change of state 267

Valency-changing derivation 305, 313
Valency classes 2, 19, 34, 40, 77–79, 211, 321
Verb semantics 3, 116, 120, 210
Verbal nouns 89, 94–98, 107, 109, 112–114, 120–125, 228

Voice
- alternation 9–10, 139–140, 143, 145–146, 155–156, 161, 169, 175, 176–180, 181, 184, 186–188, 192, 196–200, 202–204, 236, 239, 242, 253, 256, 258–260
- medio-passive / mediopassive 42, 60, 133, 185–186, 194–197, 200, 265, 269, 270, 274–275, 305, 325–326
- middle 41, 139, 145–147, 159–162, 169–170, 175, 178–179, 181, 189–191, 193–194, 197–198, 202, 204
- system/systems 10, 148, 170, 180, 235–237, 252, 256–257, 260, 272, 275, 277

Word order 15, 33–35, 49, 66, 90, 94, 99, 102–103, 159, 289

Wordlist-based typology 211

Index of Languages

Abaza 20
Armenian
– Classical 172
– Western 138–139
Athpare 21

Baltic languages 7, 32, 44, 177, 223–224
Bambara 305–306
Bantawa 21
Bashkir 23
Beng 307
Bikol 254

Camling 21
Cebuano 254–255, 257
Chichewa 14
Coptic 7, 23–24

East Khanty 215, 231
English 5–7, 22, 65, 97, 100, 112, 136, 138, 160, 170–173, 183, 248, 267–268, 296, 306
– Modern 36, 43, 139, 160
– Middle 24
– Old 41, 43, 64, 134, 139, 160
Erzya 215, 217–218, 222–223, 226–229
Estonian 215, 217, 219, 222–224

Finnic languages 7, 217, 219, 222, 224
Finnish 210, 213, 216, 223
Florentine, Old 277, 280, 283, 298
Fongbe 20
French 16, 22, 112, 159, 202, 265–268, 276, 293–294, 295–298
– Classical 284, 287–288
– Contemporary 284, 287–288
– Middle 284, 286–288, 298
– Modern 284, 286–287, 290
– Old 16, 24, 265, 284, 286–288, 290, 298
– Pre-Classical 288

German 3, 6–7, 32, 34, 36, 47, 51, 139, 160, 202, 267, 268

Germanic languages 31–32, 34, 36, 41–42, 44, 50–51, 59–60, 134, 139, 160, 171, 223–224
Gothic 7–8, 31–46, 49–51, 54–61, 63, 65–67, 69–71, 134, 139, 160
Greek 7, 14–15, 23–24, 31, 33–34, 42–44, 48, 50, 52–53, 55, 58–59, 61, 65–67, 69–72, 139, 154, 157, 169–170, 173, 180, 182–183, 197, 201–203
– Ancient 48, 51–54, 145–146, 155, 175, 178–180, 182–183, 185, 188, 192–212
– Classical 9, 169, 175, 177–178, 188, 191–199, 201–204
– Hellenistic Koine 175, 193–194, 196, 198–201, 203
– Homeric 7, 9, 32, 53, 134, 139, 144, 169, 175–181, 184–185, 188, 191–193, 198, 201–204
– Katharévousa 183, 188, 195, 201
– Medieval 175, 186, 192–193, 195–200
– Modern 9, 139, 169–171, 173, 175, 181–183, 185–186, 188, 191, 193–205
– New Testament 48, 50, 53, 55, 57–59, 61, 65–66, 69
– post-Classical 192, 194
– post-Homeric 192

Haitian Creole 19–20
Hausa 138
Hittite 7, 32, 134, 138–139, 141, 145, 146, 150–151, 155, 172
Hungarian 215, 218, 221–223, 226
Hup 20

Icelandic 32, 34, 51
– Old 41, 50, 65
Inari Saami 216, 219–222, 226, 228–229
Indo-Aryan languages 32, 153
Indo-European languages 7–9, 17–18, 31–32, 40, 42, 45–47, 49, 50, 53, 56–58, 60, 70–71, 89, 91, 133–134, 139, 160, 170, 178, 180–181, 194
Ingrian 219

Irish, Old 6, 8, 89–102, 105, 107–109, 115, 121–123, 125–127
Italian 6, 10, 35–36, 59–60, 65, 92, 112, 158, 171–172, 265–268, 276–277, 282, 284, 293–295, 297–298

Jakarta Indonesian 171–172
Japhug 22–23

Kamas 215, 221
Kabardian 20
Karelian 219
Kartvelian 19
Kechwa (Lamas Kechwa) 21
Khoe 14
Kildin Saami 215, 227
Kiranti 21
Komi 215, 218, 221

Lai 138
Latin 6, 8–10, 32–33, 43, 53–55, 64, 90, 98, 101, 111, 113, 123, 126, 133–135, 137, 140–143, 145–162, 180, 265–266, 269, 271–272, 290, 297–298
– Classical 8, 141, 147, 157, 161, 270–274, 297
– Early 151–152, 154, 271, 275
– Late 148, 151, 154, 273–278, 282, 295
– Vulgate 48, 59, 65–66
Laz 19
Livonian 215, 223–224

Madurese 255–257, 259
Manchu 21
Mapudungun 20
Mari 215, 218, 221, 223, 226, 228–229
Michif 22
Moksha 218, 227
Mordvinic languages 218, 227

Nadahup languages 20
Nakh-Daghestanian languages 7, 18
Nepali 21
Nganasan 215
Norse, Old 32, 41, 60

North Khanty 215, 217–218, 221, 223–226
North Mansi 212
North Saami 211–212, 216, 223, 226, 229

Old Church Slavonic 160

Pennsylvania German 20
Permic languages 231
Pisan, Old 280
Plains Cree 22
Portuguese 159
Proto-Germanic 32, 42, 47, 63, 64, 134, 139
Proto-Indo-European 7, 9, 32, 41, 47, 53, 60, 63, 64, 71, 133–134, 170, 177–179, 181, 205
Proto-Uralic 217, 222, 226, 229
Puma 21

Quechua 21

Romance languages 8–9, 133, 135, 147–148, 152, 157–161, 171, 265–267, 269, 275–277, 282, 290, 298
Romani 19
Romanian 208
Russian 3, 18, 20, 22–23, 52, 138–139, 146, 219

Saamic languages 212, 214, 217, 221
Samoyedic languages 214, 226, 228
Sanskrit 134, 177
Selkup 215, 223, 226
Siberian Yupik 138
Sinitic languages 26
Slavic languages 7, 19, 44, 166, 171
Soninke 8, 10, 305, 307–309, 311–317, 319–321, 323–326
South Saami 216, 221
Spanish 14, 20–21

Tagalog 238, 253–255, 257–259
Tatar 23
Tibetan 22–23
Totoli 8–10, 235–245, 247–252, 254–260
Tucanoan languages 20

Tundra Nenets 215
Turkish 19, 184
Tuscan, Old 277

Udmurt 22–23, 202, 215, 218, 220–223
Ugric languages 224, 228
Uralic languages 7–9, 18, 22–23, 209–230

Veps 215, 218–219
Votic 215, 219

Waray-Waray 254
Western Austronesian languages 9–10, 235–237, 252–253, 260

www.ingramcontent.com/pod-product-compliance
Lightning Source LLC
Chambersburg PA
CBHW031420150426
43191CB00006B/339